Alternate & Innovative Construction Systems for Housing

Alternate & Innovative Construction Systems for Housing

A joint initiative of

Building Materials & Technology Promotion Council
Ministry of Housing & Urban Affairs
Government of India

School of Planning & Architecture
New Delhi

I.K. International Pvt. Ltd.
NEW DELHI

Published by:

Building Materials & Technology
Promotion Council (BMTPC)
Ministry of Housing & Urban Affairs,
Government of India
Core-5A, First Floor, India Habitat Centre,
Lodhi Road, New Delhi-110 003
Tel.: 91-11-2463 6705, Fax: 91-11-2464 2849
E-mail: info@bmtpc.org;
Website: www.bmtpc.org

I.K. International Pvt. Ltd.
4435-36/7, Ansari Road, Daryaganj
New Delhi-110002 (India)
E-mail: info@ikinternational.com
Website: www.ikbooks.com

A Joint Publication of BMTPC & IKI

ISBN 978-81-94867-64-7

Printed by Krishan Makhijani for I.K. International Publishing House Pvt. Ltd., 4435-36/7, Ansari Road, Daryaganj, New Delhi-110002 at Rekha Printers Pvt. Ltd., Okhla Industrial Area, Phase II, New Delhi-110 020.

Ministry of Housing and Urban Affairs
Government of India

नवरीतिः

NAVARITIH

(New, Affordable, Validated, Research Innovation Technologies for Indian Housing)

CERTIFICATE COURSE ON INNOVATIVE CONSTRUCTION TECHNOLOGIES

REFERENCE MATERIAL

A joint initiative of

School of Planning & Architecture
New Delhi

and

bmtpc

Building Materials & Technology Promotion Council
Ministry of Housing & Urban Affairs
Government of India

सत्यमेव जयते
DURGA SHANKER MISHRA
Secretary
Ministry of Housing & Urban Affairs
Government of India

Preface

In the PRAGATI meeting held on 12th July 2017, Hon'ble Prime Minister emphasized and exhorted the States to accelerate the adoption of new construction technologies to improve the pace and quality of work under PMAY (U) in order to address the challenges of rapid urban growth and its attendant requirements. Under this scheme nearly 11.2 million houses are to be constructed by 2022; over 10.8 million houses have already been sanctioned so far. Out of about 6.7 million houses which have been constructed/under construction; around 1.5 million are using new technologies. Construction of houses at this scale offers an opportunity for new and alternative technologies from across the globe which may trigger a major transition through introduction of cutting-edge building materials, technologies and processes.

The Government of India has further emphasized the need to accelerate the adoption of new construction technologies to fast track and improve quality of construction under the Pradhan Mantri Awas Yojana (Urban) – Housing For All Mission in order to address the challenges of rapid urban growth and its attendant requirements. Recently, Ministry of Housing and Urban Affairs (MoHUA), Government of India successfully conducted a Global Housing Technology Challenge - India (GHTC- India) to identify and mainstream a basket of innovative housing technologies from across the globe which are cost effective, speedier, sustainable and disaster-resilient and ensure a higher quality of construction of houses, meeting diverse geo-climatic conditions and desired functional needs. It furthers the transformative vision of the Hon'ble Prime Minister and his belief in technological advances to rapidly deliver low-cost housing that meets stringent environmental, societal, quality and economic standards.

Through GHTC-India, 54 new proven technologies have been identified. These technologies are now being showcased through execution of Light House Projects (LHPs) across six States. These LHPs will act as live laboratories to establish clean and green construction practices across India and will help in sustainable construction. GHTC-India is also planning to incubate and accelerate identified potential future technologies through Affordable Sustainable Housing Accelerator (ASHA) - India.

In order to mainstream these new systems in the construction sector there is need to create an enabling eco-system to facilitate field level applications. Under PMAY-U Mission, MoHUA has setup a Technology Sub-Mission (TSM) which aims to encourage the use of sustainable & safe practices across States/ UTs with the help of IITs/NITs/SPAs and other institutes of repute. Also, Building Materials and Technology Promotion Council (BMTPC), an autonomous organization under the aegis of MoHUA operates Performance Appraisal Certification Scheme (PACS) through which any innovative systems can be evaluated and certified. In order to give further impetus to these technologies, MoHUA has assertively pursued Central Public Works Department (CPWD), Bureau of Indian Standards (BIS) and State/ UT departments to come out with notifications, circulars, Schedule of Rates (SORs), specifications etc. which will authorize State/UT Governments to use these new construction technologies in housing projects. The National Building Code of India has also made provisions to ensure utilization of number of new/alternative building materials and technologies in the construction sector.

Promotion of awareness and extension efforts on new technologies is one of the key aspect to create enabling eco-system for usage of these technologies in the construction projects. Therefore, in order to familiarise and create awareness amongst building professionals about the new and emerging building materials and technologies for housing and building construction, the need of the hour today is to introduce a Certificate Course on Innovative Construction Technologies. Accordingly, my Ministry in collaboration with School of Planning & Architecture (SPA), New Delhi and Building Materials & Technology Promotion Council (BMTPC) is launching NAVARITIH/**नवरीतिः** (New, Affordable, Validated, Research Innovation Technologies for Indian Housing) – A Certificate Course on Innovative Construction Technologies.

To start any course, it is necessary to develop the course contents and reading material. As regards, innovative systems, information is available in bits & pieces and there are no text books available summarizing all systems. Therefore, information from various resources have been collected and compiled in concise form to develop this reading material by BMTPC, SPA and resource persons from CPWD, IITs and CSIR Laboratories. It is collection of technical information available on technologies worldwide and it is first of its kind on the subject. We are sure, it will help the readers to comprehend these innovative systems and implement them in their future construction projects. The Course will be conducted through class room lectures and field visits for hands-on exposure to innovative technologies. The Course will help in capacity building of professionals in use of new technologies.

I place on record the commendable work done by BMTPC in association with SPA New Delhi and other academic & research institutions and wish them success.

New Delhi
October 20, 2020

(Durga Shanker Mishra)

Acknowledgements

The idea behind initiating a certificate course for professionals on alternate & emerging housing technologies emanated during construction Technology India -2019, an expo-cum-conference on alternate & innovative construction technologies under GHTC-India on 2-3 March 2019 which was inaugurated by Hon'ble Prime Minister of India. The need to create an ecosystem to foster & mainstream housing technologies which can help build quality, cost-effective, sustainable houses speedily was one of the key takeaway of the GHTC-India. Thanks & heartfelt gratitude to Shri Durga Shankar Mishra, Secretary, Ministry of Housing & Urban Affairs (MoHUA), Govt. of India for immediately asking BMTPC & SPA for its grounding & giving valuable pragmatic guidance during the development of the course and its reading material. Shri Amrit Abhijat, Mission Director & JS (HFA), MoHUA deserves special mention here as he has always been the pillar of strength & guide for giving tips & ideas for making the course lucid. We would also like to thank profusely Shri R.K. Gautam, Director (HFA-5), MoHUA for his unstinted support & encouragement.

We would be failing in our duties, if we do not acknowledge all the technology providers from all over the world who shared technical details of technologies and supported our cause as & when required. We would also like to thank our academic fraternity who helped us to consolidate the idea of emerging technologies and its design & field level application. The chapters written by Dr. K.M. Soni, Former ADG, CPWD, Prof. Amlan K. Sengupta & Prof. Meher Prasad, IIT, Madras, Dr. N. Gopalkrishnan, Director, CBRI, Prof. Subrata Chattophadhaya & Prof. Haimainti Banerjee, IIT, Khargpur, Prof. M. Madhavan, IIT, Hyderabad for contributing chapters in this reading material. SPA and BMTPC also would like to show its gratitude to CBRI Roorkee and IIT Roorkee to support the cause and extending technical help for developing the course contents & reading material.

We also duly acknowledge the immense literature & wealth of information available on various internet sites of technology providers, academic institutions, practioners, developers & world housing encyclopaedia. Thanks to Shri Sharad Kr. Gupta, Shri C. N.

Jha & Shri Dalip Kumar of BMTPC for collecting the technical details of alternate technologies and putting them in concise form.

Last but not the least, the support by PMU team at MoHUA and Faculty at SPA is also duly acknowledged.

Prof. Dr. P.S.N. Rao
Director, SPA, New Delhi

Dr. Shailesh Kr. Agrawal
Executive Director, BMTPC

Contents

Contributors

- Dr. Shailesh Kr. Agrawal, Executive Director, BMTPC
- Prof. P.S.N. Rao, Director, SPA, New Delhi
- Dr K M Soni, ADG(Retd), CPWD, New Delhi

  Chapter

  Formwork Systems
- Dr. N. Gopalakrishnan, Director, CBRI, Roorkee

  Chapter

  Stay In Place Form Work Systems
- Prof. Meher Prasad, Professor, Department of Civil Engineering, IIT Madras

  Chapter

  GFRG (Glass Fibre Reinforced Gypsum) Panel System
- 1. Dr. Umesh Kumar Sharma, Professor, Department of Civil Engineering, IIT Roorkee, Durability and Serviceability Assessment of Concrete Sandwich EPS Panel - Report
  2. Dr. Yogendra Singh, Department of Earthquake Engineering, IIT Roorkee, Structural Stability Assessment and Development of Design Guidelines for EPS Core Panel System towards Safe and Affordable Housing - Report
  3. Manual for Expanded Polystyrene (EPS) Core Panel System and its fieldApplication – CSIR-CBRI Report No.: S.E(G)/ 0605

  Chapter

  Precast Sandwich Panel Systems
- Dr. Subrata Chattopadhyay, Professor and Dean, Dept. of Architecture & Regional Planning, IIT Kharagpur

Chapter

Steel Structural Systems- Concepts and its Features

- Dr. Haimanti Banerji, Associate Professor, Dept. of Architecture & Regional Planning, IIT Kharagpur

  Chapter

  Steel Structural Systems- Construction methodology, implementation and Case studies

- Dr. Mahendrakumar Madhavan, Associate Professor, Department of Civil Engineering, Indian Institute of Technology Hyderabad

  Chapter

  Light Gauge Steel Frame Systems

- Dr. Amlan K. Sengupta, Professor, Department of Civil Engineering, IIT Madras

  Chapter

  Precast Concrete Building Systems –An Overview

About the Course

NAVARITIH/नवरीतिः

[New, Affordable, Validated, Research Innovation Technologies for Indian Housing]
A Certificate Course on Innovative Construction Technologies

0.1 PROLOGUE

The School of Planning & Architecture, New Delhi and Building Materials & Technology Promotion Council (BMTPC), Ministry of Housing & Urban Affairs is offering acertificate course on alternate & innovative Construction technologies for construction sector.

The housing problem in India is huge, with urban housing shortage pegged at 11.2million dwelling units. In order to meet the requirements of this housing shortage, it is incumbent that speedy and affordable housing construction mechanism be devised. For long, Indians have been building either by the brick masonry or random rubble masonry method or by using a cast-in-situ RCC framed structure with infill walls. This system of housing construction is time consuming process, with wastages and inherent difficulties of quality control besides pollution & GHG emissions. Further, there is a shortage of building materials also such as sand, bricks and so on. Therefore, there is an urgent need for us to look at alternate and innovative building materials and construction systems.

In the last few decades, several new technologies have been researched. We now use many waste materials for housing construction. Similarly, there are industrialized methods of manufacturing building components and construction. Robotics, automation, 3D printing, pod element, prefinished factory-made houses are some of the innovation being successfully implemented in the construction. Also, sophisticated machinery, equipment and technologies for construction in a speedy manner are available at door step.

To achieve the goals of Housing for All by 2022 and to bring about major transition in the building construction industry by mainstreaming alternative and innovative technologies, Government of India through the Ministry of Housing and Urban Affairs (MoHUA) launched Global Housing Technology Challenge- India (GHTC-India) on January 14, 2019. GHTC- India aims to identify and mainstream a basket of innovative technologies from across the globe that are sustainable, green and disaster-resilient, cost effective, speedier, complying with quality standards, meeting diverse geo-climatic conditions and desired functional needs. It aspires to develop an eco-system to deliver on the technological challenges of the housing construction sector in a holistic manner.

As a party of GHTC-India, Construction Technology India (CTI)-2019: Expo-cum-Conference was held at Vigyan Bhawan, New Delhi during 2-3 March 2019 to bring together multiple stakeholders involved in innovative and alternative housing technologies through an exhibition, thematic sessions, panel discussions and master classes. Technology providers from across the globe exhibited their proven technologies and made presentations during CTI-2019. About 3500 visitors including 2500 delegates from 32 countries participated in CTI-2019, Expo-cum-Conference. The exhibition had 188 stalls in which 60 exhibitors comprising of 54 proven technologies from 25 countries showcased their technologies.The Hon'ble Prime Minister while inaugurating the CTI-2019, declared the year 2019-2020 as "Construction Technology Year.

It is important at this stage to define alternate & innovative technologies as the technologies which will replace the conventional construction practices such as:

- Load bearing masonry building, i.e., walls built with masonry made of brick, cement concrete solid, hollow blocks and any other masonry, and with roof made of RC.
- Cast in-situ Reinforced Concrete (RC) frame building with masonry infill walls and cast in-situ RC slab.

Under GHTC-India, proven innovative and alternate construction technologies along with future potential sustainable technologies were identified. The proven technologies are further being showcased through execution of Light House Projects (LHPs) across six States. These LHPs will act as live laboratories to establish clean and green construction practices across India and will help in sustainable construction. It has also been planned to incubate and accelerate identified potential future technologies through Affordable Sustainable Housing Accelerator (ASHA) - India.

A series of activities have been envisaged by the Ministry of Housing & Urban Affairs for implementation under GHTC-India. As part of Construction Technology Year 2019-20, it has been decided to start a Certificate Course on Innovative Construction Technologies by BMTPC in collaboration with School of Planning & Architecture, New Delhi.

0.2 OBJECTIVES

The objectives of this certificate course are to:

(a) Familiarize the professionals with the latest materials and technologies being used worldwide for housing,

(b) Provide an awareness of the state of art of materials and technologies in terms of properties, specifications, performance, design and construction methodologies so that professionals can successfully employ these in their day to day practice, and

(c) Provide exposure to executed projects where such materials and technologies have been implemented.

The course will sensitize and provide firsthand basic information to the participant about the alternate construction systems. The knowledge gained will be sufficient to initiate field level application using the technologies, however, the architectural planning & structural design can only be undertaken by professionals having specialized degrees in the respective fields.

0.3 DURATION

The duration of the Course shall be 7 days.

0.4 CLASSES

The Course will preferably start on Friday and classes shall be held in the evening from 5.30 pm to 8.30 pm on weekdays. However, there shall be two classes on Saturday and Sunday from 2.00 pm to 5.00 pm and 5.30 pm to 8.30 pm. There shall be one day off during the course preferably on Monday. The candidates shall have to make their own transport arrangements for attending the classes.

Field visits shall be conducted for hands-on exposure to innovative technologies, which shall be optional.

0.5 CURRICULUM

The curriculum shall cover various new innovative materials and technologies that have emerged in the recent past in the area of housing and given in the Table below.

DAY 1 : Friday	**Session 01**
1730 to 1900 hrs.	Emerging Construction Systems – Introduction, opportunities, challenges
1900 to 2030 hrs.	Emerging Construction Technologies promoted through PACS/ BMTPC/ CPWD/ GHTC-India/MoHUA
DAY 2 : Saturday	**Session 02**
1400 to 1530 hrs.	Formwork Systems – Introduction, Concepts and its features, design philosophy
1530 to 1700 hrs.	Formwork Systems – Construction methodology, implementation and case studies

DAY 2 : Saturday	**Session 03**
1730 to 1900 hrs.	Stay-In-Place Formwork Systems– Introduction, Concepts and its features
1900 to 2030 hrs.	Stay-In-Place Formwork Systems– Construction methodology, implementation and case studies
DAY 3 : Sunday	**Session 04**
1400 to 1530 hrs.	Precast Sandwich Panel Systems (EPS based) – Introduction, Concepts and its features
1530 to 1700 hrs.	Precast Sandwich Panel Systems (EPS based) – Construction methodology, implementation and case studies
DAY 3: Sunday	**Session 05**
1730 to 1900 hrs.	Precast Sandwich Panel Systems (other than EPS) – Introduction, Concepts and its features
1900 to 2030 hrs.	Precast Sandwich Panel Systems (other than EPS) – Construction methodology, implementation and case studies
DAY 4: Monday - Off Day	
DAY 5 : Tuesday	**Session 06**
1730 to 1900 hrs.	Steel Structural Systems– Introduction, Concepts and its features
1900 to 2030 hrs.	Steel Structural Systems– Construction methodology, implementation and case studies
DAY 6 : Wednesday	**Session 07**
1730 to 1900 hrs.	Light Gauge Steel Frame Systems– Introduction, Concepts and its features
1900 to 2030 hrs.	Light Gauge Steel Frame Systems – Construction methodology, implementation and case studies
DAY 7 : Thursday	**Session 08**
1730 to 1900 hrs.	Precast Concrete Construction Systems – Introduction, Concepts and its features
1900 to 2030 hrs.	Precast Concrete Construction Systems – Construction methodology, implementation and case studies

DAY 8 : Friday		OPTIONAL
	Field visits to innovative technologies projects for hands-on exposure	
	Online Final Examination	

0.6 VENUE

All the classes will be held at the School of Planning and Architecture, New Delhi located at 4-B, Indraprastha Estate, New Delhi 110002.

0.7 FACULTY

The faculty willbe experts in the area of alternative technologies drawn from Academic Institutions, Industry, SPA New Delhi and BMTPC New Delhi.

0.8 TARGET GROUP

Any person who has successfully completed and in possession of a minimum qualification of B.E. / B.Tech. (Civil) or B.Arch. (or equivalent) or Diploma in Civil with 5 years' experience shall be eligible to take up the Course. Self-Attested photocopy of Degree/Diploma certificate (or equivalent) to be submitted with application.

0.9 APPLICATION

Candidates desirous of applying for this course shall have to register online on the website as link available on www.spa.ac.in. The dates for registration shall be announced on the www.spa.ac.in.

0.10 ADMISSION

Admission to the course shall be online through the website www.spa.ac.in. As and when candidates apply for the course, they shall be asked to fill the Application Form and deposit course fee. After submission of duly filled-in online form, an email will be generated to Applicant. After verification of the details and receipt of course fee by Course Coordinator in SPA-BMTPC, an email will be sent to Applicant for successful enrolment to the Course and also USER ID (Applicant's ID) and machine generated PASSWORD will be sent. A list shall be made online of the enrolled applicants.

After successful registration, the candidates can download the Welcome Kit containing General Instructions, Reading Materials, Reference Material, Presentations, Case Studies, etc. using USER ID and PASSWORD. Before commencement of the Classes, candidates are advised to go through the reading material.

Admission shall be on a 'first come first serve' basis.Candidates who are not admitted in the first batch shall be considered for the next batch and so on.

0.11 HOW TO APPLY?

Step-1: Please go to www.spa.ac.in

Step-2: On the Home Page go to "Courses offered -> e-courses -> NAVARITIH-Course on Innovative Construction Technologies -> click on the link given for course

Step-3: Once you are on the Course portal, read about the Course on Innovative Construction Technologies

Step-4: Click on Register and read General Instructions carefully

Step-5: Fill up the online Registration Form

Step-6: Deposit Course fee (Rs.10000/- + applicable GST) using Bank transfer/ NEFT/ RTGS and SBI Collect only.

Step-7: Fill in payment transaction details such as UTR No. and date of payment in the Registration Form.

Step-8: Click Submit. You will receive an email confirming successful submission of registration form.

Step-9: After verification of the details and course fee by Administrator, an email will be sent to you containing USER ID and machine generated PASSWORD. You are advised to change the machine generated PASSWORD immediately.

Step-10: Upon successful login, please complete your profile

Step-11: Download the Reading Material.

0.12 BATCH SIZE

The size of each batch of training shall be limited to 30 candidates so as to achieve a manageable class size and encourage good participation and interaction.

0.13 COURSE FEE

Rs.10,000/-(Rupees ten thousand only) + GST as applicable, per participant (One-Time, non-refundable). Payments to be made using Bank Transfer/NEFT/RTGS and SBI Collect only. The course fee includes course fee, reading material and High Tea everyday &closing Dinner on last day.

The Course is Non-Residential programme and the candidates shall have to make their own boarding and lodging arrangements at their own expenses.

Bank details for payment of Course fee through NEFT/RTGS:

Account Name	BMTPC
Name of Bank	Canara Bank

Branch Name	Parliament Street Branch
Branch Address	Parliament Street Branch, New Delhi
Type of Account	Savings
Account No.	1098101023050
Bank IFSC Code	CNRB0001098

0.14 TEACHING PEDAGOGY

The teaching pedagogy shall comprise of class room lectures, presentations, discussions and Q & A sessions.

0.15 ATTENDANCE

It is advisable that the candidates attend all the 8 sessions so that they do not miss on any of the aspects of the subject.

0.16 EXAMINATION

At the end of the course, there will be ONLINE examination based on Multiple Choice Questions (MCQ).The Multiple-Choice Questions (MCQ) based examination will be held online. This may be taken at any time at any day within 45 days after conclusion of the Course.

0.17 CERTIFICATE

A Certificate shall be awarded to each of the students on successful completion of the course after passing the examination.

0.18 CHIEF COORDINATORS

Prof. Dr. P.S.N.Rao
Director, SPA New Delhi
SPA, New Delhi
E-mail: drpsnrao@hotmail.com

Dr. Shailesh Kr. Agrawal
Executive Director,
BMTPC, New Delhi
E-mail: shailesh.agrawal@gov.in

1

Introduction to Alternate & Innovative Construction Systems

1.1 PREAMBLE

Housing for all by 2022 is the firm resolve of Govt. of India to provide pucca shelter to each household of India and is a humble beginning towards building New India. To realize the objectives of housing for all, two unprecedented missions have been started by the Govt.

1. Pradhan Mantri Awas Yojana - Urban (PMAY-U) to provide affordable housing for Urban Poorsince June 2015.
2. Pradhan Mantri Awas Yojana - Gramin (PMAY-G) to provide houses to all houseless households in rural areas since April 2016.

The number of housing units need to be constructed are huge in both the missions. There is requirement of 11.2 million dwelling units in urban areas by 2022 whereas the target for rural is 29.5 million. Also, construction sector is emerging as third largest sector globally to take India towards $ 5 trillion economy. Conventionally houses are built with traditional materials i.e. burnt clay bricks, cement, sand, aggregates, stones, timber & steel. Do we have sufficient supply of these materials? Sand and aggregates are already in short supply and due to irrational mining, it is banned in number of states in India. Burnt clay bricks use top fertile soil as raw material and also its production make use of coal, a fossil fuel. Cement and steel are also energy intensive materials and produced from natural resource i.e. limestone rock and iron ores respectively. Further, the construction requires clean drinking water which is already in short supply even for drinking. The way out is (a) to make use of alternate materials which are based on renewable resources & energy (b) optimize the use of conventional materials by bringing mechanization in the construction (c) Utilize agricultural & industrials waste in producing building materials. Now, let us look at the way construction takes place. The materials are gathered at the site and then construction takes place by laying bricks layer by layer to construct walls and pouring concrete over steel cages (reinforcement) to make floors, vertical members i.e. columns and horizontal members i.e. beams through a labour intensive process with little control on quality of finished product. Also, this construction process is slow paced. Further, being cast in situ construction, there is ample wastage of materials and precious resources and at the same time there is enormous dust generated polluting the air. Therefore, there is need to bring construction methodologies which impart speed to the construction, bring in optimum use of materials, cut down wastages and produce quality product.

In today's context, a few more terms have become significant with construction and need to be dovetailed with future construction practices. These are sustainability, climate responsiveness anddisaster resilience. The construction industry poses a major challenge to the environment. As per UN Environment Programme (UNEP), more than 30% of global greenhouse gas emissions are building related and emissions could double by 2050 on a Business as Usual scenario. As per report of GRIHA, Globally, buildings consume about 40% of energy, 25% of water and 40% of resources. In addition, building activities contribute an estimated 50% of the worlds' air pollution, 42% of its greenhouse gases, 50% of all water pollution, 48% of all solid wastes and 50% of all CFCs (chlorofluorocarbons) to the environment.

Further, Disasters due to natural hazards i.e. earthquakes, cyclones, floods, Tsunamis and landslides have been happening with ascending frequency and effects. Every year due to faulty construction practices and bad performance of built environment during disasters, there are not only heavy economic losses but also losses of precious lives of humans leaving irrevocable impact on human settlements and therefore disaster resilient construction is also paramount.

With the foregoing discussion, it is obvious that construction sector requires paradigm shift from traditional construction systems by bringing innovative construction systems which are resource efficient, environmentally responsible, climate responsive, sustainable, disaster resilient, faster, structurally & functionally superior. These kind of systems are being practiced world over successfully and have shown their versatility through the passage of time. However, Indian construction sector needs to be receptive & innovative to adopt and adapt these systems to build New India leading to sustainable growth and quality living to its citizens.

Below is the chart which shows the levels of construction technologies world over and as reader of this chapter, you can place yourself at the level, we are at present in India:

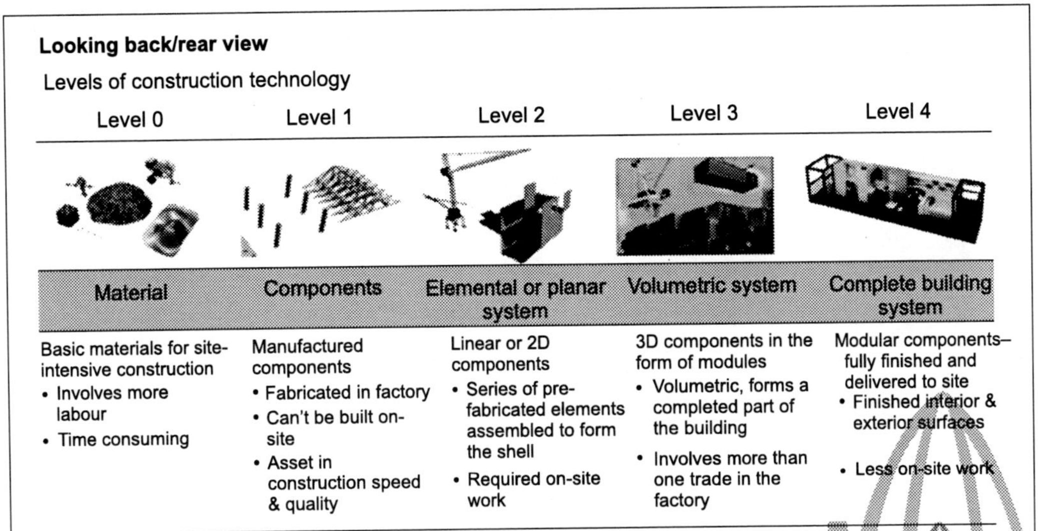

Source: Gibb., A.G.F., Off-site fabrication–Pre-Assembly, Pre-Fabrication, and Modularization

1.2 MAJOR CONSTRUCTION TYPES – WORLD OVER

There are various types of building materials & construction technologies being practiced world over since time immemorial for construction of houses. These can be broadly classified into following types as per World Housing Encyclopaedia (http://www.world-housing.net/).

1.2.1 Adobe Construction

The bricks/blocks made up of local soil/mud and dried in Sun are known as Adobe & is an age-old construction material being used world-wide. Still, in India & other countries, people make houses using adobe construction despite of its high vulnerability to earthquake & other hazards.

> Around 30% to 50% of the world's population (approximately 3 billion people) lives or works in earthen buildings. Approximately 50% of population in developing countries, including a majority of the rural population and at least 20% of the urban population, live in earthen dwellings.
>
> *Source : World Housing Encyclopaedia (http://www.world-housing.net/)*

In India, Adobe construction is primarily used in rural parts. A typical house using adobe is normally one to two storey high having thick walls. Rammed construction is another form of mud houses where the walls are cast by compacting (ramming) layers of mud.

The citadel at Bam, Iran is one of the largest adobe building in the world which was destroyed almost completely during 26.12.2003 earthquake of Iran.

Fig. 1.1: Earthen houses - adobe houses

1.2.2 Wood Houses

Wooden houses have traditionally being constructed world over and still in vogue. In areas, where wood is locally available & can be crafted for the building construction purposes using local skills, wood construction is quite popular & offer an economical & comfortable house.There are variety of wooded houses depending upon the type of wood being used, construction technique & local skills such as bamboo frame & walls with bamboo sheets; wooden plank, beam & post system; Wood frame construction like Dhajji-Dewari, Ikara houses and engineered timber houses.

Wood construction employs all kinds of wood available for the construction. Normally, wooden sections are shaped from timber logs, sawn woods, tree branches and even leaves. With the advent of latest finger & jointing techniques, readymade timber beams & columns are also available for wooden structural frame construction The wall coverings for such structures vary from region to regionsuch as plant-based coverings, light wall panelling made of reed (ikara) & mud plaster, Bamboo sheets with chicken wire mesh & cement plaster, dhajji-dewari type (small wooden frame with stone/brick masonry), mud or stone. Thatch construction is one of the most primitivewood construction. Other types as per World Housing Encyclopaedia include column (wooded post)-and-beam frame construction, walls with bamboo/reed mesh and post (waffle and daub), wooden frames with or without in fill, and stud-wall frames with plywood/gypsum board sheathing.

Fig. 1.2(a): Wood houses - Ikra Houses

Fig. 1.2(b): Wood houses - Dhajji Diwari Houses

1.2.3 Stone Buildings

Stone has also been one of the popular building materials and being used for construction since centuries. It is convenient and cheaper to construct houses using stones where it is locally available. Walls using ashlar masonry, random rubble masonry are still popular. Stone masonry blocks are also being used for walling. The historical structures world over are often built with stone masonry.

Stones used in construction can be either dressed, roughly dressed, hammer dressed or undressed. Some of the popular varieties of natural stones are slate, sandstone, granite, marble, laterite, limestone or any other local stones. Use of local stones e.g. kota stone, dholpur stone, Jaisalmer stone, Kadapa is quite prevalent in India. Stones can be laid with or without mortar. The roofs are also being constructed with bigger stone slabs supported over steel or wooden frame/truss. Another popular form in rural area is stone tile covering over sloping wooden truss.

From country to country, the construction techniques & the type of stone masonry houses vary. It also depends upon the local skills and availability of stones. However, stone buildings being heavy are vulnerable to earthquakes, if not designed for lateral forces.

Fig. 1.3: Stone masonry house

1.2.4 Brick – Unreinforced Brick Masonry Construction

This is most common housing form being used widely worldwide. Clay bricks are made using top fertile soil essentially clay to form standard sizebricks. The normal size of brick in India is 9″(230 mm) × 4.5″(115 mm) × 3″ (75 mm) or 200 mm × 100 mm × 100 mm. The bricks are fired in a kiln which can be open kiln or a draught kiln. Nowadays, energy efficient brick kilns such as Vertical Shaft Brick Kilns (VSBK) are also being used. Also, in rural areas, Sun dried bricks are being used. Brick masonry is generally laid with mortar which can either be cement based or lime/mud based. Bricks stacks without mortar are also found to be used.The roofing system vary from sloping wooden/steel truss covered with earthen/stone tiles, steel sheets to cost-in-situ reinforced concrete slab. Apart from unreinforced burnt clay brick masonry construction, there are other forms of masonry types from random rubble stone, solid & hollow block, to reinforced and confined masonry.

Bricks were first fired around 3500 BC, in Mesopotamia, present-day Iraq, one of the high-risk seismic areas of the world. From Roman aqueducts and public buildings to the Great Wall of China, from the domes of Islamic architecture to the early railway arch bridges, from the first 19thcentury American tall buildings to the 20th century nuclear power plants, bricks have been used as structural material in all applications of Civil Engineering.

Source : World Housing Encyclopaedia (http://www.world-housing.net/)

The majority of housing being constructed world over still use brickmasonry. It is normally a load bearing structures used for low to mid rise construction. The various aesthetic forms & shapes can also be created with bricks. The brick arches and brick arch construction has been very popular in India during pre-independence times and being practiced till today.

In India, as per Census 2011 Housing data based on predominant materials of walls, around 58% buildings i.e. 178 million fall under this category. During the recent earthquakes in India during 1990 to till date, collapse of brick masonry buildings was one of the probable cause for loss of lives & property.

Despite of being vulnerable to high seismic intensity, the unreinforced brick masonry construction is popular in earthquake prone regions inflicting loss of lives and property after every earthquake across the world.The earthquake codes world over have come out with prescriptive guidelines for earthquake resistant construction of such buildings. As per shape, size & height of the buildings, the provisions in the codes stipulates wall thickness, openings, resisting measures etc. The unreinforced masonry construction is now being replaced by reinforced masonry (with RC bands & vertical bars),confined masonry/composite construction of RCC beam, columns & walls. However, in India, still unreinforced brick masonry construction is practiced irrespective of seismicity of the region and mainly governed by socio-economic conditions.

Fig. 1.4: Burnt clay brick masonry house

1.2.5 Confined Masonry Construction

Confined masonry is a reinforced masonry construction where masonry walls of bricks or blocks are reinforced from all four sides of wall panel with horizontal and vertical reinforced concrete confining members. Vertical confining members are called *tie-columns* and horizontal elements as *tie-beams*. The construction resembles with reinforced concrete (RC) frame construction but here the tie-beams and columns are of much smaller x-section. These confining members here are basically ties/bands to resist tensile forces and shall not be confused with beams and columns, the way these are used in RC frame construction.Confined masonry is structurally superior system to the load-bearing brick masonry and earthquake resistant construction. Any roof/ floor form can be used with confined masonry as per the requirements & local practices. It can also be a viable cost-effective solution for social housing in earthquake prone areas.

Confined masonry has been very popular form of construction is South American countries which are prone to earthquakes as its construction is similar to unreinforced masonry construction but with different sequence of construction. It also employs same building materials i.e. brick, mortar & concrete. It is commonly believed that RCC framed construction is inherently strong for lateral loads but RCC buildings need to be properly designed, detailed & built for better performance during earthquake. In contrast, confined masonry construction's design is simple, construction follows a sequence and walls carrying lateral loads along with confinement with reinforced concrete provide superior performance during earthquakes.

Fig. 1.5(a): Confined masonry house (under construction)

Fig. 1.5(b): Confined masonry house (finished)

1.2.6 Reinforced Concrete Frame Construction

Ever since, Portland cement came into existence in the 19thcentury, concrete structures became very popular replacing old forms of load bearing construction. Concrete being weak in resisting tensile forces, steel reinforcement along with concrete i.e. Reinforced cement Concrete (RCC) became ubiquitous building material and RCC framed construction gained popularity across nations. Concrete can also be given any shape, size and form making it very versatile method of construction. Normally, RCC framed construction comprises of structural skeleton and infill walls. The skeleton is a frame composed of RCC beams primarily horizonal members & RCC columns i.e. vertical slender members. The vertical spaces between the beams & columns are infilled with brick masonry or any other building material/panel whereas the horizontal spaces are traditionally cast-in-situ RCC plate i.e. slab. The RCC frame construction is presumed as superior structural system than the masonry construction.

The basic ingredients for RCC construction are cement, coarse & fine aggregates, water and steel which are widely available as household items and being taken as granted materials for construction with which anyone can construct using thumb rules & without adequate knowledge about concrete. RCC construction is being taken up quite unprofessionally in India in the residential sector where individuals are building their own houses. However, the line of caution here is that RCC framed construction needs to be done through professionals preferably with civil engineering background. Most of the RCC framed construction which is supposed to be effective as regards earthquake resistance perform badly during earthquakes on account of bad execution, poor workmanship & low quality control. All earthquake disasters in the history world wide stand testimony to this fact.

Fig. 1.6: Reinforced concrete frame construction

1.2.7 Reinforced Concrete Shear Wall

The RCC concrete walls act as shear walls when placed in the specific bays in the plan of the RCC framed building. These shear walls also known as structural walls are very effective in resisting lateral forces and supplement framed construction by improving its seismic resistance. Owing to unprofessional approach towards RC framed construction and its potential hazards during earthquake, nowadays structural engineers prefer to provide shear walls in the building in high seismic area. These shear walls are regular in plan & elevation, however, its design & construction calls for inputs from experts. The multi-storey structures in urban areas are normally built on stilt to cater for parking & other requirements. During past earthquake, the performance of such building has been poor leading to collapse and loss of lives. Therefore, world over, shear wall buildings are being preferred and constructed replacing traditional RCC framed buildings with infill walls.

In the earthquake prone areas of the world, India being no exception, the RCC shear walls coupled with RCC frame buildings are the new norm of construction.During 2001 Bhuj earthquake, there was widespread damage leading to collapse to RC framed construction and at that time, new clauses were added into relevant Indian standards to introduce shear wall construction.

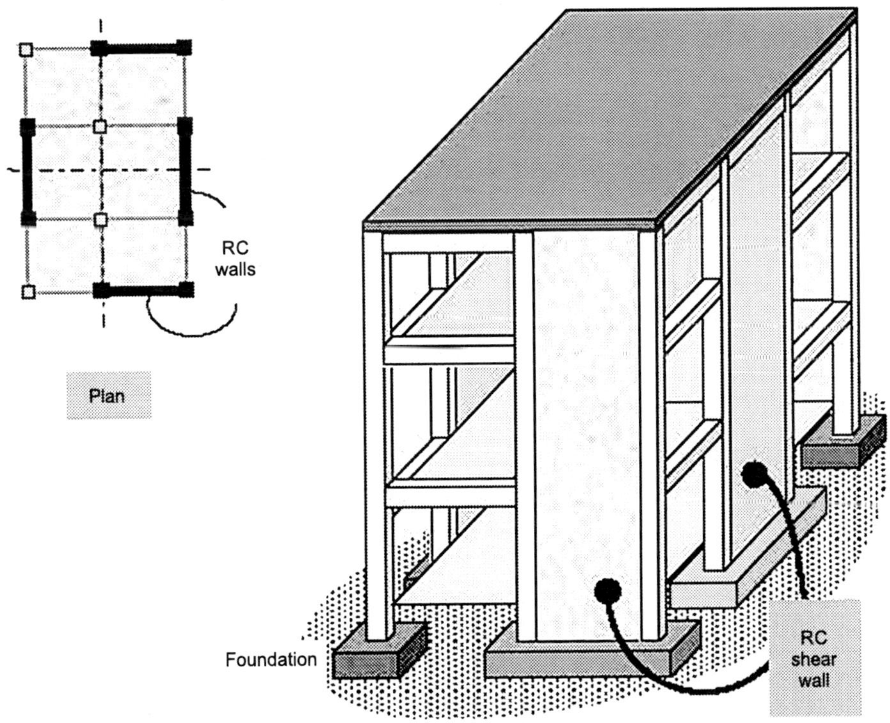

Fig. 1.7: Reinforced concrete shear wall in building

1.2.8 Structural Steel Frame Buildings

Use of steel frame buildings dates back to 19th century when the production of steel became more efficient in US. The steel frame buildings consists of verticaland horizontal structural members i.e. columns & beams which are rolled steel sections. These sections are I sections, channel sections, angle sections, tubular including rectangular & square sections. Built up sections are also used. The spaces in between beams and columns can be infilled by variety of ways such as stone/brick masonry, wooden/sandwich panels or concrete panels. The steel buildings also provide flexibility to meet the requirements of any architectural shape & size.

Indian standards provide hot-rolled structural steelshapes such as wide-flange beams and columns including their geometric & other properties. With the advent of better technology for steel fabrication, the hollow structural steel sections formed using steel plate are being used now. These sections makeconstruction durable, reliable, cost-effective&sustainable for low-rise, mid-rise and high-rise buildings.

Use of steel frame construction is some what slow in residential sector in India and restricted to pre-engineered industrial buildings but with the push from Government to enhance use of steel in housing sector, it is bound to pick up. The other potential exciting option for low-rise structures is thin sections of cold rolled steel also known as light gauge steel. The hot rolled steel structural system can be replaced by skeleton of light gauge beams, columns & panels known as light gauge steel frame system.

Fig. 1.8: Structural steel frame buildings

1.2.9 Precast Concrete Buildings

As early as after second world war in 1945, the precast concrete buildings were constructed in former USSR & some of the eastern European countries for social mass housing. Later it was picked up by the others countries as well to cater to the growing urban population & to meet the demand of housing especially low-income housing. The concept is simple, manufacture building or its components in a controlled environment using industrialized methods, transport them to the site & then erect & assemble. It comes very handy when buildings/components are standardized and mass produced thus bringing down the cost & time. Nowadays, the concept of DFMA (design for manufacture & assembly) have also been introduced where project specific customized plant, its production & assembly is designed. The end product is quality & durable house delivered in short time. Precast concrete construction is also known as offsite or prefabricated construction. The factory for production of components can be setup near the site or at a centralized location away from the site. Some of the companies are coming with mobile production plants as well.

The production in the factory is primarily done in two ways (a) 2D planar structural elements i.e. beams, columns, structural & non-structural walls, slabs, staircases, landing, sunshades. Sometimes, large wall panel having door & window openings are also cast as per requirement (b) 3D volumetric construction where the entire room/dwelling unit is cast. Also, Pod elements comprising of toilet units, bath units are also cast separately. These components are high quality factory made products are then transported and assembled at the site through dry & wet jointing procedures. In case of 3D volumetric constructions, the units are placed one over other like Lego blocks to get a multi-storey structure. The prestressed hollow core slab & walls arc is also one of precast elements gaining popularity & can be used for higher spans.

The basic premise for precast building to get overall economy is economies of scale, standardization & mass housing, regular & simple configuration. In general, when compared to conventional cast-in-situ RCC framed construction, precast buildings offer cost-effective & faster solution for quality housing in the long run. Singapore is the living example where the only form of construction which exists is precast concrete construction. At present, in India its scope is limited to mass housing projects in urban areas.

Fig. 1.9: Precast concrete buildings

1.2.10 Closure

There are umpteen number of local vernacular housing technologies practiced world over and are not being discussed here.As per socio-economic conditions, local materials, skills & architecture, the types of housing vary from thatch houses to mud houses to stone houses to wood houses. However, the construction can be classified broadly into two structural types world over, (a) load bearing masonry structures and (b) reinforced concrete framed structures. The RCC buildings continue to dominate the world construction scenario till today on account of rapid urbanisation, fast pace of development in the real estate sector. Also, RCC construction is projected as a better & durable practice.

1.3 STRUCTURAL SYSTEMS (CONSTRUCTION SYSTEMS)

Any building being constructed comprises of load carrying structural system (beams and columns, slabs, wall) and non-structural systems (in fill walls, partitions, false ceilings, wall claddings, fittings & fixtures). The basic objective of structural system is to transfersafely the action of loads (dead loads & live loads) and other environment loads (lateral forces, wind forces, hydrodynamic forces etc.) to the supporting ground without significantly disturbing the geometry, integrity and serviceability of the structure.

The structure thus constructed must satisfy three basic requirements (Reinforced Concrete Design by Pillai & Menon, 1998).

Stability, to prevent overturning, sliding, buckling of the structure, or parts of it, under the action of loads

Strength, to resist safely the stresses induced by the loads

Serviceability, to ensure satisfactory performance under service load conditions providing adequate stiffness to contain deflections, crack widths and vibrations within acceptable limits and also providing **impermeability, durability** (including corrosion-resistance)

Economy & **Aesthetics** are two other requirements, one should keep in mind while designing the structure.

1.3.1 Prevalent Structural Systems

The prevalent construction systems in India as well as across globe are:

Load Bearing Structural System

In this system, walls are constructed using bricks/stone/block masonry and floor/roof slabs are of RCC/stone/composite or truss. It is cast in-situ system and known as load bearing system as load of structure is transferred to foundation and then to ground through walls.

RCC Framed Structural System

This is also cast-in-situ system, however, the walls are replaced by the skeleton of RCC columns and beams with RCC slabs. The spaces between skeleton are filled with infill walls which can be of bricks/blocks/stone /panels. The loads of the structure are transferred through beam and column frame to the foundation. RCC framed structural system coupled with shear walls is also used for high rise structures in seismically prone areas.

Steel Frame Structural System

Here RCC beam and columns are replaced by hot rolled steel sections. For multi-storied buildings, the RCC sectionsare larger than steel section as the compressive strength is lower in the case of RCC. For low to mid rise structures, nowadays, cold rolled steel sections can be used instead of hot rolled steel.

Closure

Over the years, the cast in situ masonry construction and RCC construction is quite popular in India or rather ubiquitous. As per census data of 2011, more than 50% houses in India are load bearing masonry structures. The popular use of these systems for housing has been on account of availability of local skills, materials and ease of construction. However these houses are good under vertical (gravity) loads but masonry having low tensile strength is not capable of taking lateral loads and perform poorly in the event of earthquakes. Masonry degrade faster under extreme weather conditions and absorbs moisture requiring proper maintenance. Further, these constructions make use of basic materials namely brick, cement, aggregates, sand& steelwhich are based on finite natural resources, contribute for greenhouse gas emissions and energy-intensive and therefore are not sustainable. Also, masonry construction is aslow construction process wherein material is assembled and then brick by brick, construction takes place through a labour intensive manual process. ***Imagine, if the brick by brick wall is replaced by a wall manufactured in the factory.***

The RCC construction has been popular for last 150 years only. It was year 1824, when Portland cement was invented by Aspdin by burning limestone and clay and is the most widely used material in combination with reinforcement till today. Cement is the second most used commodity after water in the world. The RCC construction has distinct advantages such as economical, low maintenance, easy to mould to any shape, good rigidity, high compressive strength, good tensile strength due to reinforcement, better fire, weather resistance, durable, requires less skilled workforce. However, it has been learnt that RCC structures begin to show early signs of distress after construction owing to poor execution, workmanship and ignorance to basic quality control & assurance factors. During 2001 Bhuj earthquake, the multi-storeyed RCC buildings became death traps and crumbled like loosely packed stones. The main constituent of these construction is concrete and it is to prepared with proper mixing, casting, and curing to achieve desired strength & durability which is often not the case being cast-in-situ construction. Further, it is also labour-intensive slow construction process. ***Imagine, factory made RCC components being brought to the site and assembled.***

Therefore, these structural systems needs to be replaced by modern innovative alternate systems which are structurally & functionally efficient, makes optimum use of building materials, produce less waste and impart speed to the construction.

Conventional Construction Systems	Alternate Construction Systems
Slow	Fast
Maximum Use of Natural Resources	Optimum use of Resources
Waste Generation	Minimum Waste
Air/Land/Water Pollution	Minimum Pollution
Labour Intensive	Industrialized System
Prescriptive Design	Cost-effective Design
Unhealthy Indoor Quality	Better health & Productivity
Regular Maintenance	Low Life Cycle Cost
Energy Intensive	Energy Efficient
Cast-in-situ Poor Quality	Factory Made Quality Products
High GHG Emissions	Low GHG Emissions
Unsustainable	Sustainable

1.3.2 Alternate Construction Systems

With the global buzz about sustainability, reduction of carbon emissions, climate change mitigation strategies, the use of greener good practices in the construction sector has gained importance and has become relevant today. BMTPC under Ministry of Housing & Urban Affairs, Govt. of India has been promoting sustainable technologies for field level applications since 1990, however, during last few years, BMTPC is in the process of mainstreaming alternate housing technologies other than conventional ones which are suitable for affordable mass housing specially in urban areas. These alternate construction systems offer a basket of appropriate structural systems which are not only superior than the existing RCC/load bearing construction practices but also deliver quality, safe & sustainable houses at a much faster rate with much improved functional performance.

BMTPC also operates Performance Appraisal Certification Scheme (Gazette Notification No. I-16011/5/99 H-II in the Gazette of India No. 49 dated December 4, 1999) under which 34 new technologies* for mass housing have been identified, assessed for their suitability in different geo-climatic regions of the country & certified for usage by public & private agencies. The certified technologies are from the specific firms/ agencies/technology providers with their specific trade names, however, they can be generalized and classified broadly. These technologies along with other potential technologies under broad classification are as follows:

1. **Engineered formwork systems**
   - Monolithic Concrete Construction using Plastic/Aluminium/composite formwork
   - Modular Tunnel form
   - Slip form work systems
2. **Lost formwork systems**
   (a) Insulated form work systems
      - Glass Fibre Reinforced Gypsum (GFRG) Panel System
      - Sismo Building Technology
      - Insulating Concrete forms - Reliable Insupacks
      - Monolithic Insulated Concrete System (MICS)
      - Plaswall – lost in place formwork system with fibre Cement board, plastic spacer & concrete

   (b) Stay-in-place Structural Formwork systems
      - Coffor
      - Stay-in-place PVC wall forms
3. **Precast sandwich panel systems**
   (a) EPS Core Panels
      - Advanced Building System – EMMEDUE
      - Rapid Panels

- Reinforced EPS Core Panel System
- QuickBuild 3D Panels
- Concrewall Panel System
- BAU Panels

(b) Other Panels

- Prefabricated Fibre Reinforced Sandwich Panels (Aerocon Panels)
- Rising EPS (Beads) Cement Panels
- Plasmolite – fibre Cement board as outer & inner skin filled with foam concrete
- Flyash EPS Cement Sandwich Panel (Bhargav Infrastructure)
- Pir Dry-Wall Prefab Panel System (Covestro)
- Nano Living System Technology (Mgo Board as inner & outer skin with core of PUF)
- Continous PUF Sandwich Panels
- V-infill Walls (lightweight EPS cement sandwich panels)

4. **Light gauge steel structural systems**
   - Light Gauge Steel Framed Structure (LGSFS)
   - Light Gauge Steel Framed Structure with Infill Concrete Panels (LGSFS-ICP)
5. **Steel structural systems**
   - Factory Made Fast Track Building System
   - Speed Floor System
   - Continuous Sandwich (PUF) Panels with Steel Structures
6. **Precast concrete construction systems**

(a) 2D Precast component-based systems

- Waffle-Crete Building System
- Precast Large Concrete Panel System
- Industrialized RCC Precast 3-S system using RCC precast with or without shear walls, columns, beams, Cellular Light Weight Concrete Slabs/Semi-Precast Solid Slab
- Pre-stressed Precast Prefab Technology Using Hollow Core Slab, Beams, Columns, Solid Walls, Stairs, etc.
- Walltech Hollowcore Concrete Panel
- Robomatic Hollowcore Concrete Wall Panels
- Precast Construction Technology (precast beams, walls, slabs, columns, staircases & other customized elements)
- K-wall Panels (Hollowcore lightweight concrete panels)

(b) 3D Precast Volumetric

- Moducast systems
- 3D monolithic volumetric construction
- 3D Printing

7. **Metal structural systems**
    - Aluminium framing structures - infinium

---

* *The Performance appraisal certificates of the approved technologies can be downloaded from https://bmtpc.org.*

These systems are being used world over successfully and now most of the states in India along with govt. agencies & departments, construction agencies, development authorities & housing boards have shown interest & are willing to adopt them. About 1.4 million houses are being constructed with alternate construction systems in India under PMAY-U and other state-run schemes. These systems are sustainable systems and have potential to replace conventional methods of construction.

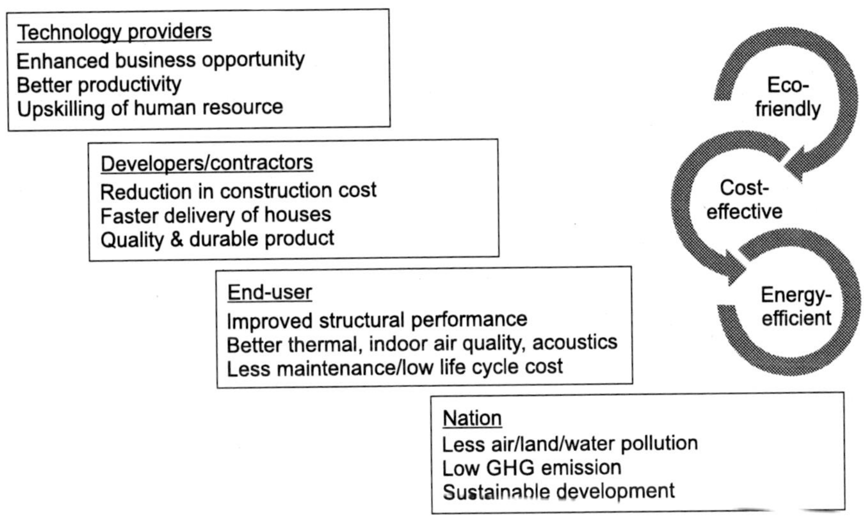

Market transformation through technology transition

1.3.2.1 Global Housing Technology Challenge (India)

To give it further impetus Ministry of Housing and Urban Affairs (MoHUA) has conceptualized the Global Housing Technology Challenge - India (GHTC-India) as a platform with which a holistic eco-system can be facilitated so that appropriate technologies from around the world and relevant stakeholders can be catalysed towards effecting a technology transition in the housing and construction sectors of India. The challenges has three components (i) Conduct of a biennial Construction Technology India, Expo-cum-Conference, to provide a platform for all stakeholders to exchange knowledge and business (ii) Identifying Proven Demonstrable Technologies from across the world, and mainstreaming them through field level applications in Light House Projects (LHPs) across India, (iii) Promoting Potential Future Technologies through the establishment of Affordable Sustainable Housing Accelerators-India (ASHA-India) for incubation and accelerator support.

GHTC-India was launched by Hon'ble Minister of State (Independent Charge), MoHUA on 14.01.2019 at Press Conference Hall, National Media Centre, Press Information Bureau, New Delhi. Subsequently, Construction Technology India – 2019 (CTI-2019) : Expo-cum-Conference was held at Vigyan Bhawan, New Delhi during 02-03 March, 2019 to bring together multiple stakeholders involved in innovative and alternative housing technologies, for exchange of knowledge and business opportunities and master classes. The Expo was inaugurated by Hon'ble Prime Minister of India in the presence of Hon'ble MoS (I/C), MoHUA.

The applications were invited online globally through a dedicated web site. 54 alternate technologies were shortlisted based on the technical parameters and are being promoted as future technologies for the construction sector. These 54 technologies have been further categorized into 6 broad categories and are given below along with brief explanation of the technology & details of the company to give the readers the idea of proven construction systems in vogue world over.

S. No.	Technology	Company
A. Precast Concrete Construction System - 3D Precast volumetric (4)		
3D Modular casting using steel moulds and high performance concrete enables to get form-finished walls cast along with the slab/roof or assembled together in the factory. The complete precast module is transported at site and erected one on another like Lego blocks. 3D construction provides faster construction, dust free environment at site, minimal wastage & disturbance at site, high quality, excellent finish, 90% work including finishing is complete in plant/casting yard, with minimum material storage at site. Since produced in factory, the technique produces better quality, durability and performance. Life cycle cost is less as compared to conventional system. Ensures faster delivery of houses. Maintenance cost initially is also comparable but in case of repair and rehabilitation required due to corrosion, if any, such cost in marine environment like in Chennai will be high. Also being thin elements, thermal performance is lower than conventional brick masonry. Monolithic connection details need to be ensured while working in seismic areas.		
1.	Pre-cast concrete system with columns, beams, walls, slabs, hollow core slabs & also 3D Volumetric components	M/s Katerra India Private Limited Velankani Tech Park, No.43, Hosur Road, E-City Ph1, Bangalore, India
2.	Vertical structural modules cast in Plant/ Casting yard are assembled together through casting of floor panel. The unit is transported & installed at site.	M/s ModucastPvt. Ltd 105 Kethana Residency, 16th Cross, 1A Main, Vignan Nagar, Bengaluru, India
3.	3D Modular casting using steel mould and high performance concrete of building modules in factory. These pods are transported to the construction site & assembled.	M/s Magicrete Building Solutions 101, Ritz Square, Ghoddod road, Surat, India
4.	Modules with 3D Volumetric Precast concrete unit, various units make on house	M/s Ultratech Cement Ltd, Ahura Centre, 3rd Floor, Mahakali Caves Road, Andheri (W), Mumbai, India

S. No.	Technology	Company
B. Precast Concrete Construction System – Precast components assembled at site (8)		
Precast Concrete Construction System is based on factory mass manufactured structural components i.e. precast columns, beams, slabs for floors and roofs/semi-precast solid slab, staircase and customized elements. These elements are cast on site/off site and then assembled with cranes and other equipment. All the components and their jointing are accomplished through on-site concerting along with embedded reinforcement to ensure monolithic resilient, ductile and durable behaviour. The establishment of factory at or near the site provides an economical solution in terms of storage and transportation. This type of construction provides high speed, elements are cast in a controlled factory condition resulting in better quality, durability and adoptable in all weather working. Life cycle cost is less as compared to conventional system. Ensures faster delivery of houses. Maintenance cost is comparable to conventional system. In case, block/brick masonry is used in infill walls, insulation may not be required else needed. Monolithic connection details need to be ensured while working in seismic areas.		
5.	Precast Large Concrete Panel (PLCP) System with structural members (wall, slab etc.) cast in a factory/ casting yard and brought to the building site for erection & assembling.	M/s Larsen & Toubro 5th Floor, B-Wing, TC-II Building, L&T Business Park, Gate No. 5, Saki Vihar Road, Powai,Mumbai, India
6.	Pre-cast Concrete Structural system comprising of pre-cast column, beam, precast concrete / light weight slab, AAC blocks/ infill concrete walls.	M/s B.G. Shirke Construction Technology Pvt. Ltd 72-76, Industrial Estate, Mundhwa, Pune, India
7.	Optimal Pre-cast concrete System through structural Analysis, design & equipment support	M/s Elematic India H-38, 1st Floor, Bali Nagar, New Delhi, India
8.	Precast concrete construction system using precast walls with precast plank floor.	M/s PG Setty Construction Technology Pvt Ltd 74, Sandesh Arcade, 3rd Floor, SahukarChenaiah Road, Kuvempunagar North, Saraswathipuram, Mysuru, India
9.	Pre cast components comprising of beams, columns, staircase, slab, hollow core slab etc. manufactured in plant & erected on site	M/s Teemage Builders Pvt Ltd Dr.no-7/67, Koduvai,SouthAvinashipalayam, c/o-MPNMJP, D.S, Chennimalai, Tiruppur, India
10.	Pre-cast sandwich panel system & Light weight Pre cast concrete slab	M/s Nordicflex House Ahura Centre, 3rd Floor, Mahakali Caves Road, Andheri (W), Mumbai, India
11.	Prefabricated Interlocking Technology (without mortar) with Roofing as Mechnized Precast R.C. Plank & Joist system	M/s AapKaAwass Adlakha Associates Pvt. Ltd F-70, Bhagat Singh Market, Gole Market, New Delhi, India

<table>
<tr><th>S. No.</th><th>Technology</th><th>Company</th></tr>
<tr><td>12.</td><td>Large Hollow wall prefab concrete Panel (lightweight, interlocking, concrete panel) using factory produced large standard hollow interlocking concrete block.</td><td>M/s William Ling
15 Mount Sinai Rise #05-01, Singapore, Pincode : 276906</td></tr>
<tr><td colspan="3">C. Light Gauge Steel Structural System & Pre-engineered Steel Structural System (16)</td></tr>
<tr><td colspan="3">Light Gauge Steel Framed Structure (LGSFS) is a factory made galvanized light gauge cold formed steel structural components assembled as panels at site. Being light weight and thin sections it has advantage over hot rolled steel. Various walling and roofing system can be used with LGSF framing.
LGSF structures provides time saving in construction and steel is recyclable. The system is low waste generation, resource efficient, clean & dust-free construction friendly, having good thermal efficiency through insulating materials like rockwool, CLC etc. In another variant, the infill wall comprises of factory made precast panels filled with light weight concrete at site. Being lighter in weight, the system provides better seismic resistance and economy. The connectivity and longevity of the system with foundation/footing need precautions.
For high rise structures, the composite structural system comprising of LGSF and hot rolled steel need to be provided.
There are variety of infill material being used in LGSF and therefore, the fire rating, thermal conductance, moisture penetration need to be ensured.
In case of hollow infill walls, sometimes the safety, impact resistance and puncture resistance is to be seen for the acceptability.
Pre-engineered Steel Structural System (PEB) is made of factory made hot rolled steel sections primarily used as columns and beams to form frame. Various walling and roofing options can be used based on the functional requirements like thermal efficiency, acoustics, fire rating, etc. This system is quick to install and provides quality construction as the components are factory made.
Steel structures have high resistance as regards to earthquake provided the connections are properly designed. In aggressive environment, steel structures need to be properly protected from corrosion. Fire coating is also required in case of steel components.</td></tr>
<tr><td>13.</td><td>LGS Framing with various walling & roofing options</td><td>M/s Mitsumi Housing Pvt. Ltd
202, RadheKishan Arista OPP Hirabhai tower Jawaharchowk - Isanpur Road Maninagar, Ahmedabad, India</td></tr>
<tr><td>14.</td><td>LGS Framing with various walling & roofing options</td><td>M/s Everest Industries Ltd
Everest Technopolis, D206, Sector 63, Noida, India</td></tr>
<tr><td>15.</td><td>LGS Framing with various walling & roofing options</td><td>M/s JSW Steel Ltd.
JSW Steel Ltd, JSW Centre, BKC, Bandra east, Mumbai, India</td></tr>
<tr><td>16.</td><td>LGS Framing with various In-situ light weight concrete walling & in-situ concrete slab</td><td>M/s Society for Development of Composites
No. 205, Bandematt, K.S.Town, Bangalore, India</td></tr>
</table>

S. No.	Technology	Company
17.	LGS Framing with various walling & roofing options	M/s Elemente Designer Homes Unit-2416, B-36, Express Trade Tower-2, Noida, India
18.	LGS Framing with various walling & roofing options	M/s MGI Infra Pvt. Ltd. 7/18 Nehru Enclave, New Delhi, India
19.	LGS Framing with various walling & roofing options	M/s RCM Prefab Pvt. Ltd 71, Mayfair Apartments, Mayfair Gardens, Haus Khas, New Delhi
20.	LGS Framing with various walling & roofing options	M/s Nipani Infra and Industries Pvt. Ltd. Nipani Industries , 2nd Floor Bhasin Arcade Main Road Gorakhpur, Jabalpur, India
21.	LGS Framing with Ecopanely boards as facing material made from agricultural wastes	M/s Strawcture Eco 52, Hari Om Nagar Colony , Phase-Ii Civil Lines, Goakhpur, India
22.	LGS Framing with walling as Lightweight concrete (Cement, sand, EPS & proprietary additive) mixed with water & poured between V Premium boards (Autoclaved Cement fibre boards) as facing sheet & various roofings	M/s Visakha Industries Ltd. A-14, I Floor, Sector-10, Noida, Noida, India
23.	Prefabricated steel structural system with Dry wall system as AAC panels, Puf panels etc	M/s RCC Infra Ventures Ltd. 14 Gf, Vipul Agora, Mg Road, Gurugram, India
24.	Hot rolled steel frame with speed floor	M/s Jindal Steel & Power Ltd. Plot no.2, Sector 32, Gurgaon,122001, Gurgaon, India
25.	Hot rolled steel section with AAC Panels as floor & slab	M/s HIL Ltd. A-76, Suraksha Building, 2nd Floor, Sector 4,, Noida, India
26.	AAC wall and roof panel system to provide integrated solution. AAC products are reinforced and used in both load and non-load bearing applications.	M/s Biltech Building Elements Ltd 71 & 83 Okhla Industrial Estate Phase III , Delhi, India
27.	AAC Panels are Wire mesh/ steel reinforced for use as wall & slab. Appears to be non load bearing panels to be used with structural framing.	M/s SCG International India Pvt Ltd Unit No. 609, 6th Floor, Emaar Palm Spring Plaza, Golf Course Road, Gurugram, India
28.	Precast Light Weight Hollow-core wall Panel is a non-structural construction material with framed structures.	M/s Pioneer Precast Solutions Private Limited Greenways Towers, 2nd Floor, No.119, St.Mary', Chennai, India

S. No.	Technology	Company
D. Prefabricated Sandwich Panel System (9)		
Precast Sandwich Panel System presented under this category comprised of; a) Expanded Polystyrene Core Panel System which are finished on site by spraying concrete, b) Dry wall system, wherein the panels are made of inner & outer boards (fibre cement /MGO) with infill core of lightweight concrete with Fly ash & EPS beads / Poly Isocyanurate (PIR). The panels are factory made components & thus quality of producing the panels can be better ensured in controlled conditions, however, material used in panels may affect the durability. The walling panels replace conventional brick & mortar walling construction thus brings in speed in construction. The dry walls do not require plastering & thus reduces the manual work on site, however, their resistance to lateral forces need to be ensured during design. EPS based panel, light weight concrete & Polyurethane brings thermal efficiency & thus brings in energy conservation/ sustainability. The technology reduces the use of natural resources to the extent of use of fly ash, EPS/ EPS beads etc. Being monolithic construction and lighter in weight, it provides better seismic resistance and economy. The details as regards claimed fire rating and toxicity in case of such panels need to be ensured. For high rise structures, the composite structural system comprising of sandwich panel and RCC/steel frame need to be provided.		
29.	Reinforced Expanded Polystyrene sheet core with sprayed concrete as wall & slab	M/s Worldhaus 301, SLV Heights , DNP Layout, Bangalore, India
30.	EPS Cement sandwich Panel): wall & slab with EPS Cement sandwich Panel to be used with RCC or Steel structural frame.	M/s Bhargav Infrastructure Pvt.Ltd B-2/20Hojiwala Ind Est Sachin Palsana Road, Surat, India
31.	EPS Cement sandwich Panel): wall & slab with EPS Cement sandwich Panel to be used with RCC or Steel structural frame. Load bearing upto G+1 storey	M/s Rising Japan Infra Private Limited I-203, SomVihar, R. K. Puram, New Delhi, India
32.	Reinforced Expanded Polystyrene sheet core with sprayed concrete as wall & slab	M/s Bau Panel Systems India Pvt Ltd, 42, 4th floor, Vigyanlok, Delhi, India
33.	Reinforced Expanded Polystyrene sheet core with sprayed concrete as wall & slab	M/s BK Chemtech Engineering 1 Jeremiah Road, Frazer town, Bangalore, India
34.	Reinforced Expanded Polystyrene sheet core with sprayed concrete as wall & slab	M/s MSN Construction No 666, 47th Street, 9th Sector, K K Nagar, Chennai, India
35.	Reinforced Expanded Polystyrene sheet core with sprayed concrete as wall & slab	M/s Beardshell Ltd. 114, Jyotishikhar Building, 8 Distt Centre, Janakpuri, New Delhi, India
36.	Pre-fab PIR (Poly-isocyanurate) based Dry Wall Panel System" as non-load bearing wall.	M/s Covestro India Pvt. Ltd. Plot 1A, Udyog Kendra, Ecotech III, Greater Noida, India

S. No.	Technology	Company
37.	Sandwich panels as wall & slab	M/s Project Etopia Group United Kingdom
E. Monolithic Concrete Construction (9)		
In this system, all walls, floors/slabs, together with door & window openings are cast in-situ monolithically in a single pour using specifically custom designed modular formwork made up of aluminium/plastics/steel/ composite, for the entire modular unit. Being modular predesigned formwork system, it acts as an assembly line production and enables rapid construction of multiple/mass scale units of repetitive type. This form of construction offers high speed, as casting cycle of 2-5 days per floor can also be achieved based on type of resources. It provides durable structure with smooth finish requiring no plastering, less maintenance. Being monolithic construction, it is excellent as regards earthquake resistance. A lead time of about 3 months is required for initiation of work, as the formwork is custom designed, manufactured and prototype approved before manufacturing required number of sets of formwork. In extreme hot climate, external insulation may be required, as the thermal conductivity of concrete is more than brick masonry wall. In case of repair and rehabilitation due to corrosion, the repair cost in multi-storeyed building is likely to be high.		
38.	Aluminium form work system for Monolithic Concrete construction	M/s Maini Scaffold Systems Pvt. Ltd. B1/A-21, Mohan Co-operative Industrial Estate, Mathura Road, New Delhi , Delhi, India
39.	Aluminium form work system for Monolithic Concrete construction	M/s KumkangKind India Pvt. Ltd 304, Jmd Regent Square, Mg Road, Gurgaon, India
40.	Aluminium form work system for Monolithic Concrete construction	M/s S-form India Pvt. Ltd. Unit No 323, 3rd Floor, Tower B4, Spazeit Park, Sohna Road, Sector 49, Gurugram, India
41.	Aluminium form work system for Monolithic Concrete construction	M/s ATS Infrastructure Ltd. Plot Number 16, Sector 135, Noida, India
42.	Monolithic Concrete construction using MIVAN technology	M/s Innovative housing & Infrastructure Pvt. Ltd PCL House- SCO 198, Sector 7C, New Chandigarh, Chandigarh, India
43.	Aluminium form work system for Monolithic Concrete construction	M/s MFS formwork Systems Pvt. Ltd. A1/268 1st Floor Indusand Bank Neelam Bata Road, NIT Faridabad, Faridabad, India
44.	Aluminium form work system for Monolithic Concrete construction	M/s Knest Manufacturers LLP. Khanna House, Plot 39 & 40, Nehru nagar, pimpri., Pune, India

S. No.	Technology	Company
45.	'Tunnel form' construction technology, an cast in situ RCC system, based on the use of high-precision, re-usable, room-sized, steel forms or moulds for monolithic concrete construction	M/s Outinord Formworks Pvt. Ltd. Gate No. 628, 629, Tal KhedKuruliChakan, Pune, India
46.	Aluminium form work system for Monolithic Concrete construction	M/s Brilliant Etoile Information Not Provided
F. Stay In Place Formwork System (8)		
The lost formwork systems are left in the structure and can either act as insulation or part of structural system. These formworks are made of Expanded Polystyrene (EPS) blocks/panels which are known as insulated concrete forms, steel cage filled with concrete/lightweight concrete known as structural forms, Panels, PVC formworks etc. Stay in place Formworks act as guide for fast construction of walling & slab as applicable. Being factory produced components, better quality of product is ensured. Formworks using EPS as outer core, Alleviated concrete using EPS bead as in-fill walling brings thermal & resource efficiency. There are certain systems such as Factory made prefab Glass fibre reinforced panels which use phosphogypsum (a waste product from fertilizer industry) as major component & thus saves natural resources/ brings sustainability. Being sacrificial formwork systems, the formwork acts either as insulation or as reinforcement, therefore saving cost on insultation/ reinforcement/ formwork. Being monolithic construction, better seismic resistance. In some of the stay-in-place formwork systems, functionality with respect to fire resistance, moisture penetration, jointing and maintenance need to be ensured.		
47.	Expanded-Steel Panel reinforced with all-galvanised Steel Wire-Struts serving both as the load-bearing steel structure and as the stay-in-place steel formwork filled with EPS-alleviated concrete.	M/s JK Structure 59 Hyde Park Gate, London, United Kingdom, Pincode : SW75ED
48.	Factory made prefab Glass fibre reinforced Gypsum cage panels suitable for wall & slab with reinforcement & concrete as infill as per the requirement.	M/s FACT RCF Building Products Limited, FRBL, Fact Cd Campus, Ambalamedu Post, Kochi, Kerala, India
49.	Structural Stay In Place Galvanized Steel formwork system for walling with the same bottom single layer formwork for slabs/ in-situ slab	M/s Coffor Construction Technology Pvt. Ltd Chandan Metal Compound, Near Gorwa BIDC, Gorwa, Vadodara, Gujarat, India
50.	Factory produced PVC Stay in place formwork with concrete & reinforcement in walling units with cast in-situ RCC Slab.	M/s Joseph Jebastin (Novel Assembler Private Limited), 1418 B-Wing, Dalamal Tower, F.P. Journal Marg, Nariman Point, Mumbai City, India
51.	Fully load bearing walls with 150 mm monolithic concrete core sandwiched inside two layers of EPS as walling.	M/s Reliable Insupack Building Solutions Sector-82, Noida, India

S. No.	Technology	Company
52.	Ready to use Stay in place polymer formwork, light weight, with flooring slab (combination of ferro cement and natural stone) placed on RCC precast joists)	M/s Kalzen Realty Pvt. Ltd 2-22-223/1/G1 Aruna Co-Op Society, Hyderabad, India
53.	FastBloc, Insulated Concrete Form (ICF), acts as formwork for concrete and rebar, Coloumn/post and beam construction, creating an strong skeleton in the walls.	M/s Fastbloc Building Systems 48 Tapadero Lane, Las Vegas, United States, Pincode : 89135
54.	Formwork system "Plaswall" with Two fibre cement boards (FCB) & HIMI (High Impact Molded Inserts) bonded between two sheets of FCB in situ and erected to produce a straight-to-finish wall with in-situ concrete.	M/s FTS Buildtech Pvt.Ltd 302, Vishakha Arcade, Opp. Courtyard Hotel, Off Veera Desai Road, Andheri West, Mumbai, India

Construction of Six Light House Projects under GHTC (India)

The above shortlisted global technology providers are invited to plan & construct Light House Projects (LHPs) within the framework of PMAY(U) on pre-selected sites across six identified PMAY(U) regions. These light house projects shall serve as open *live laboratories* for different aspects of transfer of technologies to field applications. Through online Request for proposal (RFP) & bidding process, the construction agencies along with technology have been finalized and are as follows:

S. No.	Location	DUs, Storeys	Technology	Technology Provider
1.	Indore, MP	1024, S+8	Precast sandwich panel system (precast RCC columns & beams, hollow core slabs, EPS cement sandwich panel walls)	M/s Rising Japan Infra Private Limited
2.	Rajkot, Gujarat	1144, S+13	Monolithic concrete construction (tunnel form)	M/s Outinord Formworks Pvt. Ltd.
3.	Chennai, Tamil Nadu	1152, G+5	Precast concrete construction precast components assembled at site	M/s BG Shirke Construction Technology Pvt. Ltd.
4.	Ranchi, Jharkhand	1008, G+8	Precast concrete construction - 3D volumetric construction	M/s Magicrete Building Solutions Pvt. Ltd.
5.	Agartala, Tripura	1000, G+6	Light gauge steel structural system & pre-engineered steel structural system	M/s Mitsumi Housing Pvt. Ltd.
6.	Lucknow, UP	1040, G+13	Stay-in-place formwork system (steel structural system, composite decking floor & stay-in-place formwork for walls)	M/s Novel Assembler Private Ltd.

1.3.3 Why Alternate Construction Systems are needed?

Resource Efficiency

A conventional building tends to focus on the use of basic materials namely cement, bricks, sand, aggregates, steel which are based on natural resources. Also, there is over dependence on fossil fuels for production & transportation. These natural resources are finite and cannot be replenished quickly. Also, their extraction and manufacturing have direct and indirect consequences on environment & energy requirements and pose danger to our planet in terms of greenhouse gas emissions, land & air pollution etc. Therefore, natural resources are to be used efficiently which is one of the key features of alternate construction systems as they employ industrial techniques to produces building components and use cement, steel and other aggregates optimally. The other feature of alternate construction systems is to make use of renewable resources.

Structural Design Efficiency

The alternate systems follow the path of optimization. Right from the concept & design stage, the building components including structural configuration is designed in a manner to optimize the performance. The performance-based design instead of prescriptive design philosophy is the key for design efficiency while dealing with these alternate construction systems.

Disaster Resilience

The alternate construction systems designed to be resilient in terms of natural hazards as it entails performance-based design of buildings.

Cost & Payoff

The most criticized issue about alternate construction systems is the price. The stigma is between the knowledge of up-front cost vis-à-vis life cycle cost. The cost of a building is defined as follows:

Total Cost = Initial construction cost + Running cost during life of building + disposal cost

This is also known as life-cycle cost.

Most of the time, the criterion in selection of technology is cost per m² which is initial cost and can be incongruous, if green aspects are to be considered. The buildings with alternate systems may cost 10-15% higher initially as of now (*It can also be questioned as today these systems require initial push but once mainstreamed the initial cost will also be equivalent to cost of conventional construction*) but will be less by couple of times over the entire life of the building. During life span of building, the financial payback will exceed the additional initial cost of using alternate systems several times. And broader benefits, such as reductions in greenhouse gases (GHGs) and other pollutants have large positive impacts on surrounding communities and on the planet.

Energy Efficiency

Alternate construction systems often include measures to reduce energy consumption i.e. the embodied energy required to extract, process, transport and install building materials and the operating energy to provide services such as heating and power for equipment. The buildings with alternate systems use less operating energy, embodied energy. These buildings will have a lower embodied energy than those built primarily with brick, mortar, concrete, or steel.

Water Efficiency

The conventional construction systems primarily are cast-in-situ reinforced concrete systems which require large quantity of potable water for curing and most of the time, the water of curing go waste. The new systems employ better techniques of curing such as pressurized curing, chemical curing etc. which help in conserving the water during construction.

Material Efficiency

Building materials typically considered to be sustainable, if they are based on renewable/waste resources and can be reusable and recyclable. Most of the alternate construction systems either make use of industrial waste, renewable resources, energy efficient building materials or optimizes the use of basic raw materials i.e. cement, sand, aggregates, steel consumption. For example, The GFRG panels makes use of phospho-gypsum which is a by-product of fertilizer plant, sandwich panels make use of EPS beads which are energy efficient.

Indoor Environmental Quality Enhancement

The Indoor Environmental Quality refers to provide comfort, well-being, and productivity of occupants. Indoor Air Quality seeks to reduce volatile organic compounds, or VOCs, and other air impurities such as microbial contaminants. The alternate systems employ construction materials and interior finish products with zero or low VOC emissions during the design and construction process which enhance indoor air quality. Also, well-insulated and tightly sealed envelope reduce moisture problems which often leads to dampness.

Operation & Maintenance Optimization

The construction systems identified are based on factory made building components which are manufactured with high precision under strict quality control and therefore, more durable requiring no or minimum maintenance. The alternate technologies are industrial products having SOPs for building's O & M.

Waste Reduction

Alternate construction systems not only seeks to reduce waste of energy, water and materials used during construction but also generate less construction & demolition waste after completion of the building. Well-designed buildings also help reduce the amount of waste generated by the occupants.

When buildings reach the end of their useful life, they are typically demolished and disposed to landfills. In case of alternate systems, most of the deconstructed components can be reclaimed into useful building materials.

1.3.4 End-User Benefits with Alternate Construction Systems

- Improved structural & functional performance
- Safer and disaster-resilient house
- Better quality of construction
- Low maintenance, minimum life cycle cost
- Speedy construction resulting in early occupancy
- Cost effective and environment friendly
- Better fire resistance & thermal efficiency
- Less air pollution and waste generation

Emerging construction systems help to build

SAFER structures

S: Sustainable	(resource efficient, climate responsive, environmentally responsible)
A: Affordable	(cost effective, faster construction)
F: Functional	(better thermal, acoustics, water tightness & fire performance)
E: Economical	(low life cycle cost, better quality)
R: Resilient	(disaster resistant, structurally superior)

A Journey Through Traditional Housing

Source: Various images depicted above have been taken from world wide web (www)

2

Alternate & Innovative Construction Systems Explained

2.1 PREAMBLE

As explained in the previous chapter, the cast-in-situ conventional construction systems need to be replaced by industrialized systems which reduce the construction time and produce quality, resilient and sustainable structures. These emerging systems can be broadly classified into following categories

1. Formwork system *replaces conventional formwork*
2. Sandwich panel system *replaces brick-mortar with dry wall*
3. Steel structural system *replaces cast-in-situ RCC frame with rolled steel sections*
4. Precast concrete construction *replaces cast-in-situ construction with factory made RCC components*

The above broad classification will help comprehend the readers the underlying concepts of new technologies and difference with the conventional systems.

2.2 FORMWORK SYSTEMS

2.2.1 What is Formwork

It is defined as temporary or permanent moulds conventionally made of timber or steel in which concrete is poured and once the concrete is set, the moulds are struck off and the finished set product will have the shape of the mould. In a conventional RCC framed construction to cast columns&beams, first formwork of columns of desired shape is assembled at the site and then concrete is poured. Later, formwork is removed typically after 7 to 28 days depending upon the structural element being cast. The beams are normally cast with slab and the formwork for both are assembled together and then concerting is done. The formwork for slab normally consists of plywood/ steel shuttering plates supported on steel props or wooden ballies called falsework.

For these form works, once the concrete has been poured into formwork and has set (or cured), the formwork is struck or stripped (removed) to expose the finished concrete. The time between pouring and formwork stripping depends on the job specifications, the cure required, and whether the form is supporting any weight.

In typical construction, more time & cost are required to make, erect and remove formwork than the cost & time to place the concrete and reinforcement. Formwork has significant impact on the cost, time & quality of the finished building and Nowadays, customized factory made formwork is trade-off and become very popular across globe.

2.2.1.1 *Traditional Timber/Steel Formwork*

The formwork is built on site out of timber/plywood/steel plates. It is easy to produce but time-consuming for larger structures. It is still used extensively where the labour costs are lower than the costs for procuring reusable formwork. It is also the most flexible type of formwork, so even where other systems are in use, complicated sections may use this formwork.

Imagine replacing this traditional formwork which is made in bits & pieces by engineered formwork where the formwork for entire unit is assembled first & then casting is done for entire unit in a single pour. This will eliminate joints and the construction will be monolithic & faster. This kind of formwork can be repeated more than 100 times depending upon material & quality. Further visualize, if the formwork is left within the concrete to act either as an insulation or as reinforcement. This kind of formwork is known as insulating concrete formwork (ICF) & structural stay in place formwork respectively. The ICF systems will provide better insulation without any added cost and structural stay in place form will supplement the steel requirements thus adding to economy.

2.2.1.2 Engineered Formwork

This formwork is built out of prefabricated modules with a metal frame (usually steel or aluminium) and covered on the application (concrete) side with material having the wanted surface structure (steel, aluminium, timber, etc.). The two major advantages of formwork systems, compared to traditional formwork, are speed of construction (modular systems pin, clip, or screw together quickly) and lower life-cycle costs. These formwork systems can achieve up to more than 200 uses depending on care and the applications. Metal formwork systems are better protected against rot and fire than traditional timber formwork. The formwork for the entire room including floor is erected and concrete is cast in single pour. Once the concrete is set, the formwork is stripped and taken to the floor above & so on. It works like assembly line production and facilitates repetitive monolithic modular construction.

In this system of Industrialized production of housing, the structure consists of load bearing RCC walls and slabs cast at site. Engineered formwork for casting of the entire house including the walls, floor slabs, openings, stairs, and balconies is assembled in position and concrete is placed in one continuous operation. Various construction activities, such as, erection of formwork, placement or reinforcement, concreting, stripping, etc., are performed in a pre-defined step. It is ideally suited for construction of buildings involving repetitive type of work where the floor layout is repeated on every floor. It is fast, simple and adaptable to varying architectural requirements.

2.2.1.3 *Tunnel Forms*

Tunnel forms are large, room size forms that allow walls and floors to be cast in a single pour. With multiple forms, the entire floor of a building can be done in a single pour. Tunnel forms require sufficient space exterior to the building for the entire form to be slipped out and hoisted up to the next level. A section of the walls is left uncast to remove the forms. Typically castings are done with a frequency of 4 days. Tunnel forms are most suited for buildings that have the same or similar cells to allow re-use of the forms within the floor and from one floor to the next, in regions which have high labour prices.

Tunnel form is a formwork system that allows the contractor to build monolithic walls and slabs in one operation on a daily cycle. It combines the speed, quality and accuracy of factory/offsite produced ready-mixed concrete and formwork with the flexibility and economy of cast in-situ construction.

This fast-track method of construction is suitable for repetitive cellular projects, such as hotels, apartment blocks and student accommodation. It offers economy, speed, quality and accuracy, as well as utilising the inherent benefits of concrete, such as fire and sound resistance.

The formwork sections for tunnel form are large and need to be swung by crane out from the side of the building when the concrete is being struck. This means that it is not suitable for tight sites.

In the tunnel-forms, the two half tunnels when assembled together form a full tunnel unit. Each half tunnel is made up of a horizontal and vertical panel connected by two inclined struts. In the engineered formwork, the entire room unit consisting of four walls & slab is cast together whereas here the tunnel is cast, leaving two shorter walls to be placed later.

2.2.1.4 *Insulated Concrete Formwork*

Insulating concrete formwork (ICF) systems, are forms used to hold fresh concrete that remain in place permanently to provide insulation for the structure they enclose. Insulating concrete forms (ICFs) result in cast-in-place concrete walls that are sandwiched between two layers of insulation material. These systems are strong and energy efficient. Common applications for this method of construction are low-rise buildings. Traditional finishes are applied to interior and exterior faces, so the buildings look similar to typical construction, although the walls are usually thicker. Insulating concrete forms systems offer performance benefits like strength and energy efficiency.

All major ICF systems are engineer-designed, code-accepted, and field-proven.

The two insulating faces are separated by some type of connector or web. Large preassembled blocks stack quickly on site. The insulating faces are of which is most often expanded polystyrene (EPS). The ties that interconnect the two layers of insulated forming material can be plastic, metal, or additional projections of the insulation.

The joints between individual forms can feature interlocking teeth or a tongue and groove configuration moulded into the forming material, or simple butt jointed seams. Special units for corners, floors, and roof assemblies round out the product lines and improve the engineering of the system and energy efficiency of the final construction.

Installation of insulating concrete form systems is similar to masonry construction. Utilities are typically recessed into cutouts in foam after concrete has been placed.

2.2.1.5 *Stay-in-Place Structural Formwork*

This formwork is assembled on site, usually comprising of galvanized horizontal & vertical ribs, steel sheets, channels, etc. These are usually for columns, beams and walls. The slab can be conventional RCC slab or any other form as per the usage & requirements.

The formwork stays in place after the concrete has cured and acts as axial and shear reinforcement, as well as serve to confine the concrete and prevent against environmental effects, such as corrosion and freeze-thaw cycles.

2.2.1.6 *Climbing Formwork*

Climbing formwork is a special type of slipformsfor vertical concrete structures that rises with the building process. While relatively complicated and costly, it can be an effective solution for buildings that are either very repetitive in form (such as towers or skyscrapers) or that require a seamless wall structure (using gliding formwork, a special type of climbing formwork). It is slipform method of concrete construction where the concrete is cast in one continuous operation.

Various types of climbing formwork exist, which are either relocated from time to time, or can even move on their own (usually on hydraulic jacks, required for self-climbing and gliding formworks).

Another engineered formwork system being used is flying deck form which is a system of components that are assembled into units called decks for forming concrete slabs in multi-storey buildings. The same set of flying deck forms is used repeatedly to form multiple floor slabs in a building. After the concrete that has been placed in a slab is sufficiently cured, the flying deck form for the slab is lifted and taken without disassembly to another level of a building to cast another concrete slab.

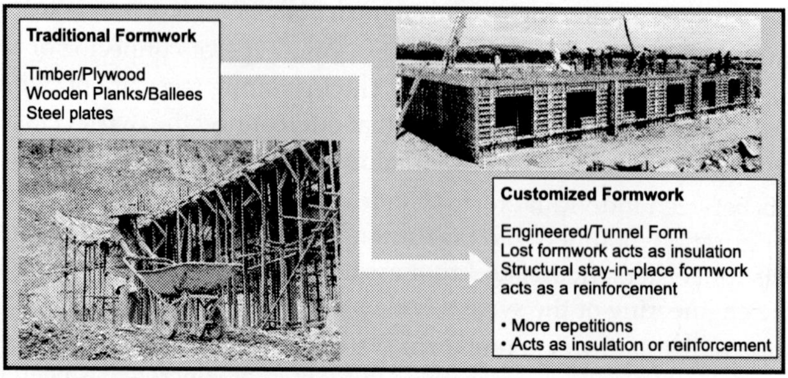

Source: Images depicted above have been taken from world wide web (www)

2.3 SANDWICH PANEL SYSTEMS

Traditionally walls are constructed with laying of modular units i.e. bricks with binding material i.e. mortar. The bricks can be replaced by concrete blocks, adobe, stone blocks or any other kind of masonry such as random rubble masonry. These walls can be infill walls or load bearing walls depending upon the strength & composition of brick &mortar. This brick & mortar construction is labour-intensive slow placed wet construction. If these brick & mortar walls can be replaced by stronger & durable readymade panels, the construction can be done pretty fast with better quality control & less wastages & human resource. There are variety of panels available which are being used world over in the construction sector for replacing these walls and are known as sandwich panels.

Imagine replacing masonry walls with factory made prefinished ready-made walls known as sandwich panels. These panels are stronger, durable with better quality control. Also, their functional performance in terms of acoustics, thermal, fire, rain water penetration, termite is much superior than cast-in-situ walls. Depending upon structural strength, these panels can be used as load bearing structural panels to build single to three storey houses or as non-load bearing infill walls to replace brick masonry walls between RCC frame. As per the requirements, these panels can be cut to suitable sizes, made hollow so as to minimize wastages & accommodate services.

Sandwich panels (also known as structural insulating panels(SIP) or composite panels) consist of two layers (wythes) of rigid material bonded to either side of a lightweight core. The three components act together as a composite wall. The lightweight core keeps the two faces in the correct position, resists shear forces, and provides insulation, while the two faces provide durability, weather and impact resistance, and resist in-plane forces of tension and compression.Sandwich panel systems include the panels themselves, the joints between them, fixing arrangement and a support system.Theyare generally pre-fabricated with good structural strength and a high level of insulation and low weight. Because of the time saving in installation, Sandwich Panels have become relatively common in residential buildings as replacement of infill walls specially internal walls.

Sandwich Panel walling system is drywall construction, where thewallsare put in a dry condition without the use of mortar. It is in contrast with the brick walls which are cast with use of plaster, which dries after application. These walls are large & rigid sheets and fastened directly to the structural frame of the building with nails, screws, or adhesives or are mounted on furring (thin strips of wood/metal nailed over the studs, joists, rafters, or masonry, which allow free circulation of air behind the wall).

Specialized tools for hanging drywall include the drywall hammer and the joint tool, which is similar to a plastering trowel but made of flexible steel with a concave bow. It is used to apply and smooth a plasterlike compound in joints between wall boards, feathering it out so that the outer edges virtually disappear and the joint, when painted, effectively becomes invisible. Nail heads, slightly depressed or "dimpled" by the hammer, disappear when similarly treated.

Sandwich Panel systems can be used to avoid delays, because the walls do not have to dry before other work can be started, and to obtain specific finishes. Panels are manufactured in both finished and unfinished forms. Finished panels can be faced with paints or other materials in a variety of permanent colours and textures, so that they need not be painted when installed. Backing materials and composition of the panel base determine the degree of insulation, fire resistance, and vapour barrier afforded. Wallboards are fire-rated from 1 hour to 4 hours according to the time that a fire's progress would be retarded by the wallboard.

The most commonly materials used for the outer layers of sandwich panels are:

- Hot-dip galvanized steel sheet
- Aluminium
- Zinc
- Pre-cast concrete or in-situ shotcrete
- Cement board
- Glass fibre reinforced polypropylene
- Poly vinyl chloride (PVC)
- Magnesium oxide board (MgO)
- Plywood
- Glass reinforced plastic (GRP)
- Glass Fibre Reinforced Gypsum (GFRG)

Whereas the core material is normally a rigid polyurethane core, but other core materials include:

- Expanded polystyrene (EPS)
- Extruded polystyrene (XPS)

- Mineral wool (rock fibre) (MWRF)
- Modified Phenolic foam (MPHEN)
- Polyisocyanurate (PIR)
- Honeycomb materials (such as Polypropylene)

Sandwich panels can be selected because of their ease and speed of installation, rigidity, thermal, fire and sound insulation, airtightness, robustness and durability, low maintenance/cleaning requirements, low capital cost, low lifecycle costs, chemical and biological resistance, light weight, weather resistance& dimensional stability.

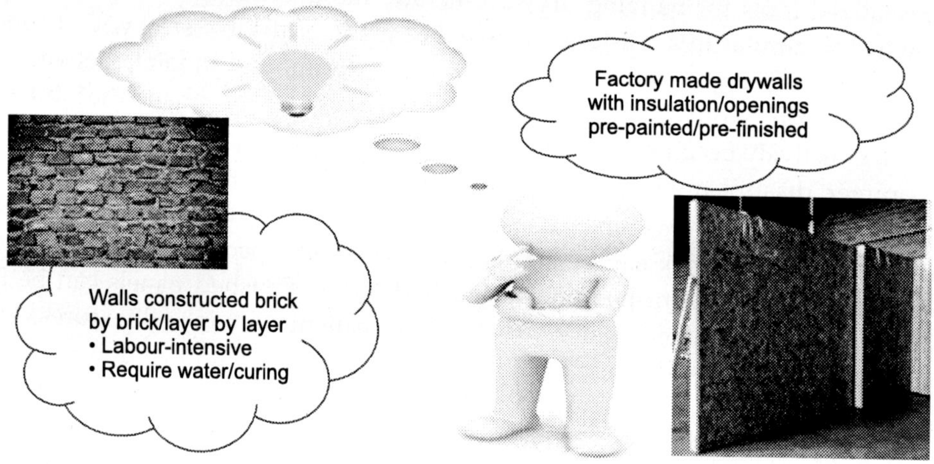

Source: Various images depicted above have been taken from world wide web (www)

2.4 STEEL STRUCTURAL SYSTEMS

The most prevalent building typology world over has been RCC framed construction where cast-in-situ RCC columns, beams& slabs are cast. The RCC frame is a structural system which transfers the loads through beam & columns to foundationsstrata. The cement was developed in 1824 as Portland cement & reinforced cement concrete (RCC) came into existence in 1849 with the first structure built in 1853. More than 150 years & RCC framed construction continues to rule the construction sector as the most convenient & easy way to construct. There are inherent advantages with RCC, however, it is time to look beyond & replace it with more efficient alternate systems. One, such system is to replace RCC frame with steel skeleton comprising of steel columns & beams. Steel is the world's most popular construction material because of its unique combination of durability, workability, and cost. It's an iron alloy that contains 0.2-2 percent carbon by weight. The early use of steel frame structure has been in late 19th century, however with the passage of time, in countries like India use of steel structural systems has not been much until recently as compared to USA & other European countries.However, Methods for manufacturing steel have evolved significantly since industrial production began in the late 19th century and today, steel production makes use of recycled materials as well as traditional raw materials, such as iron ore, coal, and limestone making it potential material for future. Based on manufacturing process, there are two type of steels which can be used for structural purposes:

Hot rolled steel

Hot rolling is a mill process which involves rolling the steel at a high temperature (typically at a temperature over 1700° F), which is above the steel's recrystallization temperature. When steel is above the recrystallization temperature, it can be shaped and formed easily, and the steel can be made in much larger sizes. When the steel cools off it will shrink slightly thus giving less control on the size and shape of the finished product when compared to cold rolled.Hot rolled steel is used in situations where precise shapes and tolerances are not required.

Cold rolled steel

Cold rolled steel is essentially hot rolled steel which is processed further in cold reduction mills, where the material is cooled (at room temperature) followed by annealing and/or tempers rolling. This process will produce steel with closer dimensional tolerances and a wider range of surface finishes. It can be used in any project where tolerances, surface condition, concentricity, and straightness are the major factors.

Hot rolled steel sections are used for steel structural systems whereas cold rolled thin sections are used for light gauge steel frame systems.

Cast-in-situ RCC framed construction can be suitably replaced by factory manufactured prefabricated steel column & beam sections and can be assembled at site by bolting/ riveting or any other suitable method. These steel sections with the advancement in manufacturing & technology are lighter, durable & offer a resilient system which can be erected pretty fast. Also, the wastages are minimized. Nowadays, all industrial & large span structures are constructed with steel structural systems. They are also termed as pre-engineered structures.

2.4.1 Structural Steel Frame System

Steel frame is a structural system with a skeleton frame of vertical steel columns and horizontal beams, constructed in a rectangular grid to support the floors, roof and walls of a building which are all attached to the frame. The development of this technique made the construction of the skyscraper possible.

The hot rolled steel profile or cross section of steel columns are normally hot rolled sections as specified in standards. Square and round tubular sections of steel can also be used and can be filled with concrete depending upon the structural requirements. Steel beams are connected to the columns with bolts and threaded fasteners, and historically connected by rivets.

Wide sheets of steel deck can be used to cover the top of the steel frame as a "form" or corrugated mould, below a thick layer of concrete and steel reinforcing bars. Another popular alternative is a floor of precast concrete flooring units with some form of concrete topping.

The frame needs to be protected from fire because steel softens at high temperature and this can cause the building to partially collapse. In the case of the columns this is usually done by encasing it in some form of fire-resistant structure such as masonry, concrete or plasterboard. The beams may be encased in concrete, plasterboard or sprayed with a coating to insulate it from the heat of the fire or it can be protected by a fire-resistant ceiling construction.

The exterior skin of the building is anchored to the frame using a variety of construction techniques & huge variety of architectural styles. Bricks, stone, reinforced concrete, architectural glass, sheet metal etc. have been used to cover the frame to protect the steel from the weather.

2.4.2 Light Gauge Steel Frame System

Light gauge or Cold form steel construction is very similar to wood framed construction in principle - the wooden framing members are replaced with thin steel sections. The steel sections used here are called cold formed sections made from cold rolled steel, meaning that the sections are formed, or given shape at room temperature. This is in contrast to thicker hot rolled sections, that are shaped while the steel is molten hot. Cold formed steel is shaped by guiding thin sheets of steel through a series of rollers, each roller changing the shape very slightly, with the net result of converting a flat sheet of steel into a C or S-shaped section.

The steel used here is coated with zinc (called galvanized) or a mixture of zinc and aluminium (called zincalume or galvalume) to protect it from corrosion. The thickness of this coating can be varied to suit a range of environments. Typically, marine environments require the most protection, and dry, arid regions the least.

The thicknesses of steel used here range from about 1 to 3 mm for structural sections, and 1 to 2 mm for non-structural sections. The members are sized to roughly correspond to wood members: 2"x4" and 2"x6" are common sizes.

Like in wooden framed construction, a frame of steel members is first constructed, and then clad with dry sheeting on both sides to form a load bearing wall. The walls can be of any material ranging from precast boards, blocks, EPS panels or an external layer of insulation material and outer leaf of cement fibre/particle board or dry mix shotcrete. The floor/roof can be RCC/steel truss/steel deck om joists. Connections between members are made with self-tapping self-drilling screws.

These sections are usually pre-punched sections i.e. sections with factory-made holes in them - so that wires and plumbing can be easily passed through the walls.

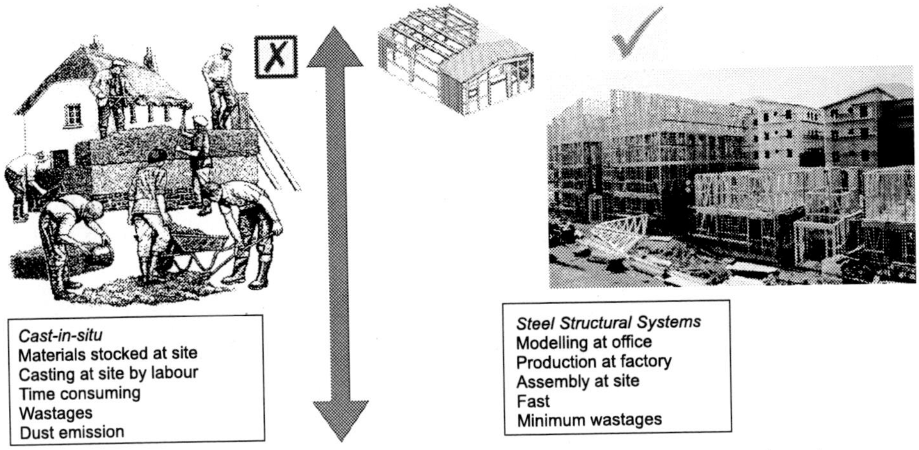

Source: Images shown above have been taken from world wide web (www)

2.5 PRECAST CONCRETE CONSTRUCTION

Precast concrete is an alternative to cast-in-situ concrete. While cast-in-situ concrete is cast in its actual location, precast concrete is cast at another location, either at the building site or in a factory, and is then lifted to its final resting place and fixed securely. Unlike cast-in-situ construction, which is monolithic or continuous, precast concrete buildings are made of separate pieces that are bolted or connected together at site.

Precasting is great for producing large numbers of modular components. Let's say we are building an affordable housing project with 1,000 identical dwelling units. We could then use precasting to produce wall slabs and floor slabs for all units, and then lift them into place and assemble them.Since it is done in a customized pre-casting yard or factory, it makes construction easier for the following reasons:

(a) The construction is done on the ground rather than at a height.

(b) It can be done inside a climate-controlled structure, eliminating problems of rain, dust, cold, or heat.

(c) Specialised formwork (moulds) can be built for doing many repetitions of the same component.

(d) Specialised equipment can be used to make, move, and pour the liquid concrete.

(e) Curing of the concrete can be done in a controlled environment.

Being manufactured under controlled conditions, the quality of precast components is very high. Further, since the components are cast beforehand, construction is very quick. In cast-in-situ construction, engineers have to build in stages after the previous stage has finished, which does take time, as concrete generally takes 28 days to reach its full strength.

However, there are certain precautions which need to be kept in mind while undertaking precast concrete construction. Since each building component is made separately, the structural frame or system is not monolithic or continuous like regular concrete construction. The joints between these components create structural discontinuity. The forces of the building will pass through these joints, so they have to be designed to transfer these forces safely and properly. Also, as the building is made of discrete components, the joints between adjacent members have to be sealed with special sealants to make them waterproof.

Precast concrete components can be connected in a number of ways:

- They can be bolted together. In order to do this, steel connectors are embedded in the concrete at the time of casting. This must be done with great precision.
- They can be grouted or concreted together. In this method, loops of steel reinforcement are left protruding out of the precast concrete members. Two members are placed in position, and reinforcement is threaded between the loops. Fresh concrete is then poured around this reinforcement, in a space left for this purpose.

Each precast component is usually large and heavy. This means that cranes are required to lift them in position; these cranes are required to operate over the entire building volume. Since there will only be a few cranes at site, the time taken by the cranes to pick up a piece and shift it to its final position becomes critical in determining the building schedule.

Reinforced concrete is a material usually used for structural systems due to its strength, durability, and affordability. Precast concrete can be used in variety of ways (a) to make beams, columns, floor slabs, foundations, and other structural members of buildings (b) to make wall or cladding panels for buildings (c) to make precast pre-stressed elements for buildings (d) to make components for infrastructure projects: elements such as bridge spans, or metro line viaducts are often precast in a casting yard (e) to make products for sale: precast water tanks, septic tanks, drainage chambers, railway sleepers, floor beams, boundary walls, water pipes are all available (f) Since it can be moulded into any shape, it can also be used to create one-off unusual forms such as boats, sculptures and suchlike.

Precasting can be done at a casting yard, in or near the site, or in a factory. A key aspect of determining whether to use site or factory precasting are the transport costs. Factory work offers superior quality for obvious reasons, so if there is a factory close to the site, it makes sense to use it.

A typical pre-casting yard must accommodate the activities such as (i) storing the raw materials, i.e. cement, aggregate, sand, admixtures, water, reinforcement bars, and steel or plywood sheets for formwork (ii) a formwork making and maintenance yard (iii) a concrete mixing plant (iv) a steel reinforcement yard to make rebar cages to be placed inside the concrete (v) a casting area (vi) a curing area (vii) a stacking area for finished components.

2.5.1 3D Precast Volumetric Construction

3D Volumetric construction (also known as modular construction) involves the production of three-dimensional units in controlled factory conditions prior to transportation to site. Modules can be brought to site in a variety of forms, ranging from a basic structure to one with all internal and external finishes and services installed, all ready for assembly. The casting of modules uses the benefits of factory conditions to create service-intensive units where a high degree of repetition and a need for rapid assembly on-site make its use highly desirable. This modern method of construction offers the inherent benefits of concrete, such as thermal mass, sound and fire resistance, as well as offering factory quality and accuracy, together with speed of erection on-site.

2.5.2 Precast Flat Panel System

Floor and wall units are produced off-site in a factory and erected on-site to form robust structures, ideal for all repetitive cellular projects. Panels can include services, windows, doors and finishes. Building envelope panels with factory fitted insulation and decorative cladding can also be used as load-bearing elements. This offers factory quality and accuracy, together with speed of erection on-site. This type of construction is normally called cross-wall construction.

2.5.3 Hybrid Concrete Construction

Hybrid concrete construction combines all the benefits of precasting with the advantages of cast in-situ construction. Combining the two, as a hybrid frame, results in even greater construction speed, quality and overall economy. Hybrid concrete construction can answer demands for lower costs and higher quality by providing simple, buildable and competitive structures that offer consistent performance and quality.

2.5.4 Flat Slabs

Flat slabs are built quickly due to modern formwork being simplified and minimised. Rapid turnaround is achieved using a combination of early striking and panelised formwork systems. Use of prefabricated services can be maximised because of the uninterrupted service zones beneath the floor slab; so flat slab construction offers rapid overall construction, as it simplifies the installation of services.

In addition to saving on construction time, flat slab construction also places no restrictions on the positioning of horizontal services and partitions. This offers considerable flexibility to the occupier, who can easily alter internal layouts to accommodate changes in the use of the structure. Post-tensioning of flat slabs enables longer and thinner slabs, with less reinforcement, and hence offers significant programme and labour advantages.

2.5.5 Hollow Core Wall-Slab Construction

A hollow core slabis a precast slab of prestressed concrete typically used in the construction of floors in multi-story apartment buildings. The slab has been especially popular in countries where the emphasis of home construction has been on precast concrete. Precast concrete popularity is linked with economical constructions because of fast building assembly, lower self-weight (less material), etc. Precast hollow-core elements are also known as the most sustainable floor/roof system and has far smaller CO_2 footprint.

The precast concrete slab has tubular voids extending the full length of the slab, typically with a diameter equal to the $\frac{2}{3}-\frac{3}{4}$ the thickness of the slab. This makes the slab much lighter than a massive solid concrete floor slab of equal thickness or strength. The reduced weight also lowers material and transportation costs. The slabs are typically 120 cm wide with standard thicknesses normally between 15 cm and 50 cm. Reinforcing steel wire rope provides bending resistance.

Hollow core slabs in prestressed concrete are usually manufactured in lengths of up to 200 meters and cut to customised sizes. The process involves extruding wet concrete along with the prestressed steel wire rope from a moving mould. The continuous slab is then cut to required lengths by a large diamond circular saw. Factory production provides the obvious advantages of reduced time, labour and training.

Another fabrication system produces hollow-core floor slabs in Reinforced Concrete (not prestressed). These are made on carousel production lines, directly to exact length, and as a stock product. However, the length is limited to about 7-8 meters.

Hollow-core slabs and wall elements without prestressed steel wire can be formed by extruders. The size of these elements will typically range in width from 600 to 2400 mm, in thickness from 150 to 500 mm, and can be delivered in lengths of up to 24 m.

The voids of the hollow core can be used as conduit for installations. The interior of the core can be coated in order to use it as a ventilation duct.

2.5.6 Prefabricated Prefinished Volumetric Construction (PPVC)

Prefabricated Prefinished Volumetric Construction (PPVC) refers to a construction method whereby free-standing 3-dimensional modules are completed with internal finishes, fixtures and fittings in an off-site fabrication facility before it is delivered and installed on site.

The key benefits of PPVC include (1) Improved Productivity (2) PPVC can potentially achieve a productivity improvement of up to 40% in terms of manpower and time savings, depending on the complexity of the projects (3) Better Construction

Environment (4) As bulk of the installation activities and manpower are moved off-site to a factory controlled environment, it can minimise dust and noise pollution and improve site safety (5) Improved Quality Control (6) Off-site fabrication can result in higher quality end products through quality control in a factory-like environment.

Conventional RCC construction takes place at the site with the availability of all materials, equipment, labour at a time and productivity heavily depends on environment & availability. The precast concrete construction takes place in an ideal factory setup giving stable working conditions for uninterrupted production with consistent quality, durability, faster delivery, optimising use of materials & therefore promoting sustainability & affordability. Try to visualize casting building component-wise at a site is being replaced by manufacturing the entire apartment in the factory.

Source: Images shown above have been taken from world wide web (www)

3
Formwork Systems

3.1 FORMWORK

Formwork is the system to support the plastic state concrete and to cast and keep in desired shape till it attains sufficient strength to support its own weight. Sometimes, low cost formwork is not removed in some of the new technologies, known as stay in place formwork or lost in place formwork.

In BIS code IS 14687, Formwork is described as Falsework and defined in the foreword as "In the widest meaning it is the total system of support for freshly placed concrete including the mould or sheathing which contacts the concrete as well as supporting members, hardware and necessary bracing, etc."

Thus, formwork is used as a temporary mould into which concrete is poured and formed. It is a vertical or horizontal arrangement made to keep concrete in position until it gains strength & shape and as such is a system consisting of props, staging and shuttering systems.

3.2 REQUIREMENTS OF A GOOD FORMWORK

Safety and integrity: The formwork has to be safe for permanent constructions and workers. For the same, it shall be adequately braced laterally and diagonally.

Rigidity and deflection: Formwork has to be rigid enough so that the deflections under the dead load and live loads and forces caused by ramming and vibration of concrete and other incidental loads imposed upon it during and after casting of concrete are well within permissible limits. The rigidity can be achieved by suitable number of ties and braces. Screw jacks or hard board wedges, where required shall be provided to control formwork settlement.

Strength and stability: The formwork must be of adequate strength and so detailed as to withstand all anticipated loads including lateral loads, vibrations and small accidental loads. The system must be such as to prevent progressive failure due to minor causes.

3.3 FUNCTIONAL REQUIREMENTS

Erection and release: Formwork has to be so designed and constructed that they can be removed in parts or as planned in the desired sequence without damaging the surface of concrete or disturbing other sections or causing collapse of the formwork systems. The connections joining various components of the formwork should be capable of being easily removed while formwork stripping.

Ease of inspection: The system should that it has adequate and safe access to all areas for easy inspection.

Shape and size: The formwork shall be erected such that the shape and dimensions of the concrete structures are conforming to the drawings, the specifications and tolerances. Chamfers, bevelled edges and mouldings if specified, should be provided in the forms.

Finish: The formwork should be hard enough so as to not to get damaged due to operations of reinforcement fixing, pouring and vibrating of concrete and removal of forms.

Reuse and number of repetitions: The formwork has to be designed and planned to permit maximum reuses/repetitions to reduce the cost of concrete and the work.

Thus, the essential requirements of formwork are:

(a) It should be strong enough to take the dead loads, live loads, incidental loads and other loads expected during construction before attaining the strength by the concrete.

(b) The joints in the formwork should be rigid so that the bulging, twisting, or sagging due to loadings is within permissible limits.

(c) The construction lines in the formwork should be true and the surface plane so that the cost finishing the surface of concrete on removing the shuttering is the least.

(d) The formwork should be easily removable without damage to itself or the concrete.

(e) It should provide ease of inspection.

3.4 COMPONENTS OF FORMWORK

As mentioned earlier, the formwork (Figure 1 & 2) may consist of the following components:

- Centring system
- Staging system
- Shuttering system

Fig. 3.1: Formwork for slab

Fig. 3.2: Formwork for wall

Centering system is a temporary arrangement and part of formwork which is arranged to support horizontal members or the formwork for floor beams & slabs.

Staging is a temporary members system which is used to support centering or shuttering. It is done by props, jacks, H frames, cup lock system, wooden ballies, etc.

Shuttering is a part of formwork or derivative of formwork as a vertical temporary arrangement used to bring concrete in a desired shape or formwork which supports vertical arrangement.

Formwork system includes accessories which are required in case of conventional formwork as well as in specialised formwork and have to be provided as per codes and manufacturer's specifications. In conventional formwork, it may include form ties, form anchors, form jacks, spreaders/spacers, column clamps, sealing strips, chamfer fillets, steel props etc and in case of specialised formwork there are large accessories which depend upon manufacturer to manufacturer and type of formwork.

3.5 TYPES OF FORMWORK

Formwork according to materials used to fabricate formwork may be timber, plywood, steel, aluminium, PVC, plastics, ferro-cement or any engineering material.

Now timber is not preferred in formwork applications due to environmental considerations and cost. Steel is used in conventional formwork. In case of specialised formwork like Tunnel formwork, steel is used. In Aluminium formwork, aluminium is used as the name indicates and in plastic - aluminium formwork, PVC and aluminium. In stay in place formwork, EPS panels, ferro-cement panels or other similar materials are used.

3.5.1 Formwork Coatings and Releasing Agents

Formwork in contact with concrete is treated with a coating or releasing agent of approved composition. The type of coating and its composition depends upon the type of shuttering material used and its surface which would be in contact with concrete. Coating and release agent should provide a clean easy release or strike without damage to either the concrete face or the form, contribute to the production of blemish free concrete surface, have no adverse effect upon either the form or concrete, be easy to apply evenly at the recommended coverage, and not inhibit adhesive of any finish applied to the formed surface.

Shuttering should be coated with suitable form release agents for easy stripping before each use. The form release agents are temporary coatings consisting of fatty acids which react with the alkaline cement and leave behind soap like substance on the contact surface. This helps release of the form. These may be oils, emulsified wax, oil phased emulsions with water globules, petroleum based products, catalysed polyurethane foam, etc.

Careful consideration should be given to the choice of release agent taking account of the type of surface to which it is to be applied, the conditions under which it is to be used, the type of concrete, the quality of finish, the area of form and the ease of application. The conventional use of waste oil as release agent should not be encouraged since it does not contain fatty acids.

3.6 DESIGN OF FORMWORK

Formwork shall be designed to meet the requirements of the permanent structure using relevant Indian Standards for materials selected for formwork and also for the loadings expected during casting of concrete including incidental loads. The design should take into account the conditions of materials to be actually used for the formwork, environment and site consideration. The checks for safety, overturning, overall stability and progressive collapse shall be implicit in design. The formwork system shall preferably be so designed that the vertical members are subjected to compressive force only under the action of combined horizontal and vertical loads. The design should also take into account the sequence of concreting, especially in construction of cantilevers, domes, etc. The design should consider the site investigation report, expected loading scheme of load transfer, sequence of erection and releasing, procedure of concreting and time frame. In case of specialised formwork, design should also consider the strength of concrete on which formwork is placed or supported, ease of curing existing concrete, and loading expected from equipment if any.

Thus the design philosophy of formwork is that the formwork shall be properly designed for self weight, weight of reinforcement, weight of fresh concrete, and various live loads likely to be imposed during the construction process such as workmen, materials, equipment, impact and other incidental loads, vertical or lateral.

3.6.1 Loads on Formwork and Combination of Loads

Formwork shall be designed to resist the expected dead load, imposed construction load, environmental load, construction load and incidental loads. Loads on formwork may be any combinations of the same during erection and operation, and lateral pressure.

Dead Loads include formwork structure, self weight of formwork and any ancillary temporary work connected or supported by formwork, weight of freshly placed concrete for the permanent structure directly supported by the formwork; and additional weight of fittings. The unit weight of wet concrete including reinforcement shall be taken as mentioned in the code and according to mix of the concrete used.

Imposed Loads during constructional operation shall constitute the imposed loads for which IS 875 (Part 2) may be referred for formwork design. Such loads may occur due to construction personnel, plant and equipments, vibration and impact of machine delivered concrete, lateral pressure of fresh concrete, unsymmetrical placement of concrete, concentrated load and storage of construction materials. Imposition of any construction load on the partially constructed structures shall not be allowed unless specified in the drawings or approved by the engineer-in-charge. Allowance shall be made in the formwork design to accommodate force or deformation in the post tensioned members.

Due consideration shall be given that the concrete is not dropped from a free height or accumulated to such a height that it exceeds the loading allowance else the same shall be considered in the design. Load from the permanent works shall be assessed from the self weight of the permanent structure to be supported by the formwork including the weight of plastic concrete which may actually be determined or taken as per IS 875 (Part 1). The effect of impact or surge wherever it may occur shall be suitably considered and catered for. Where pumping is resorted to, additional loads should be considered in design.

Lateral pressure due to fresh concrete depends on the temperature of concrete as placed, the rate of placing of concrete and the concrete mix proportion. This shall be considered as per IS 14687.

Environmental loads include wind or seismic loads, earth pressure, water pressure, snow loads or ice loads, and thermal load, etc. Wind loads should be taken for design in accordance with IS 875 (Part 3) subject to a minimum horizontal load equal to 3 percent of the vertical loads at critical level. Snow loads should be assumed in accordance with IS 875 (Part 4). Ice loads are required to be taken into account in the design of members of formwork in zones subjected to ice formation as mentioned in IS 14687. Earth pressure can occur on formwork as in the case of retaining walls and these shall be catered for. The rise in the water table may increase pressure on the formwork. Shrinkage and early thermal movements in the freshly placed concrete should be assessed and accommodated in the design of formwork.

Permissible stresses shall not exceed the values specified in the relevant Indian Standards for permanent structures and IS 14687.

3.6.2 Deviation Limit

The formwork shall be designed so as to remain sufficiently rigid during placing and compaction of concrete. The total calculated deflection of formwork including initial imperfection in the members shall not exceed the flowing;

a. For beam span < 3000 mm: Deflection not greater than 3 mm
b. For beam span >3000 mm: Deflection least of 3 mm and span/1000

3.6.3 Stability

The formwork shall be designed to check against overturning and sliding. A factor of safety of 1.5 may be used in design against overturning and sliding.

3.6.4 Forces Resulting from Erection

Such forces are important both in conventional formwork and more particularly in specialised formwork.

The acceptable erection tolerances on a nominally vertical members result in horizontal erections in association with the applied vertical forces. Provided the maximum permissible erection tolerances are not exceeded, and the centroid of the member applying the vertical forces is not more than 25 mm in plan from the centroid of the foot of the supporting vertical member, provision should be made for a horizontal reaction equal to 1 percent of the applied vertical forces. These recommendations relate to individual tubes, props and structural steel sections and to proprietary components used as support towers.

3.6.5 Bracing

The formwork system should be designed to transfer all horizontal loads to the ground or to completed construction in such a manner as to ensure safety during construction. Diagonal bracings should be provided in vertical and horizontal plane to resist lateral loads and to prevent instability of individual members. These should be provided where restraint is actually required and should be as close to the point of application of vertical and horizontal forces and at the intersection of vertical and horizontal members.

3.7 FOUNDATION

Formwork shall be designed to meet the requirements of the permanent structure using relevant Indian Standards for materials selected for formwork and also for the loadings expected during the casting of concrete including incidental loads. The design should take into account the conditions of materials to be actually used for the formwork, environment and site consideration. The checks for safety, overturning, overall stability and progressive collapse shall be implicit in design. The formwork system shall preferably be so designed that the vertical members are subjected to compressive force only under the action of combined horizontal and vertical loads. The design should also take into account the sequence of concreting, especially in construction of cantilevers, domes, etc. The design should consider the site investigation report, expected loading scheme of load transfer, sequence of erection and releasing, procedure of concreting and time frame. In case of specialised formwork, design should also consider the strength of concrete on which formwork is to be placed or supported, ease of curing the existing concrete, and loading expected from equipment if any.

Thus, the design philosophy of formwork is that the formwork shall be properly designed for self weight, weight of reinforcement, weight of fresh concrete, and various live loads likely to be imposed during the construction process such as workmen, materials, equipment, impact and other incidental loads, vertical or lateral.

3.7.1 Loads on Formwork and Combination of Loads

Formwork shall be designed to resist the expected dead loads, imposed construction load, environmental load, construction load and incidental loads. Loads on formwork may be any combinations of the same during erection and operation, and lateral pressure.

Dead loads include formwork structure, weight of formwork and any ancillary temporary work connected or supported by formwork, weight of freshly placed concrete for the permanent structure directly supported by the formwork; and additional weight of fittings. The unit weight of wet concrete including reinforcement shall be taken as mentioned in the code and according to the mix of the concrete used.

Imposed loads during construction constitute the imposed loads for which IS 875 (Part 2) may be referred for formwork design. Such loads may occur due to construction personnel, plant and equipment, vibration and impact of machine delivered concrete, lateral pressure of fresh concrete, unsymmetrical placement of concrete, concentrated load and storage of construction materials. Imposition of any construction load on the partially constructed structures shall not be allowed unless specified in the drawings or approved by the engineer-in-charge. Allowance shall be made in the formwork design to accommodate force or deformation in the post-tensioned members.

Due consideration should be given that the concrete is not dropped from a free height or accumulated to such a height that it exceeds the loading allowance else the same shall be considered in the design. Load from the permanent works shall be assessed from the self weight of the permanent structure to be supported by the formwork including the weight of plastic concrete which may actually be determined or taken as per IS 875 (Part 1). The effect of impact or surge wherever it may occur shall be suitably considered and catered for. Where pumping is resorted to, additional loads should be considered in design.

Lateral pressure due to fresh concrete depends on the temperature of concrete as placed, the rate of placing of concrete and the concrete mix proportion. This shall be considered as per IS 14687.

Environmental loads include wind or seismic loads, earth pressure, water pressure, snow loads or ice loads, thermal load, etc. Wind loads should be taken for design in accordance with IS 875 (Part 3) subject to a minimum horizontal load equal to 3 per cent of the vertical loads at critical level. Snow loads should be assumed in accordance with IS 875 (Part 4). Ice loads are required to be taken into account in the design of members of formwork in zones subjected to ice formation as mentioned in IS 14687. Earth pressure can occur on formwork as in the case of retaining walls and these should be catered for. The rise in the water table may increase pressure on the formwork. Shrinkage and early thermal movements in the freshly placed concrete should be assessed and accommodated in the design of formwork.

Permissible stresses should not exceed the values specified in the relevant Indian Standards for permanent structures and IS 14687.

3.7.2 Deviation Limit

The formwork should be designed so as to remain sufficiently rigid during placing and compaction of concrete. The total calculated deflection of formwork including initial imperfection in the members shall not exceed the following:

(a) For beam span < 3000 mm: deflection not greater than 3 mm

(b) For beam span >3000 mm: deflection least of 3 mm and span/1000

3.7.3 Stability

The formwork should be designed to check against overturning and sliding. A factor of safety of 1.5 may be used in design against overturning and sliding.

3.7.4 Forces Resulting from Erection

Such forces are important both in conventional formwork and more particularly in specialised formwork.

The acceptable erection tolerances on a nominally vertical member result in horizontal erections in association with the applied vertical forces, provided the maximum permissible erection tolerances are not exceeded, and the centroid of the member applying the vertical forces is not more than 25 mm in plan from the centroid of the foot of the supporting vertical member. Provision should be made for a horizontal reaction equal to 1 per cent of the applied vertical forces. These recommendations relate to individual tubes, props and structural steel sections and to proprietary components used as support towers.

3.7.5 Bracing

The formwork system should be designed to transfer all horizontal loads to the ground or to the completed construction in such a manner as to ensure safety during construction. Diagonal bracings should be provided in vertical and horizontal planes to resist lateral loads and prevent instability of individual members. These should be provided where restraint is actually required and should be close to the point of application of vertical and horizontal forces and at the intersection of vertical and horizontal members.

3.8 FOUNDATION

If soil is incapable of supporting superimposed loads without appreciable settlement, it should be stabilized or other means of support applied. The loads from the formwork supported on the ground shall be applied to the ground through distribution members made of timber, steel base plate or precast concrete. For details, IS 14687 may be referred.

When it is required to proceed with the upper storey construction before the floor below has developed required strength, or its strength is not enough to withstand the construction loads including dead and live loads, the formwork below the lower floors should be retained or it should be repropped, ensuring that the props are directly one under the other so as to stress the lower floors to the minimum and within the permissible limits. In any event, shock loading through the formwork to the structure below shall be avoided. Also the lower props shall be checked against buckling.

The formwork should be so designed and constructed that vertical adjustment can be made to compensate for taking up any foundation settlement.

The design and erection of formwork shall be done as per IS 14687.

3.8.1 Common Deficiencies in Design

Following common design deficiencies leading or contributing to failure should be avoided:

i. Lack of allowance in design for such loadings as wind, power buggies placing equipment and temporary material storage
ii. Inadequate anchorage against uplift due to battered form faces
iii. Insufficient allowance for eccentric loading due to placement sequence
iv. Inadequate reshoring
v. Overstressed reshoring.
vi. Inadequate provisions to tie corners of intersecting cantilevered form together
vii. Failure to investigate bearing stresses in members in contact with shores and struts
viii. Failure to provide proper lateral bracing or lacing of shoring
ix. Failure to investigate the slenderness ratio of compression members
x. Failure to account for loads imposed on anchorages during gap closure in aligning formwork

3.9 SHUTTERING FOR CONCRETE AND OTHER DETAILING

Footings: Slopped footings will normally require formwork for vertical sides only. If the slope of the top faces exceeds angle of repose of the vertical concrete, formwork may be required for the top face. Stepped footings may be provided to avoid the top form.

Columns: Forms should be capable of being stripped easily. In tall forms it is desirable to provide windows at appropriate levels on at least one face to facilitate inspection, concrete placement and vibration. Any method (standard or patented) such as adjustable clamps, bolts, purpose made yokes, etc, to hold the panels in place may be used. The spacing and size of these clamps shall depend upon the lateral pressure of fresh concrete.

Walls: The shuttering shall be fixed at required distance equal to the required wall thickness. The two faces of shutters of the wall should be kept in place by appropriate ties with spacer tubes or bolts, braces and studs.

Beams and Floor Slabs: When single post prop is used, it should be adequately braced and connected to the nearest props.

Members inclined to horizontal may have a single bottom shuttering if the angle of inclination is less than or equal to 40 degrees otherwise double shuttering shall be required.

For timber connections, bolting is preferred to nail joints to avoid damage to formwork material. The splices can be made by using a pair of mild steel or timber fishplates connected with bolts in timber. The splice piece should be at least 600 mm long, 50 mm thick with width not less than the width of the prop.

3.10 SITE OPERATION AND MANAGEMENT

3.10.1 Safety Precautions

Construction procedures should be planned in advance to ensure the safety of personnel and equipments and the integrity of the finished structure. Some of the safety provisions which need to be considered are;

i. Erection of safety signs and barricades to keep unauthorized personnel clear of areas in which erection, concrete placing or stripping is under way

ii. Providing experienced form watchers and engineers during concrete placement to assure early recognition of possible form displacement or failure. A supply of extra shores or other material and equipment that might be needed in an emergency should be readily available.

iii. Provision for adequate illumination of the formwork and work area. Inclusion of lifting points in the design and detailing of all forms which will be crane handled. This is especially important in jump forms or climbing forms and tunnel form. In the case of wall formwork, consideration should be given to an independent scaffold bolted to the previous lift.

iv. Incorporation of scaffolds, working platforms and guard rails into formwork design and all formwork drawings.

v. A programme of field safety inspections of formwork.

vi. In case of structural elements such as cantilever beams/slabs, where overturning is an important parameter, stripping of formwork shall be done only after mobilization of full restraining forces.

3.10.2 Erection of Formwork

Following should be checked during erection of formwork:

i. All provisions of the design and drawings are complied with.

ii. Any member which has to remain in position during or after the general releasing of formwork is clearly marked.

iii. The materials used are checked to ensure that undesirable or rejected items are not used.

iv. Any excavations nearby which can influence the safety of the formwork is accounted for in the planning and design.

v. The bearing soil is safe and suitably prepared. The sole plates should fully bear on the ground without possible settlement.

vi. Safety measures are taken to prevent impact of traffic, scour due to water, etc.

vii. Adequate bracings, struts and ties are installed with the progress of erection to ensure strength and stability of formwork at intermediate and final stages.

viii. Inclined forms which give rise to very high horizontal forces are taken care of by trussing and diagonal bracing.

ix. The places of stacking of materials are marked as per provision in formwork design and it should be ascertained that the stacking is done only at proper places.

x. The deterioration of materials due to storage, reuse and misuse is checked and corrective steps taken for safety.

xi Wedges are provided for adjustment of the formwork to the required position, after any settlement or elastic shortening of props occur.

xii. The inclined plane of the wedges is not too steep and the pair nailed down after adjustment to prevent their shifting. A pair of two matched and equal wedges should be used in opposition and not one wedge only by itself. The wedges should not induce eccentricity.

3.10.3 Reuse and Maintenance of Formwork

Timber Formwork: Though not generally used, timber if used, should be examined for any visible damage during use and be discarded or its safe capacity suitably reduced if signs of rot, cuts on the edge greater than 1/20 of the thickness of the section, bolt holes in the two outer third lengths or width, undue distortion of shape, any other mechanical damage or splitting is observed.

Metal Formwork: Forms which are to be reused shall be carefully cleared and properly repaired between uses, mortar film sticking to the form face or the joining surface shall be completely removed after each use when not required for use, and the formwork material shall be properly stored. The component shall be cleaned and painted periodically. Threaded parts shall be oiled greased after thorough clearing and removal of dirt or slurry. Free movement of the telescopic components shall be ensured by periodic cleaning/oiling.

3.10.4 Concreting Operations and the Application of Loads

Following shall be checked, before and during concreting operations or load application:

i. Adequate access ramps, gangway, etc in the proper positions are provided for the smooth flow of men, materials and machines.

ii. All precautions are taken to prevent accidental impact, scouring or flooding of foundations.

iii. Adequate precautions should also be taken to keep unauthorised people away from the formwork.

iv. The forms shall be clean and free from wood shavings, grit, etc.

v. Forms and joints are such that they prevent leakage of mortar and slurry. Only approved coating or form release agent are applied, and the reinforcement are clean from the same.

vi. The sequence, rate of concreting, and method of placement and position of construction joints are as per the design brief.

vii. In some cases, the load of fresh concrete and the live load at one place may cause uplift of the forms at another place and thus result in displacement of the forms and danger to the props by loosing wedges, etc. Positions of such possibilities are to be checked.

viii. The reinforcement and formwork have been checked and permission to commence the placement of concrete has been accorded.

ix. The thickness of the concrete is maintained all along the member as per drawing, even when camber has been provided.

x. The props and bracings should be watched during the placement of concrete and its vibration.

xi. Any members or wedges which may tend to become loose or shift should be attended immediately.

xii. An agreed system of communication between the man below and the man in charge of concrete operations should be established so that corrective actions as required may be taken and concreting can be stopped instantly if at all it becomes necessary to do so.

xiii. Platforms for the movement of workers and mechanized concrete buggies are separate and are not placing load upon the reinforcing steel. If this is unavoidable, steel chairs should be placed under the reinforcement at adequate spacing to prevent deformation of the reinforcement.

3.10.5 Stripping of Formwork

Stripping of formwork is also known as releasing or dismantling or removing or de-shuttering. "Striking" word has also been used in case of tunnel formwork later.

Soffit formwork shall not be released until the concrete has achieved strength of at least twice the stress to which the concrete may be subjected, at the time of removal. The strength referred to shall be that of concrete using the same cement, aggregates and admixture, if any with the same proportions and cured under conditions of temperature and moisture similar to those existing on the work.

While the above criteria of strength shall be the guiding factor for removal of formwork, in normal circumstances where ambient temperature does not fall below 15"C and where Ordinary Portland cement is used and adequate curing is done, following stripping/striking period may deem to satisfy the guideline:

Vertical formwork to columns, walls, beam	16-24 h
Soffit formwork to slabs (props to be refixed immediately after removal of formwork)	3 days
Soffit formwork to beams (props to be refixed immediately after removal of formwork)	7 days
Props to slabs.	
Spanning up to 4.5 m	7 days
Spanning over 4.5 m	14 days
Props to beams and arches	
a) Spanning up to 6 m	14 days
b) Spanning over 6 m	21 days

Above period is for conventional formwork and not for specialised formwork like aluminium formwork, tunnel formwork, and aluminium PVC formwork etc for which manufacturers provide the details but the strength of the concrete should be found out by the engineer based on specialised formwork and the methods used before stripping the formwork considering minimum requirements of the concrete.

For other than OPC and lower temperature, the stripping time, recommended above may be suitably modified. When formwork to vertical surface, such as beam sides, walls and columns, is removed at early ages, care should be exercised to avoid damage to the concrete especially to arises and features. If necessary, the provision of relevant curing methods should immediately follow the removal of the vertical formwork at such age and the concrete should be protected from low or high temperatures by means of suitable insulation.

Supporting forms and shores must not be removed from the beams, floors and walls until these structures/units are strong enough to carry their own weight and any approved superimposed load. Supporting forms and shores should not be removed from the horizontal members before concrete strength is at least 70 percent of design strength.

As a general rule, the forms for columns and piers may be removed before those for beams and slabs. Formwork and supports should be so constructed that each can be easily and safely removed without impact or stuck to permit the concrete to carry its share of the load gradually and uniformly.

Following should be checked before and during release of formwork:

i. The person concerned and the workers are in the knowledge of the sequence of releasing of forms and the props to be left in position.
ii. All formwork material are properly stacked and maintained in good condition. Any items which may be damaged or wrecked while stripping are segregated. Any member should not be allowed to be dropped from a height but should be carefully brought down.
iii. Forms are eased off from concrete faces such as to prevent damage to both concrete and forms.
iv. The sequence of dismantling, as laid down, is adhered to. If not laid down, the sequence is planned by the agency doing formwork, and that is safe for the workers and the permanent construction.

3.10.6 Tolerance in Formwork

The formwork shall be such that the finished concrete shall be in the proper position in space measured with respect to certain predefined reference points. Formwork should be of the proper dimensions and shape as per drawings. The tolerances on the shape, lines and dimensions shown in the drawing shall be within the specified limits given below:

a. Deviation from specified dimensions of cross-section of columns and beams: -6 mm and + 12 mm
b. Deviation from dimensions of footings

i. Dimensions in plan	- 12 mm and + 50 mm
ii. Eccentricity	0.02 times the width of the footings in the direction of deviation in the direction of deviation but not more than 50mm
iii. Thickness	(+/-) 0.05 times the specified thickness

Accuracy of Formwork: As per IS 14687

3.10.7 Check List

Following is the check list which may be used by foremen, supervisors and inspectors (including engineers) of formwork. Actual points to be checked should be suited to job conditions and will vary for different types of construction.

a. When adjustable steel props are used, these should be undamaged and not visibly bent, having the steel pins provided by the manufacturer for use, restrained laterally near each end, and have means for centralizing beams placed in the forkheads.
b. Sole plates are properly seated on their bearing pads or sleepers.
c. The screw adjustments of adjustable props have not been over-extended.
d. Horizontal load bearing members are not eccentric upon vertical members.
e. Steel sections (specially deep sections) are adequately restrained against tilting andoverturning.
f. There are enough restraints in the formwork against horizontal loads.
g. All securing devices and bracing are tightened.
h. Standard components of proprietary systems are used. This particularly applies to pins.
i. Adequate measures are taken to prevent accidental impacts. etc.
j. Washers under all bolts heads and nuts have adequate bearing area.
k. Steel parts on timber members should have adequate bearing areas.
l. There should be no splitting of timber due to nailing and the number of nails and boltsshould be adequate.
m. The cantilever supports should be more than adequate and be rechecked.
n. Bolted timber connections are staggered where necessary.
o. Supports are in plumb within the specified tolerance.
p. Props are directly one under another in multistage or multistorey formwork.
q. Bearing plates of props are not distorted and are flat.
r. Guy ropes or stays are tensioned adequately.
s. The dimensions of formwork are within prescribed tolerances.
t. There are adequate provision for the movement and operation of vibrators and otherconstruction plant.
u. Cambers are provided as per drawings. This may be specifically needed for long spans and cantilevers.

Measurements shall be recorded by the junior engineer/assistant engineer level officers and final go ahead for casting of concrete given by the engineer in charge after inspection.

3.11 SPECIALISED FORMWORK SYSTEMS

Specialised formwork is generally used for Monolithic Concrete Construction. Monolithic concrete construction is a method in which concreting is done in walls, beams, slabs and other structural members and thus structure is built monolithically using concrete. Such construction requires special formwork, normally prefabricated for speed. Since the formwork is prefabricated and customized for a work, it is preferred for repetitive units for the economy in construction.

Various types of formwork used for monolithic construction are as given in the followings;

1. Jump formwork
2. Aluminium formwork
3. Tunnel formwork
4. Plastic Aluminium formwork
5. Stay in Place/Lost in Place formwork

Quality in case of monolithic construction is better than cast in situ conventional construction due to specialised formwork and strict quality controlled concrete normally self compaction concrete being used.

3.11.1 Jump Formwork System

Introduction

Jump formwork or climbing formwork or sometimes referred as self lifting system is the formwork used for monolithic concrete construction which supports itself on the concrete earlier cast. Thus, such system does not need the support or access from other parts of the building. The formwork is also used for cleaning and steel fixing. Since the formwork rises or climbs or jumps with the building construction process, it is known as climbing or jump formwork. In this technique, formwork is used in repetitive form.

Such system is suitable for construction of vertical monolithic concrete elements in high-rise structures or towers or skyscrapers, such as core walls, lift shafts, stair shafts and bridge piers i.e. identical or repetitive storeys. Once, the core is available, other construction can be taken up even in conventional way by utilising the services of the lift provided in the core hence construction becomes easy and economic.

Systems are normally modular and can be joined to form long lengths to suit varying construction geometries.

Concept

A frame is constructed from structural steel members over the central core. Steel formwork panels are hung from this frame/supported on rollers. Once the reinforcement is ready and formwork is installed, concreting is done, formwork released and rolled back from the concrete face. Jacks are then used to lift the whole frame up by one level and all the formwork panels attached to this frame and concreting done.

The process takes approximately one and half days. Once the formwork is in position, the formwork panels are closed, next concreting done.

Jump form systems (Fig. 3) are typically used on buildings of five storeys or more; fully self-climbing are generally used on structures with more than 20 floors. However, a combination of crane-handled and self-climbing systems can be viable on lower structures. Jump form systems are suitable for multi storeyed construction of Shear walls, Core walls, Lift shafts, Stair shafts and Bridge pylons.

Fig. 3.3: Jump formwork

Types of Jump Formwork and their Features

Three types of jump form are in general use:

Normal jump or climbing form in which units are individually lifted off the structure and relocated at the next construction level using a crane.

Guided climbing jump form in which units also use a crane but often provide greater safety and control during lifting as the units remain anchored to or are guided by the structure.

Self-climbing jump form systems do not require a crane as they climb up rails on the building by means of hydraulic jacks, or by jacking the platforms off recesses in the structure.

Working platforms, guard rails and ladders are generally built into the completed formwork systems, along with complete wind-shield protection when necessary.

Advantages

- Faster construction
- Minimizes labour and has better productivity
- Minimize the use of scaffoldings and temporary working platforms
- Increases safety
- Self-climbing frame work cuts the requirement for the crane time to a great extent.
- The formwork is supported independently so that the shear walls as well as core walls may be completed before the rest of the structure of the main building
- Good quality surface finish
- High seismic resistance
- Can sustain high wind force
- Easy to clean the formwork
- Highly engineered jump form system nature permits precise and quick adjustment of formwork in the planes
- Transporting materials at higher levels is easy once core is cast and lift is installed
- A very small but highly skilled work force is needed on the site
- It's very easy to plan the construction activities because of the repetitive nature of work

Limitations

i. Costly for low rise structures
ii. In case lifting is required, it may have safety problems
iii. High rise structures do not have only core walls and as such other parts of the buildings are to be taken up with conventional methods.

3.11.2 Aluminium Formwork

Introduction

Aluminium formwork is used for monolithic concrete construction, the panels of which are made of high strength aluminium alloy. Since the system is made of aluminium, it is light weight and does not require the use of cranes. Individual workers can handle the elements of the formwork.

Aluminium formwork by the brand name "Mivan" was developed by one of the construction company from Europe. In 1990, the Mivan Company Ltd from Malaysia started the manufacturing of such formwork system. Aluminium formwork has been used extensively in many countries and is currently in use in India also. The technology is suitable for constructing large number of repetitive units at a faster speed.

In this system of formwork construction, cast - in - situ concrete wall and floor slabs cast monolithic provides the structural system in one continuous pour. Large room sized forms for walls and floors slabs are erected at site. They can be used for large number of repetitions, claimed to be 250. The system may not be economical if a project is having less than 500 repetitive units.

In the walls, normally single layer of reinforcement is provided at the centre. Such construction was adopted in the design of staging of overhead water tanks which has been stopped for a long time as such design was not found suitable. Therefore effect of single layer reinforcement at the centre needs to be observed for long period. Also, it becomes very difficult to repair/retrofit single layer reinforcement provided at centre if corroded.

Special care must be taken at the lift shafts. The interior panels will align properly on their own because they are set of the kicker from the formwork below. It is to be ensured that the kickers are level and will not affect the vertically of the lift shaft. If the concrete is too high in place, it can distort the alignment of the four sides of the lift shaft and must be broken out to allow a level base. Also, it should be ensured that the concrete and in particular the reinforcement does not become contaminated due to excessive or negligent application of the releasing agent. The ends of walls and door openings should be secured in position and checked for plumb.

Concept and its Features

The formwork system is made of aluminium alloy andthe panels are held in position by simple pin and wedge (Fig. 4) arrangement system requiring no bracing. The walls are held together with wall ties, while the decks are supported by beams and props. The formwork is designed based on requirements of dwelling units and the project.

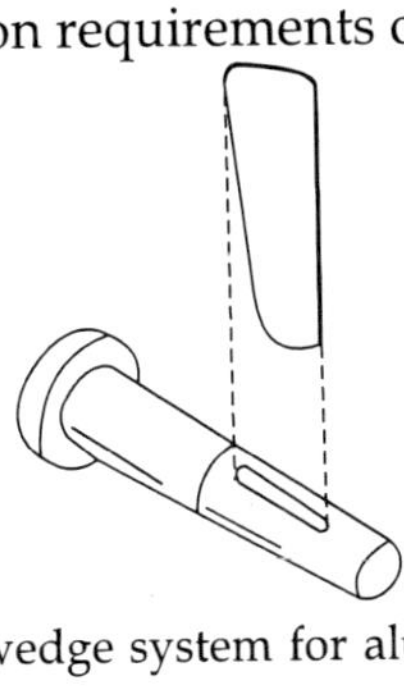

Fig. 3.4: Pin-and-wedge system for aluminium formwork

In this system, all the components in a building including slabs, beams, walls, columns (if any), staircases, balconies and sunshades are of concrete and there is no need for block work or brick work. All panels are labelled for easy identification at site. The system consists of four components as beam components (Fig. 5), deck components (Fig. 6), wall components (Fig. 7) and other components (Fig. 8).

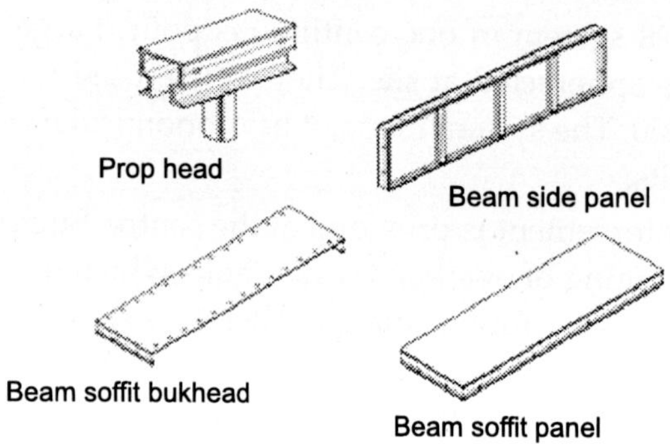

Fig: 3.5: Beam components

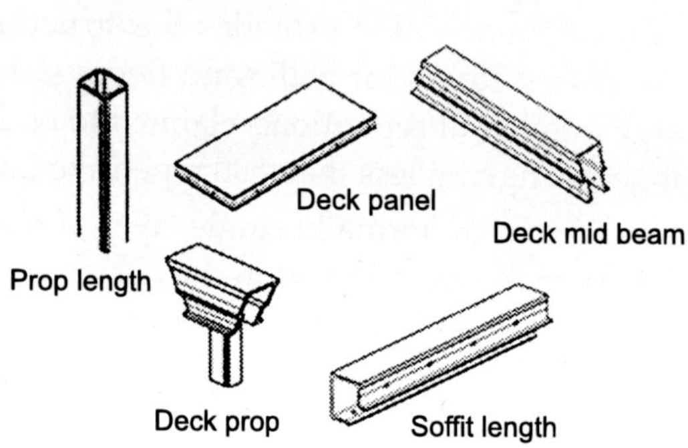

Fig. 3.6: Deck components

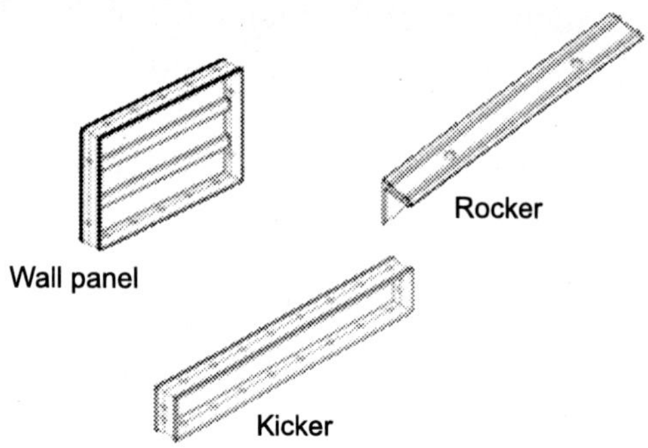

Fig. 3.7: Wall components

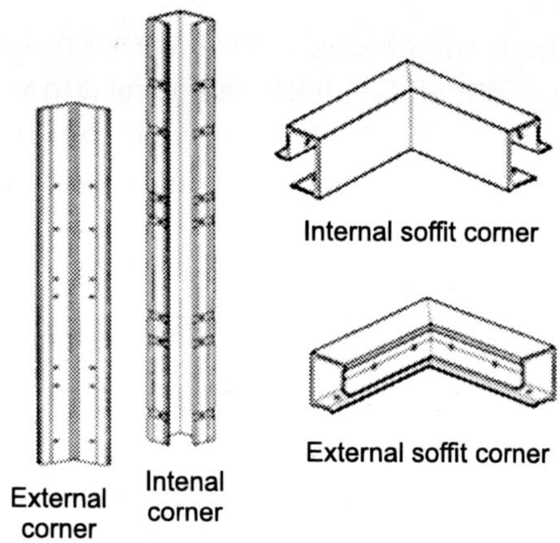

Fig. 3.8: Other components

Implementation

The system usually follows a four-day cycle as given below:

Day 1: Erection of vertical reinforcement bars and one side of the vertical formwork for the entire floor or part as the case may be

Day 2: Erection of other side of vertical formwork and formwork for the floor

Day 3: Reinforcement fixing for floor slabs and casting of walls and slabs

Day 4: Removal of formwork panels after 24 hours leaving props in place for 7 days and floor slab formwork in place for about 3 days.

Procedure

Main steps involved in the concreting are:

1. Setting up the wall reinforcement as per the design.
2. Shuttering oil is then applied and wall panels placed.
3. Placement of service ducts.
4. After the wall panels, installation of door and window panels is done.
5. Installation of Beam system.
6. Slab system is then placed.
7. Tie panels are then installed.
8. Installation of staircase wall panels is then installed.
9. Reinforcement in slab and electric conduits.
10. Concreting in walls and slab/beams.

Advantages

i. Placement of the formwork does not require heavy machines/cranes
ii. The formwork can be handled by semiskilled/unskilled workers
iii. Speedy construction compared to conventional construction
iv. Repetitive units make it economic due to economy of scale/number of uses
v. Good quality construction
vi. Plaster may not be essential
vii. Better seismic resistance
viii. Time saving in completion of project
ix. Increased durability
x. Lesser number of joints
xi. Higher carpet area within same plinth area due to less thickness of walls/shear wall construction
xii. Uniform quality
xiii. Less manual labour
xiv. Suitable for low rise to high rise structures

Limitations

i. Post construction changes not feasible
ii. Less insulation due to less wall thickness and RCC walls
iii. Less acoustic properties compared to brick walls
iv. May not be economic in case of non repetitive units
v. Lead time of about 3 months required for fabrication of formwork
vi. All the services are to be planned in advance and cannot be changed at a later date

vii. Difficult to nail or make holes in shear walls

viii. Repair and rehabilitation in coastal area of shear walls may be difficult in case of corrosion in multi-storeyed construction

ix. Initial cost of formwork is high

x. Very limited architectural features feasible

xi. Limited spans. As per BMTPC guidelines, maximum spacing between cross walls shall be limited to 1.5 times the floor height if supported on two edges and 2 times the floor height when supported on all four edges.

xii. Finishing lines seen on concrete surface

xiii. Large number of formwork components to be handled.

xiv. Higher repair cost for aluminium.

xv. Probability of theft of forms due to higher cost.

Large numbers of such formwork manufacturers/suppliers are available in the country now and monolithic construction using aluminium formwork is being carried out at number of places in the country.

Plastic Aluminium formwork manufactured by M/s Sintex Industries Ahmadabad is made of aluminium extruded sections and PVC. Other properties are similar to aluminium formwork. Plastic formwork has to be ensured for various properties mentioned for conventional formwork.

Case Study of Aluminium Formwork

CPWD has taken up Construction of 76 Multi Storied Flats for Hon'ble MPs of Lok Sabha at Dr. B.D. Marg, New Delhi with aluminium formwork. The plot has an area of 23046 sqm. The plinth area of buildings having three towers is 23046sqm approx. And buildings are having basement+stilt+13 storeys. The estimated cost of the project is 169.44 Crores. Schedule period of completion has been kept as 40 months which includes 4 months for pre tendering activities, 6 months for local body clearances and design and 30 months for execution of work. Parking and services are planned in the basement and stilt.

The work was started in August, 2018 when all the bungalows were still not available and the last Bungalow was vacated in February 2019. The work is planned to be completed within the stipulated time frame, i.e. June 2020.

Construction of basement and Stilt floor has been taken with conventional formwork and 13 upper floors with Aluminium Formwork with monolithic construction. The concrete sections in monolithic construction provided are thin as compared to conventional construction. Shear walls are provided with 200mm thickness and non shear walls as 100mm thick. Entire flat is cast in one operation. Self compacting of M 30 grade concrete has been provided for casting.

Casting of one flat is being done in 10 days which can be compressed to 8 days by reducing the time for reinforcement and conduit laying. The schedule is as given below;

Day 1 and Day 2:	Fixing of reinforcement of shear wall.
Day 2 and Day 3:	Laying electric conduits, fixing junction & switch boxes.
Day 3 and Day 4:	Fixing of formwork of wall.
Day 5:	Fixing of formwork of slab.
Day 6:	Laying of reinforcement of beam.
Day 7 and 8:	Laying of bottom layer reinforcement of roof slab.
Day 8 and 9:	Laying of electric conduits and top reinforcement.
Day 10:	Casting of complete structure.

Construction with Conventional Formwork					
	Description of Item	**Unit**	**Quantity**	**Rate/Rs.**	**Amount/ Rs.**
1.0	Cantering and shuttering including strutting, propping, etc., and removal of form for:				
1.1	Suspended floors, roofs, landings, balconies	Sqm	370	693.05	2,56,428
1.2	Lintels, beams, plinth beams, girders	Sqm	340	552.05	1,87,697
1.3	Columns, pillars, piers, abutments, posts and struts	Sqm	240	733.70	1,76,088
2.0	Providing and laying RCC – M-30	Cum	140	9,871.95	13,82,073
3.0	Steel reinforcement	kg	17136	83.50	14,30,856
4.0	Brickwork with cement mortar 1:6	Cum	107	7,590.45	8,12,178
5.1	6 mm cement plaster on ceiling 1:3	Sqm	370	227.35	84,119
5.2	12 mm cement plaster on wall 1:6	Sqm	600	254.25	1,52,550
5.3	15 mm cement plaster on wall 1:6	Sqm	650	292.85	1,90,353
				Total	46,72,343

Construction with Monolithic Aluminium Formwork					
1.	Providing and laying RCC M-30	Cum	180.00	9,871.95	17,76,951
2.	Extra for M-30 Self-compacting Concrete	Cum	180.00	650.00	1,17,000
3.	Steel Reinforcement	kg	26100.00	83.50	21,79,350

4.	Aluminium Formwork	Sqm	1615.00	202.45	3,26,957
				Total	44,00,258

Though it has been worked out that monolithic construction using aluminium formwork is economic by 6%, it depends upon the rates of the contractor. Still, it may be assumed that the cost of conventional construction and monolithic construction using aluminium formwork is almost comparable.

Considering shuttering procurement for one and half floor				
		Aluminium Formwork		**Conventional Formwork**
S. No.	**Activity**	**Time (Days)**		**Time (Days)**
1.	Mobilization	30		30
2.	Earthwork and raft	75		75
3.	Basement	60		60
4.	Stilt floor	45		45
5.	Completion of structure of one and half tower	1 × 30 = 30 12 × 10 = 120	150	13 × 18 = 234
6.	Completion of structure of remaining one and half tower	1 × 20 = 20 12 × 10 = 120	140	13 × 18 = 234
7.	Completion of structures above 13th (top) floor with conventional formwork	30		30

Saving in time has been worked out as 25% in such construction as compared to conventional construction.

As per BMTPC compendium, third edition 2018, the following projects have been completed using plastic aluminium formwork:

i. 5008 houses at Kanjhawala Narela, Delhi for DSIIDC
ii. 512 houses at Bhawan, Delhi for DSIDC
iii. 3000 houses in Ahmadabad Municipal Corporation
iv. 3000 houses in Lucknow for Lucknow Development Authority
v. 4,52,656 houses under PMAY(U) in various parts of Andhra Pradesh
vi. 4586 houses under PMAY(U) in Naya Raipur, Chhattisgarh
vii. 30,000 houses under PMAY(U) in Maharashtra

Further, the following projects have been mentioned using aluminium formwork:

i. Houses in Bangalore for Karnataka Slum Development Board
ii. Houses in Mysore for Karnataka Slum Development Board
iii. 2112 houses under PMAY(U) in Tamil Nadu
iv. 34,928 houses under PMAY(U) in Gujarat
v. 1136 houses under PMAY(U) in Puducherry
vi. Houses in Bangalore for Karnataka Development Authority & several other projects in major cities of India, among many others

CPWD has also taken up large number of projects using aluminium formwork in Delhi, Amethi, Lucknow and few other places.

3.11.3 Tunnel Formwork

Introduction

Tunnel form construction technique was invented over 50 years ago for monolithic concrete construction. **Tunnel formwork** comes in half units, in the form of an inverted two numbers of "L" which on bolting together at the top form a tunnel. The inbuilt wheels and the jacks help the formwork move in and out of the position and are adjusted to the final height. In practice, when the two halves are bolted together, the tunnel formwork will appear like shown in the following figure. Since the tunnel form is moved in and out, alignment of shear walls has to be according to the walls of formwork. Also no sunshade, openings or niches can be provided in these walls.

Concept and its Features

Two inverted "L" when joined together forms the tunnel. Two of such tunnels are placed together leaving the space for walls in which reinforcement is placed prior to placement of tunnel forms. Third half tunnel is also placed so that the wall can be casted. Thus two and half tunnels are placed at a time.

The formwork system is supported with hot air blowers which accelerates the setting of the concrete to achieve 24 hours cycle of casting of one slab.

Components of tunnel formwork are as follows:

1. Vertical, Deck and back panel to retain fresh concrete until it gets set and cured.
2. Stripping platform, gable end platform and working platform to provide for movement and working of labours and machinery and also for stripping out tunnels.
3. Push-pull props, wheeled prop to maintain line and level of tunnel.
4. Lifting triangle to place at centre of mass of tunnel form deck panel for lifting by tower crane.
5. Kicker form to provide as starter formwork at slab level to maintain position of next level tunnel form.
6. Slab stop end, wall stop end to provide as stopper to retain fresh concrete up to wall and slab line.
7. Block outs are fixed at vertical panels to provide door, window and ventilation windows in walls.

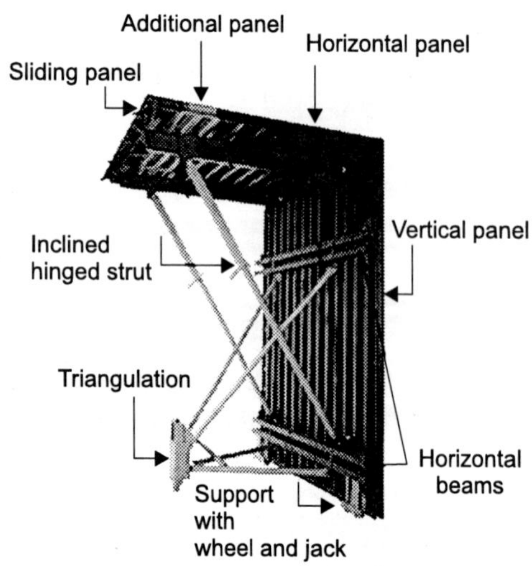

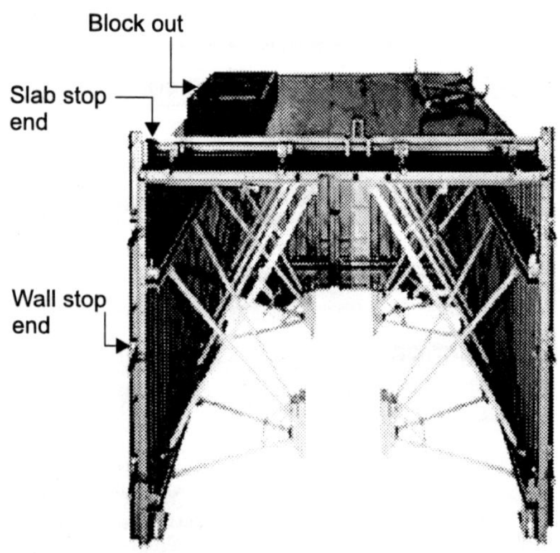

The formwork which is made of steel can be reused up to 600 times suiting to a variety of module sizes. Therefore, it is suitable for repetitive type of units. The construction is faster as the tunnel formwork allows a 24-hour construction cycle to be achieved.

Procedure

The casting process of tunnel formwork is as given below:

Step 1: Placement of Reinforcement of the Walls: Prefabricated wall reinforcement is placed by crane along the entire wing. Services if any are then placed.

Step 2: Placement of Tunnel form: Tunnel formwork is thereafter placed with the help of crane, bolted together and ties are installed.

Step 3: Slab Reinforcement and Electric Conduits: Slab reinforcement and electric conduits are then placed.

Step 4: Concreting in Walls and Slabs: Concreting is done in the walls and slabs.

Step 5: Removal of Formwork: The tunnel forms are removed the next day.

Advantages

i. Tunnel formwork is suitable and cost effective for repetitive units
ii. Since the concrete finish is good, no plaster is required
iii. The construction is very fast.
iv. Due to monolithic construction, seismic resistance is high
v. The formwork reduces joints
vi. It is suitable for high rise construction and repetitive units
vii. The formwork can be repeated for 500 times or more.
viii. Higher carpet area is achieved due to lesser thickness of walls compared to conventional construction.

Limitations

i. The formwork requires use of cranes
ii. The layout of building has to be in conformity to box type structure hence there is limitation of designing the building
iii. Niches are not feasible in design in the structure
iv. Services like plumbing and electric conduits etc are to be pre planned, placed in position before casting of concrete.
v. Basement cannot be constructed with this technique
vi. Post construction changes are not feasible
vii. Since the wall thickness is less and of RCC, it is not energy efficient in hot climate without insulation
viii. Providing shafts for services from outside is not feasible
ix. Very limited architectural features can be provided in such structures
x. Limited span is feasible due to limit on dimensions of the formwork
xi. Skilled workers required
xii. Three sides and slab are cast in one go and generally front (facade) is to be left out for removal of formwork
xiii. Sunken areas difficult to cast

Working cycle

Working Cycle of Tunnel form system is mainly divided into three parts viz Striking of Formwork, Setting of Formwork and Concreting Operation. These activities are carried out as follows:

i. Formwork panels are cleaned and oiled at the time of Deshuttering itself
ii. Ready wall reinforcement is placed in position.
iii. Forms are placed in position guided by concrete starters
iv. Slab reinforcement mesh and electrical-plumbing conduits are fixed in reinforcement
v. Walls, slab along with kickers (starters) are cast in one continuous pour
vi. Formwork panels are ready to de shutter and shift to next location by crane.

Tunnel form is widely used in the construction of cellular structures with high degree of repetition such as mass housing, prisons, hotels, hostels etc.

Guidelines for planning of buildings using Tunnel form

i. 3 side walls and slab as one room are cast in one go while 4th side (generally façade) is left out for removal of formwork.
ii. Layout should be such that tunnel forms/room forms can be retrieved from all four side of the building. Preferably from the entire periphery in any of the orthogonal directions.

iii. Width of tunnel/internal dimensions of rooms to be in multiples of 50mm preferably and there should be 2 to 3 different widths or combinations, while proportioning the room layouts for economy.
iv. Preferable room span is from 2.4m to 6.0m (width of room[s]). Larger widths can be accommodated with a table form between two Inverted 'L' forms called half tunnels.
v. Length of tunnel form/room size can be in multiples of 625mm for economy. Otherwise can be made to suit.
vi. Building plan should be symmetrical as for as possible either in one or both directions.
vii. Load carrying walls must be in same plane (one above the other)
viii. Internal beams with end column will be treated as wall with reservations/ block out forms.
ix. A minimum separation distance should be of 6m for detached buildings. Generally the maximum size of tunnel form +2m required. Typically 10m from neighbouring building as a best practice. But, specific details can be worked out.
x. Preferably no sunken areas. Bottom flush with tile drop. If present, to be cast separately (parallel activity: 1 floor below).
xi. Sunken areas in kitchen to be adjusted in flooring & Toilets areas to be under slung.
xii. Typical story height ranges from 2.7 to 3.1m.
xiii. Typical structural walls density is 4%. Ranging from 2 to 6% but can go up to 10% for high rise depending on thickness. Both principle directions generally have same density of walls.
xiv. Façade may be masonry with textured finish, stone cladding, precast panels or light weight panels with partial/full glazing.

Case Study with Tunnel Formwork

A project has been undertaken by CPWD in Anna nagar, Chennai for construction of 532 quarters for income tax department having a sanctioned cost of Rs 208.95 crores. The project consists of 4 towers of G+18 floors of Type II (1 tower having 8 quarters on each floor), III (2 towers having 8 quarters on each floor) and IV (1 tower having 4 quarters on each floor) quarters, having 8, 8 and 4 quarters on each floor respectively. Total plinth area of buildings is 57706 sqm. The buildings are founded on pile foundation. Tunnel formwork was received from Turkey for this project.

Initially architectural plans were prepared but had to be revised suiting to tunnel form construction as shown in the following:

Architectural planning

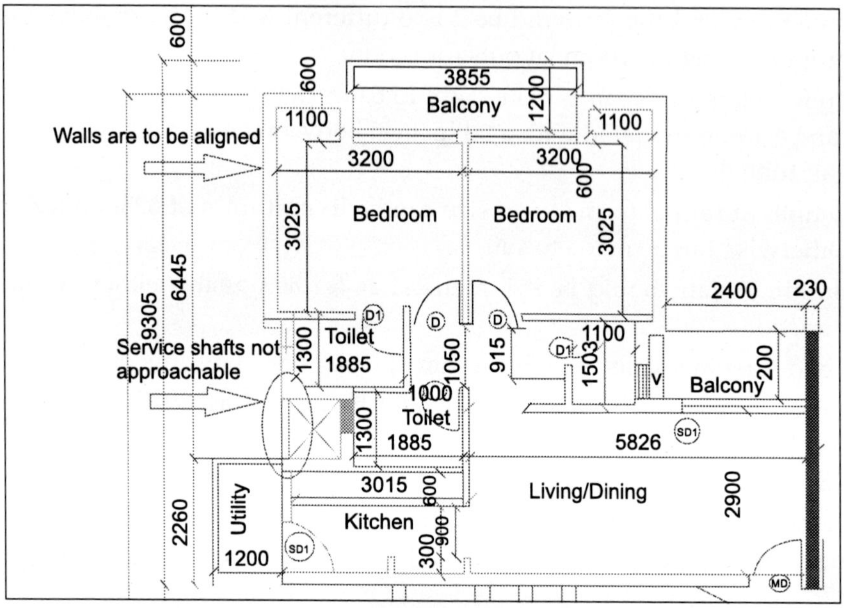

As per conventional conception

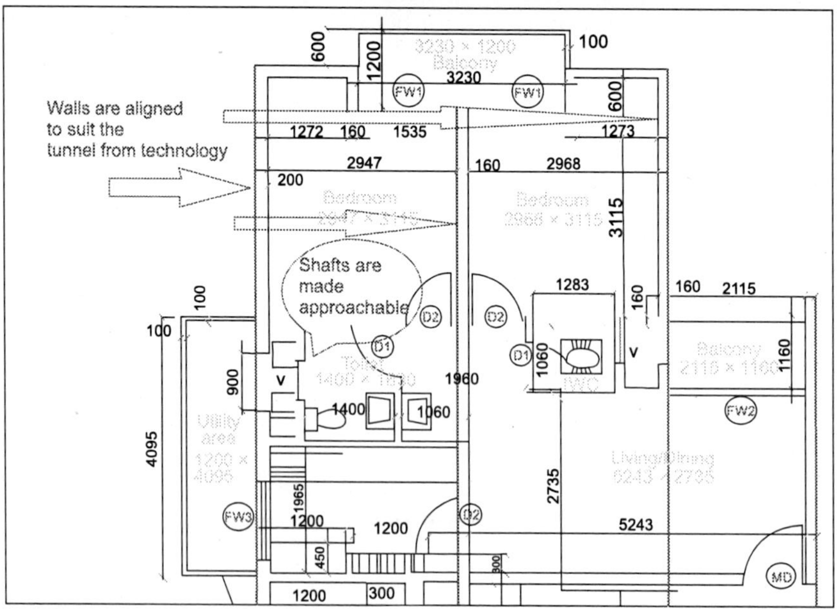

As per tunnel form conception

It may be seen that large modifications were made and all structural walls were aligned in line, openings of service shafts from outside closed and projections on tunnel form side removed. Also, structural arrangements were made accordingly as shown in the following.

Structural planning

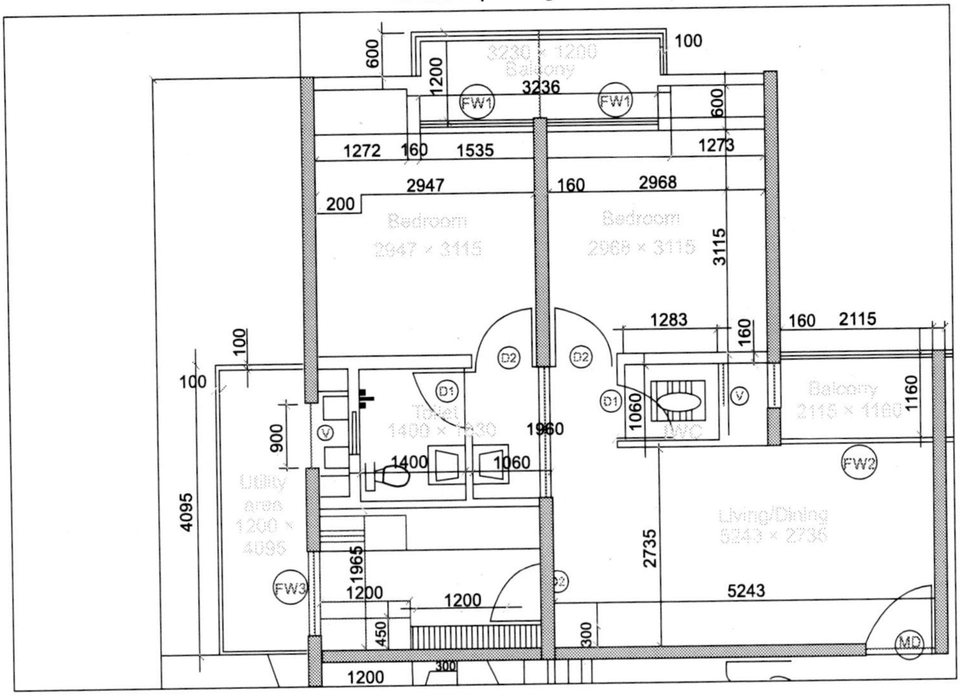

Structural wall configuration

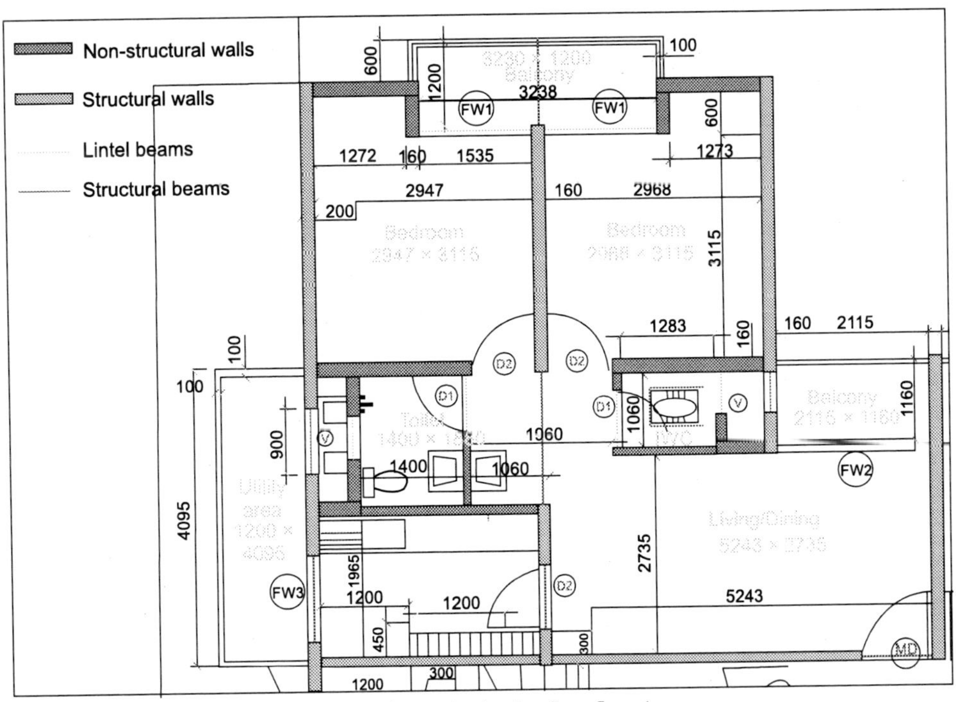

Structural and non-structural wall configuraton

BMTPC has mentioned in third edition of compendium (2018), the following major projects undertaken with this technology:

i. Apartments by M/s Runwal Group in Mumbai in 2000.
ii. Apartment complexes by M/s B G Shirke Construction Co. Pvt Ltd, Pune at Navi Mumbai and Tirupati in 2001.
iii. Apartments by L & T South City Projects Ltd at Chennai in 2008.
iv. Slum rehabilitation by M/s Pawar Patkar Construction Pvt Ltd at Nasik in 2014.

3.11.4 Stay-in-Place Formwork

For low rise structures, formwork may be provided in the form of Expanded Polystyrene (EPS) blocks from both sides for walls and then casting of concrete is done. Such EPS blocks are not removed. Since EPS blocks act as formwork and not removed (stays), such a system is called stay in place formwork.

In place of EPS blocks, ferrocement board sheets or fibre cement boards are also used as the formwork and they continue to remain with the structure. This can also be called as stay in place formwork though technology providers call it as lost in place formwork system.

In yet another technology, the formwork system consists of two filtering grids made of rib mesh reinforced by "C" channel vertical stiffeners. These grids on both faces stay with the structure hence qualify for being called as stay in place formwork.

Thus stay in place formwork is a formwork which is used for concreting and stays with the structure and is not taken out from the structure. The formwork may be manufactured with various types of materials.

Seismo Building Technology (*Source*: BMTPC)

Coffor technology (*Source*: BMTPC)

Insulating concrete form (*Source*: BMTPC)

Monolithic insulated concrete system (*Source*: BMTPC)

Lost-in-Place - Plaswall panel system (*Source*: BMTPC)

Lost-in-Place – Plasmolite wall panel (*Source*: BMTPC)

Advantages

i. The formwork does not require use of cranes or heavy machinery.
ii. The formwork provides insulation to the structure.
iii. The formwork is economic compared to other materials.
iv. It saves the cost of stripping of formwork.
v. The structure is light weight.

Limitations

i. The structure is suitable for low rise structures only.
ii. The formwork is not reusable hence kept with the structure.
iii. The wall thickness increases hence carpet area is reduced.
iv. The walls have less strength compared to RCC walls as in such case light reinforcement is placed.
v. Post construction changes are not feasible.
vi. In case of drilling or nailing, formwork material can get damaged.

How to Achieve Economy in the Cost of Formwork Construction?

1. As far as possible, use single framing scheme for the entire project. This would improve learning of labours, reduce mobilization and formwork material cost.
2. Use the same depth for all beams
3. Try to stick with the same beam outlines even if the loads and spans are not the same by modifying reinforcement ratio to resist the loads.
4. Space columns uniformly to achieve uniform sizes for columns, and beams.
5. Increase reuse of forms by using the same size for columns, horizontally in one storey and vertically in one stack.
6. Constant floor-to-floor height reduces the cost of formwork.
7. Enforce site management for proper erection and stripping, permit reasonable tolerances, specify strict tolerances only in locations where they are needed.
8. Follow time limit for stripping of formwork. Ensure quality and time management of other activities.

3.12 SAFETY REQUIREMENTS

Safety of building is related to safety of structure being cast, safety of workers and site staff hence designing, installation, placement and inspection of formwork is very important and must not be compromised.

Under Global Housing Technology Challenge-India, Expo-cum-Conference on "Construction Technology India – 2019" was organised in New Delhi where new construction technology providers from all over the world participated. Amongst other technologies, construction technology with monolithic construction was also approved. In other technologies like Pre cast/Pre fab concrete construction, Light Gauge Steel Framed Construction, and Sandwich panel system formwork used is normally of steel, timber or any other similar material.

REFERENCES

1. http://www.concrete.org.uk/fingertips-nuggets.asp?cmd=display&id=860
2. https://en.wikipedia.org/wiki/Climbing_formwork#/media/File:Kletterschalung_Detail.jpg
3. https://constructionduniya.blogspot.com/2012/02/mivan-aluminium-formwork.html
4. https://civilread.com/mivan-aluminium-formwork-shuttering/
5. http://www.zn903.com/cecspoon/lwbt/Formwork/Aluminum_Formwork/AluminumFormwork.htm
6. https://theconstructor.org/concrete/tunnel-form-construction-technique/8574/
7. Manas A. Shalgar, Manas A and Aradhye, D Tejas (2017), Introduction to advanced Tunnel Formwork system: Case study of 'Rohan - Abhilasha'. International Research Journal of Engineering and Technology (IRJET) e-ISSN: 2395 -0056 Volume: 04 Issue: 03. https://www.irjet.net/archives/V4/i3/IRJET-V4I397.pdf
8. Reddy, IAS (2018). Housing for all, Construction Technologies, Challenges, Tunnel Form Method of Construction. http://www.pessi.in/pdf/IAS%20HFA_CTC_221018.pdf
9. CPWD Specifications (Civil) 2019, Director general, CPWD, Nirman Bhawan, New Delhi
10. http://www.bmtpc.org/DataFiles/CMS/file/PDF_Files/ET_Pocket_Book_May2018_s.pdf
11. http://bmtpc.org/DataFiles/CMS/file/PDF_Files/39_PAC-MTF.pdf
12. http://www.formworkscaffoldingsystems.com/sale-9574369-professional-fast-working-jump-form-shuttering-system-steel-raw-material.html
13. https://www.ischebeck-titan.co.uk/formwork-props/
14. https://www.shutterstock.com/image-photo/formwork-construction-shuttering-concrete-1178150329
15. IS 14687:1999 Guidelines for Falsework for Concrete Structures.

4
Stay-in-Place Formwork Systems

4.1 STAY-IN-PLACE FORMWORK SYSTEMS

4.1.1 Formwork

Formwork is a technical term used in construction industry which offers defined shape to structural elements in which fresh concrete will be poured. This form work is also well known in the name of shuttering in civil engineering industry. These form work systems are temporary structures to make the reinforced concrete structures/ structural elements. Timber is a traditional form work materials predominantly used across the world. Similarly many different materials such as ply boards, steel sheets, plastics are also in practice. The form work system varies with respect to the type of structural elements. Many other parameters such as type of materials used, connections between the system, adequate support (shoring), alignment of the form work decides the quality outcome. The materials used for the form work should be strong and light in weight to handle and to hold the concrete without any intermittent failure. Adequate support to the system plays important role in deciding the safety execution. This part consumes 40-50% of total budget in terms of materials, labour and time. Many advanced techniques and methods have been developed but the maintenance and limitation in repeatability of the form work materials leads to expensive capital.

4.1.2 The Need of Stay In Place Formwork

In construction industry form work plays important role in execution. Different materials such as wood, steel sheets/plates, ply boards etc... are commonly used form work materials. But formwork costs around 40-50% of the total construction cost in reinforced concrete construction. The storing of formwork materials and limitations in reusing the materials increases the capital investment in construction industry. In construction activity placing the formwork and its alignment consumes more time compared to the concreting work. Much advancement has been occurred in form work materials, methods and in implementation techniques. Aluminum form work, steel form work, vinyl based form work, rubber and glass form works are also available.

But still the capital investments are high and requires maintenance, transportation, storing unit etc.. Stay in place (SIP) form work system is an effective and advanced way of formwork system offers integrated solution in construction work and alternative to the conventional construction.

In SIP the formwork material become an integral part of the structural elements and offer additional advantages such as thermal comfort, external protection to resist the durability issues, additional confining pressure and reduces the construction time and offers viable economical solution. Many evolutions have been occurred in the SIP system since the introduction of this concept. Different materials such as fibers reinforced polymers (FRP), polyvinyl (PVC), cementitious composites, extended polystyrene (EPS), glass fiber reinforced concrete/composites (GFRP), steel composites, steel meshes etc... have been in practice. Numerous researches have been focused on improving the SIP system more systematically and efficiently. Problems such as the bond between the fresh concrete and the form work materials influence on the elemental behavior, failure pattern, life span etc… have been identified as issues in SIP systems and research level and practical level solutions also had been proposed.

4.1.3 Insulated Concrete Forms

Insulated Concrete Form (ICF) is one of the SIP system which offers diverse option in construction. Many ICF systems are in practice. In EPS based ICF system, expanded-polystyrenes are used with proper interlocking mechanism which accommodates the EPS blocks together. There are two external EPS layers and hollow interior part offers space for fresh concrete option. In this type EPS blocks are fixed in order over a defined height followed by reinforcement placement and concreting. The connectors between the EPS layers as shown in Figure1 interlink the EPS blocks/panels and hold the reinforcement in vertical and horizontal directions. Based on the lateral pressure due to the concreting the EPS panels and interlinking mechanisms are designed and also it

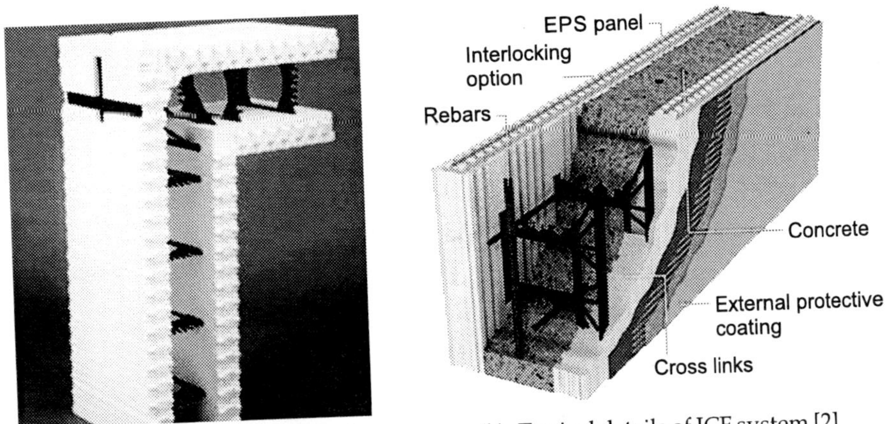

(a) EPS based ICF system [1] (b) Typical details of ICF system [2]

Fig. 4.1: EPS based insulated concrete forms

allows layer by layer construction. It further helps to achieve quality construction without the additional form work materials. The insulation property of EPS layers enhances the internal thermal comfort of the structure. In addition to that an external plastering will be done over EPS panels for protection. Figure 2 schematically shows a construction of residential buildings using ICF system.

Figure 3 shows anther module for ICF. In which a lattice made up of galvanized steel wire along with EPS is used for construction. In this system the cross links are also same as the galvanized steel wire and offers space for binding vertical and horizontal rebars as per the design requirement. In particular the small segment EPS panels are getting inserted into the lattice and got confined. This ensures stability of the system subjected to the lateral pressure during concreting. Different modules with respect to the structural elements are show in Figure 3. The external steel wire mesh offers better bonding between the external coating/plastering.

Advantages

- Offers resistance to gravity and lateral loading due to its monolithic construction technique.
- Energy efficiency and thermal comfort
- Noise reduction
- Resistant to corrosion.
- Easy to install and time saving construction technique.
- Cost effective solution.

Fig. 4.2: Typical construction of residential building using ICF system [1]

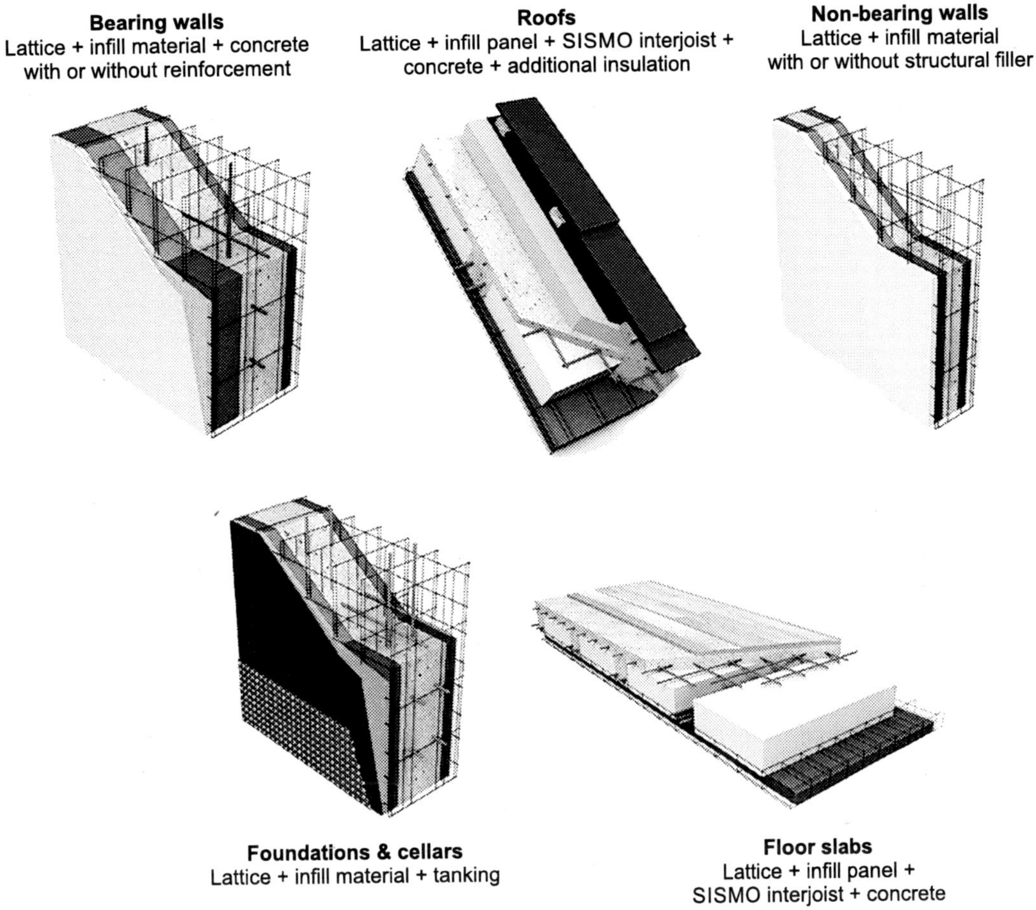

Fig. 4.3: Lattice based ICF system and its different modules [3]

The concept of ICF remains same but the materials differ with respect to the needs. Fiber boards and other materials are also in practice instead of EPS as an external layer. These fiber boards are made up of cement based composites with discontinued fibers or using fiber grids in lesser thickness. In order to connect two boards interlinks have been used in which reinforcement will be positioned. The cavity can be filled using concrete or foam based composite depend on the requirements. This kind of system can be used for internal partition and as external wall panels. This system doesn't require additional plastering until unless it is necessary.

4.1.4 Structural SIP System

In this SIP system two steel grid mesh as sacrificial form work with "C" channel section interconnectors used to connect two layers of grid mesh. Fresh concrete will be used inside the cavity similar to the other ICF systems. Instead of EPS any other insulating materials can be affixed with the external grid mesh to improve the thermal and acoustic comfort. In this method the steel channels are acting as reinforcements instead of conventional rebar and if requires additional reinforcements can also be used. Connection methods and procedures are varies with respect to the elemental sections.

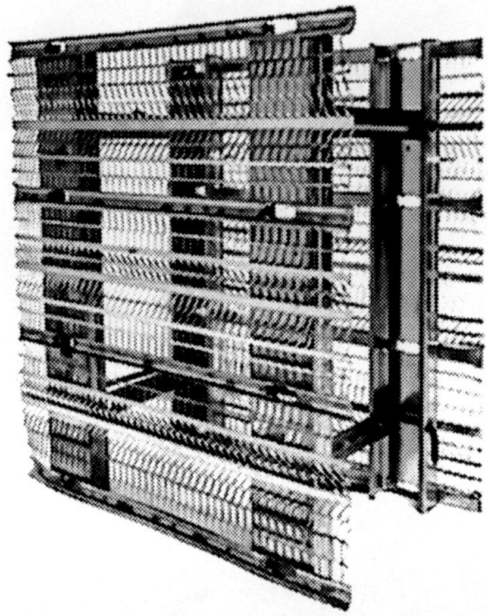

Fig. 4.4: Steel mesh based ICF system [4]

In corners and near openings additional longitudinal and transverse reinforcements will be used to make the monolithic construction more resistant against the severe loading and offers better stability as shown in Figure 5. The external grid mesh are provided with very fine gaps which will not allow the concrete t flow out and also offers better confining pressure. IS 456:2000 ; IS 1893:2016 and IS 13920:2016 are used in designing the structure to resist the gravity and seismic loading. These walls are generally considered as shear walls and designed. This panel act as light reinforced RCC walls. The steel based form work systems are considered without steel reinforcement in designing for bending/axial load and wind load using the following equation.

$$m_d + m_t < m_u \qquad \text{[Ref: 4]} \qquad (1)$$

where,

m_d = the design value for the limit state of collapse, of the max. bending moment per unit length, due to the loads liable to act on the structure, *(live load, dead load of wall, support reaction and moment from slab)*,

m_t = the design value for the limit state of collapse, of the accidental restraint moment *(moment developed at the junction of wall and slab generated due to lateral force)*,

m_u = the ultimate bending moment per unit length occurring with the design value of the axial load applied to the centre of gravity of the cross section *(moment capacity of the wall made with structural stay-in-place system)*

Here,

$m_d = m_a + V_a \times (e_{min})$

$m_t = mh$ (moment due to lateral load)

m_u = Ultimate bending capacity of the wall

m_a = Support moment for slab

V_a = vertical axial load.

R_a = Slab reaction part of vertical axial load calculation, V_a.

m_h = moment due to lateral load.

e_{min} = Minimum eccentricity.

PVC Based SIP System

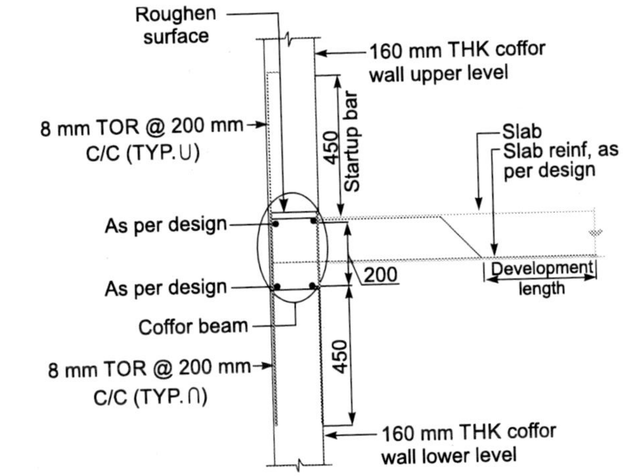

(a) Slab and outer wall connection

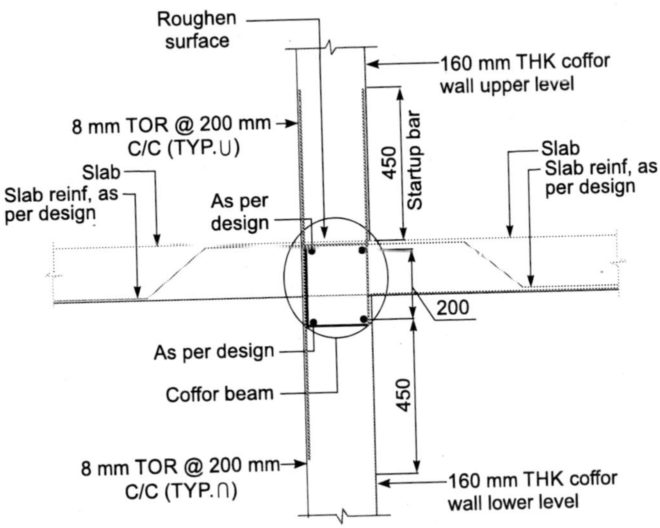

(b) Slab and inner wall connection

Fig. 4.5: Different connections adopted in constructions [4]

4.1.5 PVC Based SIP System

The poly-vinyl chloride (PVC) based form work system consists of hollow members with different interlocking internal patterns to make the connection more sustainable. In this system external plastering similar to other ICF is not mandatory and requires less maintenance. These form works are well reinforced with internal webs, ribs which acts as stiffener against the bending and provides rigidity to the form works. These PVC formworks are made in different segments with respect to the structural elements and can be integrated through the shear connectors. Inside the panels hollow spaces are available in vertical and horizontal directions for the placement of reinforcement. Additional reinforcements in both the directions to be provided at corner of the walls and in interconnections for integrity. The provided PVC panels restricts the evaporation of moisture present in concrete, makes the structure durable and resistant to corrosion and seismic.

Figure 6 shows the PVC based SIP system. These panels are placed over the extruded reinforcement with perfect alignment and adequate support. Upon interlinking all the panels, concrete will poured into the panel hollow areas. Many studies with respect to the structural behavior and fire resistance of PVC based SIP systems have been carried out across the worlds. Figure 7 shows the different connections near the corners and interconnections of PVC SIP system.

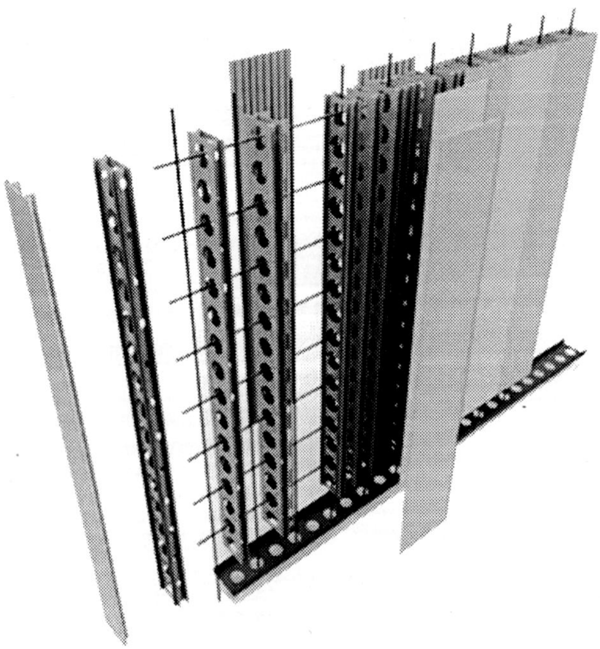

Fig. 4.6: PVC based ICF system details [5]

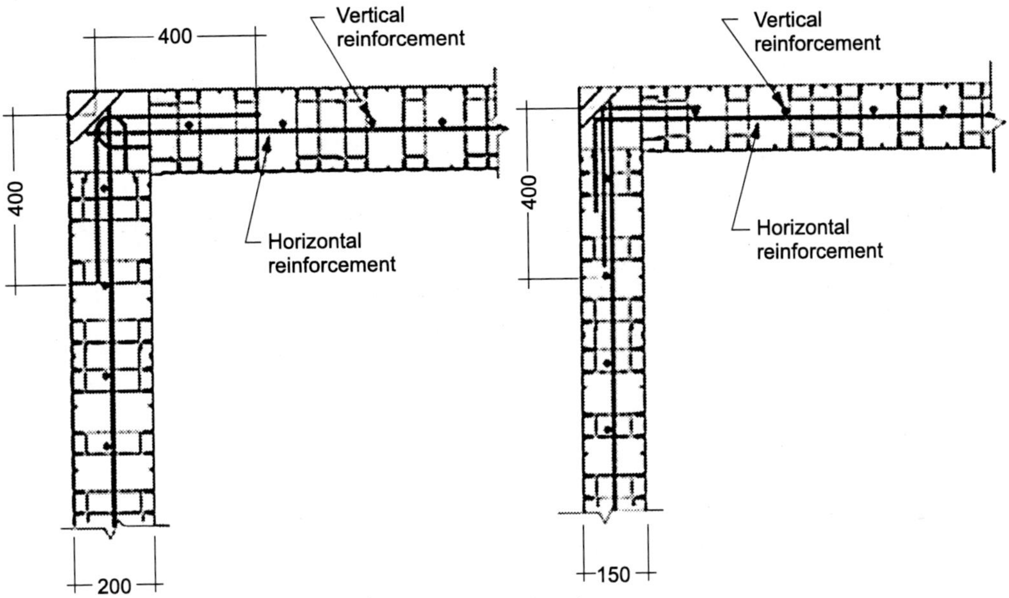

(a) Reinforcement details at corners

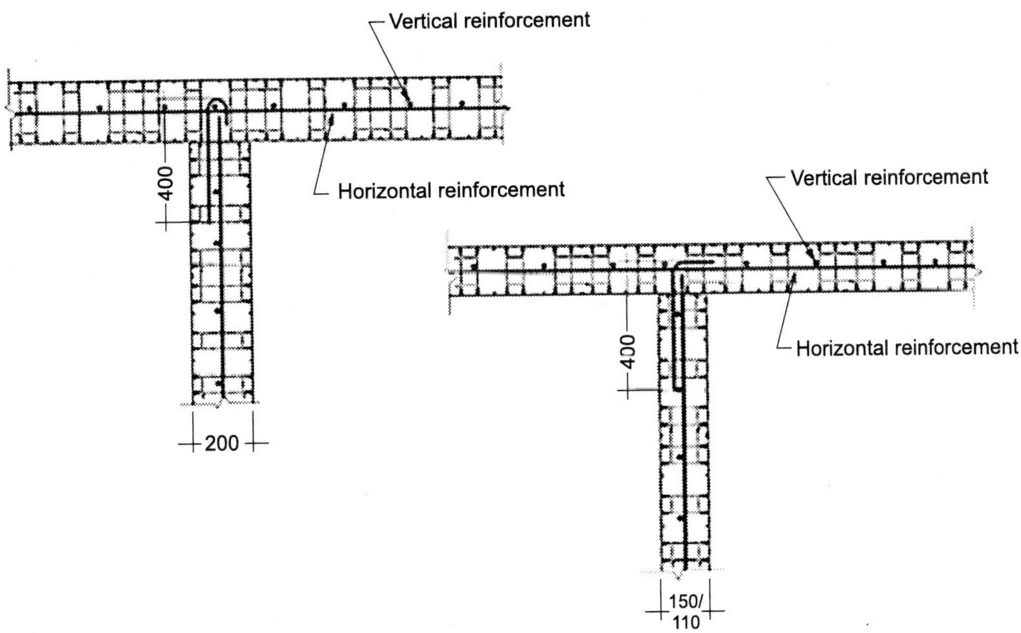

(b) Reinforcement details at interconnections [5]

Fig. 4.7: Detailed reinforcement configurations in PVC-SIP system connection [5]

Fig. 4.8: Execution of PVS-SIP system at site with adequate lateral support [5]

Michel et al. (2019) carried out an experimental study on the fire resistance behaviour of PVC based SIP system using different grade of concrete strength. Figures 4.9-4.11 show the PVC panel subjected to fire testing. The fire tests have been carried out as per ISO 834[30] and EN 1991-1-2:2002 Standards, equation 2.

$$\theta_g = 20 + 343\ \mathrm{Log10}(8t + 1) \tag{2}$$

During testing few panels lasted less than 30 min and a few panels lasted more than 50 min. In majority of cases the panel maintained its integrity for the initial 30 min. Later smoke appeared on the panel's external surface because of the fissures development and passages of gases. Finally, it is concluded that the PVC SIP system exhibits slightly better thermal performance compared to the conventional concrete elements.

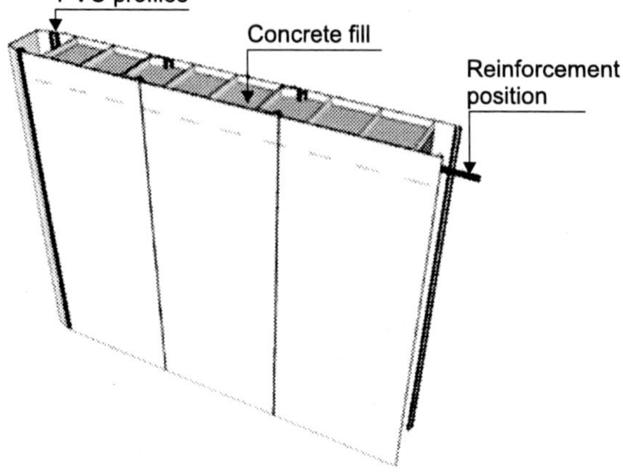

Fig. 4.9: Typical details of PVC panel SIP system used in the study [6]

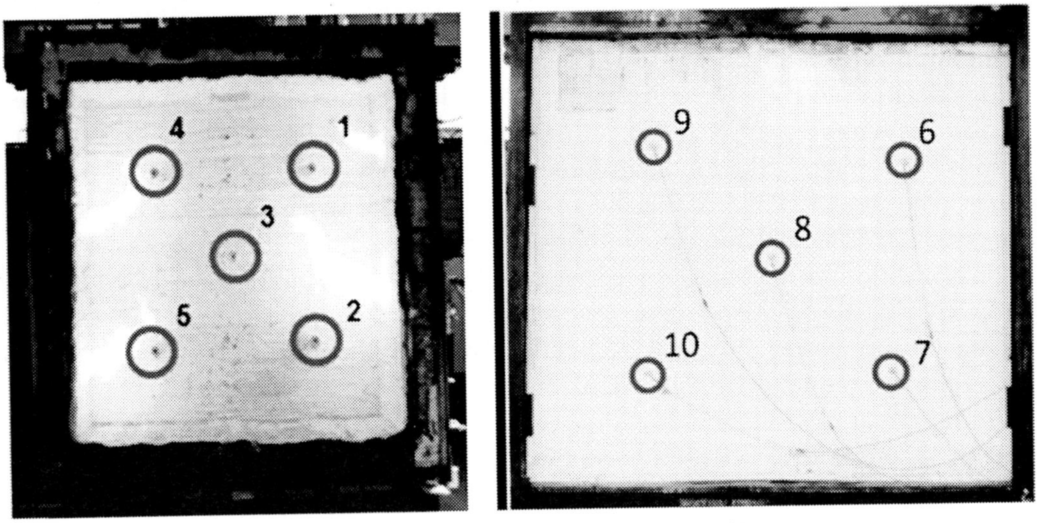

(a) (b)

Fig. 4.10: Fire testing through four points using gasoline [6]

Fig. 4.11: Failure of PVC panels during fire testing [6]

4.1.6 FRP based SIP Formwork System

Fiber Reinforced Polymer (FRP) composites are very effective in retrofitting and strengthening work. FRP based materials such as rebars, flats, pultruded sections are also available with enhanced strength and durable property. This FRP is used as SIP form work materials as also acts as reinforcement in slabs, shown in Fig.12-14. In which the FRP is made into the shape of I section with flat bottom to have resistance to the applied load. Fig. 13-15 shows the typical FRP SIP used in construction of slabs/ bridge decks. Generally the corrosion of steel reinforcement causes severe detoriates and affects the life span of the structure. In particular the bridge decks exposed the humid atmosphere, alkaline environment and adverse condition causes durability issues. The corrosion of rebars leads to volumetric enlargement and spalling of cover concrete. The effective usage of non corrosive materials like FRP as an external source significantly protects the reinforced elements and eliminates the need of additional protective coatings. Also offers less maintenance compared to the conventional technique. Commonly the use of FRP for flexural strengthening has shown incremental strength with reduction in deflection. Similarly, the use of multiple layers increases the strength and affects the ductility. These are the main considered advantages of FRP in SIP work. This FRP SIP system is predominantly used in construction of bridge decks and slab structures. In which pultruded FRP planks are used between the girders and left as SIP after concreting. This FRP increases the stiffness and control the cracks and acts as ideal solution for bridge deck construction. Many research works across the world have been focused to study the effectiveness of the FRP SIP system in bridge decks. The stress distribution of FRP deck panels are similar to the conventional design but the tension contribution of FRP panels to be considered for effective utilization as shown in Fig.17. Also the failure pattern of FRP slabs is dissimilar to the conventional slabs due to then SIP forms, shown in Fig. 16. It demands a detailed design with adequate bonding effect to take the advantage of FRP.

Fig. 4.12: Typical details of FRP deck panels with pultruded FRP sections and shear connector (Dieter et al., 2002)

Fig. 4.13: FRP section with shear connector [17]

Fig. 4.14: FRP concrete deck preparation

Fig. 4.15: FRP (grating) stiffened deck panel [19]

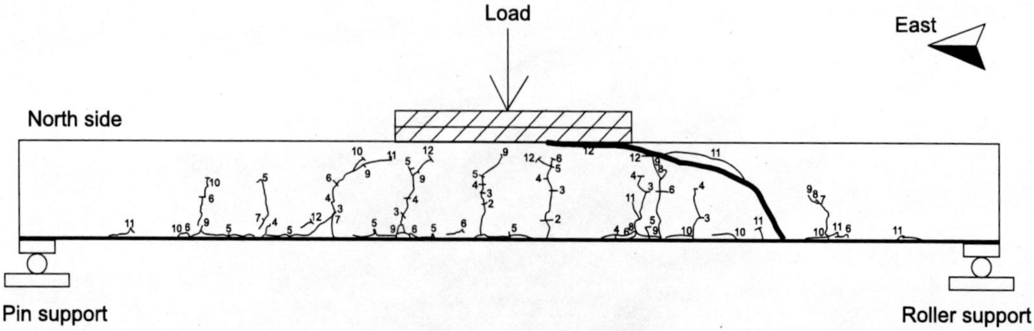

Fig. 4.16: Crack pattern of FRP deck slabunder concentrated load [20]

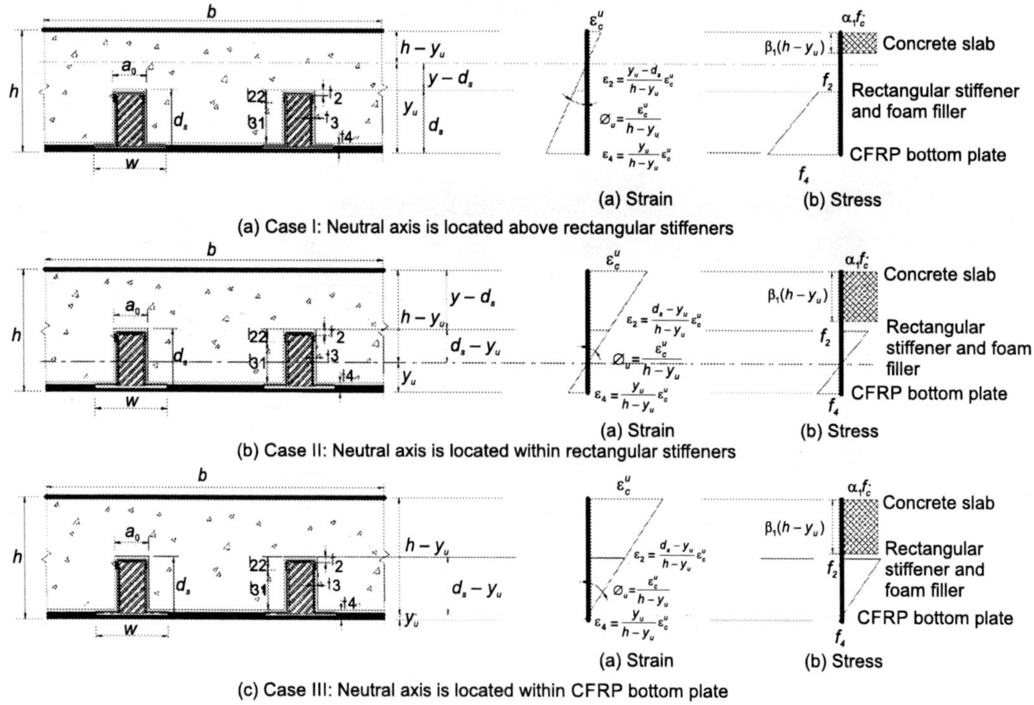

Fig. 4.17: Stress and strain distribution of FRP deck slab

Many research works have been carried out to examine its effectiveness under punching shear, bending. The usage of different shaped pultruded FRP sections are combined using the cross links as shown in Figure 12 and used over the planks instead of conventional reinforcement. Due to the smooth surface the bonding between the concrete and FRP surface were observed as a week plane. This leads to the sand blasted FRP deck panel as shown in Figure 18. These panels are kept between the girder as shown in Figure 19 and then concrete will be filled to a desired depth.

Fig. 4.18: FRP panel with sandblast coating [20]

Fig. 4.19: Placing of FRP Planks between the girders [18]

FRP molded grating-concrete composite based deck slab has been developed by Larralde, 1992 and experimentally studied its behavior. Figure 20 shows the FRP grating panel. To make use of the advantage of FRP stiffness the composite has been developed and observed that the composite panel offer better stiffness than the individual FRP grating stiffness. It is concluded that the FRP molded grating-concrete composite will fail in shear if the shear-span to depth ratio is lower than 5.

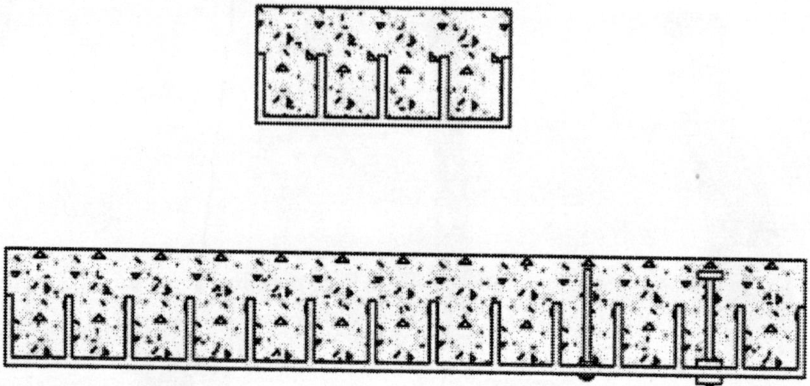

Fig. 4.20: Transverse and longitudinal cut-through views of beam specimens [7]

4.1.7 Hybrid FRP Panels

In Hybrid FRP panels light weight concrete/foam based concrete used as core material over a thin layer of normal concrete will be used. Figure 21 shows the Hybrid FRP panels. The bottom most FRP planks are offering better resistance to tension and the top most concrete layer offers resistance to compression. The inner core resists the shear force and acts as insulated materials. This principle increases the stiffness and strength without increasing the density of the elements.

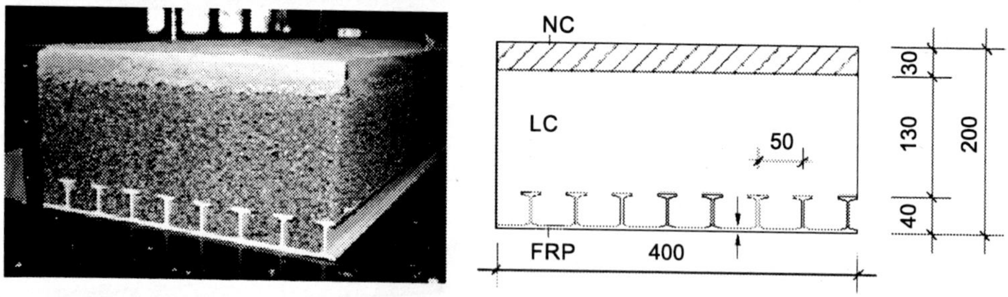

Fig. 4.21: Hybrid FRP panels [8]

Using lightweight materials/concrete in near the neutral axis region where low flexural stress exists considerably reduces the dead load of the panel without affecting the strength and stiffness. However, this technology to be designed to one that is limited by its shear strength (Honickman, 2008).

4.1.7.1 FRP box beam with concrete in the Compression Zone [21]

Descovic et al. (1995) proposed a hybrid concepts using GFRP box section with concrete on the top as shown in Figure 22. The concrete in the compression zone is also encased by the GFRP channel behaves like flange. This SIP ease the construction of deck work and rapidly increases the speed of construction. Similar to the FRP planks the bond between the concrete and FRP is ensured by the application of epoxy coating over

FRP prior to concrete placement. In order to increase the flexural stiffness CFRP layer is affixed at the soffit of the box section as depicted in Figure 22. The advantage of CFRP lower failure strain can be effectively used to provide warning before the occurrence of flexural failure (pseudoductility). Because both the materials used in this system are brittle in nature and will fail abruptly. Many research work in order to improve the system is going on across the world. Still detailed investigation for practical application by considering bonding, shear and flexural strength to be carried out to make use of this hybrid system. Similarly concrete filled FRP tube is also developed with concrete on top as shown in Figure 23.

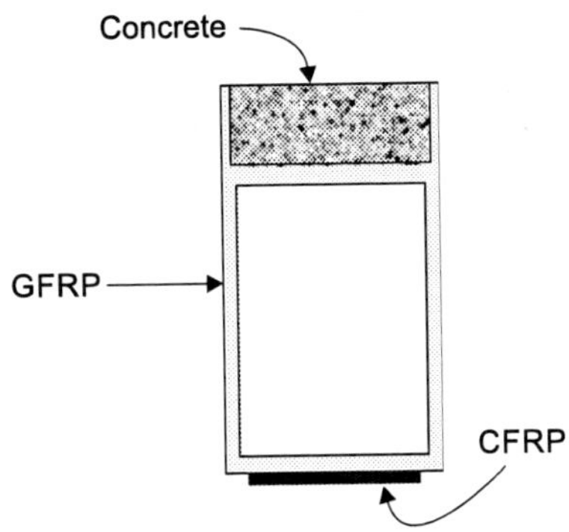

Fig. 4.22: GFRP-concrete hybrid flexural member (Deskovic et al., 1995)

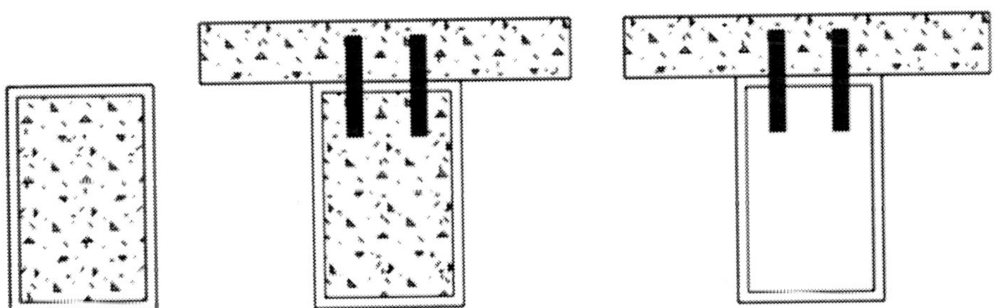

Fig. 4.23: Concrete-filled FRP tubes with a concrete slab on top [11]

In order to take the advantage of FRP SIP in structural application such RC Column, an experimental study with FRP SIP with and without FRP strips as stirrups were carried out. There are six different system of FRP SIP based RC columns with conventional reinforcement were used and tested under cyclic loading to examine its seismic behavior. Figure 24 shows the column details and detailed configurations. In this type CFRP fabrics were converted into the SIP form system and reinforcements were kept inside and then concrete were poured. However, the provide FRP SIP form syst5em offers better confining pressure and improved the ductility of column. The CFRP sheet converted Sip system did not rupture suddenly as experience in the deck panels. FRP experience layer by layer failure thus it shows better inelastic behavior as shown in Figure. This FRP based SIP for different RC elements needs extensive study and design methodology.

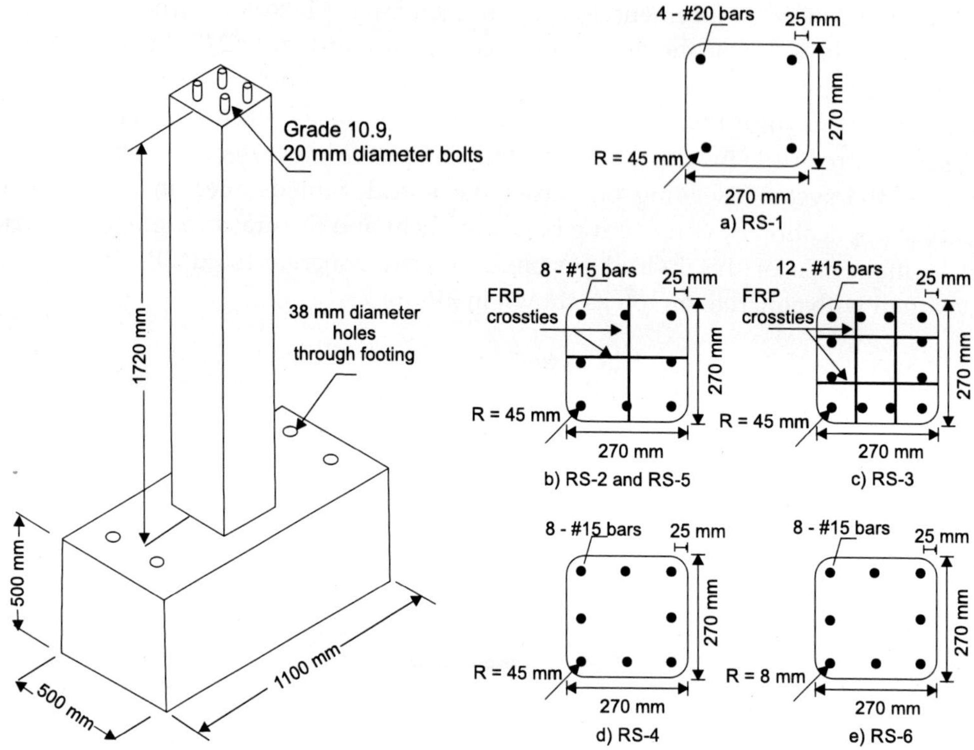

Fig. 4.24: Typical column reinforcement and FRP SIP form details

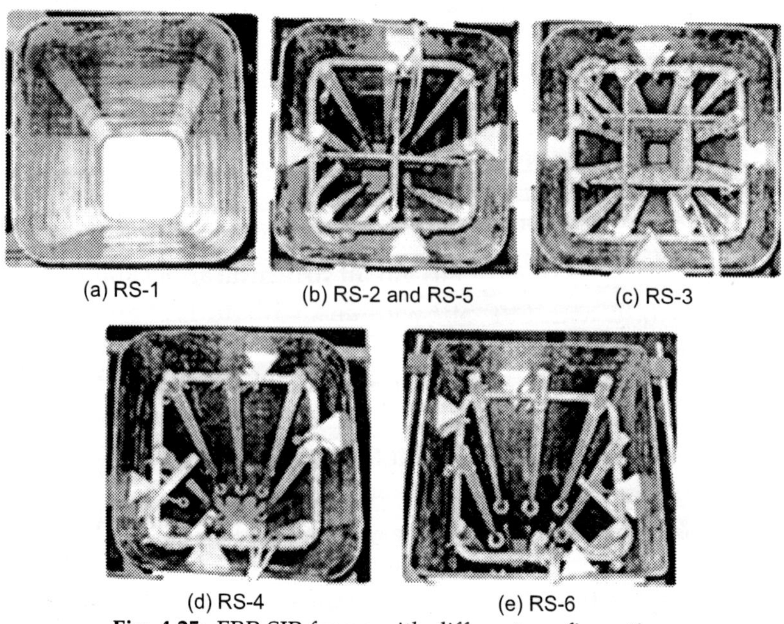

Fig. 4.25: FRP SIP forms with different configuration

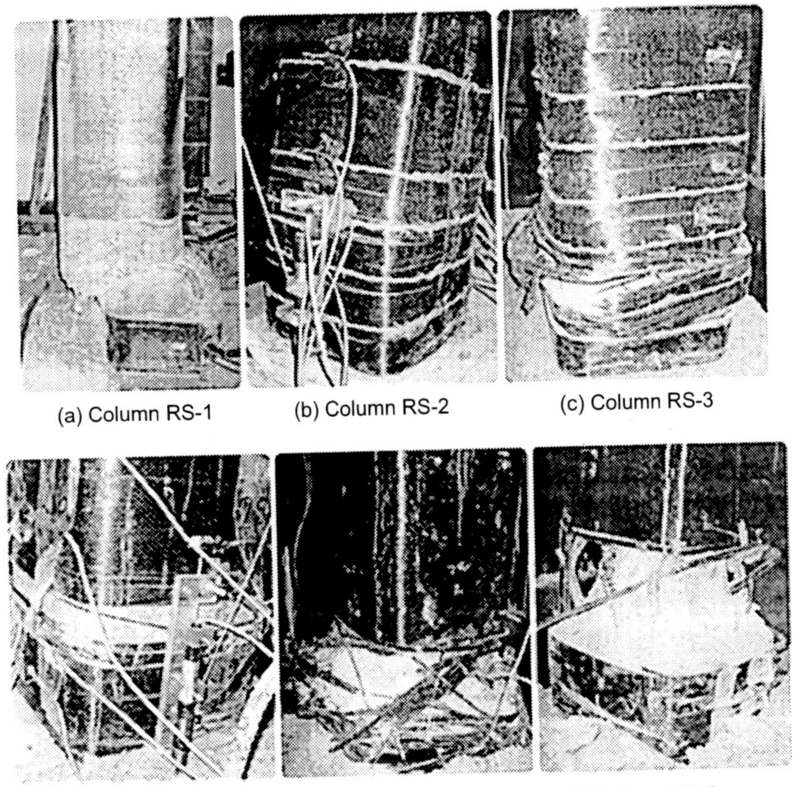

(a) Column RS-1 (b) Column RS-2 (c) Column RS-3

(d) Column RS-4 (e) Column RS-5 (f) Column RS-6

Fig. 4.26: Failure pattern of RC column under lateral loading

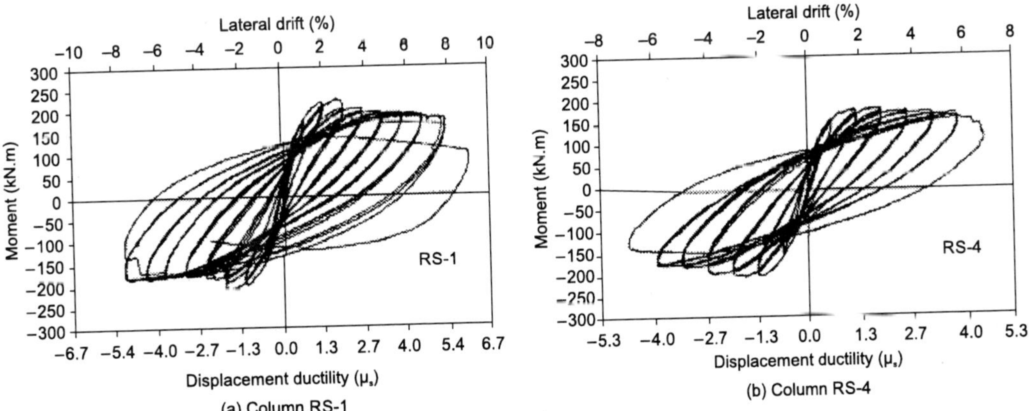

(a) Column RS-1 (b) Column RS-4

Fig. 4.27: Hysteresis behaviour of RC column with FRP-SIP form

4.1.8 Ductility in FRP-Reinforced Concrete Structures [21]

FRP and concrete are brittle material, when employs together it is difficult to get a ductile structure. Thus it is important to design theses structure similar to over reinforced so that the concrete crushing will occur prior to the FRP rupture. This behavior will provide certain ductility with warning of failure prior to collapse. If the composite structures to be over reinforced then it is necessary to provide confining reinforcement in compression zone to increase the strain capacity of the concrete. Burgoyne (2001)

4.1.9. Concreting and its influence on the Formwork [ACI 347-04] [14-16]

In SIP the concreting procedure is crucial due to the lateral pressure created by the fresh concrete during placing inside the cavity. Following factors to be considered carefully:

1. Density of concrete
2. Method of compaction
3. Mode of Concrete placement
4. Rate of concreting between the two external layers
5. Height of form work
6. Lateral support to the form system
7. Alignment of the form work

As per the American Concrete Institute 347 the maximum pressure on formwork is

$$P_m = wh \tag{3}$$

where,

P_m is the maximum lateral pressure, lb/ft^2

w is the unit weight of newly placed concreted, lb/ft^3

h is the depth of the plastic concrete ft.

Lateral Pressure on Wall Formworks [14-16]

ACI 347 considers the wall in two forms based on the height of placement and rate of placement of concrete. Equation 4 calculates the lateral pressure for wall having the placement height less than or equal to 14 ft having rate of placement less than 7 ft/hr. Similarly, Equation 5 estimates the lateral pressure for wall having height greater than 14 ft and the placement rate varies from 7 to 15 ft/hr.

$$P_m = C_w C_c [150 + 9000R/T] \tag{4}$$

where,

P_m = maximum lateral pressure, lb/ft^2

C_w = unit weight coefficient

C_c = chemistry coefficient

R = rate of fill of concrete in form, ft/hr

T = temperature of concrete in form, °F

Minimum value of P_m is $600C_w$, but in no case greater than wh. Applies to concrete with a slump of 7 inches or less. Applies to normal internal vibration to a depth of 4 ft or less.

For all wall forms with concrete placement rate from 7 to 15 ft/hr, *and for walls where the placement rate is less than* 7 ft/hr *and* the placement height exceeds 14 ft.

$$P_m = C_w C_c [150 + 43400/T + 28000\, R/T] \tag{5}$$

where,

P_m = maximum lateral pressure, lb/ft^2

C_w = unit weight coefficient;

C_c = chemistry coefficient;

R = rate of fill of concrete in form, ft/hr;

T = temperature of concrete in form, °F.

Minimum value of P_m is $600C_w$, but in no case greater than wh. Applies to concrete with a slump of 7 inches or less. Applies to normal internal vibration to a depth of 4 ft or less.

Lateral Pressure of Concrete on Column Forms [14-16]

For determining pressure of concrete on formwork ACI 347 defines a column as a vertical structural member with no plan dimensions greater than 6.5 ft. As previously presented, the American Concrete Institute recommends that formwork be designed for its full hydrostatic lateral pressure as given by Eq. (6), $P_m = wh$, where P_m is the lateral pressure (lb/ft^2), w is the unit weight (lb/ft^3) of the newly placed concrete, and h is the depth (ft) of the plastic concrete. Concrete is often placed rapidly in columns with intense vibration or with self-consolidating concrete. Therefore, h should be taken as the full height of the column form. There are no maximum or minimum values given for the pressure calculated from Eq. (6).

For concrete with a slump 7 inches or less and placement by normal internal vibration to a depth of 4 ft or less, formwork for columns can be designed for the following lateral pressure.

$$P_m = C_w C_c [150 + 9000R/T] \tag{6}$$

where,

P_m = calculated lateral pressure, lb/ft^2;

C_w = unit weight coefficient;

C_c = chemistry coefficient;

R = rate of fill of concrete in form, ft/hr;

T = temperature of concrete in form, °F.

Minimum value of P_m is $600C_w$, but in no case greater than wh. Applies to concrete with a slump of 7 inches or less. Applies to normal internal vibration to a depth of 4 ft or less.

Equation (7) may be used to determine the maximum pressure produced by concrete having a density other than 150 lb/ft³.

$$P'_m = [D'/150] \times P_m \tag{7}$$

where,

P'_m = modified pressure, lb/ft²;

D' = density of concrete, lb/ft³;

P_m = maximum pressure for concrete whose density is 150 lb/ft² when placed under the same conditions.

Notes:

1. Do not use design pressure greater than *wh*.
2. Concrete placement with normal internal vibration to a depth of 4 ft or less.
3. Values are based on concrete with $C_w = 1$ and $C_c = 1$.
4. Concrete without additives with a maximum slump of 7 inches.
5. Minimum pressure is $600C_w$ lb/ft², but in no case greater than *wh*.
6. For pour rates greater than 15 ft/hr, use pressure $Pm = wh$.

REFERENCES

1. Web page https://www.theplancollection.com/house-plan-related-articles/icf-construction-why-you-should-care-about-it-for-your-new-house-
2. Web page https://www.sismo.eu/product-0
3. BMTPC PACS report,PAC No.:1035-S/ 2018 "Structural Stay-in-Place Formwork System" M/s Coffor Construction Technology Pvt. Ltd., Gujarat.
4. Web page www.bigrivergroup.com.au
5. Michel Murillo A., Bernardo F. Tutikianc, Vinicius Ortolanc, Marcos L.S. Oliveirad, Carlos H. Sampaioe, Leandro Gómez Pa, Luis F. Silva Oa "Fire resistance performance of concrete-PVC panels with polyvinyl chloride (PVC) stay in place (SIP) formwork" Journal of Materials Research and Technology, 2019, 8(5); 4094-4107.
6. Dieter, D., Dietsche, J., Bank, L., Oliva, M., and Russell, J. (2002). Concrete Bridge Decks Constructed with Fiber-Reinforced Polymer Stay-in-Place Forms and Grid Reinforcing. *Transportation Research Record, Journal of the Transportation Research Board, 1814*(-1), 219-226.
7. Larralde, J. (1992). Feasibility of FRP moulded grating-concrete composites for one-way slab systems.
8. Keller, T., Schaumann, E., and Vallee, T. (2007). Flexural behavior of a hybrid FRP and lightweight concrete sandwich bridge deck. *Composites Part A-Applied Science an Manufacturing, 38*(3), 879-889.

9. Deskovic, N., Meier, U., and Triantafillou, T. C. (1995). Innovative design of FRP combined with concrete - long-term behaviour. *Journal of Structural Engineering, ASCE, 121*(7), 1079-1089.
10. Deskovic, N., Triantafillou, T. C., and Meier, U. (1995). Innovative design of FRP design of FRP combined with concrete - short-term behaviour. *Journal of Structural Engineering, ASCE, 121*(7), 1069-1078.
11. Fam, A., and Skutezky, T. (2006). Composite T-beams using reduced-scale rectangular FRP tubes and concrete slabs. *Journal of Composites for Construction, 10*(2), 172-181.
12. Burgoyne, C., Leung, H. Y. (2007). Model for concrete confined by aramid FRP. FRPRCS-8, Univeristy of Patras, Patras, Greece, July 16-18.
13. Hurd M, Formwork for Concrete SP 04, American Concrete Institute.
14. Robert L. Peurifoy; Garold D. Oberlender "Formwork for Concrete Structures" Fourth Edition, McGraw-Hill.
15. ACI. "ACI 347-04–guide to formwork for concrete." (2004).
16. Web page https://www.miyafrp.com/fiberglass-grating/frp-pultruded-grating.html
17. Oliva, M., et al. "FRP stay-in-place formwork for floor and deck construction." *FRP Stay-in-Place Forms for Concrete Structures, ACI Special Publication* (2008): 106-129.
18. Cheng, Lijuan, and Vistasp M. Karbhari. "Design approach for a FRP structural formwork based steel-free modular bridge system." *Structural Engineering and Mechanics* 24.5 (2006): 561-584.
19. Olivia M.G, Bank L.C, Bae H, Litow C.R. Aggregate Coated FRP Plank as Formwork and Crack Controlling Device fro Reinforcement Free Bridge Decks, The 2nd Official International Conference of International Institute for FRP in Construction for Asia-Pacific region. Seoul, Korea, 2009, 319-324.
20. Gai, Xian "Fibre Reinforced Polymer (FRP) Stay-in-Place (SIP) participating formwork for new construction" Ph.D Thesis, University of Bath (2012).
21. Cheng, Lijuan, and Vistasp M. Karbhari. "Design approach for a FRP structural formwork based steel-free modular bridge system." *Structural Engineering and Mechanics* 24.5 (2006): 561-584.

4.2 GLASS FIBRE REINFORCED GYPSUM PANEL SYSTEM

4.2.1 Introduction

GFRG (Glass Fibre Reinforced Gypsum) is a new building panel product, made essentially of gypsum plaster, reinforced with glass fibre rovings. This product, originally developed and used since 1990 in Australia by Rapid Building Systems, is suitable for rapid mass-scale building construction. The technological breakthrough of combining glass fibre strands with gypsum plaster, produced in an energy-efficient fluidized bed calcining process, resulted in GFRG wall panels with the desired properties of strength and water resistance. The addition of glass fibres, 300 - 350mm long, randomly spread, imparts tensile strength to the gypsum plaster, which is otherwise brittle. GFRG can be manufactured out of any kind of gypsum such as natural gypsum (used in Australia), flue gas gypsum, mineral gypsum or phospho-gypsum, with purity of not less than 90%. GFRG is of particular relevance to India, where there is a tremendous need for cost-effective mass-scale and rapid housing, and where gypsum is abundantly available as an industrial by-product waste (64 million tonnes of stockpiled gypsum). In India, GFRG panels are made out of phospho-gypsum (recycled industrial waste from the fertilizer industry), and are currently manufactured at FRBL (FACT-RCF Building Products Ltd.) Kochi. There is no health hazard reported in the use of panels, either with phospho-gypsum or glass fibres.

GFRG panels, considered to be the world's largest light-weight, load-bearing, pre-fabricated building panels, weighing only 44 kg/m^2 are manufactured to a standard size of 12m length, 3m height and 124 mm thickness, with modular cavities aligned along the height, as shown in Figures 1 and 2.

Fig. 4.1: GFRG panel (12 m × 3 m)

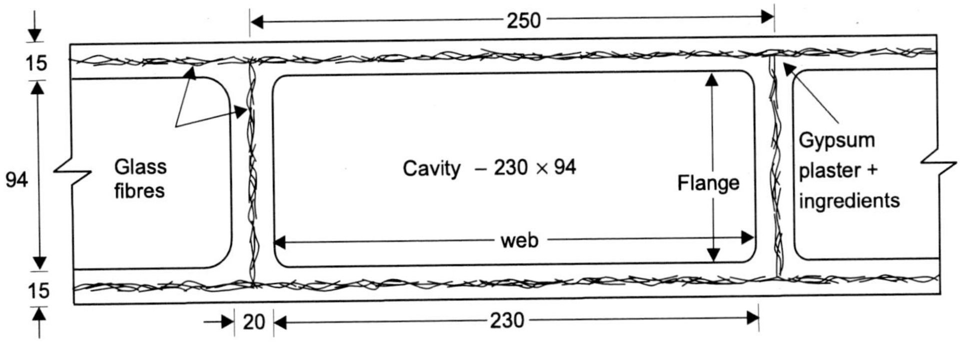

Fig. 4.2: Typical cross section of a GFRG panel (all dimensions in mm)

The manufacture of the GFRG panels are done in 'casting tables' in the factory using gypsum beta plaster, obtained from calcination of raw gypsum. Gypsum panels made using alpha-plaster (commercially known as plaster of paris) reinforced with glass fibres are in use as non-structural or partition walls, mostly used for architectural works. These are also known as glass fibre reinforced gypsum or GRG. The panels can be cut to desired lengths and transported to construction sites; however the maximum length that can typically be transported in India at present is 6m. Although the panels can also be cut at the site using a chain saw, it is more convenient to have this done at the factory itself, using an automated cutting facility. The height of the panel is typically fixed as 3m, corresponding to standard storey height, but can be suitably changed. The cellular cavities are formed between the two outer skins (15 mm thick), which are inter-connected by solid 'ribs' (20 mm thick), spaced at 250 mm intervals. These cavities can be conveniently filled with concrete and reinforced with steel, if required, to provide for additional strength and to improve ductility. Filling with some inert material, like quarry dust mixed with about 5% cement, is also found desirable, providing security and enabling convenient fixing of nails, etc. GFRG has been approved as a green building material by the United Nations Framework Convention on Climate Change (UNFCCC).

The GFRG building system can be designed to provide affordable mass housing for a wide variety of applications - from single storey to medium rise (multi-storey) structures. It is necessary to plan meticulously all the details related to the design and construction, especially issues related to optimal use of the GFRG panels, concrete and reinforcement, as well as issues related to transportation, erection, provision of services and deployment of manpower and equipment. Ideally, plants manufacturing GFRG panels need to be set up in many regions, to minimize transportation costs, and to cater to the immense and urgent need for mass housing in India - for which the GFRG building system holds promise as providing an effective solution, when scaled up in its application.

4.2.2 Concepts and Features

The GFRG panel is a structural member that is capable of resisting axial (gravity) load (P), lateral shear (V) and in-plane bending (Mi) (due to shear wall-like action against lateral loads - wind and earthquake) and out-of-plane bending (Mo) (due to eccentric gravity loading from slabs and due to lateral wind loading on external walls). Infilling the cavities with nominal concrete is found to increase significantly the axial load capacity. Providing reinforcement bars in the concrete-filled cavities is not found to increase further the axial load resistance, but can enhance the resistance to both in-plane and out-of-plane bending. GFRG buildings exhibit ductile behaviour under cyclic lateral loading. This capability is essential in an earthquake prone country like India.

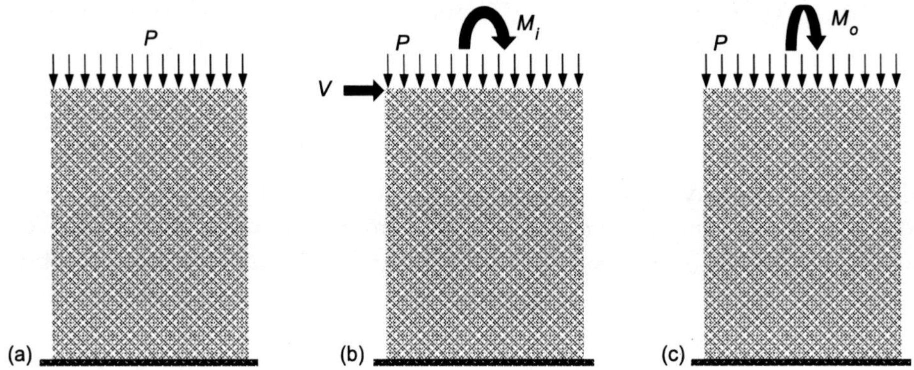

Fig. 4.3: GFRG panels subjected to: (a) axial load, (b) in-plane shear and bending along with axial load, and (c) out-of-plane bending with axial load

All components of building, such as walls, floor / roof slabs, stair cases and parapet walls can be constructed using prefabricated GFRG panels. The use of GFRG panels for walls, floors and staircases in combination, appropriately designed for composite action with RC (reinforced concrete), with tie beams / tie connection at all the wall-floor junctions, provides for a complete GFRG building system. In India, unlike Australia, more than fifty percent of the population lives in seismically prone areas of moderate to severe earthquakes. Hence, the GFRG building system has to be designed to meet the requirements of the prevailing standards of seismic resistance. Extensive studies were conducted at IIT Madras on the use of panels as structural members for earthquake resistant design, and a detailed design methodology has been developed. Tests have been carried out on a number of wall panels to assess and predict the lateral load capacity under different levels of axial loading (up to ten storeys). It was observed that GFRG, along with the concrete core, acts in a composite manner, while developing vertical shear cracks in the panels (at the junction of the web and flange), with the RC cores remaining relatively undamaged. Slipping at the interface of the core and the GFRG is found to occur, contributing to dissipation of seismic energy. The energy dissipation due to slipping and cracking of GFRG (and yielding of longitudinal bars in the case of slender walls) is found to generate significant ductility and shear wall behaviour in resisting shear and in-plane bending.

Based on the research work carried out at IIT Madras, and the research reported elsewhere (Australia and China), Building Materials & Technology Promotion Council (BMTPC), Government of India, has accorded approval of GFRG panels for construction in India. It is possible to design such buildings up to ten storeys in low seismic zones (and to lesser height in high seismic zones). However, such construction needs to be properly designed by a qualified structural engineer. Research has also been carried out in identifying waterproofing chemicals that are suitable for both GFRG and concrete, for ensuring prolonged life of these buildings.

The following manuals have been published by BMTPC for adoption in GFRG design and construction practice.

(a) GFRG / Rapidwall Building Structural Design Manual

(b) Manual on waterproofing of GFRG / Rapidwall Buildings

(c) Schedule of Items and Rate analysis for GFRG Construction

(d) GFRG / Rapidwall Construction Manual

The Bureaus of Indian Standards (BIS) are finalising publication of two standards for GFRG – i) material specification, and, ii) method of analysis and design of GFRG buildings. These standards and guidelines serve to assist architects, structural engineers and construction engineers on the design and construction of GFRG buildings in India.

Currently, GFRG panels are manufactured at FRBL Kochi and are transported to different parts of the country. There are plans to set-up more factories in the country. It is also possible to set up the calciners at one location (ideally, near a port), and to set up small-scale units with tables for manufacturing the GFRG panels at several other places which can be supplied with the calcined gypsum plaster produced in the calciners (and having a shelf life of one year, when stored in bags) by convenient transportation by road or by rail.

Some of the key features of this building system are its intelligent building design features, green building, earthquake resistant design and fire resistance. The life of these buildings are estimated to be more than that of conventional buildings.

4.2.3 Advantages and Limitations

The advantages of GFRG building construction over conventional buildings are as follows:

(a) High speed of construction with less manpower.

(b) Less built-up area for the same carpet area: wall panels are only 124 mm thick.

(c) Less embodied energy and carbon footprint: significant reduction in use of cement, sand, steel and water; recycling of industrial waste gypsum.

(d) Lower cost of structure: savings in materials; no plastering.
(e) Lower building weight (panels weigh only 44 kg/m^2), contributing to savings in foundation and reduction in design for earthquake forces, particularly in multi-storeyed construction.
(f) Buildings up to 8-10 storeys can be designed using this load-bearing system, without the need for beams and columns.
(g) Excellent finishes of prefabricated GFRG panels – used for all the walls, floors and staircases, with minimal embedded concrete: no need for additional plastering.
(h) Saving of energy and reduced CO_2 emissions contributes to environmental protection and mitigating climate change due to reduced consumption of resources and recycling of industrial waste gypsum; hence GFRG is considered as a green product.
(i) Use of reprocessed / recycled industrial by-product, viz., waste gypsum, to manufacture GFRG panel, helps to abate pollution and protect the environment.
(j) Save fertile agricultural land and energy intensive burnt clay bricks.
(k) Saving of 8-10% built-up area for the same carpet area.
(l) Better thermal performance, resulting in saving in energy required for cooling and heating a building.
(m) Manufacturing and construction at controlled conditions can give better quality of building.
(n) Resistant to water and fire.
(o) Suitable for rapid affordable mass housing.

The following are the limitations of GFRG building construction over conventional buildings:

(a) The shorter span of slab (floor/roof) should be restricted to 5 m in residential use and 4m for commercial or public use.
(b) It is ideal only if the same floor/roof is replicated for all floors in multi-storey structure.
(c) Curved walls or domes should be avoided. In case these are essential, masonry/ concrete should be used.
(d) The electrical/plumbing fittings should be planned in such a way that most of the pipes pass through the cavities in order to facilitate minimum cutting of panels.

4.2.4 Design Principles

GFRG building systems, typically comprising vertical walls and horizontal slabs, are designed as load-bearing systems, without beams and columns. Selected cavities in the walls and slabs are filled with low-grade (minimum M20 grade) concrete and suitably reinforced with minimal steel (minimum 10 mm diameter rebar). In the case of walls of buildings up to two or three storeys, only few cavities need to be infilled (typically every third cavity, reinforced with one 10 mm diameter bar); but for high rise buildings, all the cavities have to be infilled with concrete and suitably reinforced (with one or two rebars in each cavity), to impart additional strength and ductility. GFRG panels in Australia had been utilized only as load-bearing walls resisting gravity loads; the slabs were made of conventional RC. The application was extended, based on extensive studies done at IIT Madras, to their use as shear walls (resisting earthquake loads) as well as floor slabs, staircases and parapets. The comprehensive use of GFRG panels, in combination with RC, for all the structural components of a building provides an alternative to conventional load-bearing and framed building systems using traditional building materials.

4.2.4.1 Design Philosophy

The design capacities are based on limit states design procedures, considering the ultimate limit state for strength design, and satisfying the serviceability requirements. The partial safety factors for the GFRG building panel (with and without concrete infill) and reinforcing steel is taken as γ_m = 1.50 and γ_s = 1.15 respectively, as recommended in IS 456 : 2000. Earthquake resistant design is carried out in compliance with the requirements of IS 1893 (Part 1) : 2002, where the response reduction factor (R) is taken as 3.0 for seismic load calculations. The external wall panels are also designed for wind loads as per IS 875 (Part 3) : 1987.

4.2.4.2 Mechanical Properties

The following table provides some of the important mechanical properties of GFRG building panel (for both unfilled panels and panels filled with concrete), which have been determined from tests conducted at IIT Madras.

Table 5.1: Mechanical properties of GFRG building panel

Mechanical Property	Nominal Value
Unit weight	44 kg/m^2
Modulus of elasticity	7500 N/mm^2
Uniaxial compressive strength, P_{uc}	160 kN/m (unfilled) 1310 kN/m (filled)
Ultimate shear strength, V_{uc}	21.6 kN/m 61 kN/m (filled)

4.2.4.3 Axial Load Capacity

The axial load capacity of GFRG building panel (under compression) has been assessed taking into consideration possible eccentricities in loading, taking into account the minimum eccentricity values as specified in IS 456 : 2000 and IS 1905 : 1987. The characteristic values of axial compressive strength of the GFRG building panel, expressed in kN/m, are obtained from compression test results on GFRG building panel for full height panel, subject to various eccentricities of loading (20 mm, 30 mm and 45 mm) and different boundary conditions. For design purposes, the nominal values have been divided by $\gamma_m = 1.5$. Axial load capacity can be calculated as: $P_{ud} = (68 - 0.9e)$, for unfilled panels, and, $P_{ud} = (600 - 13.75e)$, for filled panels.

4.2.4.4 Out-of-Plane Bending Capacity

The out-of-plane bending capacity or the flexural capacity of GFRG panels is obtained through tests conducted, with the ribs of the panels kept both along and across the span. Their significance lies in the design of GFRG wall panels against wind loads and in the design of GFRG slabs. GFRG panels exhibit nominal flexural strength while bending out-of-plane in the direction of the ribs. This strength gets considerably enhanced when the cavities are filled with reinforced concrete, providing the desired strength needed in external walls of high rise buildings under wind loading.

Unfilled GFRG panels: When tested for out-of-plane bending, a higher bending capacity was obtained when the ribs were oriented parallel to the span, in comparison to the case when the test was conducted with the ribs kept perpendicular to span. The design bending moment capacity obtained in the case of ribs placed parallel to span was, $M_{ud} = 1.4$ kNm/m, whereas in the case of latter, M_{ud} was obtained as 0.59 kNm/m.

Filled GFRG panels: When the cavities are filled with concrete, full composite action of GFRG and concrete cannot be mobilized on account of bond slip at the interface. A conservative estimate of the moment capacity can be arrived at by ignoring the contribution of GFRG and considering the action of the concrete beams occupying the cellular cavities. Accordingly, the design moment capacity was obtained as, $M_{ud} = 2.83$ kNm/m.

4.2.4.5 Shear Strength

The shear carrying capacity of GFRG panels of 3.0 m height have been tested on unfilled panels and on the panels with the cavities infilled with reinforced concrete. The unit shear strength capacity of unfilled GFRG panels was obtained as $V_{ud} = 14.4$ kN/m. When all the cavities are reinforced and infilled with a minimum grade of M20 concrete, V_{ud} was obtained as 40 kN/m. In case the cavities of the GFRG panels are partially infilled with RC, the design shear capacity can be obtained using the expression, $14.4 + 25.4\eta$ kN/m, (η is the ratio of number of infilled cavities to total number of cavities).

4.2.4.6 Design of GFRG Wall Panels

GFRG panels are used not only as load bearing walls, but also as walls transferring lateral loads, viz., lateral in-plane shear force (V) and in-plane bending moment (M), in addition to resisting axial force (P). The design of the wall panels are done with the aid of design axial load (P_u)–in plane bending moment (M_u) interaction developed for the panels.

In-plane bending capacity: The design in-plane bending capacity (M_{ud}) and its relationship with the design axial load capacity (P_{ud}) is usually described by means of a P_{ud} - M_{ud} interaction diagram. Design interaction curves were developed for GFRG wall panels that are partially and fully infilled with RC, for panels of widths varying from 1.0 m to 3.5 m with intervals of 0.25 m. Infill of RC refers to the presence of either a single or two rebars in the selected cavities or all the cavities. A typical P_u - M_u interaction curve is shown in Figure 4.

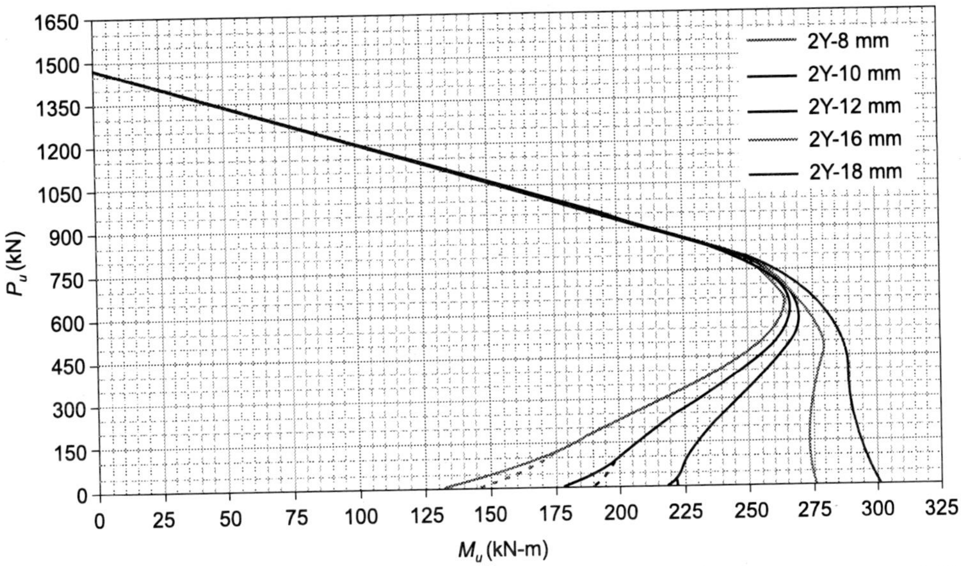

Fig. 4.4: Typical design P_u - M_u plots for 1.50 m wide GFRG panel with *M*25 concrete infill

4.2.4.7 Design of GFRG-RC Floor/Roof Slab

As GFRG panels with ribs aligned in direction of bending possess sufficient strength to resist flexure, such panels can be used as slab, whose strength can be significantly enhanced by embedding 'concealed beams', filled with RC. The ribs are to be oriented along the shorter span, supported on GFRG wall panels. For convenience in design, the contribution of GFRG towards the flexural strength can be ignored and the GFRG can be treated as lost formwork thereby eliminating the need for supporting system and shuttering, but also contributes significantly to stiffness and marginally to strength. RC concealed beams are to be provided by filling cavities at regular intervals (typically every third cavity), with a screed concrete of thickness not less than 50 mm. The cross-section of GFRG-RC slab is shown in Figure 5.

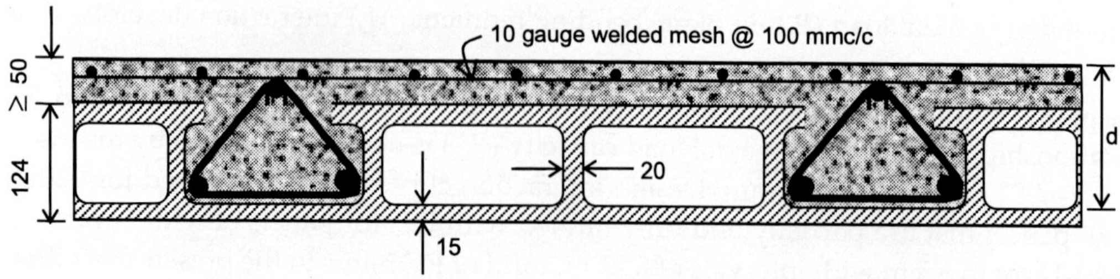

Fig. 4.5: Typical cross section of panel with concealed beams and screed concrete

The 50 mm thick screed, provided with suitable wire fabric, also serves to provide diaphragm action to the building system under lateral loading. The RC concealed beams along with the screed concrete constitute a series of T beams, which can be designed for spans up to 5 m, conforming to the requirements of IS 456 : 2000. One way slab action may be assumed for strength and deflection check. In the screed concrete, suitable welded wire fabric shall be provided.

4.2.5 Construction Methodology

Once the panels are cut in the factory, they are stacked in stillages, and are then transported to construction sites on trucks. Stillages are tackles that are used to hold intact a group of panels together in order to avoid damage during transportation (Figure 6).

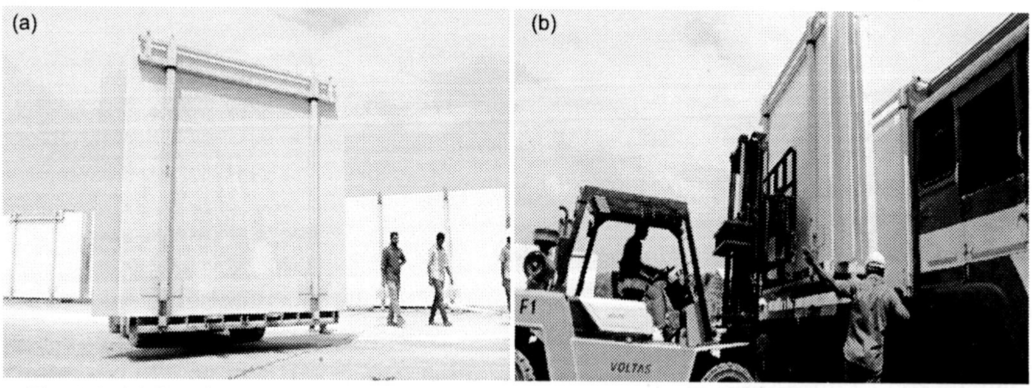

Fig. 4.6: (a) Panels stacked in stillages in the factory and, (b) loading of stillages on to trucks

Once the required materials, tools and tackles are made available at the site, the construction can make a start. The sequence of the tasks carried out for construction are summarised below.

4.2.5.1 Construction of Sub-Structure/Foundation

The foundation for GFRG system can be of the same type as that used for normal construction, as per the structural design. Generally strip footings are provided for buildings on soils which have adequate bearing capacities. If the bearing capacity is low, then pedestals can be provided on isolated footings. For multi-storeyed buildings, RC shear walls can be given. Whatever be the type of foundation adopted, a network RC plinth beams (with 'starter bars' in position) need to be provided additionally all around the foundation below the walls. These starter bars, anchored into the plinth beam, are to be located in such a way as to match with the locations of the cavities of the panel that need to be reinforced. The diameter of the starter bars shall match that of the cavity reinforcement, and these bars shall protrude vertically with adequate development length above the plinth beam (and later tied with binding wire to the cavity reinforcement). Waterproofing of the foundation especially application of a damp proof course (DPC) over the RC plinth beam is mandatory as the absorption of water by the glass fibres embedded in the GFRG wall panel can result in capillary suction. Figures 7 and 8 depict these.

Fig. 4.7: (a) Block work using fly ash blocks on strip footing and (b) pedestals on isolated footing

Fig. 4.8: (a) Insertion of rebars, and (b) foundation with starter bars in position

Activities prior to superstructure construction: After the foundation work gets over, the Architect and Project Manager is required to check the accuracy of position of the starter bars provided on the plinth beam, whose top surface is required to be perfectly horizontal. Appropriate corrections shall be made, and if required, fresh starter bars shall be installed (wherever deemed absolutely necessary) into the plinth beams through anchoring and lock setting. The cut panels delivered to the site from the factory shall have exact dimensions as per the cutting drawings. If the position of starter bars is not accurate or the plinth beam surface not horizontal, then the panels will not fit exactly. That is why it is necessary to ensure proper planning and workmanship in GFRG building construction - a requirement that is characteristic of all prefabricated construction. Proper planning shall also be done to ensure road access for the arrival of the trucks, movement of crane, and stacking of panels at site. It should be made sure that all the materials (including panels) and equipment are kept ready at site prior to the start of construction.

4.2.5.2 Construction of Superstructure

The superstructure construction starts with the lifting and erection of wall panels on to the previously prepared foundation on which a plinth beam (with starter bars) is already cast. Erection and casting of each component of the superstructure is shown in the following sections. The transportation of panels to the site is shown in Figure 9a.

Fig. 4.9: (a) Arrival of wall panels to site in trucks, and (b) wall panel being lifted using crane

Erection of wall panels: Once the foundation is completed, the wall panels can be erected over the network of RC plinth beams. For easy movement and working of the crane, the panels at the least accessible area shall be erected first, followed by others. The panels sent to the site from the factory will be marked using notations specified in the cutting drawings. Hence, the right panels have to be identified and lifted using the lifting jaws fixed to the boom of the crane and placed at the right locations, as shown in Figure 9b. Once a wall panel is erected, the vertical and horizontal levels shall be checked and corrected, if required, by making appropriate minor adjustments with the help of labour and crane. The panel shall then be supported laterally using props. The reinforcement in the appropriate cavities have to be inserted and tied to the starter bars. Next, the infill of concrete shall be done. Prior to infilling of concrete, the joint between the RC plinth beam and the panel needs to be sealed-off using appropriate waterproofing chemical, to prevent leakage of concrete slurry. The initial filling of concrete shall be limited to a depth of 300 mm (to avoid possible bursting of the GFRG skin); this filling will also serve to maintain the panel in a sturdy vertical position. It is recommended that the cavities in the panels be filled by pouring concrete in 4 stages, with an interval of 2 hours in between the successive pours. All the cavities at the location of windows other than the cut portion shall be necessarily filled with concrete. Also, in the case of door and window openings, it shall be made sure that the adjacent cavities are concrete infilled. Special care has to be taken at the wall corner joints, where two or more walls intersect. This is shown in detail in Figure 10, where two walls meet together forming a horizontal joint or a L-joint, three walls meeting together forming a T-joint and four walls forming a plus joint (4-way wall joint).

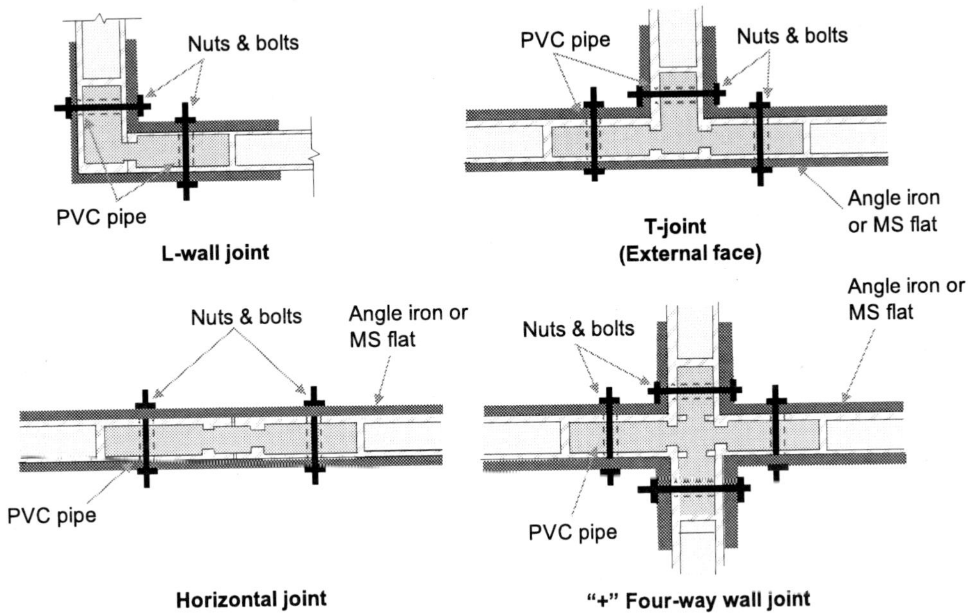

Fig. 4.10: Horizontal wall panel joints

Since the cavities house only a very small area, infilling of concrete shall be done using a hopper with a large area at the mouth and a small area (compared to 230 × 94 mm cavity) at the discharge gate, without which the infilling of concrete into typical cavities will be a difficult job resulting in spilling off of the concrete. This will cause delay in the work and utmost care need to be taken to avoid this. It is advisable to use a clamping system made of angle iron or mild steel flats to prevent movement of the panels at the joint while concreting, which can be removed after the initial set of concrete. Figure 11a shows all the ground floor walls after being completely erected, and Figure 11b shows the infilling of concrete into the wall panel cavities.

Fig. 4.11: (a) Wall panels at the ground floor have been erected, and (b) pouring of concrete into wall panel cavity

The walls of the GFRG building are likely to be subjected to nailing / screwing for various uses. The risk for the breakage of panels or for the development of cracks lies only when the cavities remain unfilled. Hence all the empty cavities shall be infilled with quarry dust mixed with 5% cement and water, or any other inert material. Wherever electrical pipelines or conduits have to be provided, the cavity can be left empty for this purpose, and subsequently infilled.

In situ construction of lintel-cum-sunshade: For all openings on the wall panels (without sunshades) up to a span of 1.2m, RC lintels need not be provided. In the case of sunshades, ribs and outer flanges of the cavities on the top portion of windows shall be cut open (including bearing) and reinforcement for the lintel beam and sunshade be inserted and concreted. Once the sunshade is concreted, then the remaining height of the cavities of the wall above this shall be infilled with concrete to a height of 2.65m. This is illustrated in Figure 12. At the top of the wall, provision shall be made for insertion of a horizontal tie beam (200 mm deep). The reinforcement cage is inserted into the top of the wall by cutting 200 mm of web prior to concreting. The embedded horizontal tie beam runs throughout the length of the walls and provides a box-like action to the building, preventing out-of-plane failure of the walls in the event of an earthquake.

Fig. 4.12: Cutting of panel, insertion of reinforcement and concreting of lintel-cum-sunshade (cast-in-situ)

Fig. 4.13: (a) Propping done for the placement of GFRG slab, and (b) panel lifted using two spreader bars

Laying of floor/roof slab panels: Before the slab panels are erected, steel beam supports ('acrospans') shall be provided at the top level of the wall panel to prevent the sudden deflection and hence failure of the GFRG slab while concreting, as shown in Figure 13a. These can be supported by means of props provided at the corners. The acrospans shall be aligned perpendicular to the direction of cavities. The laying of the floor slab is shown in Figure 13b.

The panels shall then be lifted horizontally by means of spreader bars attached with soft slings and laid on the supporting wall panels, giving a bearing of 40 mm. The use of spreader bars prevent probable damages due to bending of the panel while lifting. Once the panels are erected, the top flanges (of the cavities to be reinforced) can be cut open from the top leaving a 25 mm clear projection (from the web) on both sides. The reinforcement cage for the concealed RC beams, which are already tied and prepared, shall be placed inside the open cavities. Simultaneously service cables and pipes can also be laid. Shuttering using 6 mm plywood shall be provided throughout the perimeter of the floor slab before concreting. Then the top level of the RC screed shall be marked on the side shutter using a laser level (water tube level can also be used). A

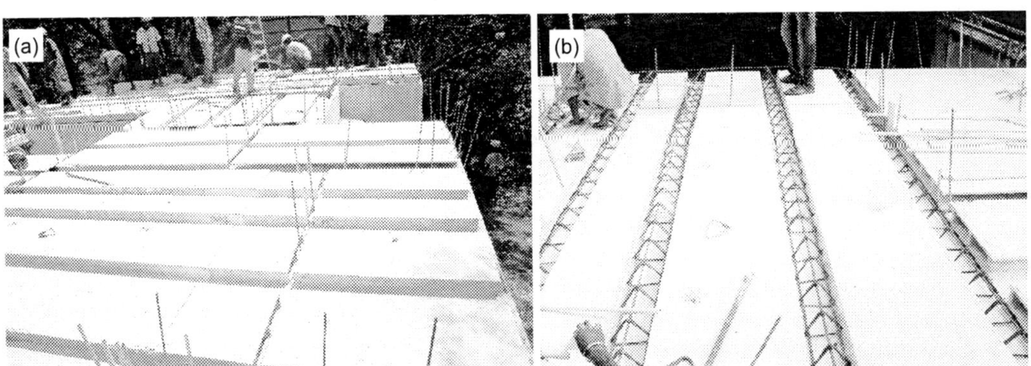

Fig. 4.14: (a) Top flange from every 3rd cavity has been cut-off, and (b) concealed beam reinforcement inside the cavities

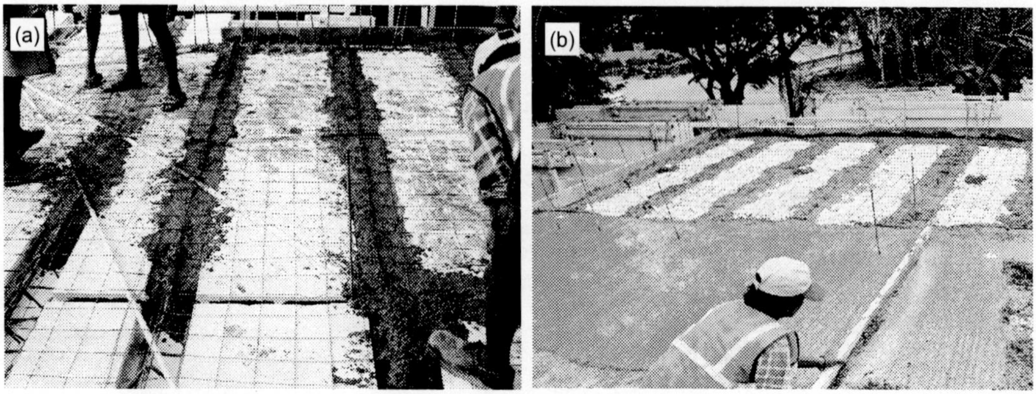

Fig. 4.15: (a) Concreting of concealed beams, and (b) concreting of 50 mm top screed

10 gauge weld mesh of 100 × 100 mm size shall then be spread over the entire slab giving a cover of 30 mm from the top of the GFRG panel at a spacing of 750 mm in both directions. After this, concreting can be done. A 20 mm needle vibrator can be used for proper compaction. The activities from flange cutting to slab concreting are shown in Figure 14 and 15.

Staircase: The staircase waist slabs and mid-landing slabs can be constructed using GFRG. Flanges from all the cavities shall be cut open from the top and infilled with RC. Landing beams shall be provided at both the floor slab and mid-landing level. These can also be constructed using GFRG panels. The laying of staircase waist slab panels and reinforcement inside the cavities is shown in Figure 16.

Fig. 4.16: (a) GFRG panel used as waist slab for staircase, and (b) reinforcement for concealed beams in waist slab

In a similar way, the construction work for the upper storey can be carried out. The parapet walls and the staircase headroom can also be constructed using GFRG.

Waterproofing of GFRG building system: Tests have shown that GFRG panels absorb very less water. The water absorption of the panels is found to be less than 2% even after 24 hours of immersion in water; the panels are therefore water resistant.But since GFRG building system is a prefabricated system, all the construction joints (including the vertical and horizontal wall panel joints) need to be treated with waterproofing compounds. These included horizontal joints between RC plinth beams and wall panels in the ground floor, floor slab and external wall panels of the upper floors, floor / roof slab and wall / parapet wall panels in wet areas like bath / toilet, open balcony and terrace, cut openings for windows and doors, reinforced concrete lintel cum sunshade and walls. Furthermore, the plinth beam top, external sides of exposed GFRG-RC floor / roof slab and wet areas of floor / roof slabs and balconies also need to be treated. Some of these treatments are to be done at the time of construction and the others after construction of structure, as part of finishing works. For terrace waterproofing, standard waterproofing technique as that used for conventional RC slab shall be used due to the presence of the screed concrete on the GFRG floor/roof slab. The methodology of waterproofing as given in the 'Manual on waterproofing of GFRG / Rapidwall Buildings' is to be precisely followed.

Finishing: Since the panels are water resistant, it is not possible to paint the walls directly, as there is likelihood of peeling of paint. Primers available in the market currently are suitable for only use on cementitious surfaces. Hence, a special primer, developed for GFRG (Manual of waterproofing of GFRG structures), need to be applied on the panel surface before painting. Alternate primers have also been identified and are now available. In addition to providing bonding to the paint, the primer also has the property of enhancing the abrasion resistance of the panel material. Even though GFRG panels do not require any plastering, it is desirable to provide 'rendering' on the external wall surfaces, by applying a thin layer of either gypsum or cementitious wall putty, to give a smooth finish. This wall putty shall be mixed with suitable waterproofing chemical in order to prevent it from peeling off from the panel, especially during rain. The methodology adopted for priming and rendering is to be carried out as per the 'Manual of waterproofing of GFRG structures'. Figure 17 illustrates these.

Fig. 4.17: (a) Spraying of primer on GFRG panel surface, and (b) glazed tiles fixed over the GFRG panel surface using special adhesive

For fixing tiles over the GFRG wall panel surface for toilets and kitchen, special additives as specified in the Manual shall be used.

4.2.6 Implementation

The major bottlenecks for large-scale use of GFRG in India is non-availability and high cost of supply of panel. Without sufficient working capital, the one and the only existing panel manufacturing plant in the country, FRBL Kochi, is running at an efficiency of 5% and lesser. With limited production, they had been supplying the panels to small builders / contractors, mainly in Kerala, Tamil Nadu, Karnataka and Andhra Pradesh. With the current increase in panel cost (Rs. 1200 per sq. m. in place of Rs. 1000 per sq. m., without GST), there is a noticeable decline in the demand of panels. In the present state, large construction companies, L&T for e.g., are not willing to take up GFRG construction without a second plant being set-up, with un-interrupted panel supply at optimal cost. These alone will create huge demand for panels in the country.

The following points may be considered for an effective marketing strategy for the GFRG panel system.

(i) Un-interrupted supply of panel at reasonable cost. Increased cost of panel is due to the large cost involved in importing of the additives used for the panel manufacture. Alternative to these can be manufactured in India, in collaboration with the Rapid Building System Company in Australia.

(ii) Publishing of the BIS code (presently, in the draft stage) on GFRG will facilitate large-scale design and construction of GFRG buildings in the country.

(iii) New plants need to be set-up, especially close to the Mumbai and Eastern regions, for the major builders to make use of the technology. Setting up of factories in will create demand for the panels.

(iv) Provide training for professionals, like, Architects, Structural Engineers and Civil (Construction) Engineers, on GFRG technology will create an eco-system for successful adaptation of GFRG construction.

(v) LPG, a major fuel in the GFRG panel manufacture, can be replaced with natural gas / LNG, to cut down the panel cost. This also adds to greenness of the product (ref. chapter 7 of this thesis)

(vi) The Central Government may consider waiving-off GST for prefabricated panels used for the purpose of affordable construction.

4.2.7 Quality Control & Assurance

Loading and Transportation of Panels

DO...

1. Mark notations on the cut panels at factory itself.

2. Load the panels stacked in stillages onto trucks based on the construction sequence followed at site (for example: panels for GF walling first, then staircase and lift walls, followed by GF roof slab, etc.).
3. Load panels of length less than 2.27m in horizontal stillages in flat position.
4. Tie the stillages properly with suitable steel rope or chain through the eyes of stillages to the hooks provided on either sides of truck platform. Provide corner angle steel sheets to protect the panel from any damage during transport.

DON'T...

1. Transport panels of width more than 2.1m without stillages.
2. Transport panels without the panel packing list indicating notation marks of panels.

Unloading of Panels on Stillages and Stacking at Site

DO...

1. Collect the packing list from truck driver
2. Stack unloaded panels at a place convenient for erection.
3. Support the outriggers of the stillage on a solid surface to prevent any movements.

DON'T...

1. Unload the stillages with panels on undulated/sandy or clayey areas.

Construction of Foundation

DO...

1. Check the level of foundation with network of RC plinth beams prior to the start of wall panel erection.
2. Complete basement infilling, compaction and floor concrete or PCC up to RC plinth beam level before start of erection of panels.
3. Apply waterproofing treatment/damp proof course (as per the GFRG waterproofing manual) on RC plinth beam/floor slab and ensure proper drying time before erection of wall panel.

DON'T...

1. Erect panel on undulated RC plinth beam/floor slab.

Lifting and Erection of Panels

DO...

1. Use lifting jaws that are in perfect working condition and spreader bars with hooks at spacing of 1250/1750/2250/2750 mm for lifting panels.
2. Lift panels of width less than 4m using a single lifting jaw.

3. Adopt spacing of the lateral props as specified in the construction manual.
4. Provide the copy of cutting drawing for each team, if multiple erection teams are deployed (as in large GFRG building construction sites).
5. Apply joint sealant to joints between plinth beam and wall panels on external sides before the first pour of concrete.
6. Infill concrete in 4 stages in the cavities with an intermittent gap of 2 hours.

DON'T...

1. Insert the lifting jaws into the same cavities as before for re-lifting.
2. Lift panel if the wind speed is more than 20 km/hr.
3. Stand under the panel when the panel is lifted using crane.
4. Erect the panel on unlevelled / undulated RC plinth beam surface or floor slab.
5. Erect the panel over RC plinth beam or floor slab without applying and curing waterproofing / damp proof course.
6. Fill concrete until it is ensured that all services (electric cables, water pipes, etc.) are installed.
7. Pour concrete until the panel is in level and plumb, and lateral props are fixed.
8. Pour concrete in one go as the panel will burst-off / crack.
9. Fill concrete in the cavity adjacent to a burst one. The infilling should be done only after the concrete in the damaged cavity is set.
10. Remove the lateral prop until horizontal tie concreting is completed and wall panels are in rigid position.
11. Infill concrete during rain
12. Keep unfilled panels on position overnight, as an unexpected wind can make the panel fall down.

Laying of Floor/Roof Slab

Do...

1. Place runners with vertical props and acrospans in position before the floor / roof slab is lifted by crane.
2. Decide whether the panel is to be lifted by holding at a single point at multiple no of points, to put holes to insert soft slings. This is to fix the under panel spreader bar below the slab. Identify the centre of gravity of the panel and mark the hole positions (equidistant from the CG) for drilling suitable holes.
3. Tie the soft sling to the under panel spreader bar through the holes put in the slab before connecting to the crane hook for craning / lifting the panel into air (with the help of trained / skilled workers or riggers).
4. Provide 40 mm bearing for floor slab panel on to the walls on all the four sides.

5. Make sure that the support system consisting of wooden runners with vertical props, and acrospans are in position before cutting the top flanges of respective cavities for providing embedded concealed RC beams leaving 25 mm protruded flanges on either sides.
6. Provide side shuttering (174/184 mm wide) with a 6 mm groove (inside) for the waterproofing treatments to be carried out after concreting and before rendering of the external walls.
7. While concreting the RC slab, an erection team member should watch the slab from below for any problems related to movement of support or sinking of panel, etc. If anything found, signal the concreting team to stop the work and resume concreting only after rectification work is done.
8. Remove vertical props / acrospan only after at least 5 days of concreting of floor / roof slab, or when the support system is required for the slab in the next floor.
9. For roof slab, the screed concrete should be 60 mm thick and necessary waterproofing admixture as per manufacturer's specification should be used. The concrete should be properly compacted using mechanical vibrators. Roof slab should be provided with necessary slope (at least 1 in 150) for rain water drainage as per the instructions.
10. Waterproofing treatment to RC roof slab should be done using approved waterproofing treatment, including staircase head room slab / lift room roof slab and following the treatment of parapet wall panel top and parapet wall-roof slab joint treatment.

DON'T...

1. Lift the floor/ roof slab GFRG panel without proper support system with vertical props is in place.
2. Concrete the floor / roof slab before electrical cables / PVC pipes for cabling or wiring, fan hooks, etc., are put in place as per the engineering service drawings.
3. Use coarse aggregate of size more than 10 mm for concreting.
4. Leave the external side of floor / roof slab (174 / 184 mm high) without water treatment and should be smooth finish by rendering afterwards.

Waterproofing Treatment of Door/Window/Ventilator Openings

DO...

1. Seal-off the joints on all exterior and interior edge of openings using approved joint sealants after installation of door / window / ventilator frames, as specified in the manual.
2. Joints between parapet wall and roof slab; parapet wall top and lintel cum sunshade joints.

DON'T...

1. Fix the window frame flushing the external wall face. It is better to keep it flush with the internal face, if not, at the centre.
2. Leave pipe joints without treating with specified sealant.

Application of Primer

DO...

1. Ensure minimum drying time as per manufacturers' specification for primer.
2. Apply primer only after completion of waterproofing treatments. Rendering (application of 1-2 mm thick rendering plaster) shall be done if fine/superior finish of external and internal wall panel surfaces and ceiling are required, and shall be applied by experienced PoP plasterers or accredited applicators having experience in rendering.
3. Mix the primer as per the proportions of components specified by manufacturer.

DON'T...

1. Add water to primer while mixing.
2. Use any primer other than the ones suitable for GFRG on the GFRG panel surfaces, as it will not have any effect on GFRG and if done, paint will eventually peel off.

Rendering and Painting

DO...

1. Use water resistant rendering compound for fine finish of surfaces of external walls and wet areas.
2. Apply painting directly over the primed panel surfaces if rendering (fine finishing) is not required.
3. Ensure proper drying (as specified by the manufacturer) after rendering.
4. Use paint primer over special primer/rendering compound applied surface, if the paint manufacturer prescribes the same.

DON'T...

1. Use locally available PoP (Plaster of Paris) for rendering or any other works in GFRG building. This is because GFRG panel is manufactured using high quality calcined beta gypsum plaster whereas the locally available PoP will be manufactured either from marine gypsum, low purity gypsum or chalk powder.

4.2.8 Case Studies

GFRG building construction is gradually gaining popularity in India, holding the promise of rapid affordable housing. Presently, there are almost 1,800 GFRG buildings built in India, mostly individual houses. Few case studies have been shown here.

GFRG Demo Building at IIT Madras

A two-storeyed demonstration building was built inside the IIT Madras campus to showcase the advantages of rapidity, affordability and sustainability. The completion of the entire superstructure and rendered it fit for occupation, within 40 days (29 days for superstructure and 11 days for foundation) after the laying of the foundation. The use of prefabricated light weight (44 kg/m^2) GFRG panels for the entire building system facilitated not only faster construction time, but also reduced labour and construction time (½ and ¾ saving in labour and construction time, compared to conventional construction), and safer working environment. This building houses 4 flats (1981 sq. ft. built-up area), two having a carpet area of 269 sq. ft. meant for the EWS (economically weaker section) and the other two with 497 sq. ft. carpet area each meant for the LIG (Figure 18).

Fig. 4.18: GFRG demo building at IIT Madras campus

This building has created widespread interest and attracted visitors (builders, architects, contractors, potential house owners, students, researchers, engineers, government officials, etc.). A video describing the construction (available at https://www.youtube.com/watch?v=UUQEUcB7cMM) has also been widely viewed across the world. IIT Madras has been providing training to architects, structural engineers, civil engineers, etc. on the design and construction of GFRG buildings based on the published manuals. The key advantages of rapidity, affordability and sustainability (less than 20% saving in energy, compared to conventional construction) have generated interest in this technology.

Water load tests on the GFRG-RC floor and terrace slabs of this building revealed that the deflection of the slabs were much lesser than estimated, due to additional stiffness offered by GFRG panels (Figure 19). Thermal comfort studies showed that the GFRG demo building was 2°C cooler compared to the adjacent conventional building. The water tightness of the joint sealant provided between door / window frames and GFRG wall panels was ensured by conducting a jet test.

Fig. 4.19: (a) Water filled in terrace up to 200 mm, (b) deflections measured at slab bottom using LVDTs

GFRG Buildings at Nellore, Andhra Pradesh

The Nellore project is the first mass housing project in the country built using the GFRG technology (BMTPC, GoI). Five two-storeyed blocks with 36 apartment units for EWS and LIG categories, have been constructed (Figure 20). Four of these comprise 8 EWS units (four in each storey), each with a built-up area of 43 sq. m. (462 sq. ft.). The fifth block comprises four duplex LIG units, each with a built-up area of 71 sq. m. (764 sq. ft.). total built-up area of 1,900 sq.m. GFRG panels have been used for the entire superstructure and the construction was finished in 5 months' time.

Fig. 4.20: GFRG building at Nellore, Andhra Pradesh

The water tightness of the joints in the GFRG building at Nellore was ensured by conducting water tightness test, after applying suitable joint sealant (as per the GFRG waterproofing manual). Refer Figure 21.

Fig. 4.21: Water pressure test for window joint

Hostel Buildings at IIT, Tirupati

Five hostel buildings each of them having four storeys and a residential apartment (1.4 lakh sq. ft. built area, in total) in the IIT Tirupati transit campus have been constructed using the GFRG technology (Figures 22 and 23).

Fig. 4.22: GFRG hostel buildings at IIT, Tirupati (1.4 lakh ft^2)

Fig. 4.23: GFRG hostel building (B1 block) at IIT, Tirupati (30,428.9 ft^2)

REFERENCES

1. IS 1905 : (1987). 'Code of Practice for Structural Use of Unreinforced Masonry', Bureau of Indian Standards, New Delhi, India.
2. IS 456 : (2000). 'Plain and Reinforced Concrete - Code of Practice'. Bureau of Indian Standards', Bureau of Indian Standards, New Delhi, India.
3. IS 1893 (Part 1) : (2000). 'Criteria for Earthquake Resistant Design of Structures. Part 1 : General Provisions and Buildings', Bureau of Indian Standards, New Delhi, India.
4. Cheng, C., Pouffary, S., Svenningsen, N., and Callaway, M. (2008). *The Kyoto Protocol, the clean development mechanism and the building and construction sector.* United Nations Environment Programme - A Report Prepared for the UNEP Sustainable Buildings and Construction Initiative, Paris, France.
5. Structural Design Manual. (2012). *GFRG/Rapidwall Building Structural Design Manual.* (IIT Madras), Building Materials & Technology Promotion Council, Ministry of Housing & Urban Poverty Alleviation, Government of India.
6. Waterproofing Manual. (2016). *Manualon waterproofingof GFRG/Rapidwall Building Structural Design* (IIT Madras), Building Materials & Technology Promotion Council, Ministry of Housing & Urban Poverty Alleviation, Government of India.

7. Schedule of Items. (2016). *Schedule of items and rate analysis for GFRG Construction* (IIT Madras), Building Materials & Technology Promotion Council, Ministry of Housing & Urban Poverty Alleviation, Government of India.
8. Paul, S., Cherian, P., Menon, D., and Prasad, A. M. (2016). 'Use of glass fibre reinforced gypsum panels with reinforced concrete infills for construction of walls and slabs'. *Indian Concrete Journal*, 90(12), 19–32.
9. IS 875 (Part 3) : (2016). 'Code of Practice for Design Loads (Other than Earthquake) for Buildings and Structures - Part 3 : Wind Loads', Bureau of Indian Standards, New Delhi, India.
10. Cherian, P., Paul, S., Krishna, S. R. G., Menon, D., and Prasad, A. M. (2017). 'Mass Housing Using GFRG Panels: A Sustainable, Rapid and affordable Solution'. *Journal of The Institution of Engineers (India): Series A* (200), 98(1–2), 95–100.
11. Construction Manual. (2018). *GFRG/Rapidwall Construction Manual.* (IIT Madras), Building Materials & Technology Promotion Council, Ministry of Housing & Urban Poverty Alleviation, Government of India.

5
Precast Sandwich Panel Systems

5.1 INTRODUCTION

Structural insulated panels (SIPs) are high performance building system for residential and light commercial construction. The panels consisting of an insulating foam core sandwiched between two structural facings are categorized as Structural Insulated Panels. The core can be made of a rigid or flexible material whose main function is to separate the facings to maximize the stiffness of the sandwich structure. When non-structural facings are used, the panels can be simply referred to as sandwich panels. These panels are divided into different categories depending upon the type of material used for the core, facings and also based on the application of these panels. The structural skins or wythes are connected to each other and to the core by connectors. These connectors are divided into different categories depending upon the material and action to be performed by the connectors.

PCI Committee Report (2011) on Precast Sandwich Wall panels gives guidelines for the use of the Precast Concrete SWPs (Sandwich Wall Panels) in construction. The primary reason of sandwich construction is the structural efficiency that can be achieved. When thin, hard, rigid and strong facings are attached to the thick, lightweight core, the geometry of the combination provides greater strength and rigidity. The strong facings provide the (a) internal couple resistant to bending, (b) resistance to edgewise loading, and (c) resistance to racking, while the core (a) resists the shear and (b) stabilizes the facings against buckling.

5.2 SANDWICH COMPOSITE PANELS

In sandwich composite panels, generally there is one inner layer or 'core' of low strength material, which is protected by two outer layers known as 'wythes' of high strength skin materials. Reinforcement or wire-mesh may or may not be provided in skin layers. The thickness and type of core depend on its thermal resistance and design temperatures. The function of wythes is to provide load resistance, cover to reinforcement, anchorage to connectors, protection against stripping, and finish.

Usually thickness of the wythes is less than the core. Two wythes are interconnected by shear connectors, webs, or combination of both. The function of shear connectors and webs is to hold the wythes and core in place, as well as to transfer the longitudinal shear in between wythes (Einea et al., 1991).

Use of sandwich panels in building construction industry was started in North America more than 60 years from now (PCI, 1997). Earlier sandwich panels were used as non-load bearing walls for partition and façade cladding. Recently, some construction companies started using these as load bearing structural elements.

The sandwich panels having inner core of Expanded Polystyrene (EPS) with shotcrete concrete and galvanized steel wire mesh reinforcement in two outer wythes are known as Reinforced Concrete Sandwich Panels (RCSP). Figures 1-7 show the schematic sketches of different types of wall, slab and staircase panels developed by different companies.

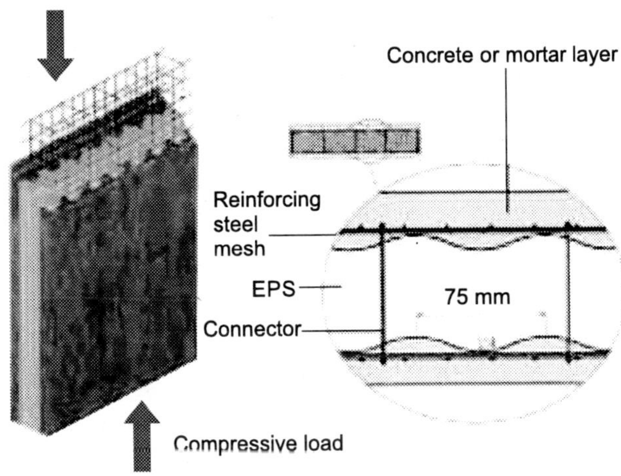

Fig. 5.1: Typical cross section of RCSP sandwich panel

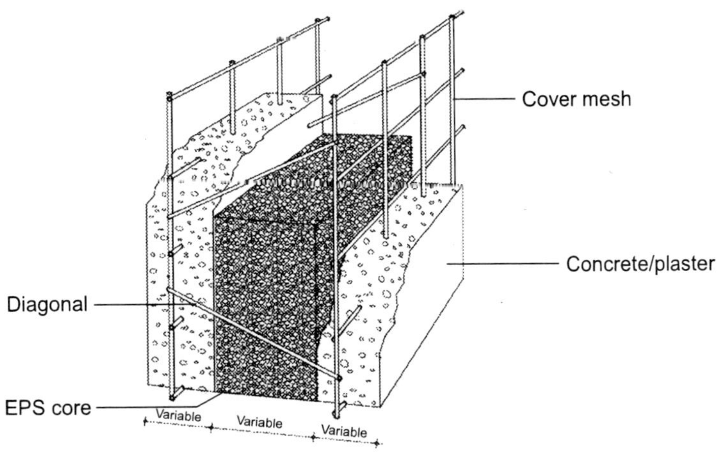

Fig. 5.2: Isometric view of typical cross section of RCSP sandwich panel

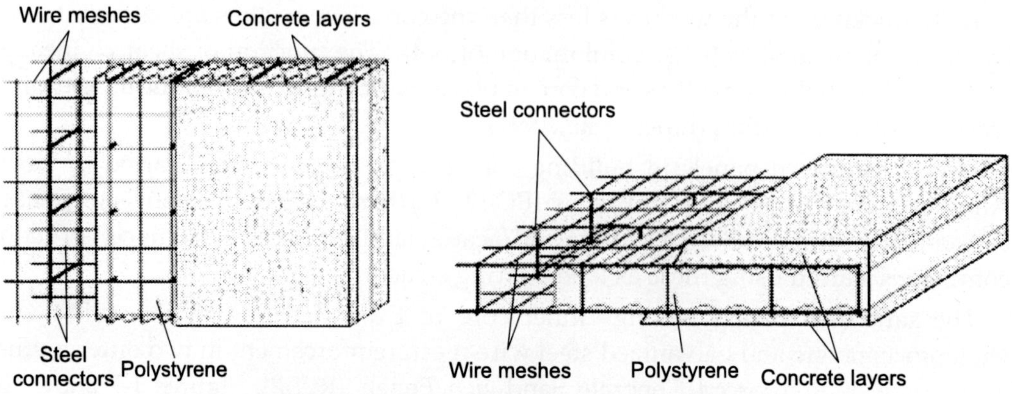

Fig. 5.3: Schematic sketches of the components of wall and floor sandwich panels

Fig. 5.4: Wall panel

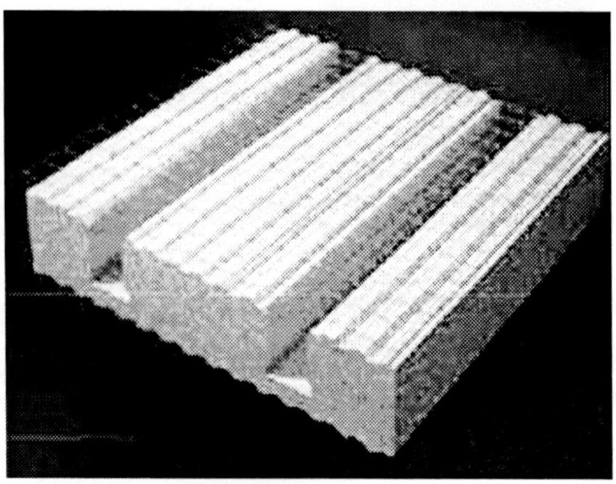

Fig. 5.5: Slab panel

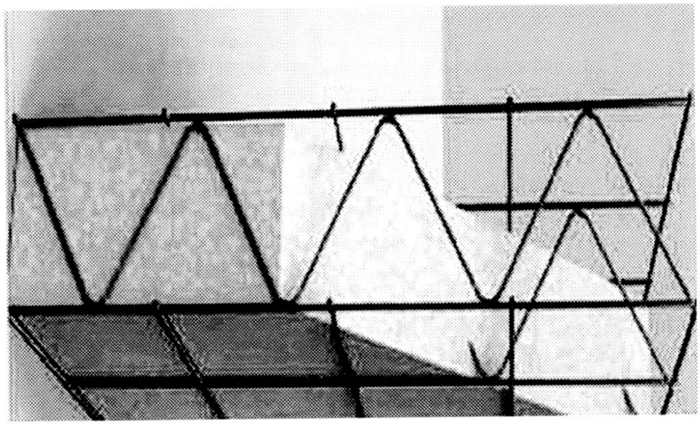

Fig. 5.6: EPS core with steel wire mesh and truss web connectors

Fig. 5.7: Staircase panel

Sandwich panels can be used to construct buildings with any geometry of walls, slabs and staircase. These provide quick, efficient and resilient building construction method with following advantages over the conventional construction system:

- Offers very high strength-to-weight ratio as well as stiffness-to-weight ratio, which enhances rigidity and strength without adding substantial weight.
- Offers high resistance against earthquake and wind forces.
- Light in weight and easy to handle and light foundation is required.
- Speedy in construction, as no shuttering is required.
- Flexibility in modifications and changes at later stage.
- Good heat, moisture and sound insulation properties, provided by the EPS core.
- Superior fatigue strength.
- Economical by avoiding formwork and skilled labour.
- Environment friendly, as it requires lesser material resulting in less severe impact on environment.

- Free from CFC and other toxic compounds.
- Offers improved blast resistance and safety against terror and sabotage activities.
- Reasonable fire rating (up to 60 minutes reported in the literature).

5.3 WYTHE CONNECTORS

Structural behaviour of the panels is dependent on the strength and stiffness of the connectors. The connectors can be categorized into a) composite connectors and b) non composite connectors as per PCI Committee report (2011). The composite connectors provide composite action to the sandwich wall panel by allowing shear transfer between the wythes.

Different types of connectors have been used in the past decades. Initially *solid zones of concrete* were used to make the panels fully composite at the cost of thermal efficiency. Later *metal connectors* were incorporated to achieve more effective thermal efficient panels and maintain the performance of the fully composite sandwich panels. Still thermal efficiency was hampered by the conductivity of the metal and the concrete solid zones. Then came the *non-metallic ties* that enhanced the thermal performance of the sandwich panels, at the cost of structural performance. Slowly, improvements were made to create panels using the non-metallic connectors that provided both thermal and structural benefits.

Use of *Fibre reinforced Polymer Grids* proved out to be the best solution for this. CFRP and GFRP grids are used as connectors in the sandwich panels that provide enhanced thermal and structural efficiency to the system.

Depending on the material used for connectors, they can be categorised as:

1. FRP Connectors: The objective is to reduce thermal bridging in the sandwich panels, while transferring shear forces to develop composite action within the panel. The panel incorporates a new system of concrete wythes and studs connected by the GFRP connectors, where the studs are not in direct contact with the wythes.
2. Metallic Connectors
3. Solid Zones of Concrete
4. Plastic Connectors

Depending on the behaviour, connectors may be classified as Shear Connectors or Non shear Connectors

1. **Shear connectors:** Shear connectors are those which can transfer longitudinal shear, resulting from flexure in the panel, from one wythe to the other (Figure 8). These connectors may resist shear in one or two perpendicular directions.
   (a) One-way shear connectors
      - Concentrated one-way connectors
      - Continuous one-way connectors

(b) Two-way Shear Connectors: These connectors have comparable shear capacity in two directions in the plane of the panel.

- **Cylindrical sleeve anchors :** These connectors are strong in resisting torsion as well as shear. They are intended for use in non-composite panels to transfer the weight of the non-structural wythe to the structural wythe.
- **Crown anchors :** They are made by bending small diameter bars into a three dimensional configuration.
- **Concrete blocks :** These blocks are also intended to encase the panel lifting inserts.

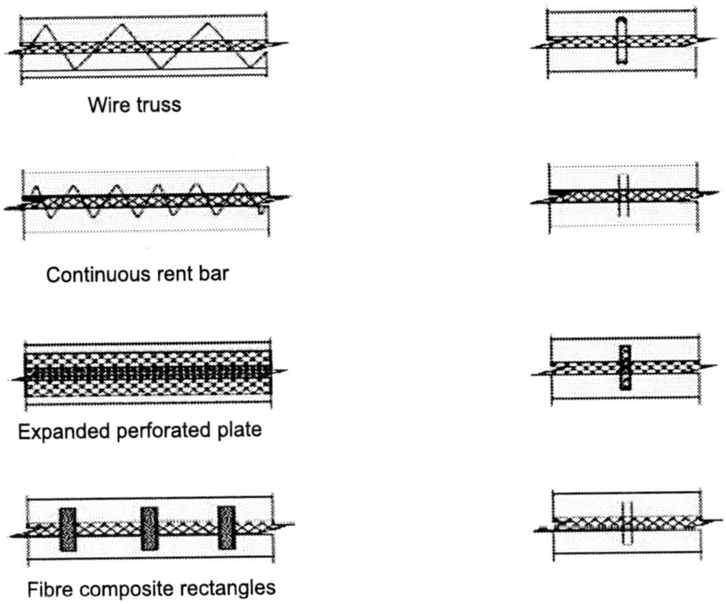

Fig. 5.8: One-way shear connectors, PCI Committee report on Precast/Prestressed Concrete Sandwich Panels (2011)

2. **Non-shear connectors :** These connectors can transfer only a negligible amount of longitudinal shear from one wythe to the other (Figure 9). They are commonly used in non-composite panels to transfer tension or compression forces due to stripping, storage, transportation, erection, wind, and seismic loads from a non-structural to a structural wythe. This type of connector can be divided into metallic and non-metallic connectors.
   - **Metallic connectors:** The most popular metallic connectors are pin connectors. They are galvanized or stainless steel bars bent into various configurations. Proper anchorage into both concrete wythes can be accomplished through deforming or hooking at the pin ends. Continuous

welded ladder connectors are also used as non-shear connectors. They are equivalent to equally spaced pins.

- **Non-metallic connectors:** These connectors are made of non-reinforced or fiber reinforced plastics. The use of plastic pins may be advantageous in avoiding condensation at connector locations inside buildings where the humidity is high. Consideration must be given to the effect of plastic connectors on the fire resistance of the panel and to the long-term creep effect of connectors.

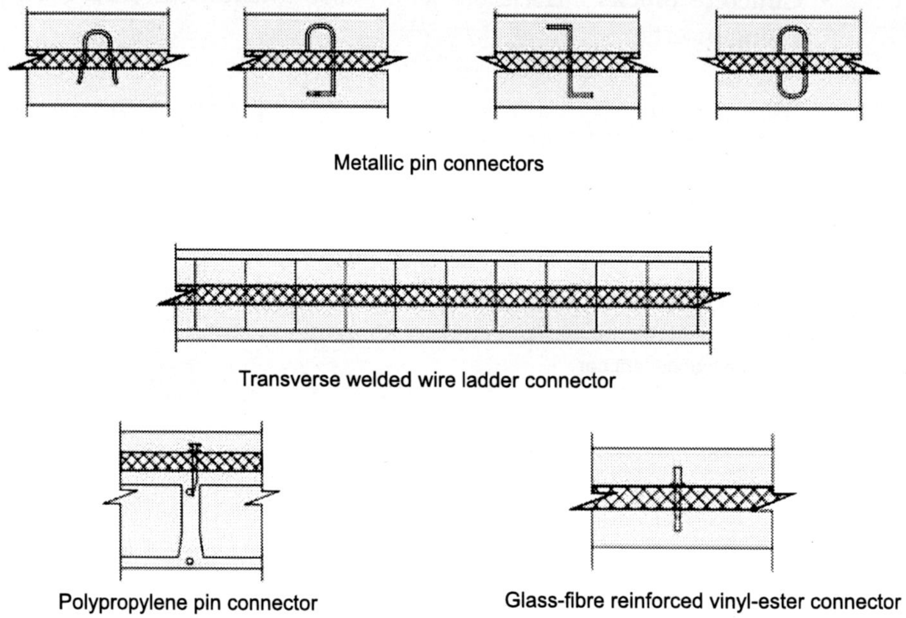

Fig. 6.9: Non-shear connectors, PCI Committee Report on Precast/Prestressed Concrete Sandwich Panels (2011)

5.4 INSULATING CORE

The properties of the insulation materials depend on their structure, the raw materials used and the manufacturing process. In the selection of a suitable thermal insulation material, the required thermal properties are of prime importance. For the functionality and safety of the building, other important criteria in the choice of insulation are mechanical strength, resistance to ageing, sound insulation properties, and resistance to moisture and fire. The selection of insulation type to enhance energy performance is as important as the reinforcement needed to enhance structural performance. The core material is normally low strength material, but its higher thickness provides the sandwich composite with high bending stiffness with overall low density.

Cellular insulation used in the manufacturing of sandwich panels comes in two primary forms:

Thermoplastic: These get deformed easily on heating and can be bent easily. The thermoplastic insulations are known as molded expanded polystyrene (beadboard) and extruded expanded polystyrene (extruded board).

Thermosetting: These when molded cannot be softened by heating. These insulations consist of polyurethane, polyisocyanurate and phenolic.

In the case of sandwich panels with concrete wythes, during the manufacture of the panel, insulation is exposed to high temperatures (60oC-66oC) from concrete hydration and possible applied heat from accelerated curing. Once the panel is cured and erected in place, the insulation may be exposed to a continuous moisture and vapor gradient that may affect the physical and thermal behavior of the insulating material.

5.5 STRUCTURAL SKINS

The structural skins are the main load carrying components of the Structural Insulated Panels. The skin should be able to a) carry the compressive loads acting on the load bearing wall, b) should be able to take up the tensile and compressive forces in case the wall is subjected to out of plane bending c) should be able to bond properly with the core insulating material d) should provide fire protection to the combustible core.

In the case of concrete panels, the thickness of each concrete wythe depends on its structural function, concrete cover, anchorage of connectors, stripping and finishing. Non composite panels have a thicker concrete wythe backing a thinner architectural wythe, whereas composite panels have wythes of equal thicknesses and act as a single structural system to carry axial and lateral loads. Composite panels generally have an overall thickness less than that of non-composite panels.

5.6 EPS CORE PANEL SYSTEM

5.6.1 Expandable Polystyrene (EPS)

Expandable Polystyrene (EPS) is a rigid cellular plastic that is made from expandable polystyrene that contains an expansion agent. It is most commonly used for packaging foodstuffs, medical supplies, electrical consumer goods and insulation panels for buildings.

Polystyrene is extracted from oil. Thousands of small units of styrene, called monomers, link together to form large molecules of polystyrene by a process called polymerization.

The expandable polystyrene (EPS) production process uses a pure hydrocarbon, which does not contain any halogens and does not damage the earth's protective ozone layer, as the expansion agent.

Process of EPS manufacturing: EPS starts as small spherical beads with a typical diameter of 0.5 -1.5 mm. They contain an expanding agent. When the beads are heated with steam, the agent starts to boil, the polymer softens, and the beads expand to about forty times their initial size.

After a maturing period to equilateral temperature and pressure, the pre-foamed beads, which now have a closed cellular foam structure, are packed in a mould and again reheated with steam.

The mould is made in the same shape as finished article. The pre-foamed beads expand further, completely fill the mould cavity and fuse together. When moulded, nearly all the volume of the expanded polystyrene (EPS) foam(98%) is air.

For EPS core panels system,EPS should be of fire retardant grade. Fire retardant grade of EPS contains a small quantity self-extinguishing and environment friendly fire-retardant agent.

When exposed to a fire source, the FR grade foam will shrink rapidly and distance itself from the heat source to reduce the likelihood of ignition, its primary benefit. The additive will further decompose and cause a reduction of flames, limiting flame spread. Note that the FR grade EPS will stop burning if the ignition source is completely removed.

5.6.2 EPS Core Panel System

Expanded Polystyrene (EPS) core Panel system is a modern, efficient, safe and economic construction system for the construction of buildings. These panels canbe used both as load bearing as well as non-load bearing elements.EPS core panel is a 3D panel consisting of 3-dimensional welded wire space frame provided with the polystyrene insulation core. Panel is placed in position and shotcrete on both the sides.

The EPS panels consist of a 3-dimensional welded wire space frame utilizing a trussconcept for stress transfer and stiffness as shown in Fig.10.EPS panel includes welded reinforcing meshes of high-strength wire, diagonal wireand self-extinguishing expanded polystyrene uncoated concrete, manufactured inthe factory and shotcrete is applied to the panel assembled at the construction site,which gives the bearing capacity of the structure.EPS panel after shotcrete has the following five components (as Fig. 10):

i. The outer layer of shotcrete.
ii. Welded reinforcing mesh of high wire.
iii. The core of expanded polystyrene sheet.
iv. Diagonal wire (stainless or galvanized wire).
v. The inner layer of shotcrete.

The welded mesh fabric connected piercing polystyrene with truss of steel wire,welded to the welded fabric at an angle. It gives a rigidity spatial structure, andsimultaneously prevents polystyrene core shifting.

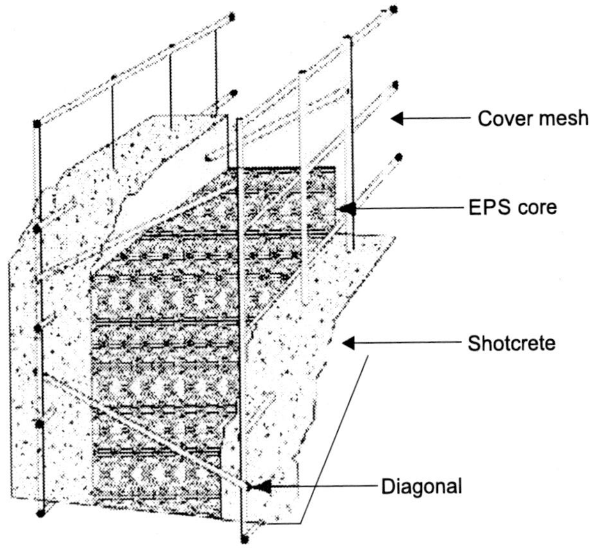

Fig. 6.10: Typical cross section of wall panels

Individually welded internal strut wires or diagonals extend through the panel corebetween each surface. These galvanized strut wires are welded continuously in therequired spacing so they form, with the welded wire fabric, into a triangulated trusssystem which greatly increases the panel strength.EPS panel is a versatile structural element designed for floors, walls, partitions, roofand stairs. Fig. 11 & Fig. 12 shows the welded reinforcing mesh of the EPS panelsat different cross-sections.

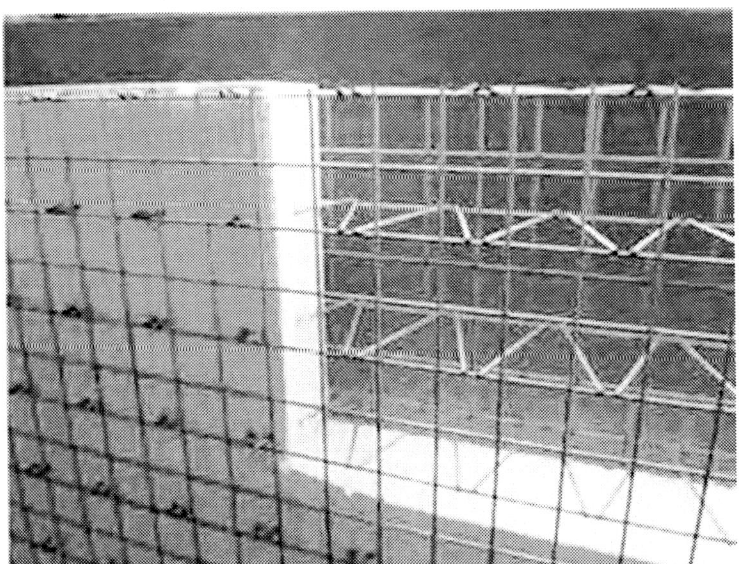

Fig. 6.11: Reinforcing mesh expanded polystyrene core and diagonal wire

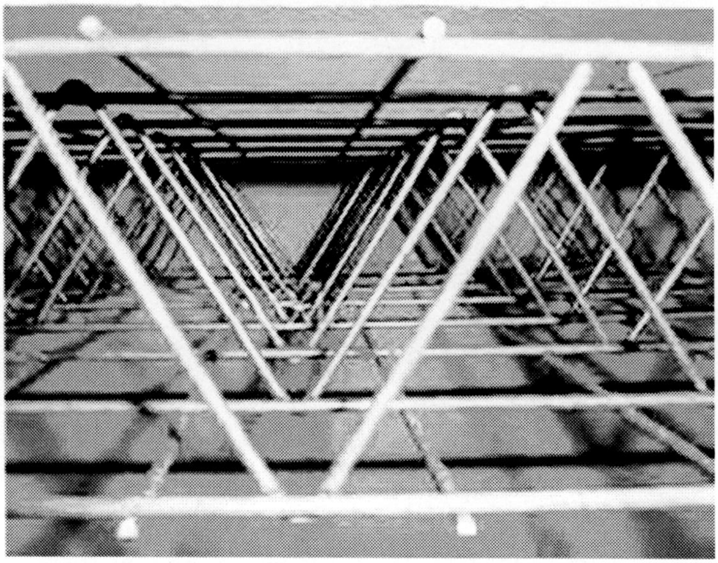

Fig. 6.12: Welded reinforcing mesh 3-D panel without expanded polystyrene core

The typical EPS panel is generally manufactured with dimensions of 1200 m width, 3000 mm length and over all thickness range of 80-230 mm.The panels are finished at the site using minimum 30 mm thick shotcreting ofcement & coarse sand in the ratio of 1:4 applied under pressure. The shotcretingcoat encases the EPS Core with centrally placed steel welded wire mesh.

Some of the advantages of the EPS Core panel systems are as follows:

i. Reduce the cost of construction
ii. Reduce Construction period
iii. Reduce transport cost. Light weight panels: do not requires cranes and otherheavy construction equipment. (A Standard panel of size (1.2×3) m withoutshotcrete weighs 20 kg).
iv. The installation does not need heavy construction equipment.
v. Ensure high levels of thermal insulation, sound insulation, as well as sanitaryand fire safety.
vi. EPS 3-D panels allow no additional cost to erect buildings in areas withmoving soil, especially heaving, subsidence, frozen ground, and remoteareas.
vii. Strength and durability - used extruded polystyrene virtually inert and doesnot absorb moisture, is durable and resistant to decay.

Some of the Limitations of the EPS Core Panel System:

i. EPS Panel construction system may only be used in the construction offoundation walls supporting 4 storeys or less, unless designed by aprofessional engineer.

ii. Concrete must be applied by either the "shotcrete dry" or "shotcrete wet" process in accordance with ACI 506 R-85, "Guide to Shotcrete," by the American Concrete Institute.

iii. Compressive strength of concrete shall not be less than 20 MPa.

iv. The steel reinforcement shall have a minimum allowable stress (f_y) of 415MPa.

The EPS Core panel system is environment friendly and aesthetically appealing. Itcan be constructed quickly resulting in savings in construction time and money. Thetechnology has been in use successfully in many African as well as European countries with involvement of different agencies.

5.7 BEHAVIOUR OF SANDWICH PANELS

The Sandwich Panels can be divided into three main categories (Figure 10) depending upon the structural behaviour as:

1. **Composite panels** : These panels are designed, analyzed, detailed and manufactured so that the facings or the wythes act together to resist the applied loads. The entire panel acts as one single unit in bending and is achieved by providing shear connectors, the details of which have been discussed in the previous sections.
2. **Partially composite panels** : These panels have shear connectors connecting the wythes, but full composite action is not achieved.
3. **Non-composite panels** : These panels are designed, analyzed, detailed and manufactured so that the wythes act independently. Generally a structural and a non structural wythe are used, with the structural wythe being the thicker of the two.

Load carrying capacity of sandwich panels depends upon the composite action of wythes and longitudinal shear stress transfer mechanism by the connectors. If the applied flexural load is resisted by both wythes integrally, panel is **fully composite** and bending stress distribution will be continuous across the section, as shown in Figure 13(a). If the connectors are not capable of transferring full longitudinal shear stress, the panel will be **partial composite** panel and bending stress distribution will be as shown in Figure 13(b). A panel is said to be **non-composite** if the connectors have no capacity to transfer longitudinal shear stress and bending stress distribution will be as shown in Figure 13(c) and 13(d) (Einea et al., 1991).

5.7.1 Studies on Compression Behaviour

Benayoune et al. (2007) conducted full scale test under axial loading, on Precast Concrete Sandwich Panel (PCSP) of various slenderness ratios varying from 10 to 20. Violent failure occurred in all cases by crushing at either one or both ends of the panels. The first cracks were noticed to appear at loads of 44–79% of the ultimate loads. Strength reduction in axially loaded panels is less as compared to eccentrically loaded

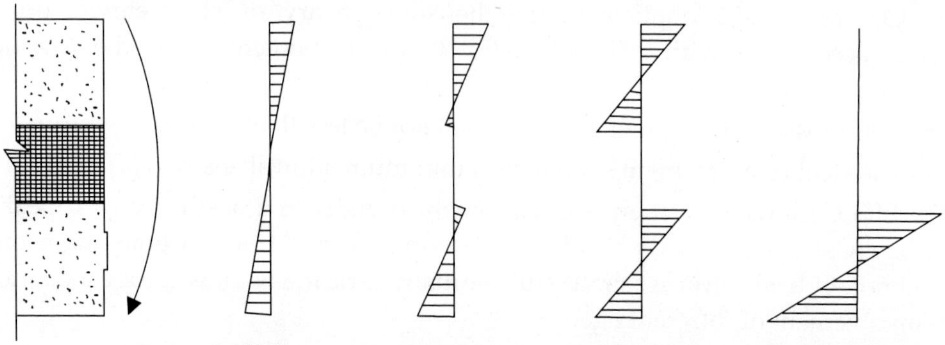

Fig. 6.13: Stress distribution in sandwich panel systems due to pure bending

panels. The results obtained using ACI equation and expressions of other researchers for solid walls are conservative as compared to FEA and experimental results. They also proposed a semi-empirical formula for calculation of load carrying capacity. Gara et al. (2012b) tested sandwich panels, under vertical in-plane load. Numerical simulations were also performed with non-linear finite element models. Numerical simulations indicated that the ultimate loads of axially loaded panels are close to the buckling load whereas ultimate loads of eccentrically loaded panels are significantly lower than the buckling loads. The results of the experiments and numerical simulations indicated that a partial degree of composite behaviour was attained by the tested panels even if non-shear connectors are used in the interior layer.

Carbonari et al. (2013) presented a characterization of behaviour of Expended Polystyrene (EPS) sandwich panels, with the variations in EPS thickness, mortar layer thickness and mixes, and panel height, through experimental results and proposed analytical formulation. Influence of length of connecter provided through EPS thickness was observed and found that as the thickness increases, the load carrying capacity decreases. Increase in compressive strength of mortar enhances the load capacity, whereas mortar thickness did not cause any considerable effect. Height of panel played considerable role in load capacity of panel. The increase in length dimension produces considerable reduction in load capacity of panels. Maximum load is also affected by position of reinforcing mesh. The load resistance is maximum when the mesh is placed at center line of mortar.

Benayoune et al. (2006) tested full scale Precast Concrete Sandwich Panels (PCSP) of various slenderness ratios from 10 to 20 under eccentric load. It was observed that panels failed in crushing. The first crack occurred at 38-55% of failure load. As the slenderness ratio increases, the load carrying capacity decreases nonlinearly. FE analysis was also performed using commercial software LUSAS. FEM results and experimental results were in good agreement, while classical expression based on reinforced concrete principle underestimates the strength of the PCSPs.

Aziz et al. (2004) preformed experiments on sandwich panels with openings and verified the theoretical ultimate load calculated using Saheb and Desayi (1990) equation for ordinary wall with opening. The average ratios of experimental to theoretical ultimate loads for sandwich panels were found to vary from 0.99 to 1.01.

Mohamad et al. (2011) tested sandwich panels of 40 mm thick lightweight foamed concrete as wythes and polystyrene insulation of 20 mm to 45 mm thickness as core. Wythes were reinforced with 9 mm diameter high tensile strength layer and 6 mm dia. mild steel bars at 45□as shear connectors. The crack pattern has shown the failure due to local buckling in all the panels. Crushing occurred in all the cases at either one or both ends of the panel. The first crack was noticed to appear at loads of 51% to 72% of ultimate loads. Mousa and Nasimuddin (2011) presented study on a new type of composite structural insulated panels (CSIPs), made of low-cost thermoplastic orthotropic glass/poly-propylene (glass–PP) laminate as a face sheet and expanded polystyrene foam (EPS) as a core with very high facesheet/core moduli ratio, under concentric and eccentric loading. CSIPs specimens failed by global buckling mode in which no de-bonding was observed. The eccentric specimens failed at load 35% lower than that of the concentric ones. Global buckling formulas for concentric and eccentric loading were presented and validated using the experimentalresults and were in a good agreement. An equivalent stiffness formula was also developed for sandwich wall under in-plane loading. Design graphs for global buckling were developed to be used as a preliminary design for CSIPs wall under conentreic and eccentric loading.

5.7.2 Studies on Shear Behaviour

Very few studies have been performed for determination of shear strength of sandwich panels. Shear strength of sandwich panels can be determined by either direct shear test or diagonal compression test. Kabir (2005) performed direct shear test on 550 mm height and 1000 mm long panel. FEM analysis with incremental loading, was also performed using ANSYS. For FE modeling of panel two types of elements were used. Non-linear 8-noded solid elements for concrete and beam elements for wythe steel and shear connectors were used. The load deflection curve is linear upto 6000 kg and first crack occurs at 7000 kg. The sample failed at ultimate load 12000 kg and crack pattern is perpendicular to the normal principal stresses. Cracks occurred over the full length of sample and shear sliding was the failure mechanism. The panel's behaviour was same as a deep beam. Load deflection curve and ultimate load obtained from experiment and FEM analysis are matching.

Gara et al. (2012b), performed diagonal compression tests to assess in-plane shear strengthof EPS core wall panels. Three types of specimens were tested: simple wall panels, prestressed wall panels and panels with transversal stiffening walls. Diagonal compression tests were carried by means of a slide push by six hydraulic jacks. Panels with transvers walls show more deformation capacity than plane wall. Cracking load of prestressed panel is more as compared with other wall panels. In all tests, there was no sudden failure. The numerical simulation was done with an elastic FEM model using SAP 2000. Concrete was modelled with shell elements of thickness equal to total thickness of concrete. Experimental load deformation curve was compared with numerical model considering elastic modulus Ec and 0.4Ec to take into account cracking of concrete. Up to the first crack load of 100 kN, the experimental load-deformation curve matches with the numerically obtained curve for full value of Ec, and after cracking, the numerical curve with 0.4 Ec simulates the experimental behavior well. Maximum value of horizontal tensile stress in central node reaches 2.3 N/mm^2, nearly equal to ultimate tensile strength of concrete.

5.7.3 Studies on Flexural Behaviour

Experimental and analytical (FEM) studies were performed by Benayoune et al. (2008) to understand flexural behaviour of precast concrete sandwich panels (PCSP). The observed crack pattern was similar to the conventional solid slab. First crack appeared at approximately 55%-60% of the ultimate load. Truss shaped shear connectors give substantial degree of composite action, and the diameter of shear connectors influences the ultimate strength and composite action. In FEM analysis, 2D and 3D models were proposed for one-way and two way slabs. In two way slabs, shear connectors were placed in both longitudinal and transverse directions, whereas in one way slabs, shear connectors were placed only in longitudinal direction. FEM analysis was done in software LUSAS using four types of elements: 3D thin shell element, 2D isoparametric plane stress element, 2D bar element and 3D bar element. In one way slab, concrete wythes were modelled using 2D isoparametric plane stress element and 2D bar elements were used to model shear connectors and reinforcement. Two way slabs were modelled using 3D thin shell element and 3D bar element. Experimental results are in good correlation with analytical study. Results obtained from 2D model are very close to experimental results. The difference is less than 4% in ultimate load and 1.5% in deflection in elastic range. In 3D modelling, the difference in ultimate load is 16% on higher side and 1.2% in deflection in elastic range. 2D model predicts reasonable value of strain in shear connectors. Accordingly, 2D model was recommended to evaluate the composite behaviour at elastic and ultimate states.

Bajracharya et al. (2012) have done structural evaluation of Concrete Expanded Polystyrene (CEPS) sandwich panels, as slabs, using FEM with 8-noded brick elements in software Strand 7. 8-noded brick finite element model accurately predicted the load deformation behaviour. Carbonari et al. (2012) performed experiments to study the flexural behaviour of sandwich panel having 90° shear connectors. Three experiments were performed, one with simply supported and two with monolithic connections between walls and slab to simulate actual conditions. It was observed that connectors' contribution to stiffness of slab is small. The slab has high deformation and cracking under normal service load. Maximum load resisted by slab may be increased by changing shear connectors from 90° to incline. High deformation and cracking is related to failure of welding between steel mesh and connectors. Special attention must be paid to the welding between the connectors and the steel mesh embedded in the concrete layers.

Gara et al. (2012a) carried out test on simply supported floor panels and on wall-floor junctions. Numerical simulations with linear and non-linear FEM were also performed. A full scale 3D single story building was also tested to assess the ultimate capacity of real floor taking into account the wall-floor connections and bi-directional behaviour. Semicomposite behaviour was observed in flexural test panel due to low slip between concrete wythes and EPS core. A tri-linear behaviour with a very small uncracked phase was identified. Formulas for estimation of cracking and failure moment have also been proposed. Wall-floor junctions showed significant restraint against rotation and it depends on arrangement of wall and floor panels at junctions. Wall-floor junctions can be constructed in two different types, in the first type, floor panels cross the wall panels, and the wall panels were interrupted at the floor level. Whereas in the second type, floor panels are interrupted and wall panels are continuous. The first system has larger stiffness and strength as compared to the second system. The bending moment resisted by first system on a 1.12 m wide panel is 7.73 kN-m and second system resists only 4.63 kN-m. Waryosh et al. (2013) conducted test on sandwich panels made of light weight concrete as core and reinforced concrete as wythes, connected by truss type shear connectors. Experiments were conducted with three variables (thickness of core, strength of wythes and type of light weight concrete in core), keeping two variables as fixed and varying one at a time. Flexural strength increases with increase in thickness of panels. Flexural strength of panel with sawdust as light weight aggregate in core is more than polystyrene and porcelenite. Central deflection decreases with increase in strength of the concrete used in wythes.

5.7.4 Studies on Behaviour Under Lateral Dynamic/Seismic Loading

Cantilever and fixed end reinforced concrete sandwich wall panels (RCSPs) with and without openings along with 2-storey full scale H-shaped walls were tested under simulated seismic loading by Pavese and Bournas (2011). All panels exhibited only a relatively gradual strength and stiffness degradation and in no case did any panel suffer from sudden shear failure. The study concluded that RCSP is a good construction system in high seismicity regions. Bournas et al. (2012) proposed a 'column model' for nonlinear analysis of RCSPs walls under cyclic loading. The model consists of an elastic column element with nonlinear flexural and shear springs concentrated at the column ends. It yields satisfactory results of flexural and shear forces in the global response of the walls if constitutive law is used properly.

Pseudo-static cyclic tests were performed by Ricci et al. (2013) on cast-in-situ sandwich panels with and without opening for determination of stiffness, strength, ductility, and energy-dissipation under seismic loading. For a drift of 0.1-0.2% damping ratio is slightly more than 0.05 and for drifts of 0.4-1.0% damping ratio is 0.1, and the ductility is in the range 5 to 8.5. The drift at yielding is approximately equal to 0.1%. Panels can withstand horizontal load up to inter-storey drift equal to 1.3% without loss of the vertical load carrying capacity. Tested panels are able to withstand high horizontal loads, approximately equal to 100 kN/m. Seismic performance of the tested sandwich panels is comparable with those of common RC panels. Trombetti et al. (2012a) developed analytical model to evaluate mechanical characteristics and seismic behaviour of lightly reinforced concrete panels. Comparison between experimental results and analytical models has been performed. Experimental results were in good agreement with analytical model. Panels do show large values of kinematic ductility. The analytical tools developed for the seismic design can be successfully used for the actual seismic design of building structures. Trombetti et al. (2012b) reported assessment of the seismic performance (stiffness, strength, ductility) of cellular structures built with lightly reinforced concrete/polystyrene sandwich panels. Horizontal loading cycles were imposed to the structures, while the vertical load was kept constant. It was observed that there is no real collapse, but just a "virtual collapse". A good degree of kinematic ductility was developed. Sliding shear with pinched mode of failure was observed.

Rezaifar et al. (2008) conducted full scale dynamic test on single storey building constructed with sandwich panel, on shake table under several ground motions. The results obtained from experiment were also compared numerically using ANSYS. 3D panel buildings have considerable resistance to high levels of earthquakes due to: (i) over strength, (ii) minor energy dissipation by inelastic deformations, and (iii) the small drift. The overall displacement ratio of 4.5 and the over strength coefficient of approximately 6.0 were found using pushover analysis.

Ricci et al. (2012), Ricci et al. (2013b), Palermo et al. (2014) performed shake table test on full scale 3-story building. The plan dimensions of building was 4.10 m x 5.50 m, height of building 8.25 m and inter-storey height 2.75 m. Construction of building was done using the sandwich panel of same specifications as used by authors in earlier papers. First the theoretical seismic capacity and expected mechanisms of failure was calculated. Three-dimensional FEM model was developed using SAP2000 to get modes of vibration and natural frequency. Modeling was done with shell-layered elements for both uncracked and fully cracked conditions, these conditions were simulated by taking different value of modulus of elasticity of concrete. For uncracked condition Ec,UC = 25000 MPa and for cracked condition Ec, FC = 2750 MPa. The fundamental frequency of uncracked building was 12.8 Hz and for cracked building was 3.3 Hz. The expected sequence of failure of mechanisms with peak shaking table acceleration were identified. The test was performed on shake table with traditional instrumentation along with an advance instrument optical monitoring system. Acceleration Time history of Montenegro -1979 earthquake was used for seismic tests.

White noise tests were performed before and after each seismic test in order to estimate the variation in the dynamic properties of prototype system. Spectrograms from white noise test were obtained and natural frequencies were presented. Up to five white noise test (i.e. till PGA of 0.5g) fundamental frequency was constant, decrease in frequency was observed after PGA of 1.0g. The record of acceleration time history is similar to the previous papers of the authors. There was dynamic amplification of acceleration between bottom of table to top storey of the order of 1.4 to 1.7. Time history was recorded and it was found that the amplitude of strain in concrete is less than 0.5x10-3. Displacement was recorded during the test. Inter-storey drift of 0.26% for first storey and 0.3% for roof was recorded. The first visible crack was observed at 1.0g PGA and were mostly concentrated around the openings. The response of shake table test was better than as anticipated by analytical calculations. The natural frequency calculated from FEM model and experiment is almost matching. The modules of elasticity required to match initial and final frequency are equal to 15,000 MPa, and 10,200 MPa. This indicates that, even after some cracks due to earthquake the building will perform similar to uncracked building. It was observed that the building is having over strength. The underestimation of strength may be due to neglecting tensile strength of concrete. The over strength of building is also explained by "Modified Compression Field Theory", the peak shear strength of panel is approximately two times the ultimate strength.

5.8 DESIGN GUIDELINES

These guidelines for analysis and design of EPS sandwich wall panel buildings have been developed by IIT, Roorkee. Requirement of thickness of wythes as per fire rating and durability is also presented. Before starting of structural design of any structure there is requirement of forces acting in various load resisting elements at critical sections due to action of various loads and their combinations. More accurate analysis can be performed using FEM with the help of software like SAP 2000 and ABAQUS or any other available FEM based software to obtain design forces, but as shown in the previous chapter, simpler calculations using 'Pier Analysis' also yield fairly good results for gravity and seismic loads. After getting the design forces, the structural elements such as walls, slabs, foundation etc. can be designed for compression, moment and shear, using simple RC design theory with some modifications.

5.8.1 Design of Wall Panels for Compression

Pure axial compression in solid panels

Ultimate load carrying capacity of sandwich panel walls under pure axial case may be calculated using following equations of ACI 318-89/Benayoune, 2007. These equations are only applicable when panel behaves fully composite, applied load is in "middle-third" of wall thickness and slenderness ratio is not more than 25.

$$P_u = 0.55\phi f_{cu} A_c [1 - kH/32t)^2]$$

$$P_u = 0.4 f_{cu} A_c [1 - kH/40t^2] + 0.67 f_y A_{sc}$$

where,

f_{cu} = Characteristic cube strength of concrete

f_y = Tensile strength of steel

P_u = Ultimate axial load

k = 0.8, for wall restrained against rotation

Φ = Capacity reduction factor = 0.7

A_{sc} = Total area of steel

A_c = Gross area of wall panel

H = Effective height of wall panel

t = Thickness of the panel section

Axial compression in panels with opening

Load carrying capacity of sandwich panels having openings may be calculated using equation given below (Saheb and Desayi, 1990). The influence of size and location of the opening(s) is taken into account through the parameter α.

$$P_{uoc}^{c} = (k_1 - k_2\alpha) P_{uc}^{c}$$

$$P_{uc}^{c} = 0.55\Phi[A_g f_c' + (f_y - f_c')A_{sy}][1 - (H/32t]^2[1.2 - (H/10L)]$$

where,

$$\alpha = \frac{A_0}{A} + \frac{a}{L}$$

$$A_0 = L_0 t,\ A = Lt,\ a = [(L/2) - \tilde{a}]$$

$$\tilde{a} = [(L^2 t/2) - L_0 t a_0] / (Lt - L_0 t)$$

P_{uoc}^{c} = Theoretical ultimate load for panel with opening

P_{uc}^{c} = Theoretical ultimate load for panel without opening

A_g = Gross area of the wall panel section

A_{sv} = Area of vertical steel in wall section

L_0 = Length of panel opening

f_c = Cylinder strength of concrete

f_y = Yield strength of steel

H, L, t = Height, length and thickness of wall panel

k_1 & k_2 = Constants

k_1 = 1.0027

k_2 = 0.779

a_0 = Distance of the centre of the opening from the left edge of the panel

a = Distance between the centres of panel with and without opening

$\tilde{a}$ = Distance of the centre of the panel without opening from the left edge of the panel.

Axial force-moment interaction

Strength of eccentrically loaded short sandwich panels may be calculated using following equations, proposed by Benayoune et al. (2006). These equations are derived using the principles of linearity in strain, strain compatibility and equilibrium as shown in Figure-14.

Following assumptions are made:

(a) The two wythes act in fully composite manner.

(b) Parabolic stress-strain curve is replaced by rectangular stress-strain curve having depth (S) = $0.9x$, x is depth of neutral axis

(c) The compressive stress in the extreme compression fibre is 0.45 f_{cu}, and the corresponding ultimate strain ε_{cu} = 0.0035.

(d) The tensile strength of concrete is neglected.

$$P_u = F_{cc} + F_{sc} - F_s$$

$$P_u = 0.45 f_{cu} BS + f_{sc} A_{sc} - f_s A_s$$

$$M_u = P_u e$$

$$M_u = F_{cc}\left(\frac{h}{2}-\frac{S}{2}\right)+F_{sc}\left(\frac{h}{2}-d_1\right)+F_s\left(\frac{h}{2}-d_2\right)$$

where,

P_u = Ultimate axial load

M_u = Ultimate moment

e = Eccentricity

f_{cu} = Characteristic cube strength of concrete

F_{cc} = Compressive force in concrete

F_{sc} = Compressive force in compressive steel

F_s = Tensile force in steel

f_{sc} = Compressive stress in compressive steel

f_s = Tensile stress in tensile steel

A_{sc} = Total area of steel

A_s = Gross area of wall panel

h = Total thickness of wall panel

S = Depth of equivalent stress block

d_1 = Distance between most compressive fibre to compression steel

d_2 = Distance between most compressive fibre to tension steel

ε_{cu} = Ultimate strain in concrete

ε_s = Strain in tensile steel

ε_{cs} = Strain in compressive steel

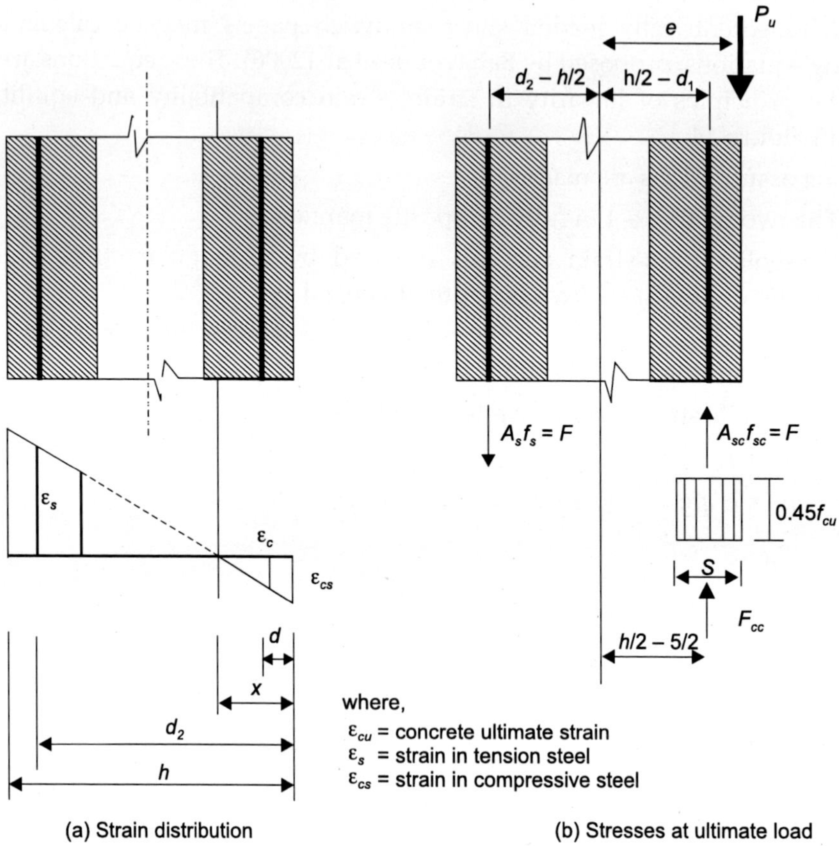

Fig. 6.14: Variation of strain and stresses on a composite panel cross section subjected to eccentric axial loading

The above described method may lead to non-conservative estimates as it assumes fully composite action between the different layers of the composite panel. Benayoune et al. (2008), and Mohamad et al. (2014) calculated degree of composite action and ultimate strength, analytically. Benayoune et al. (2008), suggested that the distribution of stress across the depth, up to linear stage can be used for evaluating degree of composite action.

Ratio of effective moment of inertia (I_e) to gross moment of inertia (I_g), (assuming full composite action) provides the degree of composite action.

$$I_e = \frac{Mh}{(\sigma_b - \sigma_t)}$$

where,

σ_t, σ_b = Stress at top and bottom

M = Applied bending moment

h = Depth of panel

Ultimate load resisted by the panel can be determined as follows:

Non-composite action	Composite action
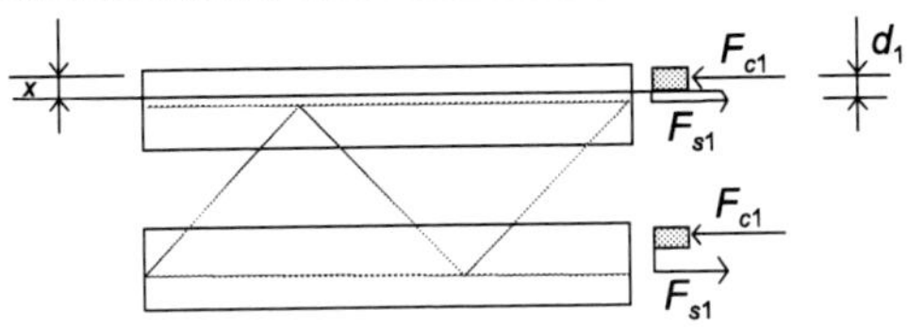 (a) Non-composite action (1 metre length) $F_{s1} = A_s f_y$, $F_{c1} = 0.85 f_{cu} b s_1$ $F_{s1} = F_{c1}$, $s_1 = F_{s1}/F_{c1}$ F_{s1} = Force in tension reinforcement (non-composite) $M_{u(\text{onewythe})} = F_{s1}\left(d_1 - \frac{s_1}{2}\right)$ $M_u = 2M_{u(\text{onewythe})}$ M_u = Ultimate moment capacity F_{c1} = Comp. force in conc. (non-composite A_s = Area of tension reinforcement b = Per metre length of wall section or connector spacing f_y = Yield stress of steel s_1 = 0.9x, Depth of neutral axis	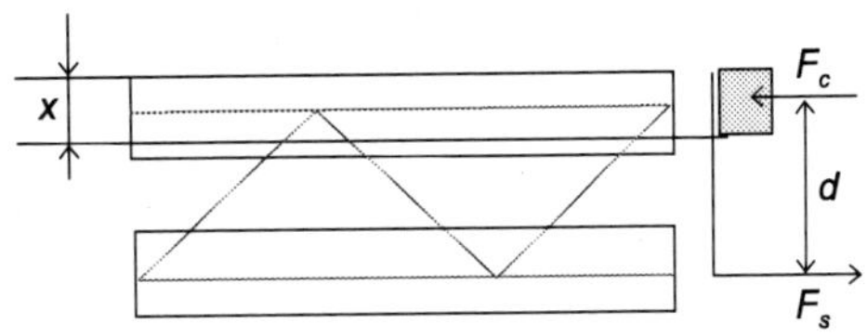 (b) Fully composite action (1 metre length) $M_u = T(d - s/1)$ M_u = Ultimate moment capacity F_c = Comp. force in conc. F_s = Force in tension reinforcement s = 0.9x, where x is depth of neutral axis

Upto 3.0m span single sandwich panels can be used for slab and roof of residential buildings, beyond 3.0 m span ribbed beam type sandwich panels serve the deflection and strength criteria. Trombetti et al. (2012b), developed analytical formulation for calculation of bending resistance, axial resistance, shear resistance and their combinations of sandwich panels, on the basis and assumptions of RC theory. These formulation can be applied to large lightly reinforced concrete (LLRCW) walls with spread reinforcement if there is full composite action and shear connectors do not buckle.

Evaluation of moment resistance (M_u) for given axial load N of LLRCW

$$\tilde{M}_u = (f_y \rho b y_u)\left(\frac{h}{2} - \frac{y_u}{2}\right) + [f_c b 0.8(h - y_u)](0.1h + 0.4y_u) + A_{s,add} f_{y,d}(h - 2c)$$

$$y_u = h\left[\frac{0.8 - \frac{N}{f_c bh}}{0.8 + \frac{f_y}{f_c}\rho}\right]$$

where,

f_y = Yield strength of steel

f_c = Compressive strength of concrete

ρ = Geometric ratio of vertical reinforcement

y_u = Position of neutral axis in ultimate condition

v = Normalised axial force

$v = N / F_c bh$

$A_{s,add}$ = Cross-sectional area of the additional bars placed at the ends of wall

c = Re-bar cover

Shear capacity

Shear strength of a sandwich panel may be calculated as per Clauses 40.2 and 40.3 of IS 456:2000. Shear stress due to design shear force acting at the section (τ_v) is to be compared with the nominal shear stress capacity of section (τ_c), shown in Table 6.1. In no case design shear strength is more than maximum shear strength ($\tau_{c,max}$) of section shown in Table 2.

$$\tau_v = \frac{V_u}{bd}$$

If deign shear stress (τ_v) is more than shear stress capacity of section (τ_c), provide additional shear reinforcement as per design. Shear reinforcement shall be provided to resist shear force equal to

$$V_{us} = V_u - \tau_c bd$$

$$V_{us} = \frac{0.87 f_y A_{sv} d}{s_v}$$

where,

V_u = Shear force due to design load

B = Length of wall

d = Effective depth

A_{sv} = Area of horizontal shear reinforcement

s_v = Spacing of horizontal shear reinforcement

f_y = Yield strength of steel

Table 6.1: Shear capacity of section without shear reinforcement (τ_c) N/mm² (IS 456: 2000)

$100\frac{A_s}{bd}$	**Permissible Sheer Stress in Concrete, τ_c, N/mm²**					
	Grade of concrete					
	M 15	M 20	M 25	M 30	M 35	M 40 and above
(1)	(2)	(3)	(4)	(5)	(6)	(7)
≤ 0.15	0.18	0.18	0.19	0.20	0.20	0.20
0.25	0.22	0.22	0.23	0.23	0.23	0.23
0.50	0.29	0.30	0.31	0.31	0.31	0.32
0.75	0.34	0.35	0.36	0.37	0.37	0.38
1.00	0.37	0.39	0.40	0.41	0.42	0.42
1.25	0.40	0.42	0.44	0.45	0.45	0.46
1.50	0.42	0.45	0.46	0.48	0.49	0.49
1.75	0.44	0.47	0.49	0.50	0.52	0.52
2.00	0.44	0.49	0.51	0.53	0.54	0.55
2.25	0.44	0.51	0.53	0.55	0.56	0.57
2.50	0.44	0.51	0.55	0.57	0.58	0.60
2.75	0.44	0.51	0.56	0.58	0.60	0.62
3.00 and above	0.44	0.51	0.57	0.60	0.62	0.63

Table 6.2: Maximum shear stress at section ($\tau_{c,max}$) N/mm²

Concrete grade	M 15	M 20	M 25	M 30	M 35	M 40 and above
$t_{c\ max}$, N/mm²	1.6	1.8	1.9	2.2	2.3	2.5

Evaluation of ultimate shear strength V_u according to the Eurocode

Ultimate shear strength (V_u) for a given axial force (N) in a lightly reinforced concrete wall (LLRCW), can be obtained using EC8 and EC2 provisions (Trombetti et al., 2012b). The shear capacity (V_u) is the smaller of shear resistance of horizontal reinforcement and the concrete strut resistance.

Shear horizontal reinforcement resistance (V_u)

$$V_u = \frac{sw}{\ } zF\,(\cot\theta + \cot\alpha)\sin\alpha$$

Concrete strut resistance (V_u)

$$V_u = 0.6bzf_c\alpha_c(\cot\theta + \tan\theta)$$

where,

A_{sw} = Area of horizontal shear reinforcement

s = Spacing of horizontal shear

z = Inner lever arm

θ = Angle between concrete compression struts and the main tension cord = 22°

α = between shear reinforcement and the main tension cord = 90°C

α_c = 1 as per EC2

Evaluation of ultimate sliding resistance according to the Eurocode

The shear stress at interface of two concrete members casted in different times must satisfy the following expressions according to the EC8 and EC2 provisions:

$$v_{Edt} \leq v_{Rdt} \leq 0.5 v f_c$$

$$v_{Edt} = \beta V_E/(zb)$$

$$v_{Rdt} = cf_{ctd} + \mu\left(\frac{}{} + \rho f_y\right)$$

$$v = 0.6\left(1 - \frac{f_{ck}}{250}\right)$$

where,

N_E & V_E = Axial force and shear force in member, respectively

μ & c = Parameters depending on roughness of the surface at contact (μ = 0.7 and c = 0.45);

β = Ratio of longitudinal force in the new concrete area and the total longitudinal force either in compression or tension zone, both calculated for the section considered

v = Effectivity factor

f_{ctd} = Tensile strength of concrete

A_c = Cross-sectional area of concrete

5.8.2 Seismic Design Parameters

For seismic resistant design of sandwich panels, the parameters like coefficient of critical damping may be taken as 5% and poison's ratio as 0.2. Seismic performance factors (SPFs) such as response modification/reduction factor (R-factor), the system over strength factor (Ω_0) and deflection amplification factor (C_d) for sandwich panel construction up to two story building may be taken as R = 3.5, C_d = 3.5 and Ω_0 = 3.0. Buildings with 4 storey or more do not pass FEMA P695 acceptance criteria (Mashal and Filiatrault, 2012).

5.8.3 Fire and Durability

RCSP building system also have good resistance against fire. Fire rating of 1.5 hours is obtained by using 1.5 inches thick wythes and 2 hour rating by using 2 inches thick wythes (Mousa 2014). The fire rating can be further increased by increasing the wythe thickness (Mousa 2014, Enbuil Manual 2012a, Enbuil Specification 2012b). Modified expanded polystyrene used in sandwich panels is non-combustible. It does not contribute to fire and simply melts when exposed to flame. For durability, provisions of IS 456:2000 may be employed.

REFERENCES

1. Aziz, F. N. A. A, Ali, A. A. A., Jaafar, M. S., Samad, A. A. A., Trikha, D. N., 2004,"Ultimate strength of precast concrete sandwich panel with opening under axial load", Journal- The Institution of Engineers, Malaysia, Vol. 65, No. 1 / 2, March/June, pp. 8-12.
2. Bajracharya, R. M., Lokuge, W. P., Karunasena, W., Lau, K.T., Mosallam, A. S., 2012,"Structural evaluation of concrete expanded polystyrene sandwich panels for slabapplications", conference paper, proceedings of the 22nd Australasian conference onmechanics of structure and materials, ACMSM22, Sydney, Australia, 11-14th December.
3. Benayoune, A., Samad, A. A. A., Ali, A. A. A., Trikha, D. N., 2007, "Response of pre-castreinforced composite sandwich panels to axial loading", Construction and Building Materials, Vol. 21, pp. 677–685.
4. Benayoune, A., Samad, A. A. A., Trikha, D. N, Ali A. A. A., Akhand, A. M., 2004,"Precast reinforced concrete sandwich panel as an industrialised building system", International Conference on Concrete Engineering and Technology, University of Malaya, Kuala Lumpur, Malaysia.
5. Benayoune, A., Samad, A. A. A., Trikha, D. N., Ali, A. A. A., Ashrabov, A. A., 2006,"Structural behaviour of eccentrically loaded precast sandwich panels", Construction and Building Materials, Vol. 20, pp. 713–724.
6. Benayoune, A., Samad, A. A. A., Trikha, D. N., Ali, A. A. A., Ellinna, S. H. M., 2008,"Flexural behaviour of pre-cast concrete sandwich composite panel– experimental and theoretical investigations", Construction and Building Materials, Vol. 22 , pp. 580-592.
7. Bournas, D. A., Torrisi, G., Crisafulli, F., Pavese, A., 2012, "Experimental investigation and analytical modelling of prefabricated reinforced concrete sandwich panels", 15thWCEE, LISBOA.
8. Buffarini, G. et al., 2009, "Seismic analysis of EMMEDUE subsystem upon shaking table: Accelerometric readings", Institution for new technology, energy and the environment ENEA-ACS.
9. Bush, T. D. and Stine, G. L., 1994, "Flexural Behavior of Composite Precast Concrete Sandwich Panels with Continuous Truss connectors", PCI Journal, Vol. 3 (2), pp. 112-121.
10. Carbonari, G., Cavalaro, S. H. P., Cansario, M. M., Aguado A., 2012, "Flexural behavior of light-weight sandwich panels composed by concrete and EPS", Construction and Building Materials, Vol. 35, pp. 792–799.

11. Carbonari, G., Cavalaro, S. H. P., Cansario, M. M., Aguado, A., 2013, "Experimental and analytical study about the compressive behaviour of EPS sandwich panels", Materiales de Construcción, Vol. 63, 311, pp. 393-402.
12. CSI (2010), SAP 2000 Nonlinear, Integrated Software for Structural Analysis and Design-Analysis Reference Manual, Computers and Structures, Inc., Berkeley, California, USA.
13. Desayi, P., and Krishnan, S. (1964). "Equation for the Stress-Strain Curve of Concrete."ACI Journal Proceedings, 61(3).
14. Einea, A., Salmon, D. C., Fogarasi, G.J., Culp, T. D., Tadros M. K., 1991. "State-of the-Artof precast concrete sandwich panels". PCI Journal, Vol. 36(6), pp. 78-98.
15. Einea, A., Salmon, D. C., Tadros, M. K., 1994, "A New Structurally and Thermally Efficient Precast Sandwich Panel System", PCI Journal, Vol. 39(4), July-August, pp. 90-101.
16. Enbuil, 2012a, Enbuil assembly manual, Revision 4.
17. Enbuil, 2012b, Specification of Enbuil System.
18. EVG-3D, Panel construction system-A brief introduction into the EVG-3D panel construction system.
19. Fam, A. and Sharaf, T., 2010, "Flexural performance of sandwich panels comprising polyurethane core and GFRP skins and ribs of various configurations", Composite Structures, Vol. 92, pp. 2927–2935.
20. Forni, M. and Poggianti, A., 2009, "Seismic analysis of EMMEDUE subsystem onvibrating table: Numerical F.E. modelling", Institution for new technology, energy and the environment ENEA-ACS.
21. Gara, F., Ragni, L., Roia, D., Dezi, L., 2012a, "Experimental behaviour and numerical analysis of floor sandwich panels", Engineering Structures Engineering Structures, Vol. 36, pp. 258–269.
22. Gara, F., Ragni, L., Roia, D., Dezi, L., 2012b, "Experimental tests and numerical modelling of wall sandwich panels", Engineering Structures, Vol. 37, pp. 193–204.
23. "Housing for All by 2022 Mission" – National Mission for Urban Housing, Ministry of Housing & Urban Poverty Alleviation, Government of India, June 17th, 2015
24. Hu, H.-T., Lin, F.-M., and Jan, Y.-Y. (2004). "Nonlinear finite element analysis of reinforced concrete beams strengthened by fiber-reinforced plastics." Composite Structures, 63(3–4), 271-281.
25. IS: 1893 (Part 1): 2002, "Criteria for earthquake resistant design of structures - Part 1 :general provisions and buildings", Bureau of Indian Standards.

26. IS: 456:2000, "Plain and reinforced concrete - code of practice", Bureau of Indian standard
27. IS: 875 (Part 3)-1987, "Code of practice for design loads (other than earthquake) for buildings and structures", Bureau of Indian Standards.
28. Jankowiak, T., and Lodygowski, T. (2005). "Identification of parameters of concrete damage plasticity constitutive model." Foundation of Civil and Environmental Engineering, 06, 53-69.
29. Kabir, M. Z., 2005, "Structural Performance of 3D sandwich panels under shear and flexural loading", Scientia Iranica, Vol. 12, No. 4, pp. 402-408.
30. Kadam, S.B. (2015). "Seismic Evaluation and Retrofit of Masonry Buildings." Ph.D. Thesis, IIT Roorkee, Roorkee.
31. Lee, A.J., Kelly, H., Jagoda, R., Rosenfeld, A., Stubee, E., Colaco, J.,Gadgil, A., Akbari,A., Norford, L., Burik, H.V., 2006, "Affordable, safe housing based on expanded polystyrene (EPS) foam and a cementitious coating" Journal of Master Science, Vol. 41, pp. 6908-6916.
32. Mashal, M. and Filiatrault, A., 2012, "Quantification of seismic performance factors for buildings incorporating three-dimensional construction system", NZSEE Conference.
33. Mlynarczyk, A. and Pessiki, S., 2000, "Experimental evaluation of the composite behavior of precast concrete sandwich wall panels", Center for advance technology for large structural systems (ATLSS), Lehigh University, Report No. 00-07, August, pp. 127.
34. Mohamad, N., Omar, W. and Abdullah, R., 2011, "Precast lightweight foamed concrete sandwich panel (PLFP) tested under axial load: Preliminary Results", Advanced Materials Research, Vol. 250-253, pp. 1153-1162, Trans Tech Publications, Switzerland.
35. Mosallam, A. S., 2014, "Structural evaluation of Schnell Home S.R.L. EPS sandwich panelslabs subjected to out-of-plane flexural loads", SETH-SCHL-FELX0114, Structural Engineering Testing Hall (SETH), Civil & Environmental Engineering Department, The Henry Samueli School of Engineering, University of California, Irvine.
36. Mourtaja, W., Karadogan, F., Yuksel, E. and Ilaki, A., 2000, 3D behaviour of shotcreted lightweight panel buildings, 12th World Conference on Earthquake Engineering (12WCEE).
37. Mousa A. and Zidan A., 2014, "3-D Panel System: A sustainable building solution for Egypt". http://www.researchgate.net/publication/266208931, (accessed on 11.12.2015).

38. Mousa, M. A. and Nasimuddin, 2009, "Experimental and analytical study of carbon fibrereinforced polymer (FRP)/autoclaved aerated concrete (AAC) sandwich panels", Engineering Structures, Vol. 31, pp. 2337-2344.
39. Mousa, M. A. and Nasimuddin, 2011, "Global buckling of composite structural insulated wall panels", Materials and Design, Vol. 32, pp. 766–772.
40. Mowrtage, W. and Karadogan, F., 2009, "Behaviour of Single-Story Lightweight Panel Building under Lateral Loads", Journal of Earthquake Engineering, Vol. 13, pp. 100-107.
41. Mowrtage, W., 2012, "Low-Rise 3D panel structures for hot regions: Design guidelines and case studies", Arab Journal of Science and Engineering, Vol. 37, pp. 587–600.
42. Murty C.V.R, 2000, Earthquake Tips (IITK-BMPTC), Learning earthquake design and construction. Indian Institute of Technology Kanpur (IITK) and the Building Materials and Technology Promotion Council (BMTPC).
43. Mydin, M. A. O., Utaberta, N., Yus of, M. Y. M., Amirudin, N. A., 2015, "Stress-strain relationships of composite foamed concrete panel with different number of shear connectors under compression", Jurnal Teknologi (Sciences & Engineering), Vol. 75:5, pp. 19–25.
44. Numayr, K. and Haddad, R., 2009, "Static and dynamic analytical and experimental analysis of 3D reinforced concrete panels", Structural Engineering & Mechanics, Vol.32(3), pp. 399-406.
45. Palermo, M., Gil-Martin, L. M., Hernandez-Montes, E. and Trombetti, T., "2013, In-plane shear behaviour of thin low reinforced concrete panels for earthquake re-construction", Materials and Structures, Vol. 46, pp. 841–856.
46. Palermo, M., Ricci, I., Silvestri, S., Gasparini, G., Trombetti, T., Foti, D., Ivorra, S., 2014,"Preliminary interpretation of shaking-table response of a full-scale 3-storey buildingcomposed of thin reinforced concrete sandwich walls", Engineering Structures, Vol. 76,pp. 75–89.
47. Pavese, A., Bournas, D. A., 2011, "Experimental assessment of the seismic performance of a prefabricated concrete structural wall system", Engineering Structures, Vol. 33, pp. 2049–2062.
48. PCI Committee on Precast Sandwich Wall Panels, 1997, "State-of-the-Art of Precast/Prestressed Concrete Sandwich Wall Panels, Second edition" PCI committee report, PCI Journal, May-June.
49. PCI Committee on Precast Sandwich Wall Panels, 2011, "State-of-the-Art of Precast/Prestressed Concrete Sandwich Wall Panels" PCI committee report, PCI Journal, spring.
50. Pessiki, S. and Mlynarczyk, A., 2003, "Experimental Evaluation of the composite behaviour of precast concrete sandwich wall panels", PCI Journal, Vol. 48(2), March-April, pp. 54-71.

51. Poluraju, P. and Rao, G. A., "Influence of longitudinal reinforcement and stiffeners on strength and behaviour of 3D wall panels under axial compression", jeaconf.org, (accessedon 20.12.2015).

52. Poluraju, P., Rao, G. A., 2014, "Behaviour of 3d-panels for structural applications undergeneral loading: A state-of-the-art", International Journal of Research in Engineering and Technology, Vol. 03, Special Issue 16, pp. 173-181.

53. Refaei, F. A. I., Mihilmy, M. T. E. and Bahaa, T. M., 2015, "Seismic Behavior of Sandwich Panel Walls", World Applied Sciences Journal , Vol. 33 (11), pp. 1718-1731.

54. Rezaifar, O., Kabir, M. Z., Taribakhsh, M., Tehranian, A., 2008, "Dynamic behaviour of 3D-panel single-storey system using shaking table testing", Engineering Structures, Vol. 30, pp. 318–337.

55. Ricci, I., Gasparini, G., Silvestri, S., Trombetti, T., Foti, D., Ivorra-Chorro, S., 2012,"Design of a shaking table test on a 3-storey building composed of cast-in-situ concrete walls", 15th WCEE, LISBOA.

56. Ricci, I., Palermo, M., Gasparini, G., Silvestri, S. , Trombetti, T., 2013a, "Results of pseudo-static tests with cyclic horizontal load on cast in situ sandwich squat concrete walls', Engineering Structures, Vol. 54, pp. 131–149.

57. Ricci, I., Palermo, M., Silvestri, S., Gasparini, G., Trombetti, T., Foti, D., Chorro, S. I.,2013b, "Shake Table Response of a Full-Scale 3-Storey Building Composed of Thin Reinforced Concrete Sandwich walls", AES-RSESS'2013 First International Conferenceon Reliability and Safety of Engineering Systems and Structures, Vancouver, CANADA,August 12 - 16.

58. Saheb, S. M. and Desayi, P., 1990, "Ultimate strength of RC wall panels with openings", Journal of Structural Engineering (ASCE), Vol. 116, No. 6, pp. 1565-1578.

59. Sarkar, A., Ahmad, A., Singh, Y., 2016, "Seismic design of expanded polystyrene corepanel based building systems", International conference on earthquake engineering and post disaster reconstruction planning, ICEE-PDRP, 24th-26th April, Nepal.

60. Schnell Home, The core wall system Schnell home, by Schnell Wire System.

61. Trombetti, T., Silvestri, S., Gasparini, G., Ricci, I., 2012a, "Results of pseudo-static tests with cyclic horizontal load on H-shaped substructure composed of concrete/polystyrene sandwich bearing panels without openings", Strategie di sviluppo sostenibile per lecostruzioni in Cina, in Europa e in Italia, pp. 489-498.

62. Trombetti, T., Silvestri, S., Gasparini, G., Ricci, I., 2012b, "Correlations between the experimental results of pseudo-static tests with cyclic horizontal load onconcrete/polystyrene sandwich bearing panels and their analytical

counterparts", Strategiedi sviluppo sostenibile per le costruzioni in Cina, in Europa e in Italia, pp. 499-508.

63. Trombetti, T., Silvestri, S., Gasparini, G., Ricci, I., 2012c, "Results of pseudo-static tests with cyclic horizontal load on concrete/polystyrene sandwich bearing panels with and without openings", Strategie di sviluppo so stenibile per le costruzioni in Cina, in Europa ein Italia, pp. 509-518.
64. Vecchio, F. (1990). "Reinforced Concrete Membrane Element Formulations." Journal of Structural Engineering, 116(3), 730-750.
65. Waryosh, W. A. and Abtan, Y. G., 2013, "Structural behaviour of composite sandwich slab panels", Journal of Engineering and Development, Vol. 17, No. 4, October, pp. 220-232.
66. www.jmt.in/what-is-expandable-polystyrene-eps.html.

6

Prefabricated Steel & Light Gauge Steel Structural Systems

6.1 PREFABRICATED STEEL & LIGHT GAUGE STEEL STRUCTURAL SYSTEMS

6.1.1 Introduction

Steel is a combination of iron and carbon. Steel is alloyed with various elements to improve physical properties and to produce special properties such as resistance to corrosion or heat.

Alloy steel refers to a type of steel that is alloyed with various elements. In theory, every steel can be referred to as alloy steel since the simplest steel is iron alloyed with up to 2.06% of carbon. However, the term "alloy steel" commonly refers to steels that are alloyed with elements other than carbon. The total weight of alloying elements can amount up to 50% to give the material improved properties such as better wear protection or ductility. A distinction is made between low-alloyed and high alloyed steels. Low-alloyed steels are characterized by their low amount of alloys, which in summation make up to less than 5%. The amount of elements in high-alloyed steels can be greater or equal to 5%, making the material more expensive. Aside from those two groups, there are also unalloyed steels which carry an extremely small amount of alloys.

6.1.1.1 Steel Grades and Properties

According to the World Steel Association, there are over 3,500 different grades of steel, encompassing unique physical, chemical, and environmental properties. In essence, as already said, steel is composed of iron and carbon, although it is the amount of carbon as well as the level of impurities and additional alloying elements, that determine the properties of each steel grade.

The carbon content in steel can range from 0.1-1.5%, but the most widely used grades of steel contain only 0.1-0.25% carbon. Elements such as manganese, phosphorus, and sulfur are found in all grades of steel, but, whereas manganese provides beneficial effects, phosphorus and sulfur are deleterious to steel's strength and durability. Different types of steel are produced according to the properties required for their application, and various grading systems are used to distinguish steels based on these properties.

According to the American Iron and Steel Institute (AISI), steel can be broadly categorized into four groups based on their chemical compositions:

Carbon steels : Carbon steels contain trace amounts of alloying elements and account for 90% of total steel production. Carbon steels can be further categorized into three groups depending on their carbon content:

- **Low carbon steel (mild steel):** Typically contain 0.04% to 0.30% carbon content. This is one of the largest groups of Carbon Steel. It covers a great diversity of shapes; from Flat Sheet to Structural Beam. Depending on the desired properties needed, other elements are added or increased like for Structural Steel the carbon level is higher and the manganese content is increased.
- **Medium carbon steel:** Typically has a carbon range of 0.31% to 0.60%, and a manganese content ranging from .060% to 1.65%. This product is stronger than low carbon steel, and it is more difficult to form, weld and cut. Medium carbon steels are quite often hardened and tempered using heat treatment.
- **High carbon steel:** Commonly known as "carbon tool steel", it typically has a carbon range between 0.61% and 1.50%. High carbon steel is very difficult to cut, bend and weld. Once heat treated, it becomes extremely hard and brittle.

Alloy steels : Alloy steels contain alloying elements (e.g. manganese, silicon, nickel, titanium, copper, chromium, and aluminum) in varying proportions, in order to manipulate the steel's properties, such as its hardenability, corrosion resistance, strength, formability, weldability or ductility. Applications for alloy steel include pipelines, auto parts, transformers, power generators and electric motors.

Stainless steels : Stainless steels generally contain between 10-20% chromium as the main alloying element and are valued for high corrosion resistance. With over 11% chromium, steel is about 200 times more resistant to corrosion than mild steel. These steels can be divided into three groups based on their crystalline structure:

- Austenitic steels are non-magnetic and non heat-treatable, and generally contain 18% chromium, 8% nickel and less than 0.8% carbon. Austenitic steels form the largest portion of the global stainless steel market and are often used in food processing equipment, kitchen utensils, and piping.
- Ferritic steels contain trace amounts of nickel, 12-17% chromium, less than 0.1% carbon, along with other alloying elements, such as molybdenum, aluminum or titanium. These magnetic steels cannot be hardened by heat treatment but can be strengthened by cold working.
- Martensitic steels contain 11-17% chromium, less than 0.4% nickel, and up to 1.2% carbon. These magnetic and heat-treatable steels are used in knives, cutting tools, as well as dental and surgical equipment.

- Duplex stainless steels are a family of stainless steels. These are called duplex (or austenitic-ferritic) grades because their metallurgical structure consists of two phases, austenite (face-centered cubic lattice) and ferrite (body centered cubic lattice) in roughly equal proportions.

Tool steels : Tool steels contain tungsten, molybdenum, cobalt and vanadium in varying quantities to increase heat resistance and durability, making them ideal for cutting and drilling equipment.

6.1.2 Steel as a Structural Material

Mild Steel is the most common type of steel used in building construction. It is strong and durable, and ensures a sturdy built. Due to the strength that carbon steel provides, it is hugely useful in buildings and has proved to be of great advantage. It does not crack when bent, it is immensely flexible, and it is ductile and has great plasticity, along with the fact that it can endure calamities like earthquakes without it causing cracks in the steel.

Structural steel is a category of steel used for making construction materials in a variety of shapes. Structural steel components are made out of mild steel, which is formed out of a precise cross section, at the same time it follows definite standards for mechanical properties and chemical composition. Structural steel comes in various shapes like I-Beam, Z shape, HSS shape, L shape (angle), structural channel (C-beam, cross section), T shaped, Rail profile, bar, rod, plate, open joist of web steel etc. Standard structural steel varies in different countries with different specifications. For example, European I-beam is Euronorm 19-57; structural steel in USA comes in carbon, low alloy, corrosion resistant high strength low alloy, quenched and tempered alloy steel etc. Structural steel materials generally used are wrought iron, cast iron and mild steel.

- **Cast iron,** only used in compressive members.
- **Wrought iron,** fibrous in nature- resists tensile stresses.
- **Mild steel,** Suitable for all structural members, equally strong in tension and compression, can replace cast iron and wrought iron.

6.1.2.1 Reason for Popularity of Structural Steel

- Rapid construction in all weathers
- Ease of Fabrication and speed of construction
- Easy field repair
- Design Flexibility
- Renewable
- Components can be re-used
- Dimensional stability
- Reduced number of columns (long Span Structures)
- Smaller beam and column section

- Thin slab
- Repairing and strengthening
- Restoration and renovation
- Structure can start to function right after its completion
- Quality and comfort

However, the weight of structural steel requires heavy trucks or trains for delivery and cranes for placement. For small-scale buildings like houses or light industrial plants, the weight adds considerable cost to the project. For homes, structural steel seems like overkill. For medium-sized commercial building, framing often uses both structural and light gauge steel.

6.1.2.2 Hot Rolled Steel

Hot rolled steel is steel that has been roll-pressed at very high temperatures—over 1,700°F, which is above the re-crystallization temperature for most steels. This makes the steel easier to form, and resulting in products that are easier to work with. To process hot rolled steel, manufacturers first start with a large, rectangular length of metal, called a billet. The billet is heated and then sent for pre-processing, where it is flattened into a large roll. From there, it is kept at a high temperature and run through a series of rollers to achieve its finished dimensions. The white-hot strands of steel are pushed through the rollers at high speeds. For sheet metal, rolled steel is spun into coils and left to cool. For other forms, such as bars or plates, materials are sectioned and packaged.

Steel shrinks slightly as it cools. Since hot rolled steel is cooled after processing, there is less control over its final shape, making it less suitable for precision applications. Hot rolled steel is often used in applications where minutely specific dimensions aren't crucial. Railroad tracks and construction projects often use hot rolled steel.

Hot rolled steel can often be identified by the following characteristics:

- A scaled surface—a remnant of cooling from extreme temperatures.
- Slightly rounded edges and corners for bar and plate products (due to shrinkage and less precise finishing).
- Slight distortions, where cooling may result in slightly trapezoidal forms, as opposed to perfectly squared angles.

Hot rolled steel typically requires much less processing than cold rolled steel, which makes it a lot cheaper. Because hot rolled steel is allowed to cool at room temperature, it's essentially normalized—meaning it's free from internal stresses that can arise from quenching or work-hardening processes.

Hot rolled steel is ideal where dimensional tolerances aren't as important as overall material strength, and where surface finish isn't a key concern. Where surface finish is a concern, scaling can be removed by grinding, sand blasting, or acid-bath pickling. Once scaling has been removed, various brush or mirror finishes can also be applied. Descaled steel also offers a better surface for painting and other surface coatings.

The various sections are fabricated from white hot steel by passing it through rolling mills or other machines. This section explains the process through a flow chart followed by three most conventional processes of iron making and steel making.

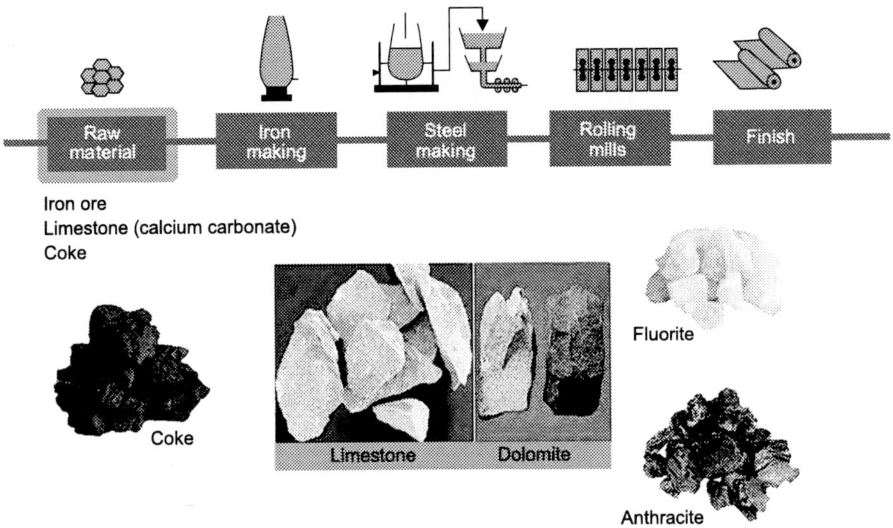

Fig. 6.1(a): Steel manufacturing process

Blast furnace for iron making: This is a vertical shaft furnace that produces liquid metals by the reaction of a flow of air introduced under pressure into the bottom of the furnace with a mixture of metallic ore, coke, and flux fed into the top. Blast furnaces are used to produce pig iron from iron ore for subsequent processing into steel, and they are also employed in processing lead, copper, and other metals. Rapid combustion is maintained by the current of air under pressure.

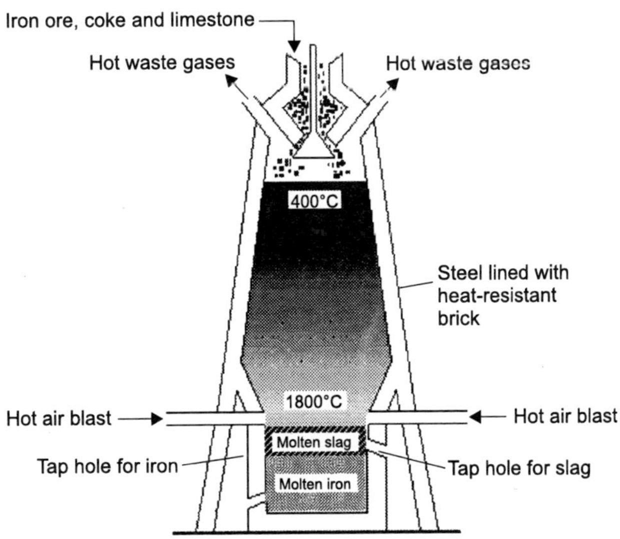

Fig. 6.1(b): Blast furnace for iron making

Electric-arc Furnace for iron making: It is a furnace that heats charged material by means of an electric arc.

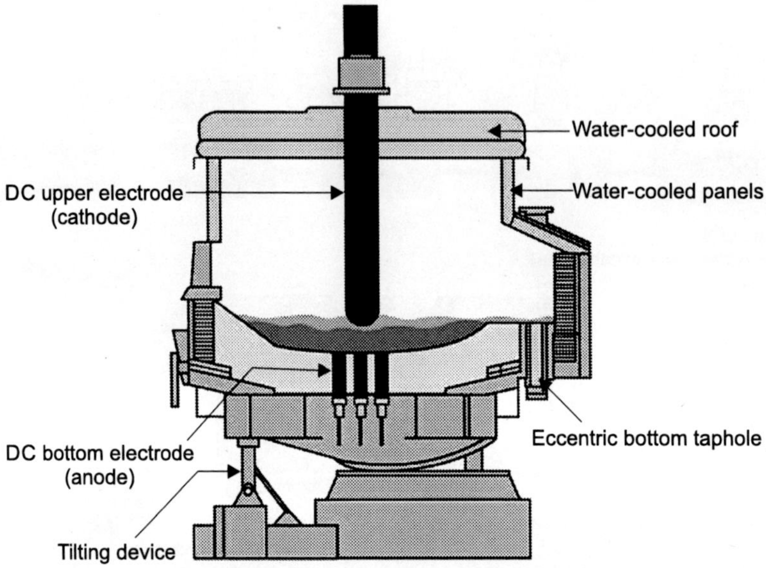

Fig. 6.1(c): Electric arc furnace for iron making

Bessemer Process for iron making : A process for the manufacture of steel from molten pig iron by oxidation of the impurities in the iron by the oxygen of air that is blown through the molten iron; the heat of oxidation raises the temperature of the mass and keeps it molten during operation. The process is carried on Bessemer converter which is made of steel and has a lining of silica and clay or of dolomite.

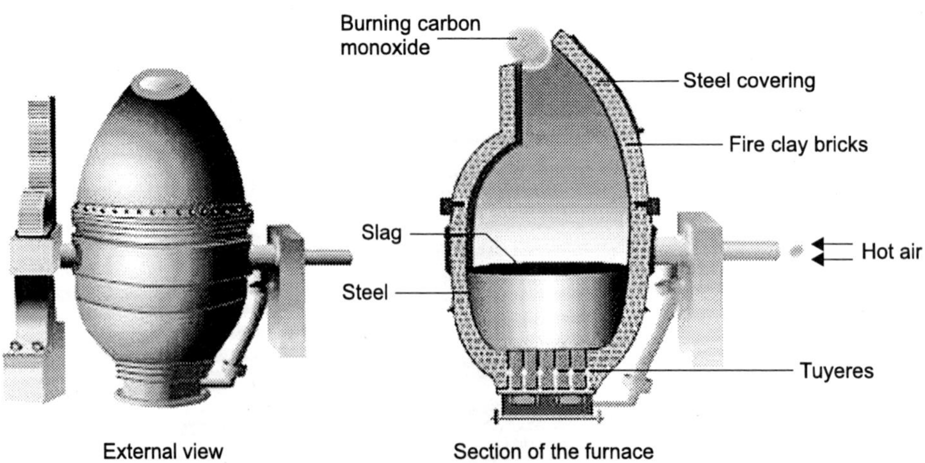

Fig. 6.1(d): Bessemer process for iron making

Electric-arc furnace for steel making : The Electric-arc Furnace employs three vertical graphite electrodes for producing arcs, striking on to the charge and heating it to the required temperature.

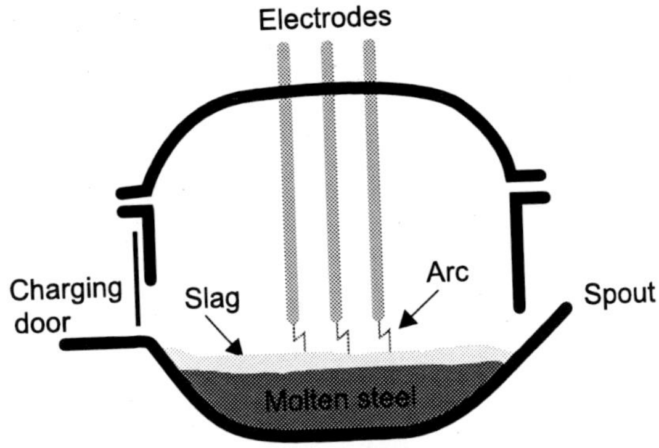

Fig. 6.1(e): Steel making through electric arc furnace

Basic oxygen steel making process: This converts the molten pig iron into steel by blowing oxygen through a lance over the molten pig iron inside the converter.

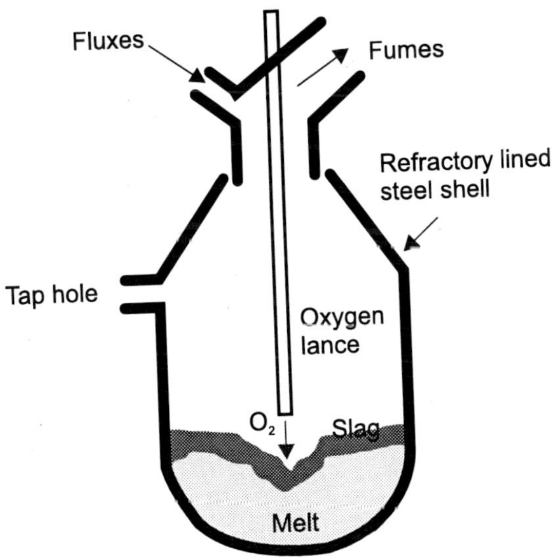

Fig. 6.1(f): Basic oxygen steel making process

A rolling mill is a complex of machines for deforming metal in rotary rolls and performing auxiliary operations such as transportation of stock to rolls, disposal after rolling, cutting, melting, piling or coiling etc., A set of rolls in their massive housing is called a 'stand'.

Fig. 6.1(g): Rolling mill

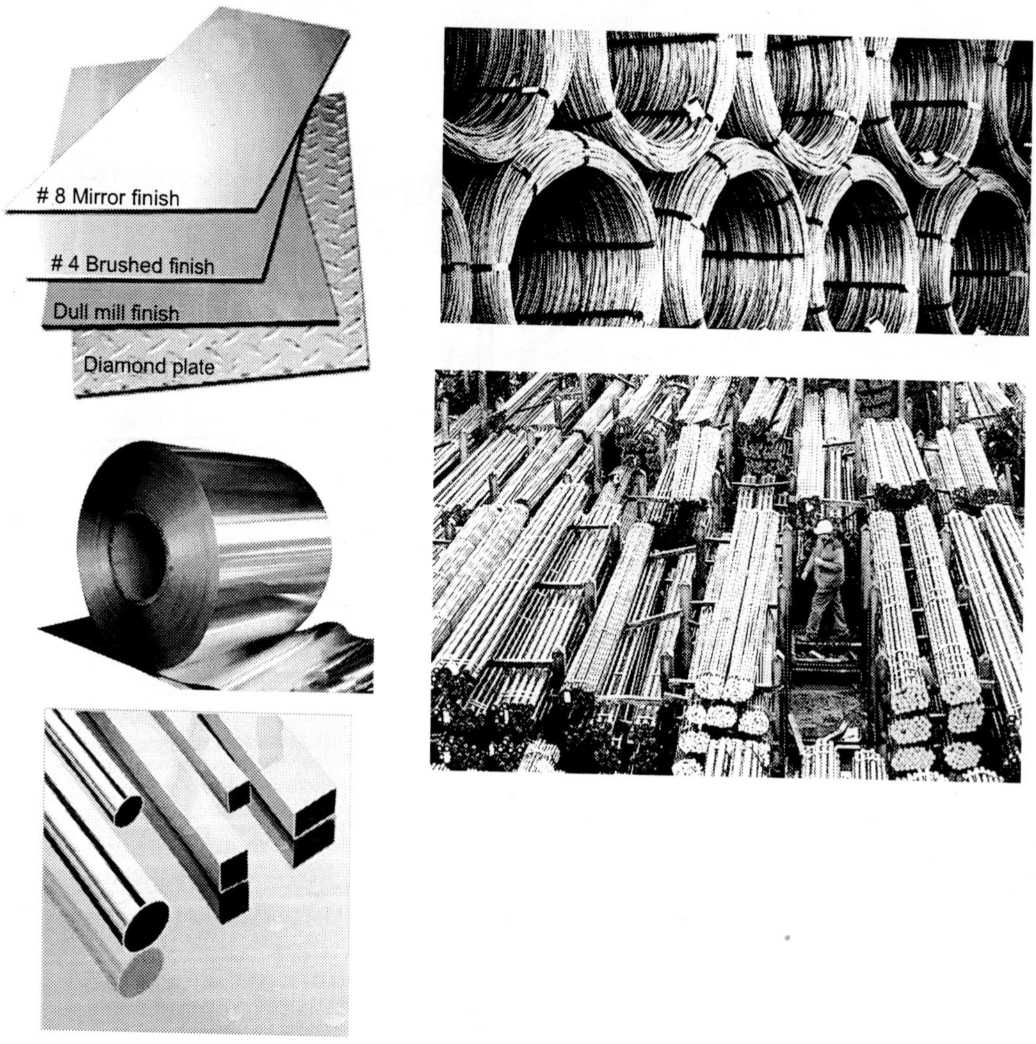

Fig. 6.1(h): Types of finishes

6.1.2.3 Cold-Formed Steel

Cold-formed steel (CFS) members are made from structural quality sheet steel that are formed into C-sections and other shapes by roll forming the steel through a series of dies. No heat is required to form the shapes (unlike hot-rolled steel), hence the name cold-formed steel. A variety of steel thicknesses are available to meet a wide range of structural and non-structural applications. Cold formed sections are produced by bending and shaping flat steel sheets at room temperature. The final shaping process involves forming the material by either press-braking or cold roll forming. Members are generally protected against corrosion through galvanization, which provides an efficient coating against corrosion.

In cold-formed steel (CFS) frame structures the skeleton is usually sheathed with sheets (metal profiled or plan sheets, sandwich panels) or panels (wood-based panels, gypsum-based panels). Connections between sheathings and CFS profiles (sheathing fasteners) are generally made of self-piercing screws.

CFS structural systems for housing may be divided in the following types: stick-built (one-dimensional), panel or panelized (two-dimensional), volumetric or modular (three-dimensional), semi-volumetric or hybrid, for which the main distinguishing factor is the degree of prefabrication.

The use of cold formed steel (CFS) in the residential market has increased over the past several years due to its price stability, consistent quality and similarity to conventional framing. Cold-formed steel solutions offer versatility in construction because of their inherent high strength-to-weight ratio, non combustibility and increasingly developing market.

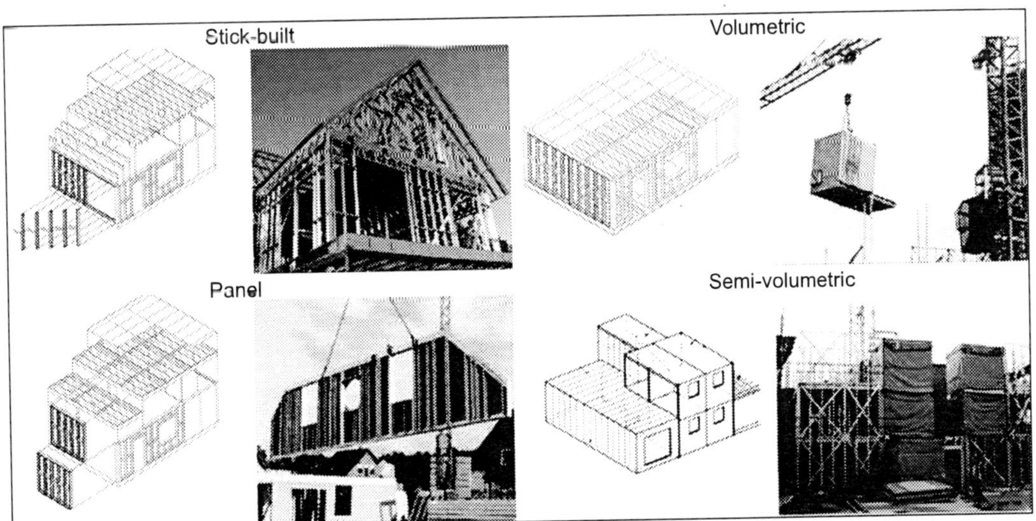

Fig. 6.2 (a): Structural systems in CFS

6.1.2.4 General Description of the Stick-Built Structural System

Two principal methodologies, namely the Platforms and the Balloon system, can be considered. In the first case, the structure is built floor by floor, so as to have the possibility to use every level as a working platform for the construction of the floors above. The walls are interrupted at the floor level and the floor system transmits the loads directly to the vertical panels.

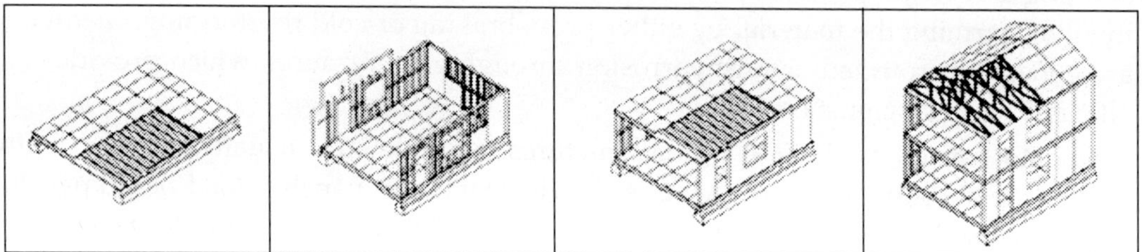

1. Construction of the foundation and of the ground floor platform	2. Assembly of the structural walls elements	3. Conclusion of the walls and construction of the first storey floor	4. Assembly of the first storey walls and of the roof

Fig. 6.2 (b): Platform system of stick built

Balloon system is characterized by continuous walls, to which the floors are connected to, without interrupting the continuity of the vertical frame elements. This kind of structural system presents a higher degree of difficulty of assembly, because of the considerable height of the walls, which typically requires the use of temporary bracings during the construction phase.

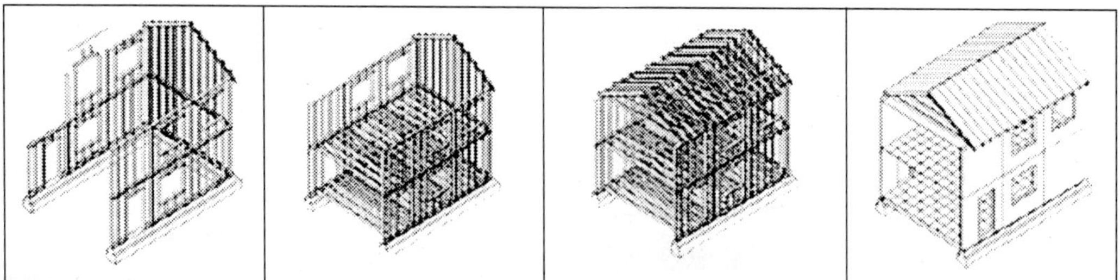

1. Construction of the foundation and of the vertical frame elements for two storeys	2. Assembly of the floors	3. Conclusion of the structure of the walls and floors and construction of the roof	4. Application of internal and external finishing

Fig. 6.2 (c): Balloon system of stick built

6.1.3 Nomenclature of various units and Technical Terms

Major terms that we come across while working with steel are different types of loads, tension, stress, safety factor, effective length etc.,

Technical term	Units
Loads	Kilo Newton's/ Esq.
Tension	Newton or kg.mtr/sec^2
Stress	Newton/ mtr^2
Safety factor	No units
Effective length	metres

6.1.3.1 Technical Terms

- **Accidental Loads:** Loads due to explosion, impact of vehicles, or other rare loads for which the structure is considered to be vulnerable as per the user.
- **Actual Length:** The length between centretocentre of intersection points, with supporting members or the cantilever length in the case of a free standing member.
- **Beam:** A member subjected predominantly to bending.
- **Bearing type connection:** A connection made using bolts in 'snug-tight' condition or rivets where the load is transferred by bearing of bolts or rivets against plate inside the bolt hole.
- **Braced member:** A member in which the relative transverse displacement is effectively prevented by bracing.
- **Buckling load:** The load at which an element, a member or a structure as a whole, either collapses in service or buckles in a load test and develops excessive lateral (out of plane) deformation or instability.
- **Buckling strength or resistance:** It is a force or moment, which a member can withstand without buckling.
- **Built-up section:** A member fabricated by interconnecting more than one element to form a compound section acting as a single member.
- **Camber:** Intentionally introduced pre-curving (usually upwards) in a system, member or any portion of a member with respect to its chord. Frequently, Camber is introduced to compensate for deflections ata specific level of loads.
- **Characteristic yield/ultimate stress:** The minimum value of stress, below which not more than a specified percentage (usually 5 percent) of corresponding stresses of samples tested are expected to occur.
- **Column:** A member in upright (vertical)position which supports a roof or floor system and predominantly subjected to compression.
- **Compact section:** A cross-section, which can develop plastic moment, but has inadequate plastic rotation capacity needed for formation of a plastic Collapse mechanism of the member or structure.
- **Corrosion:** An electrochemical process over the surface of steel, leading to oxidation of the metal.

- **Dead loads:** The self-weights of all permanent constructions and installations including thyself-weight of all walls, partitions, floors, roofs, another permanent fixtures acting on a member.
- **Dejection:** It is the deviation from the standard position of a member or structure.
- **Design life:** Time period for which a structure or a structural element is required to perform its function without damage.
- **Design load/factored load:** A load value obtained by multiplying the characteristic load with a load factor.
- **Ductility:** It is the property of the material ora structure indicating the extent to which it can deform beyond the limit of yield deformation before failure or Fracture. The ratio of ultimate to yield deformation is usually termed as ductility.
- **Earthquake loads:** The inertia forces produced in a structure due to the ground movement during an earthquake.
- **Edge distance:** Distance from the centre of a fastener hole to the nearest edge of an element measured perpendicular to the direction of load transfer.
- **Effective length:** Actual length of a member between points of effective restraint or effective restraint and free end, multiplied by a factor to take.
- Account of the end conditions in buckling strength calculations.
- **Factor of safety:** The factor by which the yield stress of the material of a member is divided to arrive at the permissible stress in the material.
- **Gauge:** The spacing between adjacent parallel lines of fasteners, transverse to the direction of load/ stress.
- **Gusset plate:** The plate to which the members intersecting at a joint are connected.
- **Imposed (live) load:** The load assumed to be produced by the intended use or occupancy including distributed, concentrated, impact, vibration and snow loads but excluding, wind, earthquake and temperature loads.
- **Limit state:** Any limiting condition beyond which the structure ceases to fulfil its intended function.
- **Main member:** A structural member, which is primarily responsible for carrying and distributing the applied load or action.
- **Normal stress:** Stress component acting normal to the face, plane or section.
- **Partial safety factor:** The factor normally greater than unity by which either the loads (actions) are multiplied or the resistances are divided to obtain the design values.
- **Period of structural adequacy under fire:** The time (t), in minutes, for the member to reach the limit state of structural inadequacy in a standard fire Test.
- **Permissible stress:** When a structure is being designed by the working stress method, the maximum stress that is permitted to be experienced in elements, Members or structures under the nominal/service load.

- **Pitch:** The centre-to-centre distance between individual fasteners in a line, in the direction of load/ stress.
- **Poisson's ratio:** It is the absolute value of the ratio of lateral strain to longitudinal strain under uni-axial loading.
- **Purloins:** Purloins are beams of light sections spanning between trusses carrying dead load of roof, live load and wind load.

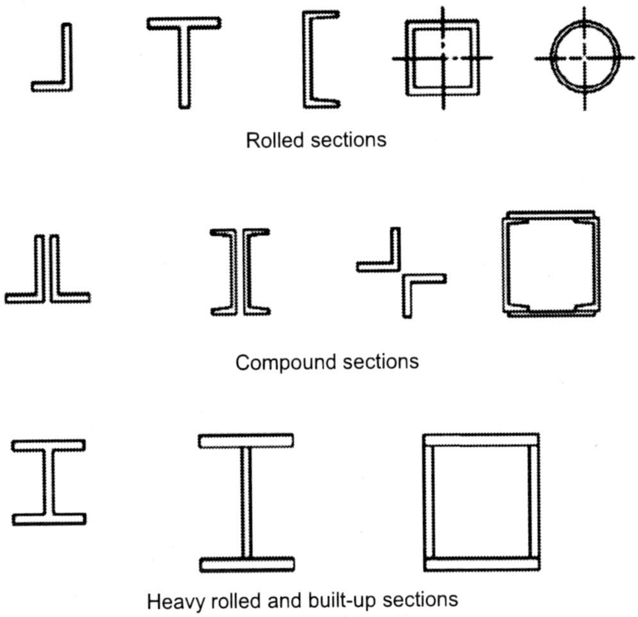

Fig. 6.3: Steel sections

- **Roof truss:** A roof truss consists essentially of the following components:
  - **Upper chord/rafter:** The upper most line of members which extend from one support to the other through the apex.
  - **Bottom chord/rafter:** Consists of the lower most line of members extending from one support to the other.
  - **Web members:** The top and the bottom chord members are connected by vertical or diagonal members called web members.
- **Secondary member:** Member which is provided for overall stability and or for restraining the main members from buckling or similar modes of failure.
- **Shear force:** The in-plane force at any transverse cross section of a straight member of a column or beam.
- **Shear Stress:** The stress component acting parallel to a face, plane or cross section.
- **Slender section:** Cross section in which the elements buckle locally before reaching the yield moment.

- **Slenderness ratio:** The ratio of the effective length of a member to the radius of gyration of the cross section about the axis under consideration.
- **Steel girders:** Girders are collector steel beams, they are the main horizontal supports of a structure which support the smaller beams.
- **Strain:** Deformation per unit length or unit angle.
- **Stress:** The internal force per unit area of the original cross section.

The relationship between the **stress and strain** that a particular type of steel displays is known as that steel's stress-strain curve.

A **stress-strain curve** typical of structural steel contains

1. Ultimate strength
2. Yield strength
3. Rupture
4. Strain hardening region
5. Necking region

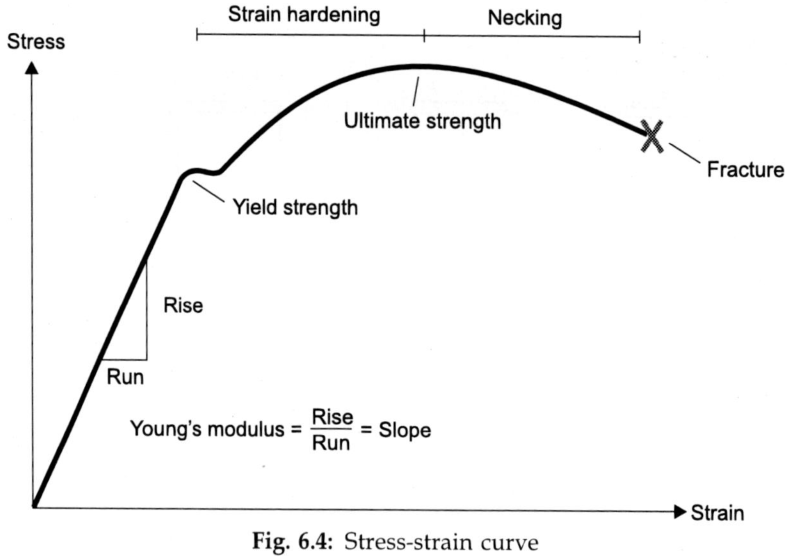

Fig. 6.4: Stress-strain curve

- **Tensile stress:** The characteristic stress corresponding to rupture in tension, specified for the grade of steel in the appropriate Indian Standards.
- **Transverse:** Direction along the stronger axes of the cross section of the member.
- **Ultimate limit state:** The state which, if exceeded can cause collapse of a part or the whole of the structure.
- **Wind loads:** Load experienced by a member or structure due to wind pressure acting on the surfaces.
- **Yield stress:** The characteristic stress of the material in tension before the elastic limit of the material exceeds, as specified in the appropriate.

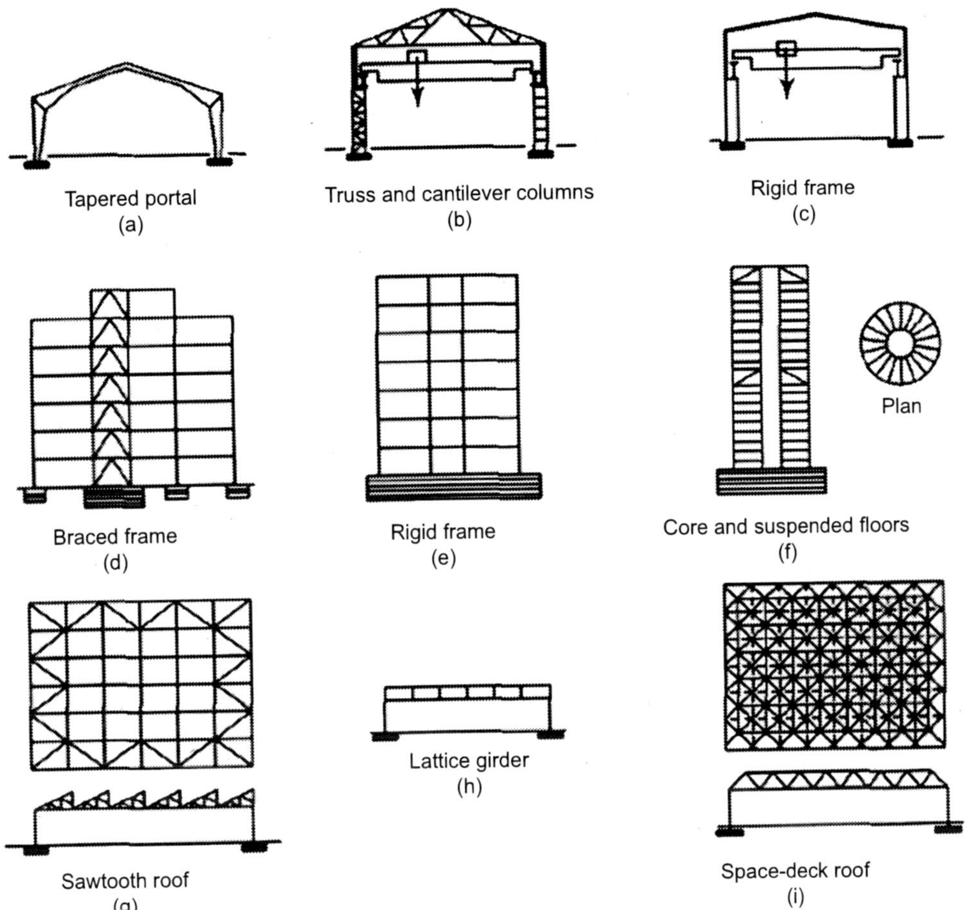

Fig. 6.5: Types of steel construction

6.1.4 History of Steel

Though iron has been in use for centuries, its usage in construction is more modern. It began around the Industrial Revolution, which was characterized by mass production and the development of new materials, including steel which is one of the great inventions in architecture.In late 1800 steel was limited to bonding masonry, tension members, doors and windows, decoration, etc.The use of innovative process of smelting by Abraham Darby III made it possible to construct the first iron bridge in Shropshire, England in 1781. The First usage of steel in structural members was during 1792.In 1852 invention of Otis by Elisha made it possible to construct the multi storeyed buildings.

In the mid-19th century, with the invention of conversion of the iron to steel, mild steel began to compete with the wrought-iron and cast-iron as a structural material. For many years steel was allowed to take stress of 78N/mm^2 which is same as of wrought iron, which made the use of steel unviable. Later on, in 1897, steel was allowed to take the stress of 125N/mm^2, which encouraged more diverse use of steel. The monumental, long span structures of Paris Exposition in 1855, 1867, 1878 & 1889 were possible by the use of steel. The 'Eiffel Tower' stood as symbol of celebration of steel usage in the 1889 exposition.With movements like Art Nouveau steel was also used as articulation element besides its structural usage.

The first structural steel frame building to be erected was Ritz hotel in London in 1904 in which the entire weight of the masonry walls, floors and roofs were carried by the steel frame. Until World War II, all tall buildings were made of steel frame structures after which the shortage of steel encouraged the construction of reinforced concrete frames.

Since 1980 due to considerable overproduction of steel the cost of steel became low, encouraging steel frame construction again. Though the use of steel was restricted to military shelter and storage building prior to World War II, but in the later half of the 20th century, steel became more versatile.

The following figures illustrate some of the world's most impressive steel buildings. At the end of 20thcentury, advanced steel production enabled railroad construction across theworld, expanding new frontiers in remote locations.

Brooklyn Bridge (1883)

Home Insurance Building (1885)

Eiffel Tower (1889)

Woolworth Building (1912)

Chrysler Building (1930)

Empire State Building (1931)

U.S. Steel Tower (1971)

Willis Tower (1973)

30 St Mary Axe, London (2003)

Burj Khalifa, Dubai (2009)

Fig. 6.6 (a): Historical evolution of famous steel buildings of the world

6.1.4.1 Use of Steel in India

The Ïron Pillar" which was built during the Ashokan Period is an excellent example of use of metal in construction. The cast iron monumental pillar is considered to be technological marvel due to its resistance to corrosion.

Though India had long legacy of metallurgical science but due to lack of technological advancements in other areas, use of steel remained limited to only arms and ammunitions. Restrictions on mining and fire arms production gradually resulted in loss of knowledge.

Steel was re-introduced in India by British rulers through various machineries, railways, transport vehicles and bridges. However due to abundant natural resources in the country steel was rarely adopted as building material.

Fig. 6.6(b): Iron Pillar, Delhi

Fig. 6.6(c): First passenger train in India

6.1.5 Uses of Structural Steel

6.1.5.1 Steel in Infrastructure

It is used for a myriad of project like:

- Transport networks: steel is required for bridges, tunnels, rail track and in constructing buildings such as fueling stations, train stations, ports and airports.

Fig. 6.7: Use of steel in infrastructure

About 60% of steel use in this application is as rebar and the rest is sections, plates and rail track.

- Utilities (fuel, water, power): over 50% of the steel used for this application is in underground pipelines to distribute water to and from housing, and to distribute gas. The rest is mainly rebar for power stations and pumping houses.

6.1.5.2 Steel in Buildings

Steel is extensively used in construction of modern architecture from skyscrapers and airports to residential homes and parks. Steel is well capable of handling high level stress both in tension compression which makes it possible to construct taller buildings. Being pre-engineered and uniform manufacturing, the quality of final output is good. Also, the dead load of steel is very less than that of concrete which creates smaller stress on foundation and saves costs. Standardised productsmade of steel speed up the process of construction. The most common applications of steel in buildings are listed below:

Structural sections: These provide a strong, stiff frame for the building and make up 25% of the steel use in buildings.

Reinforcing bars: These add tensile strength and stiffness to concrete and make up 44% of steel use in buildings. Steel is used because it binds well to concrete, has a similar thermal expansion coefficient and is strong and relatively cost-effective. Reinforced concrete is also used to provide deep foundations and basements and is currently the world's primary building material.

Sheet products: 31% is in sheet products such as roofing, purlins, internal walls, ceilings, cladding, and insulating panels for exterior walls.

Fig. 6.8: Nagakin Capsule Tower, Japan

Non-structural steel: Steel is also found in many non-structural applications in buildings, such as heating and cooling equipment and interior ducting. Internal fixtures and fittings such as rails, shelving and stairs are also made of steel.

Prefabricated modular structures: In these type of structures typical units are prefabricated and attached with central component. This type of construction is majorly used for temporary structures or structure that require quick change in spatial arrangement.

The steel frame capsules (designed to be replaceable, removable, and transportable) are prefabricated in specialist factories and assembled at a plant before being delivered to the site.

Each one was lifted by mechanical cranes and are attached to the tower shafts using 4 high-tension bolts.

6.1.6 Advantages and Limitations

Following are some of the advantages and disadvantages of steel:

6.1.6.1 Advantages

High strength/weight ratio: Steel has a high strength/weight ratio. Thus, the dead weight of steel structures is relatively small. This property makes steel a very attractive structural material for

- High-rise buildings
- Long-span bridges
- Structures located on soft ground
- Structures located in highly seismic areas where forces acting on the structure due to an earthquake are in general proportional to the weight of the structure.

Ductility: Steel can undergo large plastic deformation before failure, thus providing large reserve strength. This property is referred to as ductility. Properly designed steel structures can have high ductility, which is an important characteristic for resisting shock loading such as blasts or earthquakes. A ductile structure has energy absorbing capacity and will not incur sudden failure. It usually shows large visible deflections before failure or collapse.

Predictable material properties: Properties of steel can be predicted with a high degree of certainty. Steel in fact shows elastic behaviour up to a relatively high and usually well-defined stress level. Also, in contrast to reinforced concrete, steel properties do not change considerably with time.

Speed of erection: Steel structures can be erected quite rapidly. This normally results in quicker economic payoff.

Quality of construction: Steel structures can be built with high-quality workmanship and narrow tolerances.

Ease of repair: Steel structures in general can be repaired quickly and easily.

Adaptation of prefabrication: Steel is highly suitable for prefabrication and mass production.

Repetitive use: Steel can be reused after a structure is disassembled.
Expanding existing structures: Steel buildings can be easily expanded by adding new bays or wings. Steel bridges may be widened.
Fatigue strength: Steel structures have relatively good fatigue strength.

6.1.6.2 Limitations

General cost: Steel structures may be more costly than other types of structures.These are generally heavy and thus expensive to transport
Fireproofing: The strength of steel is reduced substantially when heated at temperatures commonly observed in building fires. Also, steel conducts and transmits heat from a burning portion of the building quite fast. Consequently, steel frames in buildings must have adequate fireproofing.
Maintenance: Steel structures exposed to air and water, such as bridges, are susceptible to corrosion and should be painted regularly. Application of weathering and corrosion-resistant steels may eliminate this problem.
Susceptibility to buckling: Due to high strength/weight ratio, steel compression members are in general more slender and consequently more susceptible to buckling than, say, reinforced concrete compression members. As a result, considerable materials may have to be used just to improve the buckling resistance of slender steel compression members.
Others

- Steel cannot be mold in any direction but it can only be used in forms in which sections originally exists.
- Has a high expansion rate in changing temperatures.
- Production of steel is energy intensive.

6.1.7 Steel Failure

Beams are structural elements that are subjected to bending forces. When bending occurs, the beam is subjected to tension and compression simultaneously.

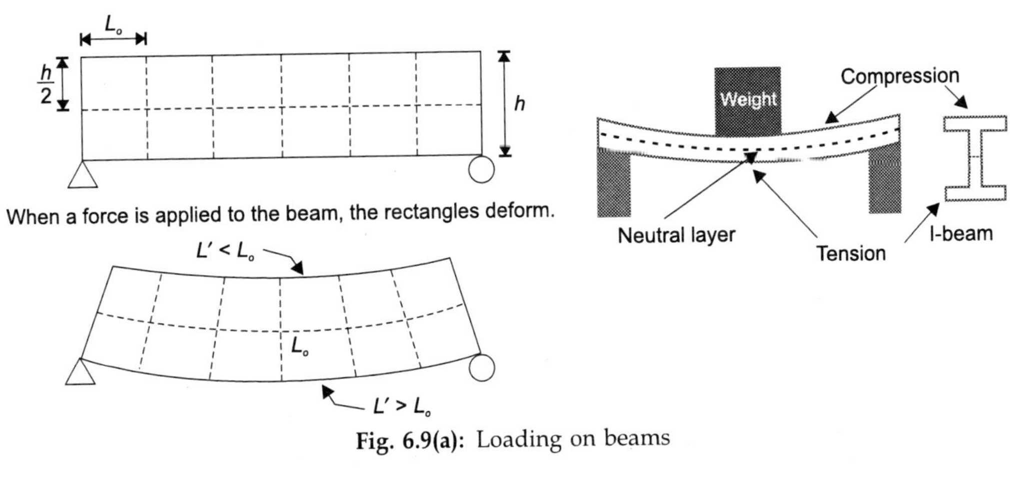

Fig. 6.9(a): Loading on beams

Columns are subjected to axial forces. When axial forces occurs, the steel column is subjected to compression and experiences strain i.e. reduction in length of column. Buckling of Columns is a form of **deformation** as a result of axial- compression forces.

This leads to **bending** of the column, due to the instability of the column.

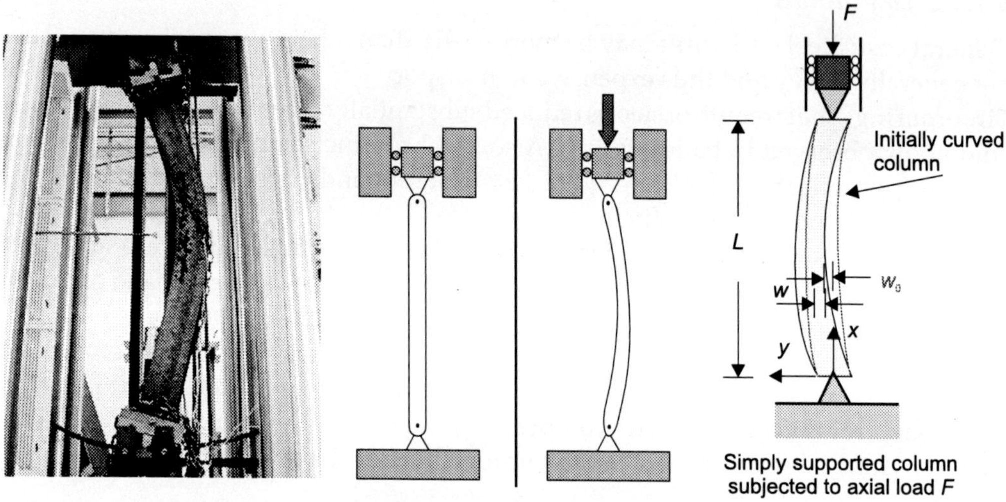

Fig. 6.9(b): Buckling of columns

Crippling is just like buckling, but it happens locally in the web of a beam when it is being **compressed**.

It often occurs at the **supports** of a beam, where the bottom flange is resting on a support, and the top flange is holding up the load.

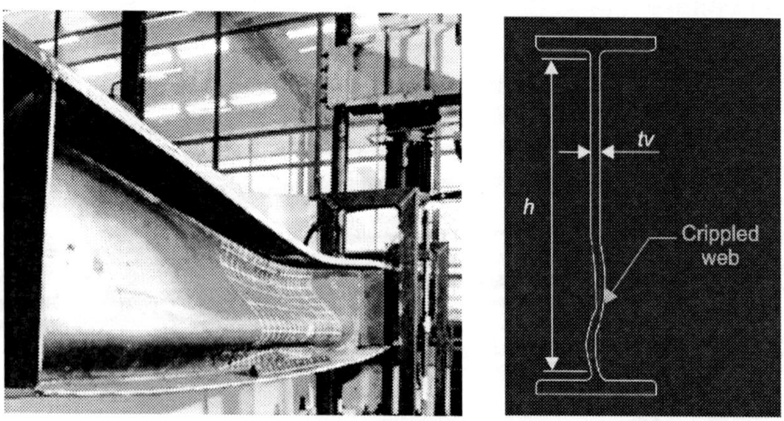

Fig. 6.9(c): Crippling

Torsion is the twisting of a steel section due to an applied torque.

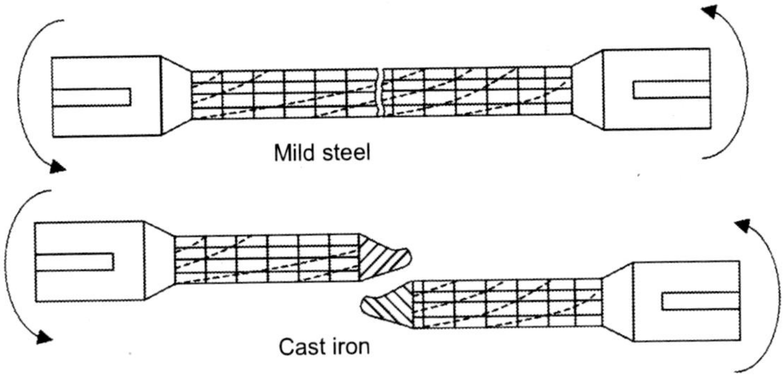

Fig. 6.9(d): Torsion

6.1.7.1 Detection of Faults in Steel Bars Using Ultrasonic Techniques

This type of testing utilizes high-frequency sound waves that are transmitted throughout the material being tested in order to conduct a thorough inspection. Ultrasonic inspection can be used to detect surface flaws, such as cracks, seams, and internal flaws such as voids or inclusions of foreign material. It's also used to measure wall thickness in tubes and diameters of bars.Depending on the test requirements, these waves can be highly directional and focused on a small spot or thin line, or limited to a very short duration.Two methods of UT are used for flaw detection –Shear and Compression Wave.

- **Shear method** uses an angled beam that is usually 45° for surface and subsurface testing. Surface cracks, seams and near surface inclusions can be detected with this method.
- **Compression method,** is also known as normal incidence. This is the primary internal inspection for bar testing. The transducer is set to exactly enter the bar surface perpendicular to the surface. This inspection method is limited to the entire bar volume except approximately a 3mm thick outer shell

6.1.8 Specialized Applications of Steel

The development of construction methods in iron and steel was the most important innovation in architecture since ancient times which helped to create stronger and taller structures at comparatively lower cost than stone, brick, or wood. Greater unsupported spans and openings became feasible.

In architecture before 1800, metals played an auxiliary role being used for bonding masonry (dowels and clamps), as tension members (chains strengthening domes, tie rods across arches to reinforce the vaults), and for roofing, doors, windows, and decoration. Cast iron, the first metal that could be substituted for traditional structural materials, was used in bridge building as early as 1779. Its ability to bear loads and to be produced in an endless variety of forms, in addition to its resistance to fire and corrosion, quickly encouraged architectural adaptations, first as columns and arches and afterward in skeletal structures.

Since cast iron has much more compressive than tensile strength (for example, it works better as a small column than as a beam), it was largely replaced in the late 19th century by steel, which is more uniformly strong, elastic, and workable, and its high resistance in all stresses can be closely calculated.

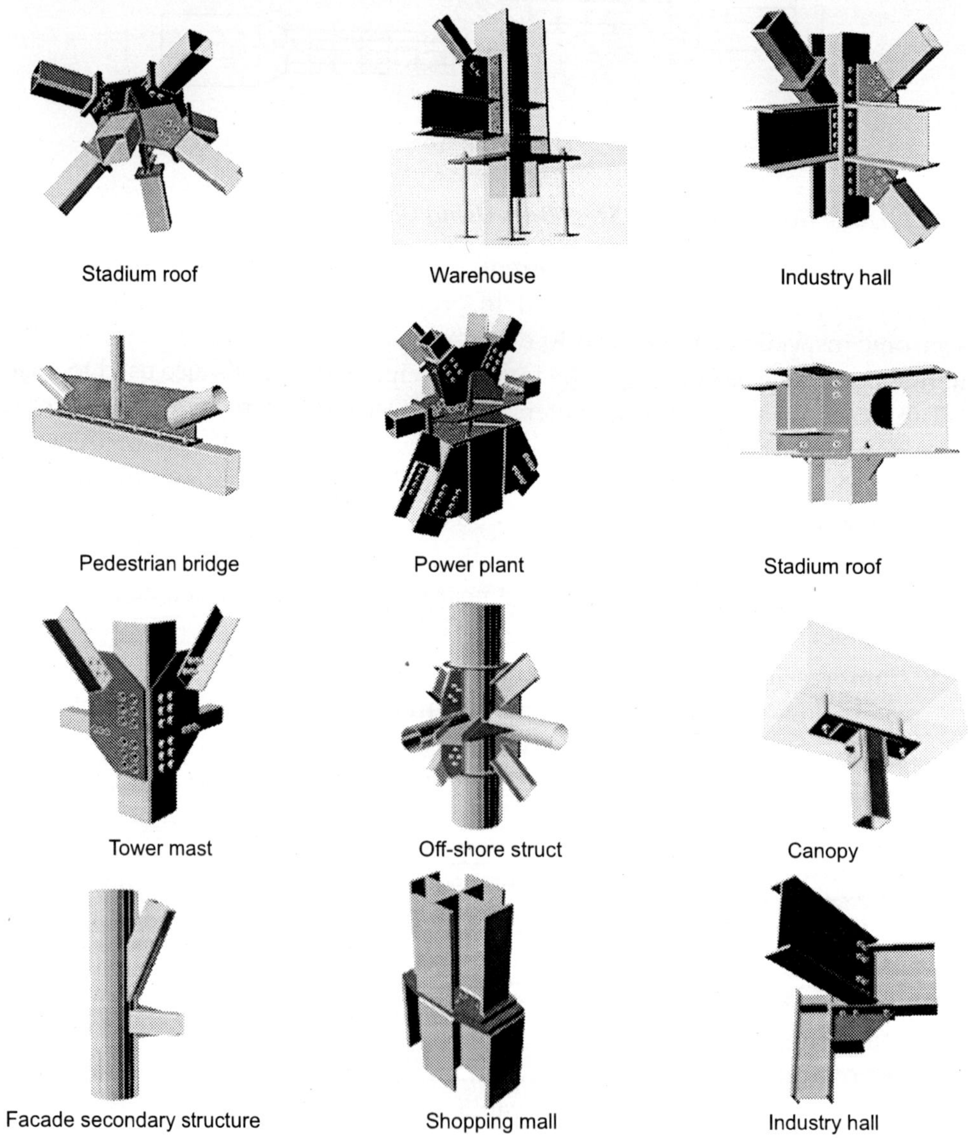

Fig. 6.10(a): Type of joining details for steel structural members

Steel structural members are rolled in a variety of shapes, the commonest of which are plates, angles, I beams, and U-shaped channels. These members may be joined by steel bolts or rivets, and the development of welding in the 20th century made it possible to produce fused joints with less labor and materials. The result is a rigid, continuous structure in which the joint is as firm as the member and which distributes stresses between beams and columns. Normally, steel needs to be protected against corrosion by surface coverings, but alloys such as stainless steel have been developed for exposed surfaces. Aluminum and other light metal alloys are favored for exterior construction because of their weather resistance.

The primary method of attachment of these two members is a simple lap joint. The plate that attaches to the inclined member on the right is connected using a simple fillet weld.

This is a flange-plated moment connection to the column. As such, it is transferring shear through the 5-bolt shear tab and the flange plates transfer the design moment.

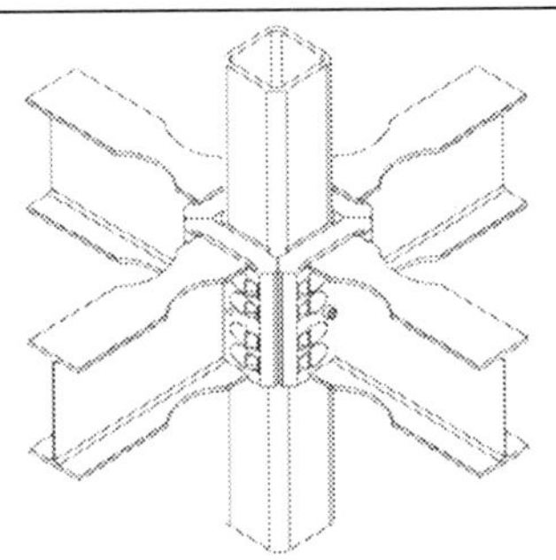

The Simmons Moment Resisting Space Frame connection is integral to the ConXtech strucutral framing system. (US patent No. 6,837,016. Other patents pending.)

Fig. 6.10(b): Type of joining details for steel structural members

Steel special moment frames (SMFs) with supplementary Viscous Damping Devices (VDDs) improve seismic resilience and reduce construction costs. The VDD dampens the motion of the SMF during an earthquake like the shocks on a car traveling down a bumpy road. The reduction in the response of the SMF yields a significant reduction in both the steel tonnage of the SMF and the foundation materials. Installation is simple, and no third-party special inspections are required. Unlike other seismic products, fluid viscous dampers do not need to be replaced after a major seismic event.

Composite floor system is an efficient and environmentally friendly steel floor system using open-web steel joists and steel deck with a concrete topping slab. The integral component of this system is the screw, which bonds the concrete slab to the top chord of the steel joist. The screw is a self-drilling, self-tapping fastener that is attached with a tool (provided). Since it also serves as the deck attachment, no additional welding is required. The system is custom-designed to the requirements of each project. A typical floor with exceptional strength and serviceability will include spans up to 60 ft., with joists spaced at 4 ft. to 6 ft. on centre. Being a composite floor system, the maximum span-to-depth ratio of the bare joist is L/30, allowing a shallower floor-to-floor height than traditional floor systems.

Structural thermal break plates are high-performance thermal insulators used between horizontal and vertical connections of internal and external structural elements to prevent thermal bridging. The plates provide simple, economical, and extremely effective thermally and structurally efficient connections to achieve the highest LEED certification levels by reducing heat loss and the risk of internal condensation. STBs are available in three grades of low-thermal conductivity, high-compressive strength material. Unlike proprietary mechanical thermal break systems, STBs are simple to incorporate into most details. This flexibility means that they can be used for an infinite variety of steel-to-steel, steel-to-concrete, steel-to-timber, and concrete-to-concrete applications, including balcony, canopy, parapet, masonry shelf angle, cladding, and external staircase connections.

Composite structural steel framing that replaces common reinforced concrete core construction. The steel plate composite wall system leverages the speed and accuracy of steel and the stiffness of concrete. The system removes the need for reinforcement placed onsite and the additional time for concrete curing that typically sets the pace for building construction. Embeds are no longer a field-measured installation, reducing onsite coordination.

6.1.9 Steel Technology Centre, IIT Kharagpur

The vision of this centre is to come up as an international interdisciplinary sustainable research centre primarily catering to the needs of steel industries, along with a strong base of fundamental research on steel allied areas, using sustainable method.

6.1.9.1 Thrust Areas of Research

- Monitoring and controlling of processes
- Utilization of low-grade ores
- Light-weight material designs foe different sectors like automotive, ship etc. (with formability, joining, & hybridization)
- Energy and emissions
- Application (surface modification, bio-compatible steel, modelling, ultrafast cooling, laser based processing)

6.1.9.2 Facilities Available

Hot rolling mill : Utilized in shaping of the metal objects between rotating rolls when temperature of the metal is kept above its re-crystallization temperature

Ultrafast cooling unit: Utilized in rapid cooling of steel

Benefits :

- less force
- greater degree of deformation
- improved structure & properties of metal
- no hardening

Benefits :

- Better mechanical properties
- Multi-phase microstructure

Forging press: Utilized in shaping of a metal by application of pressure exerted by two dies.

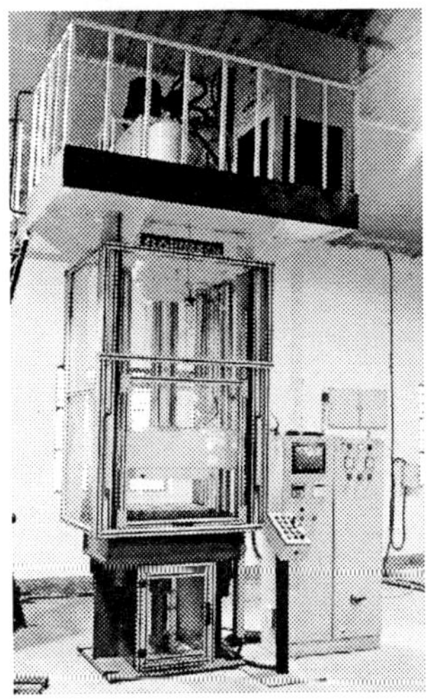

High temperature vacuum furnace

Utilized in carrying out processes such as annealing, brazing, sintering and other het treatment with high consistency and low contamination.

Benefits:

- The absence of air and other gases prevents oxidation,
- Heat loss from the product due to convection

Mechanical Testing Facilities

UTM: Utilized in determining the tensile strength and compressive strength of materials

Hardness tester: Utilized in determining the hardness of a material.

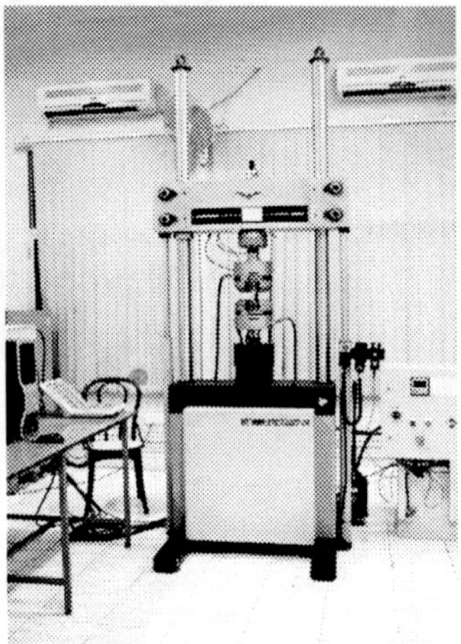

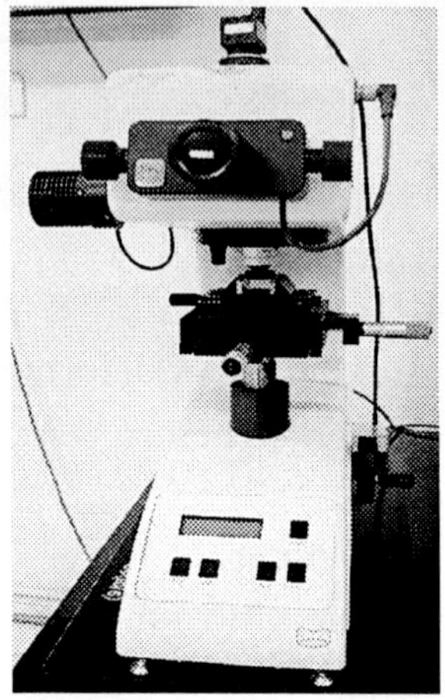

Sample Preparation and Microscopy

Abrasive cutter

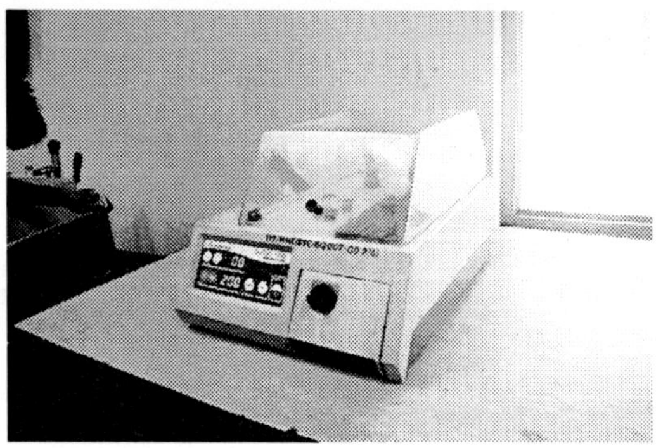

Precision diamond cutter

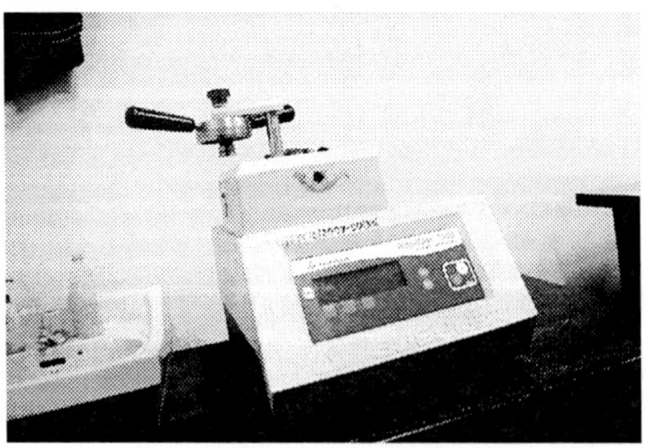

Hot mounting press

Polishing

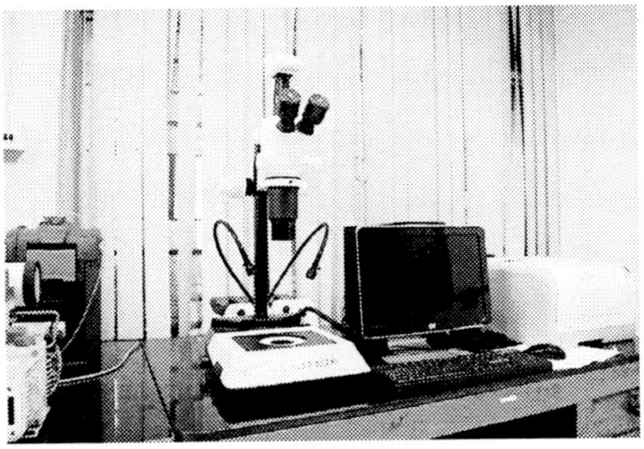

Optical macroscope

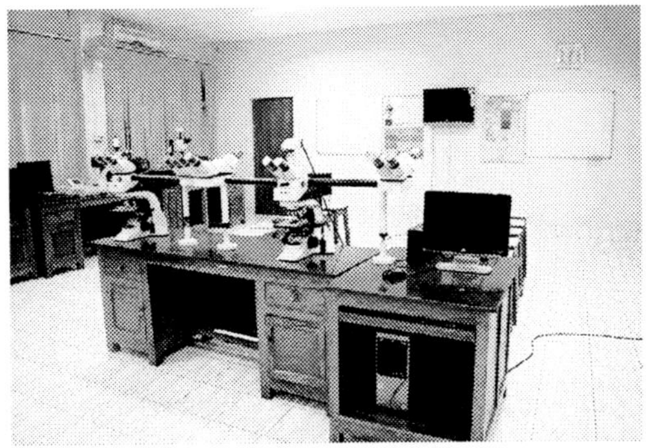

Optical microscope

Optical microscope with low magnification

Workshop

Lathe

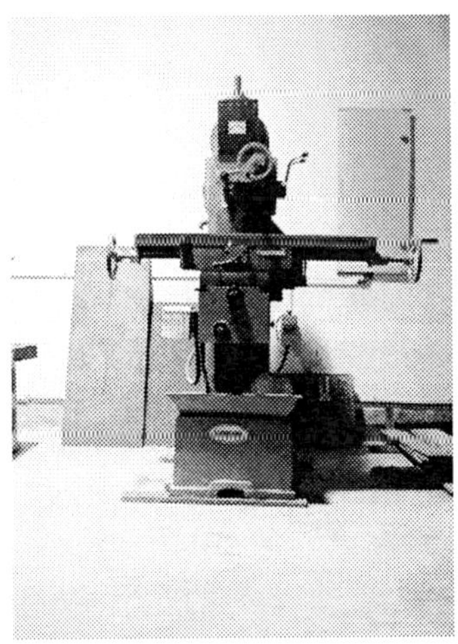

Vertical milling

Band saw

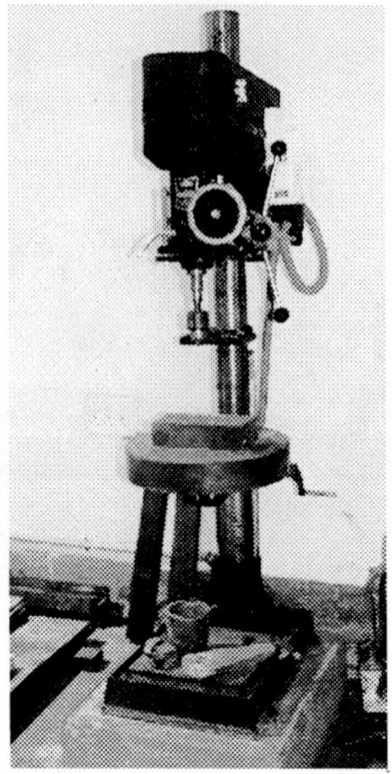

Drilling

Wheel grinding

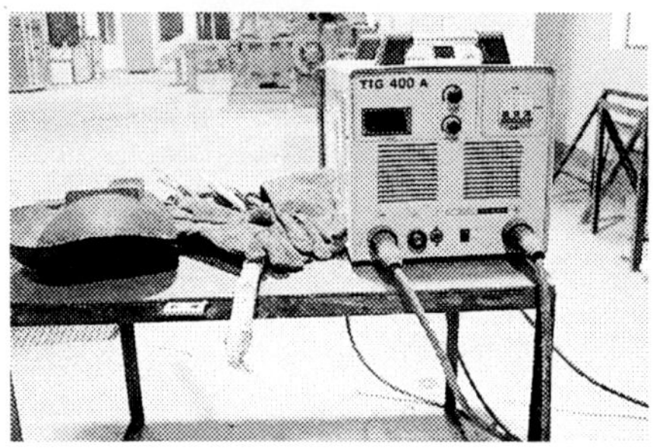

TIG welder

Fig. 6.11: Steel Technology Centre, IIT Kharagpur

6.1.10 Applications of Steel in Residential Sector

The advantages that steel offers to the construction sector have long been recognized by designers and specifiers. The versatility of steel gives architects the freedom to achieve their most ambitious visions. Building owners value the flexibility of steel buildings, and the value benefits they provide, such as the light, open, airy spaces that can be created, making it ideal for modernization, reconfiguring, extending or adapting with minimal disruption, and without costly and sometimes harmful demolition and redevelopment. Even without these benefits, steel is often the first choice just on the basis of cost . Following are the reasons to use steel in residential construction:

Strength, beauty, and design freedom: Steel offers architects more design freedom in colour, texture and shape. Its combination of strength, durability, beauty, precision and malleability gives architects broader parameters to explore ideas and develop fresh solutions. Steel's long spanning ability gives rise to large open spaces, free of intermediate columns or load bearing walls. Its capacity to bend to a certain radius, creating segmented curves or free-form combinations for facades, arches or domes sets it apart. Factory-finished to the most exacting specifications under highly controlled conditions, steel's final outcome is more predictable and repeatable, eliminating the risk of on-site variability.

Fast, efficient, resourceful: Steel can be assembled quickly and efficiently in all seasons. Components are pre-manufactured off site with minimal on-site labour. A whole frame can be erected in a matter of days rather than weeks, with a corresponding 20% to 40% reduction in construction time relative to on-site construction, depending on a project's scale. For single dwellings, on more challenging sites, steel often allows less points of contact with the earth, reducing the amount of excavation required. Structural steel's lighter weight relative to other framing materials such as concrete enables a smaller, simpler foundation. These efficiencies in execution translate to considerable resource efficiencies and economic benefits, including accelerated project schedules, reduced site management costs and an earlier return on investment.

Adaptable and accessible: These days, a building's function can change dramatically and rapidly. A tenant may want to make changes that increase floor loads significantly. Walls may need to be repositioned to create new interior layouts based on different needs and space usage. Steel-built structures can cater for such changes. Non-composite steel beams can be made composite with the existing floor slab, cover plates added to the beams for increased strength, beams and girders easily reinforced and supplemented with additional framing or even relocated to support changed loads. Steel framing and floor systems also allow easy access and alterations to existing electrical wiring, computer networking cables and communication systems.

Less columns, more open space: Steel sections provide an elegant, cost-effective method of spanning long distances. Extended steel spans can create large, open plan, column free internal spaces, with many clients now demanding column grid spacing over 15 metres. In single storey buildings, rolled beams provide clear spans of over 50 metres. Trussed or lattice construction can extend this to 150 metres. Minimising the number of columns makes it easier to subdivide and customize spaces. Steel-built buildings are often more adaptable, with greater potential for alterations to be made over time, extending the lifetime of the structure.

Endlessly recyclable: When a steel-framed building is demolished, its components can be reused or circulated into the steel industry's closed-loop recycling system for melt down and repurposing. Steel can be recycled endlessly without loss of properties. Nothing is wasted. Steel saves on the use of natural raw resources since around 30% of today's new steel is already being made from recycled steel.

Added fire resistance: Extensive testing of structural steelwork and complete steel structures has provided the industry with a thorough understanding of how steel buildings respond to fire. Advanced design and analysis techniques allow precise specification of fire protection requirements of steel-framed buildings, often resulting in significant reductions in the amount of fire protection required.

Earthquake resistance: Earthquakes are unpredictable in terms of magnitude, frequency, duration, and location. Steel is the material of choice for design because it is inherently ductile and flexible. It flexes under extreme loads rather than crushing or crumbling. Many of the beam-to-column connections in a steel building are designed principally to support gravity loads. Yet they also have a considerable capacity to resist lateral loads caused by wind and earthquakes.

Aesthetics, meet function: Steel's slender framing creates buildings with a sense of openness. Its flexibility and malleability inspire architects to pursue and achieve their aims in terms of exploring distinctive shapes and textures. These aesthetic qualities are complemented by steel's functional characteristics that include its exceptional spanning ability, dimensional stability over time, its acoustic noise dampening abilities, endless recyclability and the speed and precision in which it is manufactured and assembled onsite with minimal on-site labour.

More usable space, less material: Steel's ability to maximise space and internal width with the thinnest shell possible means thinner, smaller structural elements are achievable. Steel beam depths are around half that of timber beams, offering greater usable space, less materials and lower costs compared with other materials. Wall thicknesses can be thinner because steel's strength and excellent spanning capacity means there's no need to build solid, space-consuming brick walls. This can be particularly relevant for heavily constrained sites, where steel's space-saving properties can be the key to overcoming spatial challenges.

Lighter and less impacting on the environment: Steel structures can be significantly lighter than concrete equivalents and require less extensive foundations, reducing the environmental impact of the build. Less and lighter materials means they are easier to move around, reducing transportation and fuel use. Steel pile foundations, if required, can be extracted and recycled or reused at the end of a building's life, leaving no waste material on site. Steel is also energy efficient, as heat radiates quickly from steel roofing, creating a cooler home environment in hot climate areas. In cold climates, double steel panel walls can be well insulated to better contain the heat.

6.1.10.1 Comparison between Traditional Type and Steel Construction

This section presents a comparative analysis highlighting the advantage of use of steel in residential sector.

Social

i. Affordable houses can be constructed to address to the current shortage in the LIG and EWS groups.
ii. Can offer a quality and comfortable solution to deprived families
iii. Offers resistance to earthquakes and high winds

iv. Modules can be added on to cater for growing families

Economical

i. The cost of construction of composite steel structure is 41.28% higher when compared to RCC structure and cost of steel structure is 38.19% higher when compared to RCC structure
ii. There is a reduction in dimensions of elements in steel structure and thus it is lighter in weight than RCC structure and thus reducesfoundation cost
iii. Scrap value of concrete is almost nil, whereas steel can be used again
iv. Life span us longer
v. Insulated steel panels can reduce cost of cooling
vi. Steel is more durable

Environmental

i. On-site waste is minimized
ii. Steel scrap generated can be directly recycled
iii. Reusing or recycling of building components is possible
iv. Steel construction improve energy efficiency and thermal comfort

Time

i. Steel structure saves 18.66%, and composite structure saves 32.02% in construction time when compared with RCC, thereby providing savings in net cost.
ii. Quick to build at the site as parts are prefabricated at the factory.
iii. Ease in expansion and faster erection of the structure in case of steel.
iv. Easily transported
v. Easily assembled on site

Operation & Maintenance

i. A wide range of sections are available such as I, C, and angle sections along with joining methods such as bolting, welding, and riveting.
ii. It is easy to repair or retrofit.
iii. Skilled labour is required and time for designing connections is more as compared to RCC structures

Life cycle assessment

i. The life-cycle energy consumption of steel is found to be 75.1% as that of concrete, and the environmental emissions is half of the latter. Therefore on the life-cycle energy consumption and environmental emissions of the building materials, the steel-framed building is superior to the concrete-framed one.
ii. The average heat transfer coefficient of the envelopes of a steel-framed building is higher than that of the concrete-framed one due to the higher thermal

conductivity of steel. The life-cycle energy consumption and environmental emissions of air conditioning in-use phase of a steel-framed building are therefore larger than those of the other building type. It results in a slightly higher life-cycle energy consumption and environmental emissions of the steel-framed building. The energy consumption of the steel-framed building in the use phase will be reduced if its heat preservation can be improved.

A Comparative Study

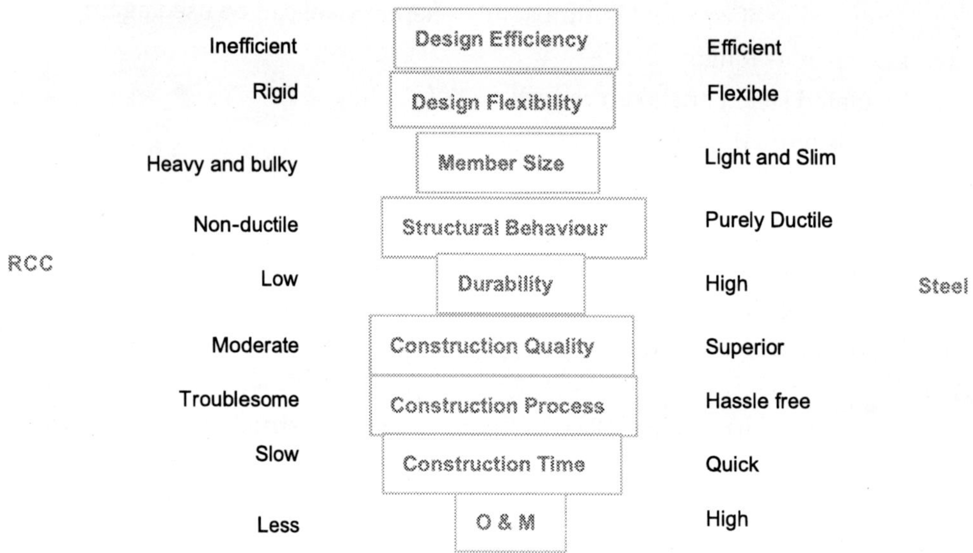

Fig. 6.12(a): Comparison of steel construction with RCC

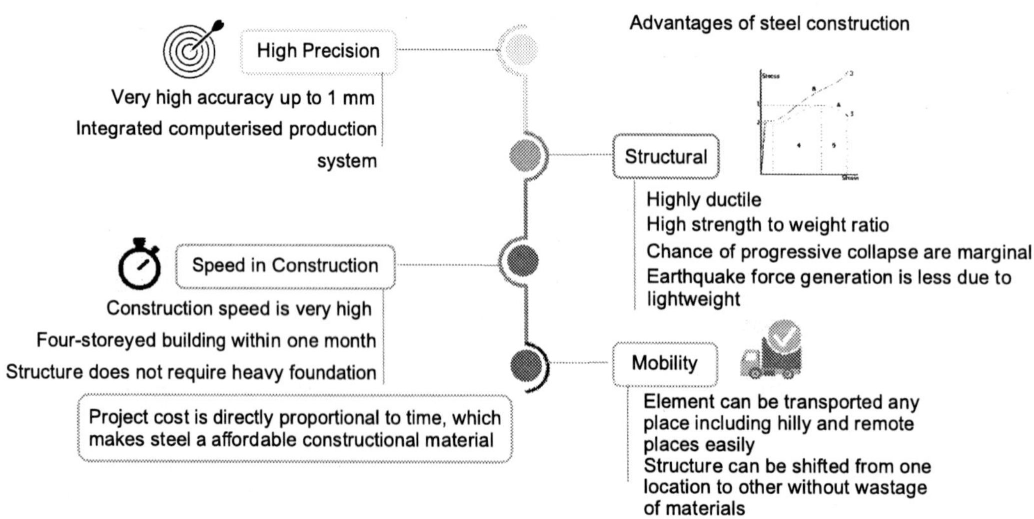

Fig. 6.12(b): Advantages of steel construction

6.1.10.2 Restello, Kolkata

The idea behind RESTELLO was to design and execute an environmentally responsible residential steel building to cater to the need of society in terms of luxury, comfort and cost and to bring customers closer to the future trends in building.

The steel 'skin' of the building comprises one perforated steel screen and a second inner skin of floor to ceiling glazing. About 90 per cent of the construction material used were manufactured at the factory end, and later assembled at site. The structure has a highly superior finish due to the steel walls. Moreover, the steel structure has allowed for long spans, creating uninterrupted living spaces. The perforated façade filters the light while providing natural ventilation.

Living Steel, a worldwide, collaborative program designed to stimulate innovative and responsible housing design and responsible housing design and construction was launched in 2005 by the World Steel Association. The program was developed to help address the unprecedented, communities and the quality of people's lives stemming from growing urban population. The members of Living Steel manufactures include Arcelor Mittal, Baosteel, BlueScope Steel, CELSA Group, Corus, Erdemir, IMIDRO, Posco, Ruukki, SeverStal and Tata Steel. Following are the unique advantages of using steel in Restello:

- The perforated steel sheets on the exterior give a unique façade, provide greater thermal comfort and reduce the need for air-conditioning. Its unique geometry with two layers of filtered light façade acts as resistance to high winds and heavy lights at the same time allowing proper ventilation and day light.

- This building also impresses in terms of utility, offering resistance to earthquakes and fires, due to its efficient designing.
- RESTELLO uses recycled steel, reducing the material used and energy intensity in the manufacturing process.
- The use of steel in Restellos construction also responds well to the demands of the local climate. Dampness is a major issue for people living in Kolkata due to the high levels of moisture content in the atmosphere. The resistance of steel to dampness and soiling is advantageous as it does not shrink or swell with time or due to humidity. This has contributed to an improved dry wall and exterior appearance.

The construction of Restello however faced the following challenges:

- The grade of concrete required was specific to the project and was not readily available
- Vendors for such a unique project were not easily found and a few had to be developed.

6.1.10.3 Innovative Architecture Application of Steel in Interior Partitions, Furniture, Fittings and Fixtures

Stainless steel is most commonly found in commercial kitchens, sterile medical facilities, and transportation hubs. It has also found its way into retail, hospitality, and residential interior designs. Stainless steel is an extremely flexible material in terms of design options. In addition to the customization and fusing of components, stainless surfaces can be highly polished. So, it is possible to get either an elegantly reflective finish or brush the steel for a soft satin finish or a standard blasted and pickled finish.

Following are some of the common application of stainless steel in residential interiors:

- Handrails and guard rails
- Elevator interior rails
- Interior glass partition framing
- Floating stair components, including structural support beams & stringers
- Display shelving
- Tables and seating
- Reflective wall and ceiling surfaces
- Exposed structural framing elements

6.1.10.4 Advantages and Effectiveness of Steel Intensive Construction for Fast Track Affordable Mass Housing

Factory Made Fast Track Modular Building System comprises prefabricated steel structure with different walling components. The advantages are:

- Minimum time usage: About 70 percent of the work is done in the factory with minimal usage of concrete, which enables system to deliver the building within a few days of work at site. The steel modules are pre-fitted with flooring, ceiling tiles, electrical and plumbing fittings.
- Structures are durable and suitable for mass housing.
- Heat preservation: Glass wool can be used as insulation and effectively avoid the phenomenon of cold bridge of the wall body. The heat preservation effect of 100mm glass wool is equivalent to 1m-thick brick wall and is good for improving indoor livability.
- Fire Resistance: By using good fire proof material, light steel system can resist fire for four hours and can effectively slow down spreading of fire which is essential for safety of residents in mass housing.

- Termite resistant: The light steel buildings can completely resist termite invasion, thus extending the life span of the house and decrease the repair cost. This is extremely essential in Indian scenario.
- Fast To Assemble: A 300m2 -building only need 10 workers for 30 days from the foundation to everything finished.
- Environmental friendly: The material used in the construction is recyclable.
- Anti-seismic: Steel structure being resistant to seismic shocks can use safety of residents.

6.1.11 Conclusion

India was the world's third-largest steel producer in 2017. The growth in the Indian steel sector has been driven by domestic availability of raw materials such as iron ore and cost-effective labor. Consequently, the steel sector has been a major contributor to India's manufacturing output. The Indian steel industry has always strived for continuous modernization and up-gradation of older plants and to attain higher energy efficiency levels. Indian steel industries are classified into three categories such as major producers, main producers and secondary producers.

6.1.11.1 Market Size

India's finished steel consumption grew at a CAGR of 5.69 per cent during FY08 - FY18 to reach 90.68 MT. India's crude steel and finished steel production increased to 102.34 MT and 104.98 MT in 2017-18, respectively.

6.1.11.2 Future

The National Steel Policy, 2017, has envisaged 300 million tonnes of production capacity by 2030. Huge scope for growth is offered by India's comparatively low per capita steel consumption and the expected rise in consumption due to increased infrastructure construction and the thriving automobile and railways sectors. The following tables summarize the national and global scenarios:

Global Scenario	Indian Scenario
Overcapacity	
• Global overcapacity >600 MT • Global production declined by ~3% in 2015 • Capacity shutdowns, job cuts and property sale offs in various countries	• National Steel Policy in place to guide rational capacity addition • Long term vision developed for growth of the steel industry • Developing a self-sustained domestic market for steel

Contd.

Demand generation

- Demand in major steel consuming countries slowed down
- Developing countries, major consumers of steel, not growing at the rates observed in the past decade
- Major steelmaking countries witnessed negative growth
- Steel facing substitution by other materials in various applications

- Make-in-India to drive manufacturing growth
- Power-for-All to drive electricity sector growth
- Smart cities to drive urbanization
- Planned investment in infrastructure to drive growth of infrastructure sector

Sustainable development

- Controlled GHG emissions
- Stringent regulations on air pollution and effluent discharge
- Reducing energy intensity in steelmaking
- Reducing use of fossil fuels for meeting energy need

- Stringent efficiency parameters specified
- Global superior energy performance partnership (GSEP)
- NEDO model projects
- UNDP-AUSAID-MOS Steel Project
- National Action Plan on Climate Change
- Committed to reducing GHG emissions

New steel products

- Need for light weight, high strength steel; driven by stringent environment norms
- New generation of transport
- Construction in earthquake-prone zones
  - Advances in defence, space and other strategic sectors
  - Changing requirements in aviation and renewable energy
  - Changing safety norms for automobiles

- Steel Research & Technology Mission of India (SRTMI) established
- Collaborations with foreign players
- Pursuing development of
  - CRGO steel sheets
  - High grade steels for automobiles
  - High strength low alloy structural grade steels
  - High strength micro-alloyed grade steels

Affordable raw material

- Volatility in market; fluctuations in iron ore and coal prices increases hedging cost
- Regulatory challenges in mine acquisitions

- Enacted MMDR Amendment Act, 2015 for increased availability of iron ore and manganese ore in the country
- Enacted Coal Mines (Special Provisions) Act, 2015 for increased availability of coal
- Increased emphasis on beneficiation and agglomeration of iron ore

Although India has been one of the biggest exporters of steel, the use of steel in Indian industry is very limited due to relatively higher cost and lack of cutting edge technology. Some other factors are poor productivity, shortage of metallurgical coal and perceived low potential utilization. These are the challenge to overcome through advanced research. The per capita steel consumption in India is at around 68 kg as against the world average of around 208 kg. The target for per capital steel consumption is 160 kg by 2030.

REFERENCES

1. Indian Standard : General Construction in Steel- Code of Practice (Third Practice) IS 800:2007
2. Rajput et al, (2013). Time and Cost Comparison of Construction of RCC, Steel and Composite Structure Building. in IUP Journal of Structural Engineering. Oct2013, Vol. 6 Issue 4, p41-59. 19p.
3. Xu Zhang, Xing Su, and Zhijia Huang, (2007). Comparison of LCA on Steel and Concrete construction office buildings - A case study. [available no-line] https://www.researchgate.net/publication/237400091

Websites:

1. http://www.bmtpc.org/
2. http://worldsteel.org
3. http://www.carbonandgraphite.org/pdf/steel_production.pdf
4. http://www.steel.org/Making-Steel/How-Its-Made/Processes/Processes-Info/The-Basic-Oxygen-Steelmaking-Process.aspx
5. https://i.ytimg.com/vi/VD5y isfVAOE/hqdefault.jpg
6. http://www.carbonandgraphite.org/pdf/steel_production.pdf
7. http://belajar-engineering.blogspot.in/2010/11/bessemer-process-bessemer-converter.html
8. http://www.marine-knowledge.com/wp-content/uploads/2011/07/aluminium-sheets-in-coils1.jpg
9. http://www.steel-insdag.org/TeachingMaterial/Chapter1.pdf
10. http://www.columbia.edu/cu/gsapp/courses/archa4125/history/history.html
11. http://www.slideshare.net/SteelBusinessBriefing/steel-construction
12. https://www.britannica.com/technology/blast-furnace

6.2 STEEL STRUCTURAL SYSTEMS- CONSTRUCTION METHODOLOGY, IMPLEMENTATION AND CASE STUDIES

6.2.1 Construction Methodology In Steel Structure

6.2.1.1 General Guidelines in Steel Structural Design

The **structural design** basis of any steel structure will depend on the type of structure and the complete process is divided into three phases: Planning, Design and Construction. The following basic information help in the process.

Site conditions:

i. Bearing capacity of the soil
ii. Maximum load capacity of the soil
iii. The foundation to be chosen for the soil
iv. Requirements of soil improvements if any
v. The water table level of the site

The Loads Acting on the Structure (refer fig. 1)

i. **Dead load:** The load due to the self -weight of the structural members forms the dead load.
ii. **Live load:** The imposed loads the structures are subjected during the occupancy period are called as live loads.
iii. **Wind load:** Wind loads act horizontally on the surface area of the building on its windward site.
iv. **Seismic load**
v. **Erection load**
vi. Secondary effects due to contraction or expansion resulting from **temperature** changes, differential settlements of the structure, eccentric connections, and rigidity of joints differing from design assumptions.

Structural design methods are selected based on the local practices. The three design methods are:

i. Working stress method
ii. Limit State Method
iii. Load Resistance Factor Design method.

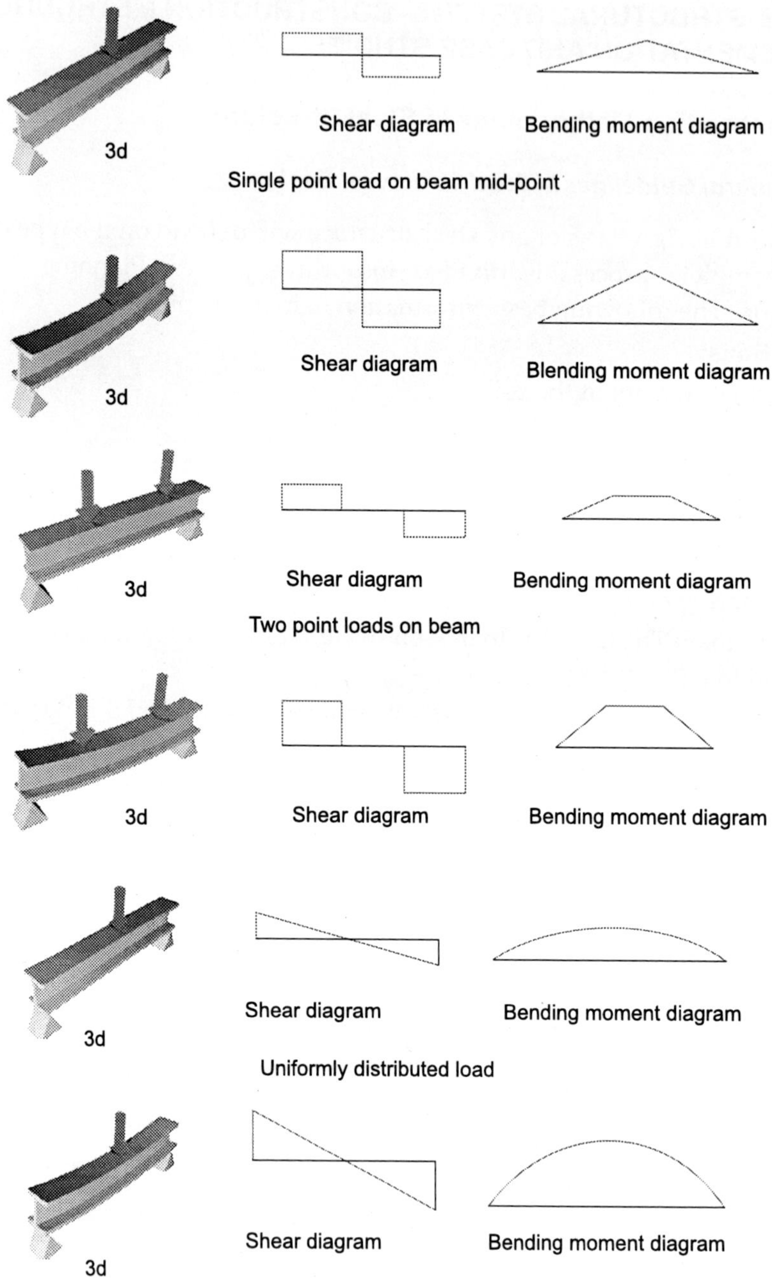

Fig. 6.1: Loading on beams

6.2.1.2 Factors to be Considered in Design of Steel Structure

i. Maximum allowable settlement of foundation/structure to be considered

ii. Vertical and lateral deflections of buildings, structures as a whole and other structural member to be considered.

iii. Sliding and overturning of buildings or structures should be checked and prevented by design.

iv. Standard detailing guidelines should be followed in the drawing.

v. All engineering and design shall comply with relevant and applicable codes of practices, local bye-laws, and rules as per Directorate of industries and factories & as listed in Project Design Basis.

vi. Environmental exposure conditions should be considered in the design and respective factors must be applied in structural member design.

vii. Types of construction materials and structural members and their properties should be used during design.

viii. Special care should be taken to provide an easy escape of occupants during emergency situations such as fire.

6.2.2 Fabrication and Erection of Steel Structure

The process of steel fabrication involves grinding, welding, cutting, bending, drilling, punching, burning or melting and other general crafting methods using various high-quality tools and CNC equipment. The entire steel fabrication process is systematic and requires utmost planning, precision, and knowledge. Steel fabricators are well aware of all the crucial steps and measures that need to be taken care of in the fabrication process. Structural steel is usually fabricated to create members like beams, trusses, hollow sections, angles and plates. These steel members must be accurately fabricated before assembling them together. All component parts of these members are fitted-up temporarily with rivets, bolts, or small amounts of welds. Various fastening methods are employed to deliver different types of finishes. Finishing is generally performed by milling, sawing or other suitable methods.

Structural steel fabrication can be carried out in shop or at the construction site. Fabrication of steel work carried out in shops is precise and of assured quality, whereas field fabrication is comparatively of inferior in quality. In India construction site fabrication is most common even in large projects due to inexpensive field labour, high cost of transportation, difficulty in the transportation of large members, higher excise duty on products from shop. The skill of personnel at site also tends to be inferior and hence the quality of finished product tends to be relatively inferior. However, shop fabrication is efficient in terms of cost, time and quality. Following steps are involved:

6.2.2.1 Surface Cleaning

Structural sections from the rolling mills may require surface cleaning to remove mill scale prior to fabrication and painting. The following techniques are adopted:

- ***Hand preparation***, such as wire brushing, does not normally conform to the requirements of modern paint or surface protection system. However in some applications manual cleaning is used and depending on the quality of the cleaned surface they are categorized into Grade St-2 and Grade St-3.
- ***Blast cleaning*** is the accepted way of carrying out surface preparation in a well-run fabrication shop. Abrasive particles are projected on to the surface of the steel at high speed by either compressed air or centrifugal impeller to remove rust and roughen the surface before applying the coating. By using shot or slag grits, both of which have an angular profile, surface oxides are removed and a rougher surface is obtained to provide an adequate key for metal spraying or special paint. Depending upon the increase in the quality of the cleaned surface, the blast cleaning is categorized into Grade - Sa2, Grade - Sa2½ and Grade Sa- 3.
- ***Flame cleaning*** is another method of surface cleaning. In this method the surface is cleaned using an oxy-acetylene torch which works on the principle of differential thermal expansion between steel and mill scale. In another method 'the steel piece is immersed in a suitable acid and the scale and rust are removed'.

6.2.2.2 Cutting and Machining

After surface preparation, the next step is cutting to and this is done by any of the following methods:

- **Shearing and cropping:** Sections can be cut to length or width by cropping or shearing using hydraulic shears. Heavy sections or long plates can be shaped and cut to length by specialist plate shears. For smaller plates and sections, machines featuring a range of shearing knives, which can accept the differing section shapes, are available.
- **Flame cutting or burning:** In this method, the steel is heated locally by a pressurised mixture of oxygen and a combustible gas such as propane, which passes through a ring of small holes in a cutting nozzle. The heat is focused on to a very narrow band and the steel melts at 1500°C when a jet of high-pressure oxygen is released through a separate hole in the centre of the nozzle to blast away the molten metal in globules. The desired cuts are obtained quickly by this process. However due to a rapid thermal cycle of heating and cooling, residual stresses and distortion are induced and hence structural sections that are fabricated using flame cutting are treated specially in the design of structural steelwork.
- **Arc plasma cutting:** In this method, the cutting energy is produced electrically by heating a gas in an electric arc produced between a tungsten electrode and the work piece. This ionises the gas, enabling it to conduct an electric current. The high-velocity plasma jet melts the metal of the work piece. The cut produced

by plasma jet is very clean and its quality can be improved by using a water injection arc plasma torch. Plasma cutting can be used on thicknesses up to about 150 mm but the process is very slow.

- **Cold sawing:** When a section cannot be cut to length by cropping or shearing, then it is normally sawn. All saws for structural applications are mechanical and feature some degree of computer control. There are three forms of mechanical saw - circular, band and hack. The circular saw has a blade rotating in a vertical plane, which can cut either downwards or upwards, though the former is more common. Band saws have less capacity; Sections greater than 600 mm × 600 mm cannot be sawn using band saws. The saw blade is a continuous metal edged, with cutting teeth, which is driven by an electric motor. Hack saws are mechanically driven reciprocating saws. They have normal format blades carried in a heavy duty hack saw frame. They have more productivity than band saws.

6.2.2.3 Punching and Drilling

Most fabrication shops have a range of machines, which can form holes for connections in structural steel work. The traditional drilling machine is the radial drill, a manually operated machine, which drills individual holes in structural steel work. This method is too slow for primary line production. Today larger fabricators have installed NC (Numerically Controlled) tooling, which registers and drills in response to keyed in data. These can drill many holes in flanges and webs of rolled steel sections simultaneously. It is also possible to punch holes, and this is particularly useful where square holes are specified such as anchor plates for foundation bolts. While this method is faster compared to drilling, punching creates distortion and material strain hardening around the holes, which increase with material thickness. Its use is currently restricted to smaller thickness plates. In order to reduce the effect of strain hardening and the consequent reduction in ductility of material around punched holes, smaller size (2 mm to 4 mm lesser than final size) holes are punched and subsequently reamed to the desired size.

6.2.2.4 Straightening, Bending and Rolling

Rolled steel may get distorted after rolling due to cooling process. Further during transportation and handling operations, materials may bend or may even undergo distortion. This may also occur during punching operation. Therefore, before attempting further fabrication the material should be straightened. In current practice, either rolls or gag presses are used to straighten structural shapes.Gag press is generally used for straightening beams, channels, angles, and heavy bars. This machine has a horizontal plunger or ram that applies pressure at points along the bend to bring it into alignment. Long plates, which are cambered out of alignment longitudinally, are frequently straightened by rollers. They are passed through a series of rollers that bend them back and forth with progressively diminishing deformation.

6.2.2.5 Fitting and Reaming

Before final assembly, the component parts of a member are fitted-up temporarily with rivets, bolts or small amount of welds. The fitting-up operation includes attachment of previously omitted splice plates and other fittings and the correction of minor defects found by the inspector.In riveted or bolted work, especially when done manually, some holes in the connecting material may not always be in perfect alignment and small amount of reaming may be required to permit insertion of fasteners. In this operation, the holes are punched, 4 to 6 mm smaller than final size, then after the pieces are assembled; the holes are reamed by electric or pneumatic reamers to the correct diameter, to produce well matched holes.

6.2.2.6 Fastening Methods

The strength of the entire structure depends upon the proper use of fastening methods. There are three methods of fastening namely *bolting, riveting* and *welding*. A few decades back, it was a common practice to assemble components in the workshop using bolts or rivets. Nowadays welding is the most common method of shop fabrication of steel structures. In addition to being simple to fabricate, welded connection considerably reduce the size of the joint and the additional fixtures and plates.

Welded connections: Welding is used extensively for joining metals together and there is no doubt that it has been a most significant factor in the phenomenal growth of many industries. The different terminology used in welds is explained in IS: 812(1957).A welded joint is made by fusing (melting) the steel plates or sections along the line of joint. The metal melted from each member of the joint unites in a pool of molten metal, which bridges the interface. As the pool cools, molten metal at the fusion boundary solidifies, forming a solid bond with the parent metal. When solidification completes, there is a continuity of metal through the joint.There are five welding process regularly employed namely:

- **Shielded metal arc welding (SMAW):** This is basically a semi-automated or fully automated welding procedure. The type of welding electrode used would decide the weld properties. Since this welding is carried out under controlled condition, the weld quality is normally good.
- **Submerged arc welding (SAW):** This is fully mechanized process in which the welding head is moved along the joint by a gantry, boom or tractor. The electrode is a bare wire, which is advanced by a motor. Since the welding is carried out in controlled conditions, better quality welds are obtained.
- **Manual metal-arc welding (MMA):** This is the most widely used arc welding process and appears to be advantageous for labour intensive Indian construction practices. As it is manually operated it requires considerable skill to produce good quality welds. Hence in the case of MMA, stringent quality control and

quality assurance procedures are needed. In India, the Welding Research Institute, BHEL, Trichy, Tamil Nadu, conducts periodical courses for welders and weld inspection personnel. Welders who are employed in actual fabrication are, in fact, graded according to their training and skills acquired.

- **Metal active gas welding (MAG)L:** This process is sometimes referred to as Metal-Inert Gas (MIG) welding. It is also manually operated. A gas that does not react with molten steel shields the arc and the weld pool. This protection ensures that a sound weld is produced free from contamination-induced cracks and porosity. Nevertheless, this procedure also depends on the skills of the welder.
- **Stud welding:** This is an arc welding process and is extensively used for fixing stud shear connectors to beam in the composite construction. The equipment consists of gun hand tool, D.C. power source, auxiliary contractor and controller. The stud is mounted into the chuck of the hand tool and conical tip of the stud is held in contact with the work piece by the pressure of a spring on the chuck. As soon as the current is switched on, the stud is moved away automatically to establish an arc. When a weld pool has been formed and the end of the stud is melted the latter is automatically forced into the steel plate and the current is switched off. The molten metal, which is expelled from the interface, is formed into a fillet by a ceramic collar or ferrule, which is placed around the stud at the beginning of the operation. The ferrule also provides sufficient protection against atmospheric contamination.This process offers an accurate and fast method for attaching shear connectors, etc with the minimum distortion. While it requires some skill to set up the weld parameters (voltage, current, arc time and force), the operation of equipment is relatively straight forward.

Defects in welds: Faulty welding procedure can lead to defects in the welds, thereby reducing the strength of the weld. Some of the common defects in welds these are: Undercut, Porosity, Incomplete Penetration, Lack of side wall fusion, Slag inclusions and Crack.

However, there is still a demand for structural members to be bolted arising from a requirement to avoid welding because of the service conditions of the member under consideration.

6.2.2.7 Finishing

Structural members whose ends must transmit loads by bearing against one another are usually finished to a smooth even surface. Finishing is performed by sawing, milling or other suitable means. Several types of *sawing machines* are available, which produce very satisfactory finished cuts.One type of milling machine employs a movable head fitted with one or more high-speed carbide tipped rotary cutters. The head moves over a bed, which securely holds the work piece in proper alignment during finishing operation.

6.2.2.8 Surface Treatment

Structural steelwork is protected against corrosion by applying metal or paint coating in the shop or at site.

Metal coatings: The corrosion protection afforded by metallic coating largely depends upon the surface preparation, the choice of coating and its thickness. It is not greatly influenced by the method of application. Commonly used methods of applying metal coating to steel surfaces are hot-dip galvanizing, metal spraying, and electroplating.

- *Galvanizing:* It is the most common method of applying a metal coating to structural steel work. In this method, the cleaned and fluxed steel is dipped in molten zinc at a temperature of about 4500°C. The steel reacts with molten zinc to form a series of zinc or iron alloys on its surface. As the steel work piece is removed, a layer of relatively pure zinc is deposited on top of the alloy layers. For most applications galvanized steel does not require painting.
- *Spraying:* An alternative method of applying metallic coating to structural steel work is by metal spraying of either zinc or aluminum. The metal, in powder or wire form, is fed through a special spray gun containing a heat source, which can be either an oxy-gas flame or an electric arc.
- Electroplating is generally used for fittings and other small items.

Paint coatings: Painting is the principal method of protecting structural steel work from corrosion. Paints are usually applied one coat on top of another, each coat having a specific function or the primer is applied directly on to the cleaned steel surface. Its purpose is to wet the surface and to provide good adhesion for subsequently applied coats. Primers for steel surfaces are also usually required to provide corrosion inhibition. The intermediate coats (or undercoats) are applied to build the total film thickness of the system. This may involve application of several coats. The finishing coats provide the first-line defence against the environment and also determine the final appearance in terms of gloss, colour etc. They also provide UV protection in exposed condition. Intermediate coats and finishing coats are usually classified according to their binders, e.g. vinyl finishes, urethane finishes.The various superimposed coats within a painting system have, of course, to be compatible with one another. They may be all of the same generic type or may be different, e.g. chloral-rubber base intermediate coats that form a film by solvent evaporation and no oxidative process, may be applied on to an epoxy primer that forms a film by an oxidative process which involves absorption of oxygen from the atmosphere.

6.2.2.9 Transportation of Structural Members

Development of the steel industry is entirely dependent on shipping and transportation services. All types of Steel materials require heavy duty vehicle to transport them from one place to another. Mostly steel frame structural members are transported by ship, barge, truck, and rail. Mode of transportation is decided according to cost efficiency of mode and time period of delivery. LGSF is becoming increasingly popular since transportation is easier and less costly.

6.2.2.10 Storage of Structural Members

Structural steel shall be stored in a way to prevent distortion, corrosion, scaling and rusting.Structural steel sections shall be coated with cement wash before stacking, especially in humid areas. In case of long time storage or storage in coastal areas, Steel sections shall be stacked at least 150-200 mm above ground level. Steel sections shall be stacked upon platforms, skids or any other suitable supports.Structural steel sections of different types, sizes and lengths shall be stored separately to facilitate issues in required sizes and lengths without cutting from standard lengths. Ends sections of each type shall be painted with separate designated colors.

6.2.2.11 Handling of Structural Members

The means of handling and manipulating steelwork within a Steelwork Contractors factory has developed over time to suit their particular operations. However, it generally involves the use of computer controlled conveyor systems and overhead gantry cranes running on either rails on the floor, or crane girders attached to the steel frame of the fabrication factory. Steel elements may be picked up using chains or strops, or temporary lifting brackets can be welded-on to facilitate the use of hooks. Tag lines shall be used to control the load in handling structural steel when a crane is used. Heavy steel sections shall be lifted and carried with the help of slings and tackles.

6.2.3 Application of Steel Structure Framing in Buildings

Steel construction is used in the following types of structures [fig. 2(a) - 2(i)]

- **Warehouse buildings & industrial buildings** because of its ability to create large span spaces at low cost.
- **Residential buildings** in a technique called light gauge steel construction.
- **High rise buildings** due to its strength, low weight, and speed of construction.
- **Office buildings.**
- **Temporary structures** as these are quick to set up and remove.
- **Rail stations.**
- **Airport:** This includes airport terminal buildings, aircraft hangers, cargo buildings, baggage handling system structure, ATC tower structure, aero bridge structure.

Fig. 6.2(a): Warehouse buildings

Fig. 6.2(b): Industrial buildings

Fig. 6.2(c): Residential buildings

Fig. 6.2(d): High-rise buildings

Fig. 6.2(e): Office buildings

Fig. 6.2(f): Temporary buildings

Fig. 6.2(g): Rail stations

Fig. 6.2(h): Aircraft hangers

Fig. 6.2(i): Airport terminal building

6.2.3.1 Techniques of Steel Frame Construction

Conventional steel fabrication: Conventional steel fabrication involves cutting steel members to the correct length and welding them to build the final structure. This construction process may be executed on site entirely which require massive manpower. Alternatively, for best results it can be done in a workshop partially to provide better working conditions and reduce work-time.

Bolted steel construction: In this technique, all structural steel members are fabricated and painted off-site, then delivered to the construction site, and finally bolted in place. The size of the steel structural members is controlled by the size of the truck or trailer used to deliver steel elements. Commonly, the maximum length of 6m m is acceptable for normal truck and 12m for long trailer. Bolted steel construction is substantially fast because only lifting the steel members into place and bolting need to be executed on construction site. It is considered to be the most preferred construction approach because the most of the fabrication can be done in workshops, with the right machinery, lighting, and work conditions.

Light gauge steel construction: Light gauge steel construction is very similar to wood framed construction in principle - the wooden framing members are replaced with thin steel sections. The steel sections used here are called cold formed sections, meaning that the sections are formed, or given shape at room temperature. This is in contrast to thicker hot rolled sections, that are shaped while the steel is molten hot. Cold formed steel is shaped by guiding thin sheets of steel through a series of rollers, each roller changing the shape very slightly, with the net result of converting a flat sheet of steel into a C or S-shaped section.

6.2.4 Light Gauge Steel Framed Structures (LGSF)

Light Gauge Steel Framed Structures (LGSF) which is currently gaining popularity is based on factory made galvanized light gauge steel components, designed as per codal requirements, produced by cold forming method and assembled as panels at site forming structural steel framework of a building of varying sizes of wall and floor.

The basic building elements of light gauge steel framing are cold formed sections which can be prefabricated on site using various methods of connection. The assembly is done using special types of screws and bolts.

Cold formed sections are widely used in construction including residential floors, industrial buildings, commercial buildings, hotels and are gaining greater acceptance in the residential sector. LGSF is already well established in residential construction in North America, Australia and Japan and is gaining ground in India. LGSF is based on established system of light gauge steel structures and designed as percodal provisions with loading requirements as per Indian Standards.

LGSF is typically ideal for one to three storey high buildings, especially in residential homes, apartments andcommercial buildings. Due to its flexibility fast construction and durability, this technology has great potential forcounties like India.

LGSF can be combined with composite steel / concrete deck resting on light steel framing stud walls. Apart fromhaving potential for mass housing, LGSF can be used for long term temporary or permanent structuressuch as schools and classroom, military and civil housing needs, post - disaster relief structures and industrial buildings. Advisable span for LGSF buildings should be 7.5 m.

In high rise commercial and multi-family residential construction, light gauge frames are typically used for interior partitions and support of exterior walls and cladding.However, in many low-rise & mid-rise applications the entire structural system can be framed with light gauge steel members. Construction of light gauge structure is very similar to wood framed construction. Being non-combustible in nature, the structure provides a good alternative to wood and a sustainable solution. Speed of construction is very fast compared to conventional RCC methods.

Fig. 6.3(a): LGS framing system

Fig. 6.3(b): Installation of LGS frames

Fig. 6.3(c): House being constructed from LGSF

6.2.4.1 Advantages and Disadvantages of LGSF

Following are the advantages and disadvantages of LGSF

Advantages

- **Easier to work with:** Light gauge steel is easily customizable.
- **Build speed:** This steel is manufactured off-site, which decreases build time on-site.
- **Strong yet light:** Light gauge steel has the highest strength-to-weight ratio. Earthquake force generation is less due to light weight. Chances of progressive collapse are marginal due to highly ductile and load carrying nature of closely spaced studs/joists.
- **Safety level:** Light gauge steel is much more durable than other building materials. Galvanized steel resists decay and corrosion.
- **Remodelling ease:** The walls attached to steel framing are often easy to remove. Since steel is highly customizable, it can form virtually any shape. As long as load-bearing parts aren't removed, nearly any part of the structure can be changed.

- **Flexibility:** The high strength-to-weight ratio allows longer spans without beams, allowing more design possibilities. With other building materials, it costs significantly more to achieve the same effect.
- **Ductility**: When the structure is subjected to great force, it will not suddenly crack like glass, but slowly bend out of shape.
- **Material costs:** It is lightweight, durable, easy to transport, and resistant to many damaging scenarios. Also, structure being light, does not require heavy foundation.
- **Environment friendly:** The highly accurate nature of the planning and manufacturing process leads to less wastage.
- **Non-combustible:** It is non-combustible and less susceptible to fire damage.
- **Resistance:** LGS is resistant to insect damage.
- **High precision:** Fully integrated computerized system with CNC machine provides very high accuracy up to 1 mm.
- **Mobility:** Structural element can be transported to any place including hilly places to remote places easily and structure can be erected fast. Structure can be shifted from one location to another without wasting materials.

Disadvantages

- Light framed structures allow the passage of sound more readily than the more solid masonry construction.
- Light gauge steel will lose strength in the advent of fire. Adequate fire protection must be used. The easiest form of fire protection is to clad the steel with fire rated sheeting or drywall.

6.2.4.2 Components of LGSF

This section discusses the various components of LGSF.

Stud profiles: These are used in a variety of applications including external curtain walls, load bearing walls, headers floors & roof joists, soffits and frame components. Studs serve as a general all purpose framing component used in a variety of applicationsincluding external curtain walls, load bearing walls, headers floors & roof joists,soffits and frame components.

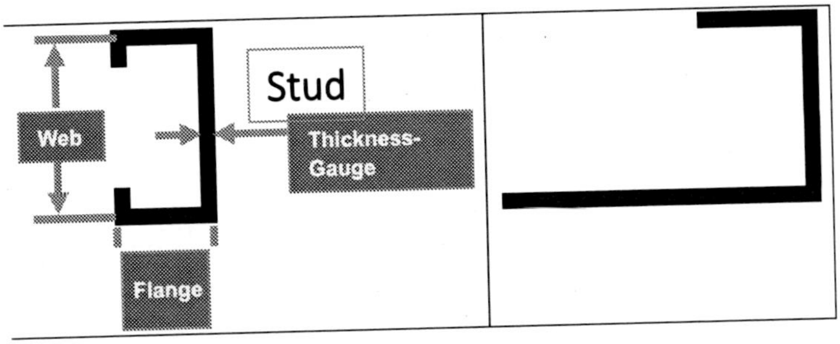

Fig. 6.4(a): Studs and flanges used in LGSF

Track profiles: Track is used as closure to stud and joists end as well as head and sill conditions. It is also used for blocking and bridging conditions. Load bearing steel framing members shall be cold – formed to shape from structural quality sheet steel complying with the requirements of one of the following:

i. ASTM A 653 / A 653 M -13 Grade 33, 37, 40 & 50 (Class 1 and 3) or
ii. ASTM A 792 / A 792 M -13 Grade 33, 37, 40 & 50; or
iii. ASTM A 875 / A 875 M – 13 Grade 33, 37, 40 & 50; or
iv. Sheets, that comply with ASTM A 653 except for tensile and elongation with requirements, shall be permitted, provided, the ratio of tensile strength to yield point is at least 108 and the total elongation is at least 10 per cent for a 5 mm gauge length or 7 per cent for a 20 mm gauge length.

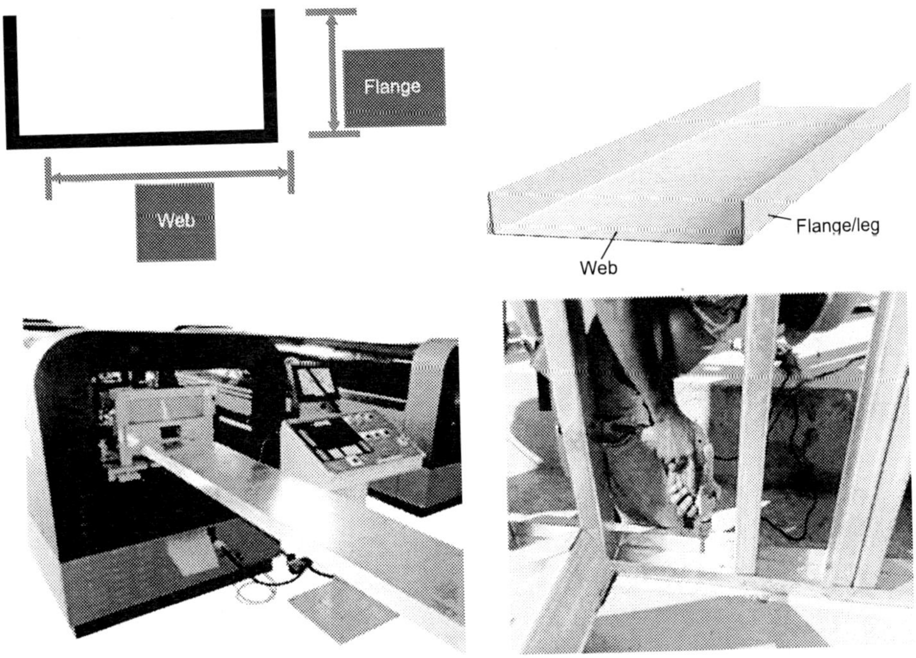

Fig. 6.4(b): Tracks used in LGSF

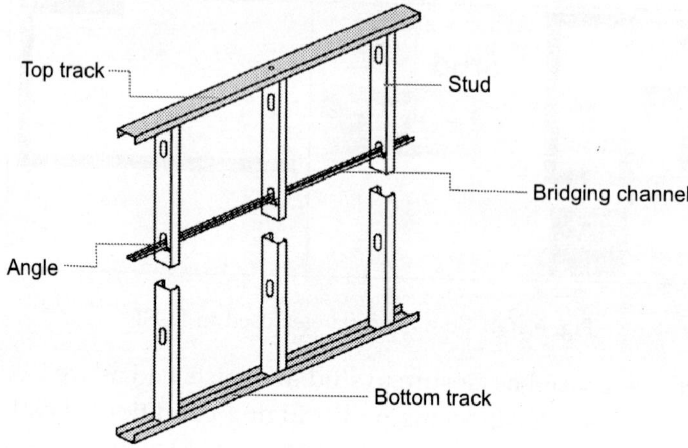

Fig. 6.4(c): Typical framing configuration in LGSF using studs and tracks

Wall frame: A typical wall frame consists of top track (U shape configuration) with a depth compatible with that of thestuds of the same nominal size. Minimum height of track flanges shall be 19 mm.

Load bearing walls

C section studs with depth of 90 and 200 mm and thickness between 2.7 mm and 2.0mm are provided at a distance of 300 mm/400 mm/610 mm to ensure the efficientuse of cladding material. Multiple studs are used at heavily loaded applicationsuch as adjacent to openings or in braced panels. C section with 94 x 50 mm is usedfor noggins. Alternation shall be required for the local details at the head & the base of the wall toensure that loads are adequately transferred without local deformation of the joists& studs.

Non-load bearing walls

It is similar to that of load bearing walls except that noggins and diagonal bracing arenot required to stabilize the studs.

Deflection limit of walls

Suggested deflection limit for external walls subject to wind loading are as follow:

- Full height glazing height / 600
- Masonry wall height / 500
- Board/reduced finish height / 360
- Steel cladding height / 250
- Other flexible cladding height / 360

Wall cladding: Wall cladding shall be designed to resist wind load. Sheet has to be screwed to the joist / purlin with maximum spacing of 300 mm c/c. All the joints of sheet in longitudinal direction require a minimum lap of 150 mm in order to make them leak proof.Following materials are generally used on wall cladding:

- Gypsum board conforming to IS 2095 (Pt. 1): 2011
- Heavy duty cement particle board conforming to IS 14862:2000.

Bracing: Bracing and bridging shall have configuration and steel thickness to providesecondary support for the studs in accordance with the relevant specification for thcdesign of Cold - formed steel structure of members.

Fig. 4(d): Bracings used in LGSF along with studs and tracks

Floor frame: The floor should be designed for the combined effect of dead and imposed load. Floor joist are pre-assembled to form floor cassettes for speed of construction. This works well for regular floor places but care shall be taken when the geometry of the building requires the cassettes to vary in size with location or when non - right angel corners are required.

Flooring boards offer resistance to the top flange of the joists.

Roof frame: Flat roof is made up of joists. Where steel decking forms a flat roof, a minimum fall of 1:4 should be introduced to ensure that any moisture runs off. To avoid local ponding to rain water, the pitch may need to be increased to overcome the effective reduction in roof angle caused by the deflection of long span roof purlin or decking.

Fig. 6.4(e): Flat roof components in LGSF

Roof truss: Use of Light Steel roof truss is very economical for larger span building. An attic oropen roof truss creates usable roof space, uses fewer components than Fink trussand provides an economical solution, since it utilizes the high strength of the steelmembers. The trusses are placed at 600 mm maximum spacing and are battened and tiled in a conventional manner.

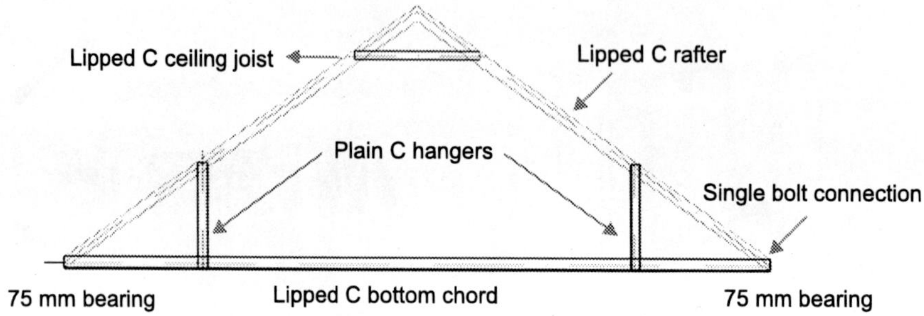

Fig. 6.4(f): Sloped roof components in LGSF

Screws: Screws as per the details given below shall be used:

- Panel Assembly – Low profile screws
- LGS-LGS wall panel to roof cassette – 12-14 × 15 mm
- LGS to concrete – Tapcon screw 14-12 × 60 mm Hex head
- Wire mesh = EPS board – SDS Hex head with Ceresin without washer
- HRS-LGS – Hex heat
- CP board 6 mm – WT 8 CSK Phillips
- Gypsum board – Flat heat self-driven type
- Deck sheet/Wire mesh – SDS WT, CSK, Flat head

Extended polystyrene panel: Shall be of minimum density: 15 kg/m^3.

Wire mesh: Shall be made of 4 mm dia wire of UTs 480 MPa with spacing 150 mm × 150 mm or 1.4 m dia of spacing 40 mm × 40 mm.

Shortcrete: Shortcrete when used shall be of minimum grade M 25.

Foundation: Foundations to light steel framing are essentially the same as for any other form of construction. All tracks should completely rest on foundation to concrete.

6.2.4.3 Process of Designing LGSF

The LGSS is designed based on provision of the following standards:

- Indian Standard IS 801: 1975 Code of Practices for use of cold-formed and welded section and light gauge steel structural members in general building construction.
- British Standard BS 5950 (Part 5):1998: Structural use of steel in Building Part 5: Code of Practice for design of cold formed thin gauge structure.

- British Standard BS 5950 (Part 1): 2000 Structure use of steelwork in Building Part with loading requirement as per IS 875 (Part 1)
- Indian Standard IS 875 : 1987 Code of practice for design loads

  Part 1 - Dead Loads - Unit Weights of Building Material and Stored Materials

  Part 2 - Imposed Loads

  Part 3 - Wind Loads
- IS 1893 (Part 1):2002 Criteria for Earthquake Resistant Design of Structures - Part 1 : General Provisions and Buildings

6.2.4.4 Process of Construction and Fabrication of LGSF

The sections are manufactured using a Centrally Numerical Control (CNC) automatic four Pinnacle Roll Forming machine having production speed of 450-900 m/h with very high precision.Construction phases of steel buildings resemble the phases of conventional reinforced concrete buildings. The sections, manufactured as per design are numbered properly.

The profiles are sent to site either as profile or panellized parts, considering the distance of the construction site and transportation conditions. Profiles are assembled by trained assembly team at the construction site in line with the architectural plan. Only special studs are used during assembly, no welding is done. Once the assembly is done, the frame is filled with insulation materials (fibreglass, rockwooletc). Walls are then covered with standard boards or similar approved materials.The sequence of erection is:

- laying of foundation
- fixing of tracks
- fixing of wall panels with bracings as required
- fixing of floor panels
- fixing of roof panels, decking sheet
- fixing of electrical & plumbing services
- fixing of insulation material & walling panels.

This section describes the process of construction.

Laying of foundation and fixing of tracks: Foundations for light steel framing are essentially the same as for any form of construction, although dead loads applied by the light steel frame will be much lower than in the concrete or masonry construction.

- All tracks should completely rest on the foundation to concrete.
- The level should be maintained for foundation if any level difference erection can be done with insert plate.
- Finally, it should be grouted at the site.

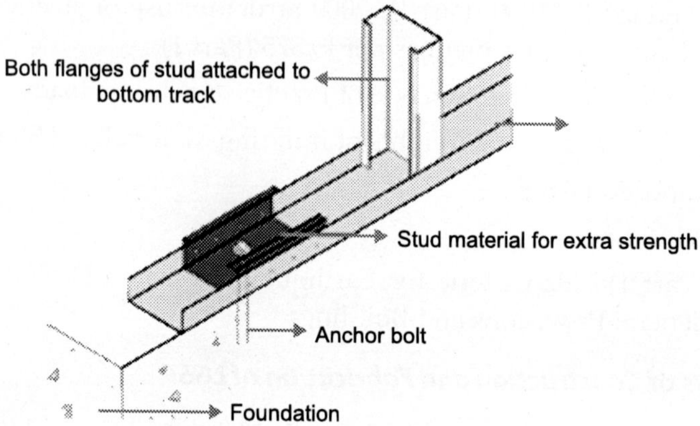

Fig. 6.5(a): Anchoring of tracks to foundation

Fixing of wall panels with bracings: Wall panels are generally made by using heavy duty Cement Particle Board and Gypsum board. It can also be made using high density extended polystyrene core plastered from outside using wire mesh and chicken mesh. Galvalume sheet of appropriate thickness can also be used as cladding. This technology is being evaluated by BMTPC under PACS.

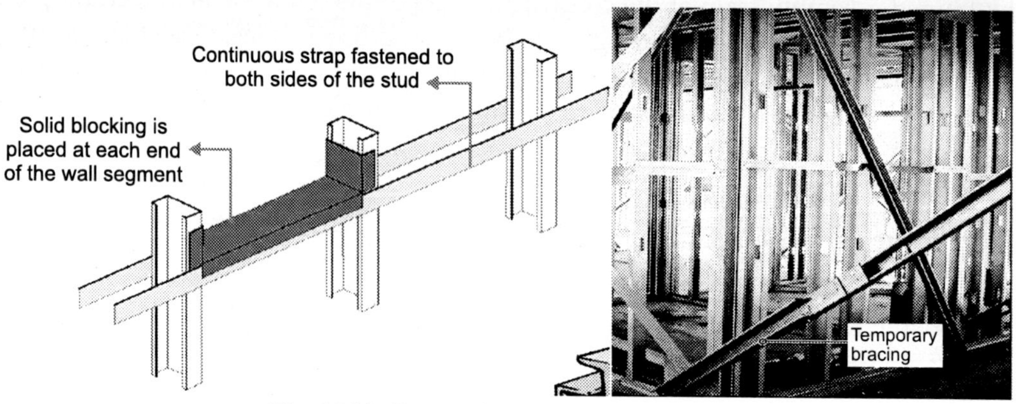

Fig. 6.5(b): Fixing of wall panels with bracing

- All load bearing studs, including king and jack studs, shall be seated in the tracks.
- Wall bridging shall use the same pattern of blocked bay at the end of each run with additional intermediate blocked bays
- Adequate temporary wall bracing shall be provided until permanent bracing has been installed.
- Maximum deviation of +/–15 mm in overall height of wall (3-storey) or +/– 10 mm in overall height of wall (2-storey) and +/– 5 mm in storey height (approx. 2.5 m)

- Support may be provided to prevent distortion and damage to framework due to wind or erection forces.

Fixing of floor panels: The construction of a suspended floor comprising cold-formed steel floor joists is similar to that for a floor using timber joists. The strength-to-weight ratio of light steel joist is higher than that of other material. Steel joists are stable and do not suffer, the long-term problems of drying out, creep and shrinkage. Joists are generally positioned at 300, 400 & 600 mm centres, depending on the spacing capabilities of the floor materials used. Following are some salient features:

- Bearing surfaces for joists shall be uniform and level.
- Anchors, hangers, tie-downs, bearing ledgers, etc., that are part of the supporting structure shall be properly placed and attached.
- Web stiffeners shall be installed at all concentrated load locations and are often required at bearing points.
- Floor joists shall not be loaded before bracing or sheathing is installed.
- Sub-flooring should be checked for squeaks. Correct as necessary.
- Small gap on either end of the floor joist to keep the floor joist away from the rim joist. The floor joist rubbing against the rim joist causes squeaks.

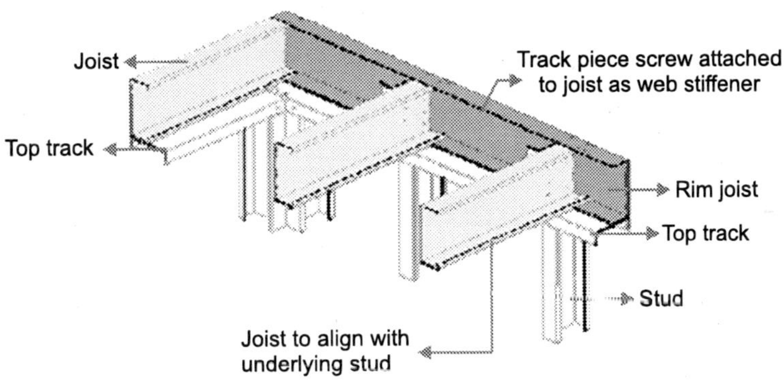

Fig. 6.5(c): Fixing of floor joists

Fixing of roof panels, decking sheet: The truss system is the most common roof system. Truss spacing is determined by the type of roof cladding, the strength and rigidity of the battens.

- Trusses that do not meet interior load bearing walls shall be shimmed for adequate bearing
- Trusses shall not be pulled down to any interior partition.
- Heavy construction loads, such as stacks of plywood, gypsum board, bricks, HVAC units, etc., shall never be placed on trusses before they are properly braced.

Fig. 6.5(d): Fixing of roof truss

Header and sill detail: Trusses shall not be placed over loose lintels, shelf angles, headers, beams, or other supporting structures not securely attached to the building.

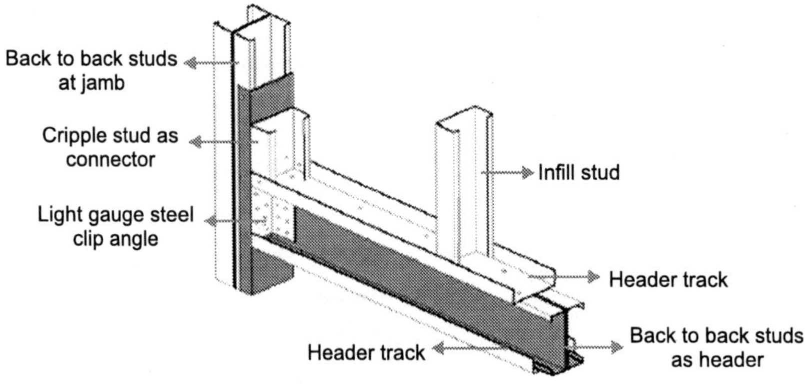

Fig. 6.5(e): Header details of LGSF

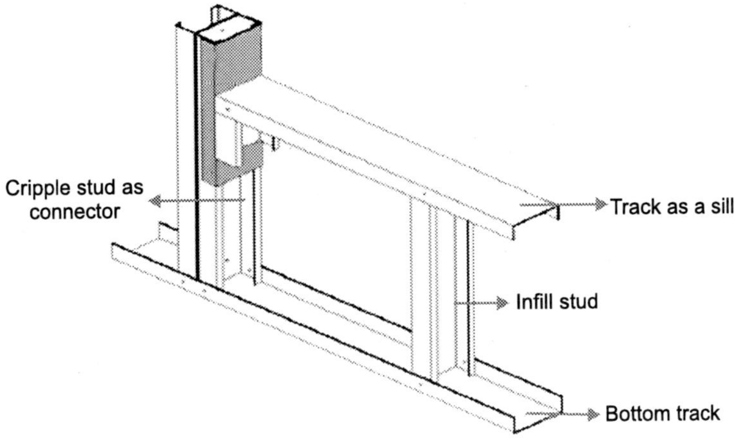

Fig. 6.5(f): Sill details of LGSF

Fixing of electrical & plumbing services: Electrical Gas and plumbing, services are installed through pre-punched service holes in the web of the steel forms. Plastic grommets and silicon seals are used to fasten and protect wiring and pipes from corrosion and damage arising from vibrations. Electrical cables running within floor insulation layer in the separating floor construction should be protected with cartridge fuses or mini circuit breaker.

Fixing of insulation material & walling panels

- Thickness and profile of sheet shall be verified with the erection drawings.
- These are normally used as roof/wall cladding and design to resist wind load.
- Sheet has to be screwed to the joist/purlin with maximum spacing of 300 mm c/c.
- All the joints of sheets longitudinal direction requires a minimum lap of 150 mm in order to make it leak-proof.
- Sealant tape/ sealant paste shall be used at joints to avoid any type of leakage

Fig. 6.5(g): Fixing of wall and roof cladding to LGSF

Fig. 6.5(h): LGSF building in different stages of construction

6.2.5 Innovative Architectural Applications of Steel

6.2.5.1 Steel as Cladding in External Façade

Steel is a good material for the exterior facade of buildings. Due to its aesthetically pleasing quality, steel wall cladding is often used in the exterior of large office buildings or hotels. Steel is easy to install on any façade and also is durable as a façade material.

Steel facades can be designed as per the lighting and ventilation requirements of the space. Mechanized facades with sensors Fig. 6(b) are also used.

Steel plate: The most common use of steel as cladding material is in the form of plates. Steel has a very high tolerance for weathering because of its self-healing qualities. Figure 6(a) shows the Len Lye Museum, New Zealand designed by Patterson Architects, which has a mirror-like facade manufactured from approximately 32 metric tonnes of austenitic 316L stainless steel sheets, which have been hung in vertical interlocking panels which exhibit an apparently seamless appearance. The highly alloyed grade 316L, containing nickel, chrome and molybdenum is particularly suited for external facades of buildings in coastal environments because of its robust resistance to corrosion.

Fig. 6.6(a): Len Lye Museum, New Zealand Designed by Patterson Architects

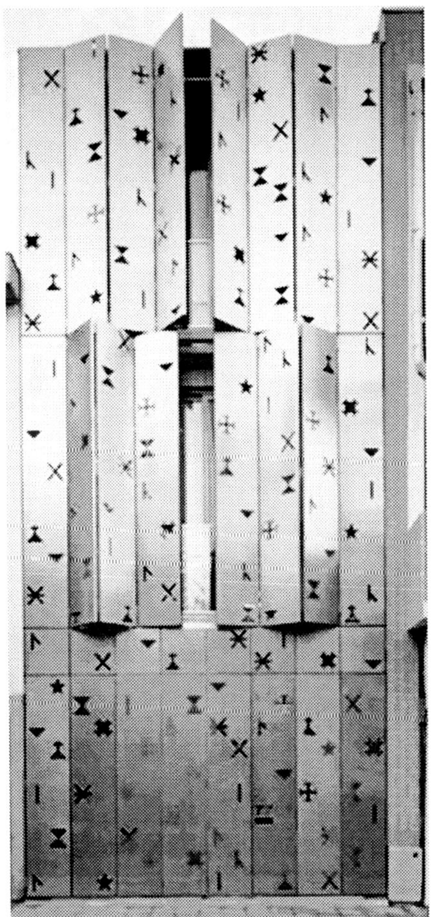

Fig. 6.6(b): Sensor controlled facades: controlling daylight and ventilation through foldable steel panel system

Steel mesh: Perforated steel mesh and steel louvers can be used for the façade. Steel wire mesh acts to bring old and new together as a façade element and also as a second façade as internal cladding or as a decorative screen. In many cases, architectural wire mesh can be tensioned over the full height of a facade. To do this, solid substructures absorbing significant loads is required at the building's upper and lower attachment points. This ensures significantly lower costs for substructures and installation compared to facade cladding with framed solutions. Depending on the size of the individual mesh elements, additional intermediate mountings fixed to each level of the building might be required. These reduce the maximum loads acting on the substructure as well as possible deflection of the mesh.

Fig. 6.6(c): Architectural mesh can be tensioned vertically over several stories

Fig. 6.6(d): Transparent architectural mesh elements combine sun protection

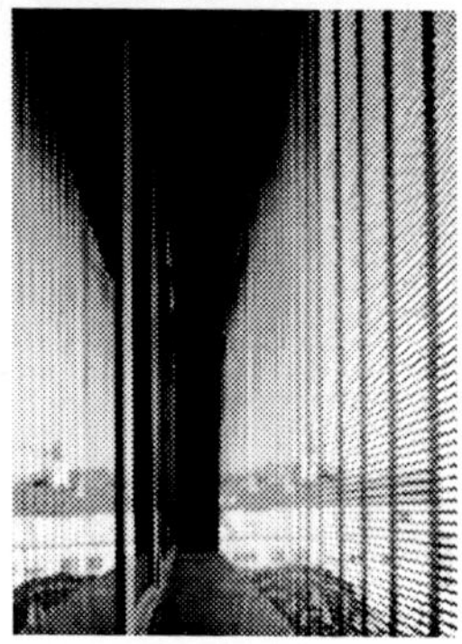

Fig. 6.6(e): ADAC Yatch School, Mohnesee, Germany

Fig. 6.6(f): Perforated steel mesh

Fig. 6.6(g): Flexibility in shape and size of openings and apertures

Architectural wire mesh can be adapted to geometrical shapes using individual elements as polygons. This includes cubes, cylinders, spheres and also more complex shapes. The high degree of dimensional stability allows even larger areas and elements to be completed.

Wire mesh is fire resistant and ensures efficient operation of ventilation, air conditioning and sprinkler systems.

Fig. 6.6(h): Open geometry of wire mesh preserves the view of the outside world

6.2.5.2 Steel Fencing Gates and Awning

Mobile trackless security barrier is a type of temporary fencing widely used to secure temporary tenancies, kiosks, pop-up shops, mall walkways, construction areas, entertainment venues and events, and other areas needing a versatile, cost-effective, short-term separation. Stainless steel railings are also used in landscaped areas due to its better weather resistance and aesthetic appeal.

Fig. 6.7(a): Some applications of stainless steel

Folding Arm Awnings offer excellent protection against sun, wind and rain. These high-quality awnings can be adapted to any size required, and are of virtually unlimited span. Curved stacking doors are suitable for securing curved or circular apertures such as curved counter tops, reception counters, restaurants, shop-fronts, shopping centre walkways, convention centers and venues, canteens, and office building entryways. Pivoting security screens or grilles with hinge can be put out of the way when not in use, allowing for a completely unobstructed opening where required. These grilles have practically no width or height limit. The grade & profile of the frame will vary according to the width & height of the unit as wider spans can require even stronger materials.

Fig. 6.7(b): Pivoting hinged security screens

6.2.5.3 Container Homes

Container homes made from the steel shipping containers are generally used for carrying goods everywhere on trains, trucks, and ships. They are used as giant lego blocks for building homes of all shapes and sizes.

The smallest container makes a tiny box home of about 100 square feet of floor space. Eight larger containers together can make a two-storey house at about 1400 square feet. Hundreds of container micro-apartments together can make a huge apartment building.

These prefabricated and modulor container homes are environmentally friendly because they are made from used containers, thus conserving metal resources. Also they have lower construction and material cost.

Fig. 6.8: Container home

6.2.5.4 Innovative Applications of Stainless Steel

Stainless steel is an extremely flexible material in terms of design options. Following are some common but innovative applications of Stainless Steel.

Application of Steel in Interiors: Steel can be used for interior design applications like tables, chairs, utensils, stairs, railings, balustrade.

Fig. 6.9(a): Woven stainless steel mesh and steel sofa

Fig. 6.9(b): Perforated steel mesh riser and tread

Fig. 6.9(c): Sofa. Painted, oxidized stainless steel and mild steel

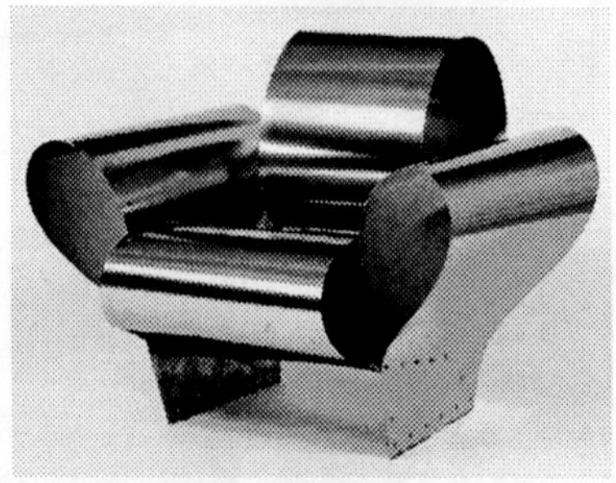

Fig. 6.9(d): Sofa. sprung stainless steel and wingnuts

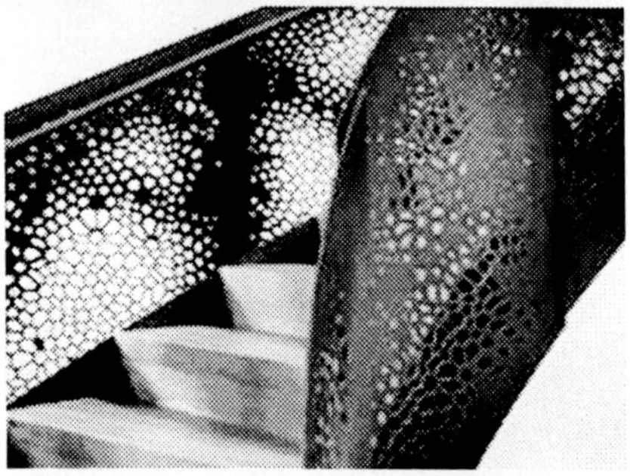

Fig. 6.9(e): Perforated steel balustrade

Fig. 6.9(f): Rusted steel finish stair

Application of steel in Art and Installation: A plethora of sculptures, artworks and installations have been made usingsteel, especially stainless steel. Stainless steel reflects the environment andhence makes the installations very dynamic.

Fig. 6.10 (a): Artworks and installations

Application of steel in Landscape: Steel may be used for making plant vases, edging of lawns, and also forcreating shaded outdoor landscaped spaces.

Steel vase

Steet canopy reflects the landscape

Steel vase

Steel edging

Steel canopy

Fig. 6.10 (b): Landscaping elements

6.2.5.5 Application of Steel as Installations in IIT Kharagpur

Fig. 6.11: Steel installations at IIT Kharagpur

6.2.6 Case Studies

6.2.6.1 R&D Centre, Mumbai

The building located in Mumbai is designed by MALIK Architecture. The site whether the building is located is filled with lush large trees and its profile have dictated the evolution of the design of the building. This building has a unique combination of earth tone terracotta walls, aluminium matte steel panels. The deeply recessed windows in the southern façade, the large glass panels on the north and east, clerestory lighting are some of the other salient features of this centre.

Fig. 6.12(a): Concrete to reduce coldness of steel

Fig. 6.12(b): Glass façade has spider joints supported by steel columns wraps over to merge with perforated steel ceiling panels

The entire R&D complex flows through the trees without being obtrusive, the dappled effect of light and shade and the movement of the sun through the trees, the reflections of this entire combination into the water contemplate a total effect of 'serenity' that is so vital in any R&D centre.

6.2.6.2 Indoor Cycling Velodrome – IGSC, Delhi, Commonwealth 2010

The structure has a built up area of 18000 sq. m. on 110 acres of land with a seating capacity of 3800 fixed seats. This is currently the largest indoor stadium in the country having green building features. It is an air-conditioned velodrome with 250-meter-long timber tracks, and the indoor has been kept completely insulated by using a double skin roof sheeting with sandwiched insulation. The structure has peripheral RCC columns for unobstructed view. The most unique features of the buildings are two main spine steel arches of 2.5-meter diameter each, curved in the horizontal profile, span 146 meters reaching a height of 38.7 meters. This is the primary support system for the roof, anchored on a 1.5-meter diameter bored cast-in-situ pile. The rectangular tube steel lattice girder, spanning from 78 to 130 meters, is supported on RCC columns at the ends, and suspension cables from the primary steel arches at two intermediate points.

Fig. 6.13: View of the massive roof structure

The radius, span and height of these trusses in the cross direction vary due to the shape of the roof. The purlins over these cross trusses are laid to hold the insulating double skin. In plan, the two primary arches can be seen to be connected through ties to form a Vierendeel girder for stability against horizontal forces. Adequate and sufficient bracing for lateral stability has been provided. All structural steel members, those are Rectangular/ Square Hollow Sections, have been painted with two coats of Zinc Anode epoxy primer, finished with two coats of Epilux 89 high build after having cleaned the surface to SA 2.5.

The structural calculations for the frame has been done for Seismic Zone 4, subject to a wind velocity of 47m/sec.

6.2.6.3 Handloom Marketing Complex at Janpath, New Delhi

The Handloom Marketing Complex is located in Janpath, New Delhi and is designed by CPWD with INSDAG as the structural consultant. The construction started on 22.09.2009 and was completed on 15.07.2012. The total cost was approximately Rs.42.63 Crores. The building has been conceived to incorporate sound structural engineering principles and innovative architectural concepts.

The superstructure has 2 towers of G+3 story which accommodate offices/ emporiums and the two basements are considered for parking. Area for first basement is 2040 sq.m and that of the second basement is 2356 sq.m.

Total height of the building is restricted within 15.0 m because of its proximity (within 200 m) to JantarMantar, which is a protected monument. Column to column spacing was kept at 6.0 m to utilize the advantages of Steel–concrete composite construction. A completely glass faceted bridge has been provided to connect the two towers at 1st, 2nd and 3rd floor levels.

Fig. 6.14(a): Front view of the building

The uniqueness of this building lies in the fact, that the columns are concrete encased steel sections acting as composite columns and the beams are steel beams with the top slab playing an effective role as the compression flange of the steel-concrete composite beam. The frame of the building was analyzed with Steel-Concrete Composite option keeping the other structural elements with RCC or steel as required for achieving an optimum solution. The building has been modeled as a 3-D frame with rigid joints between the elements of the frame. The floor slabs have not been included in the 3-D model. The entire frame was analyzed using STAAD PRO 2005 software package. The frame was analyzed for different combination of worst possible loads on the structures. This is a composite construction, in which, the bare steel sections support the initial construction loads, including the weight of structure during construction.

In conventional composite construction, concrete slabs rest over steel beams and are supported by them, whereas in this case the steel beam and the slab act as a "composite beam" and their action is similar to that of a monolithic Tee beam. By the composite action between the two, their respective advantages have been fully utilized. Generally in steel-concrete composite beams, steel beams are integrally connected to prefabricated or cast in situ reinforced concrete slabs.

Fig. 6.14(b): Stages of construction

Following are the advantages of steel concrete composite construction which is true for this building:

- The most effective utilisation of steel and concrete is achieved.
- Keeping the span and loading unaltered, a more economical steel section (in terms of depth and weight) is made possible.
- As the depth of beam reduces, the construction depth reduces, resulting in enhanced headroom.
- Composite beams have less deflection than steel beams due to its stiffness.
- Composite construction provides efficient arrangement to cover large column free space.
- Composite construction is amenable to "fast-track" construction because of using rolled steel and pre-fabricated components, rather than cast-in-situ concrete.
- Encased steel beam sections have better fire resistance and corrosion resistance.
- The lighter weight and higher strength of steel permit the use of smaller and lighter foundations.
- Additional reinforcing steel was not required for composite concrete filled tubular sections.

6.2.6.4 I-Lab, Hyderabad

The prominent shell of the I-Lab building is poised dynamically by the DurgamCheruvu lake-side. The building has a unique identity that marks it apart from the other corporate buildings in its vicinity because of the innovative use of structural systems.

The design is characterized by the use of a unique dia-grid structure used effectively to provide visual lightness and usable open office spaces inside. The self-supporting form with minimal vertical supports lends the building an innovative look and adds to its architectural character. This five-storied structure took eight months for construction. The faster construction was possible due to the use of prefabricated members which also guaranteed accuracy of construction.

The I-Lab building envelope is a 55m x 23m x 21m large shell structure actualized with the help of lightweight and strong mild-steel structural system. The use of steel has been maximized, reducing the otherwise low life cycle of the building since steel is a recyclable material.

Fig. 6.15: Views of different parts of the building

The skin of the building is a network of circular hollow M.S. sections with nodes that are welded during assembly. Steel floor beams are spanned between the peripheral nodes and central ring beam and these floor beams in turn support the composite floor slabs. The composite floor is made of concrete poured out over steel plates. This increases the strength of the slab and reduces the section. The core that houses the services has columns of reinforced concrete with optimal and varying thickness of steel usage. Thus, the net quantity of material used for structure has been minimized increasing transparency as well as lightness of structure.

The dia-grid shell is clad with hard-coated glass that ensures a high level of visual comfort and also allows a good level of reflection-free sunlight. The central portion of the building at the fifth floor, which is the roof of the board room, is covered with water resistant composite construction that reflects partial direct sunlight. Reduction in noise level between two floors is expected to be around 5 to 7 decibels achieved by means of sound insulating material. The I-Lab building has become an icon in its class - and it owes this status to the unique approach towards the structure and architectural expression.

6.2.6.5 Centre Georges Pompidou, Paris

The largest museum for modern art in Europe designed by architects Richard Rogers and Renzo Piano, the center has been envisioned inside-out with its structural and mechanical services (color coded) visible on the exterior. The centre is a vast 7-level glass and steel superstructure, including a terrace and mezzanine floor. The architectural style is based upon:

- revealed structure,
- exposed ducts, and
- machine-precision aesthetics.

Fig. 6.16(a): Front view of the building

Materials used are glass, steel, and colored tubing. Large column -free spaces with all services and structural members confined to the outsides makes the interior spaces easily rearrangeable.

This flexibility was the primary driving force for the design decisions. The proposal was able to successfully concentrate all activities within half the site, leaving the remaining half to be used as a public square.

Fig. 6.16(b): Exposed services in the interior and exterior

In plan, the superstructure of the building consists of three zones:

- The middle zone contains the 157-foot clear span across the building interior between the main columns.
- The outside two zones make up structural wall frames to support and cantilever.

The superstructure is 16000 tonnes of prefabricated steel parts. Two 10 tonne external gerberettes on both sides of the building connect the trusses supporting the floors to the vertical systems i.e the columns. These also form the ends on which the bracing system (X shaped) of the façade rests. It was custom made in Germany. The large hollow members are made of cast iron. These HSS members of the brace have been fitted with cast ends that make connecting and pinning easier.

Fig. 6.16(c): Interior vast space

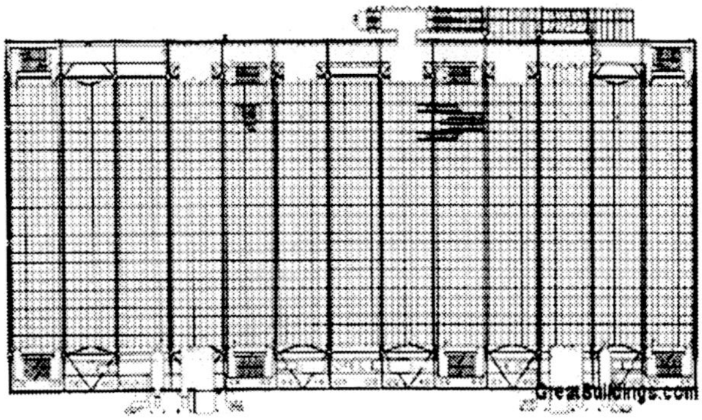

Fig. 6.16(d): Schematic plan

6.2.6.6 Lloyd's Building, London

Designed by Richard Rogers, the Lloyd's building is 88m high and has 14 floors. The cleaning cranes on top of the structure bring the overall height to 95m. The building was designed with 3 main towers and 3 service towers built round a central, rectangular space on the ground floor. This central space is the underwriting room - usually just called 'the room' - where insurance is bought and sold. It's overlooked by 4 floors of galleries. These form a 60m high atrium lit by natural light.

By early 1980 the detailed configuration of the building had emerged. The basic 'doughnut' arrangement - gallery floor plates around a central atrium - remained and the building emerged as a forceful and highly individual presence in the urban landscape.

The structure was originally conceived in steel, however during the design development the fire authorities opposed to this approach. Despite fears that a concrete frame would be overly bulky, the design team resolved to use the restriction as a learning opportunity and undertook a study tour of concrete buildings in the US as part of their research, resulting in a concrete framed building. Steel, however is widely employed in the cladding of the building, particularly in the service towers.

The third material that characterizes the external appearance of the building is glass; triple glazing incorporating rolled glass is used to achieve a sparkling quality that contrasts with the soft sheen of the stainless steel.

Fig. 6.17(a): External view

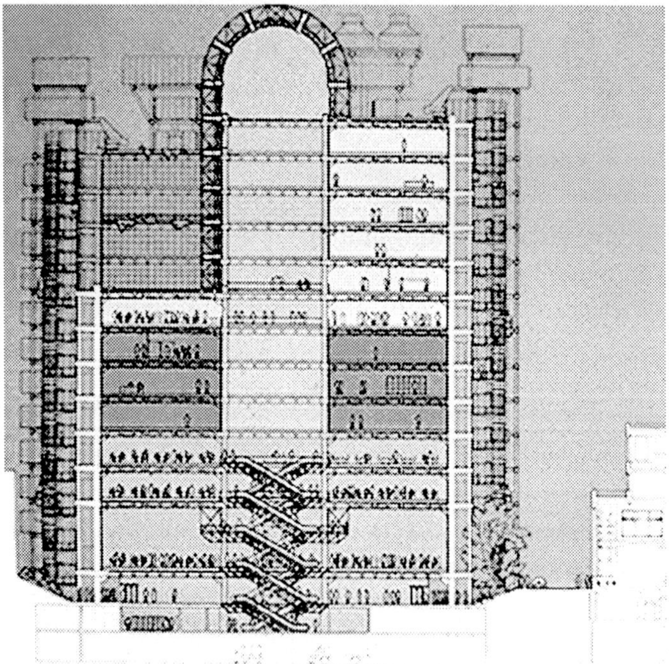

Fig. 6.17(b): Schematic section

The main floor system is predominantly an in-situ concrete raft, supported on beams spanning between the atrium and the façade columns, while the service towers are of pre-cast concrete elements. The great columns, both on the exterior and within the atrium, stand proud of the cladding, increasing the highly articulated vertical quality of the building. External steel-tube cross braces are concrete-cased for fire safety and help to maintain an appearance of a spare and elegant slenderness.

Fig. 6.17(c): Main services running vertically down towers, connected into each level of the building through raised floor and ceiling void

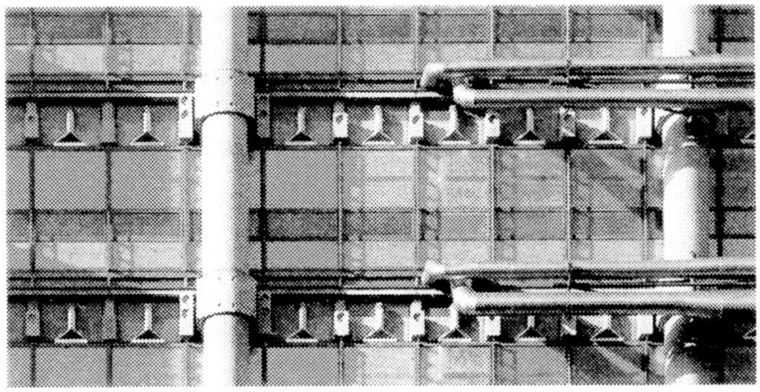

Fig. 6.17(d): The layers of structure, services and cladding articulate the elevation

6.2.6.7 *Jay Pritzker Pavilion, Chicago*

Located in Grant Park, along the edge of Lake Michigan, the Jay Pritzker Pavilion is an open-air venue designed by Frank Gehry featuring performances by the Grant Park Symphony Orchestra, as well as jazz, blues, and other world music performances. The Pavilion is visible from surrounding city streets and is intended to act as a focal point for Millennium Park. The name of the bandshell refers to Chicago's Pritzker family, owners ofHyatt Hotels and the Marmon Group.

The bandshell, built atop a sublevel municipal parking garage, is the centerpiece of the city's new Park, which was constructed partially on the site of an older park that had fallen into massive disrepair, and partially over tracks that were originally built by the Illinois Central Railroad in the early 18th century. A busway and metro rail tracks which run adjacent to Millennium Park pass beneath the Pavilion at the lowest level of the parking structure.

Seating for the audience is provided in two areas. The main seating area accommodates up to 4,000 people in fixed seats and is located immediately adjacent to the Pavilion. Beyond the main seating area, a lawn area accommodates an additional 7,000 people in a more informal environment.

The bandshell is comprised of an exposed structural steel frame (made from both round HSS and WF sections), clad on the front with stainless steel panels. The Pavilion is a highly sculptural design element clad in stainless steel panels. The stage area is clad in Douglas Fir. The Pavilion features a series of portable risers that will accommodate an orchestra of up to 120 musicians, and a choral terrace with space for a choir of up to 150 members. Back stage areas are shared with the adjacent Harris Theater for Music and Dance. Large glass doors allow the Pavilion to be used during winter months for public functions including banquets, receptions, and lectures. A decorative lighting system enhances the Pavilion with colored light washes and projections during evening performances.

Clad in stainless steel panels, that frame the stage opening and connect to an overhead trellis of curved steel pipes, the Pavilion is a highly sculptural design element. The trellis, in the shape of a flattened dome, is supported by cylindrical concrete pylons clad in stainless steel panels.

Fig. 6.18(a): Front view

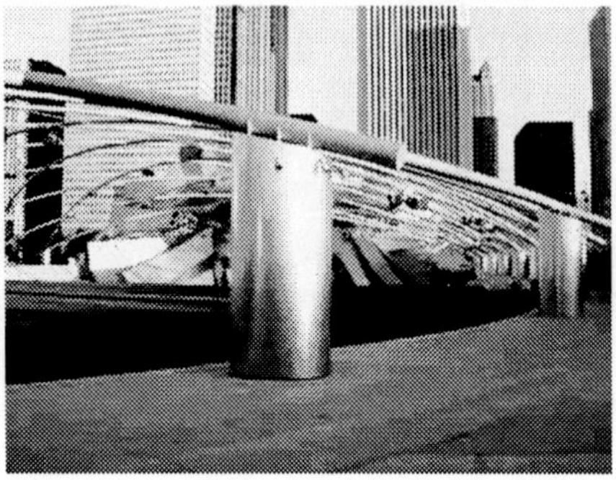

Fig. 6.18(b): Pylons supporting trellis

Fig. 6.18(c): SS panels on the bandshell facade

Fig. 6.18(d): Piers supporting HSS tubes

Fig. 6.18(e): HSS supports tying curved section

Fig. 6.18(f): Round HSS atop pier

Fig. 6.18(g): Diagonal sections with supports

Fig. 6.18(h): Junction of 5 tubes

Fig. 6.18(i): Welding of steel

Fig. 6.18(j): Edge of the shell towards seats

Fig. 6.18(k): Shell and truss support system

Fig. 6.18(l): Connection details of frames

Fig. 6.18(m): Intersection of two shells

Fig. 6.18(n): Tube intersection connection

6.2.6.8 Steel Junction, Kolkata

This is a retail space of 36000 sq. ft. meant to serve as a showcase of steel products for Tata Steel. The requirement of the project was to exhibit raw and finished metal, and so the store was built primarily in mild and stainless steel including displays, staircases, furniture and lighting. Metal in raw and hardware forms are exhibited on the ground floor, the first floor displays finished steel goods.

Fig. 6.19(a): Front view

Fig. 6.19(b): Steel staircase

Fig. 6.19(c): Steel articles displayed

Fig. 6.19(d): AC air diffuser (grill) directly on the HVAC duct. Artificial lighting recessed into a false ceiling and also hung from the structural slab

Fig. 6.19(e): Castellated beams

REFERENCES

1. http://www.bmtpc.org/
2. http://epg.modot.org/index.php/751.5_Structural_Detailing_Guidelines
3. https://www.bdcnetwork.com/best-steel-construction-12-projects-earn-structural-steel-industrys-top-building-award
4. https://www.slideshare.net/tboake/complexity-meets-craft-innovative-steel-detailing-in-architecturally-exposed-structural-steel
5. https://www.nbmcw.com/tech-articles/concrete/18714-design-of-buildings-of-steel-and-concrete.html
6. https://www.trellisdoors.com.au/product/commercial-security/security-screens-and-screen-doors/grilles-s07-1
7. http://www.steel-insdag.org/
8. http://www.worldstainless.org/Files/issf/non-image files/PDF/ISSF_Stainless_Steel_in_Architectural_Applications.pdf
9. https://www.britannica.com/topic/architecture/Methods
10. https://www.weavingarchitecture.com/fileadmin/02-c-Haver_Architekturgewebe/AG_Dokumente/P_24_E_scrg_13062017.pdf
11. https://www.superiorscreens.com.au/gallery-adjustable-louvres.html
12. https://www.pinterest.com/pin/517280707195634399/
13. http://www.compositestechnologypark.com/lgsf.html
14. http://www.fitidisgroup.com/lgsf.html

6.3 LIGHT GAUGE STEEL FRAME SYSTEMS

6.3.1 Introduction

The light gauge steel frame systems are being used for construction practices for many decades; majorly as wall assemblies, floor panels and decks, joists, trusses, purlins and rafters. The development of design standards for the CFS construction practice began since 1950s', and continues till now. There are several advantages in the construction practices of light gauge steel frame systems such as higher strength weight ratio, shape and dimensional flexibility, ease of transportation and installation speed. The countries like United States of America, Australia and China has a separate organizations to develop a design standards for light gauge steel frame systems. The Construction manuals have been developed by National Association of Home Builders (NAHB) and American Iron and Steel Institute (AISI) were approved and adopted in International code council (ICC) and American National Standard Institute (ANSI).

The following are the list of International Standards for Design and Construction of Light gauge steel frame systems:

- Australia and New Zealand Specification: AS/NZS 4600 AS/NZS 4600:2005 Similar to NAS 2007 but includes high strength steels such as G550 for all sections. Building Code: Building Code of Australia (National document) calls AS/NZS 4600:2005 (https://www.standards.org.au/standards-catalogue/sa-snz/building/bd-082)

- Brazil Specification: NBR 14762:2001 Cold-formed steel design, Procedure and NBR 6355:2003 Cold-formed steel structural profiles Building (www.abnt.org.br).

- Canada Specification: CAN/CSA S136-07 as published by Canadian Standards Association which is the same as AISI S100. Building Code: The National Building Code of Canada is the model code adopted with amendments by individual provinces and territories. (https://nrc.canada.ca/en/certifications-evaluations-standards/codes-canada/codes-canada-publications/national-building-code-canada-2015)

- China Specification: Technical Code of Cold-formed Thin-wall Steel Structures Building Code: GB 50018-2002 (https://www.codeofchina.com/standard/GB50018-2002.html)

- Ethiopia Building Codes: EBCS-1 Basis of design and actions on structures EBCS-3 Design of steel structures

- EU Countries Specification: EN 1993-1-3 (same as Eurocode 3 part 1-3), Design of steel structures, Cold formed thin gauge members and sheeting. Each European country has its own National Annex Documents (NAD).

- Germany Specification: German Committee for Steel Structures (DASt), DASt-Guidelines 016: 1992: Calculation and design of structures with thin-walled cold-formed members
- Italy Specification: UNI CNR 10022 (National Document) EN 1993-1-3 (not compulsory)
- India Specification: IS:801, Indian standard code of practice for use of cold-formed light gauge steel structural members in general building construction, Bureau of Indian Standards, New Delhi (1975) (currently under revision)
- Japan Specification: Design Manual of Light-gauge Steel Structures Building Code: Technical standard notification No.1641 concerning light-gauge steel structures
- Malaysia uses British Standard BS5950, especially BS5950:Part 5; AS4600 (from Australia) is also referenced.
- Philippines National Structural Code of the Philippines 2010, Volume 1 Buildings, Towers, and other Vertical Structures, Chapter 5 Part 3 Design of Cold-Formed Steel Structural Members is based on AISI S100-2007
- Singapore Specification: British Standards are in current use.
- South Africa Specification: SANS 10162, The Structural Use of Steel: Part 2 - Limit-state design of cold-formed steelwork Building code: National Building Regulations of South Africa
- United Kingdom Eurocode for cold-formed steel in the UK. BS EN 1993-1-3:2006: Eurocode 3. Design of steel structures. General rules. (https://www.steelconstruction.info/)
- United States Specification: North American Specification for the Design of Cold-Formed Steel Structural Members, document number AISI S100-2007 published by the American Iron and Steel Institute in October 2007. Building Code: IBC and/or NFPA may be enforced, but both reference AISI S100. (https://www.steel.org/)

6.3.2 Shape Flexibility

In general the light gage steel structures are made up of Cold-formed Steel Structural Sections/Members.

Definition of Cold-formed Steel Section: The structural steel sections that are made from bending a flat sheet at room temperature.

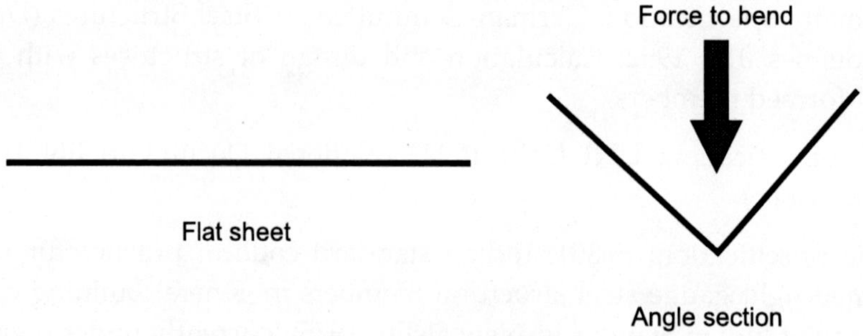

Fig. 6.1: Definition of cold-formed steel sections

The flexibility in fabrication of infinite shapes enables the use of cold formed steel sections in light gage steel structures for various applications. The cold-formed steel sections can be fabricated into various shapes based on the need. Typically, the shapes of the cold-formed steel fabricated from bending process is neither symmetric not closed due to the disability in manufacturing. The cold-formed steel shapes that are fabricated from the bending process is shown in Fig. 2.

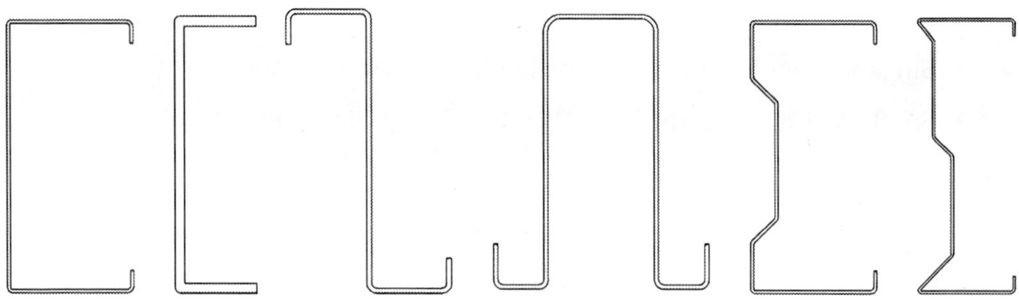

Fig. 6.2: Various shapes of cold-formed steel sections

The unsymmetric cross-sections developed from bending process are highly vulnerable to instability failures. The instability failures of the CFS sections are (i) lateral torsional buckling (beams); (ii) flexural torsional buckling; (iii) sudden collapsible flexural buckling due to high slenderness (L/ry). The instability failure modes of the unsymmetric shaped CFS sections are shown in Fig. 3. The design strength of the CFS structural members that fails in instability failures can be determined using the direct strength method of American Iron and Steel Institute which is purely empherical method. The direct strength method is formulated such that it under predicts (over conservatively) the strength of the CFS members that are highly slender to account the instability failures. The detailed description about the direct strength method of AISI is presented in the following sections.

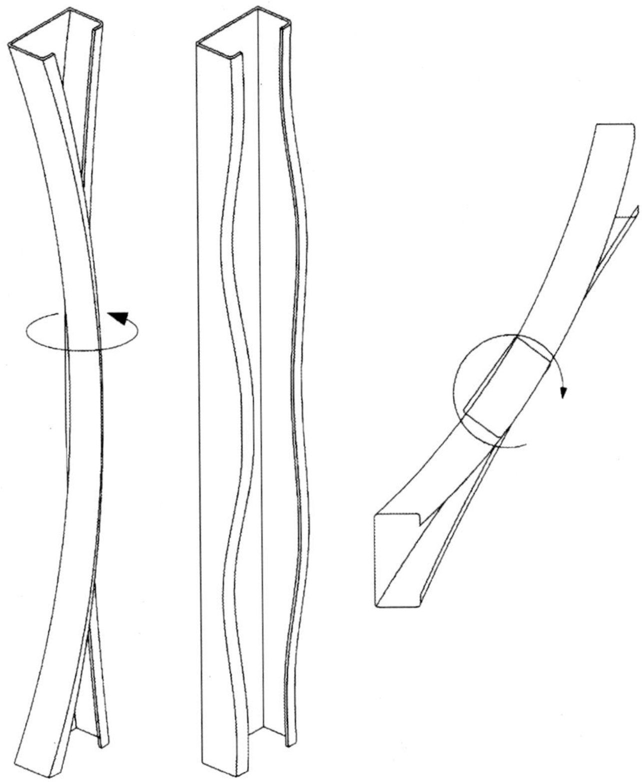

Fig. 6.3: Instability failure modes of cold-formed steel sections

6.3.3 Light Gauge Steel Frame Structure (LGSF) Installation

As the name implies the complete LGSF structure is light in weight and hence it requires minimum foundation. In general, the LGSF structures are built over the stem wall foundation and a concrete platform. After the completion of platform, it requires only minimum time to install the LGSF structure.

The following is the sequence of installation of LGSF Structure:

Fig. 6.4: RCC stem wall construction

Fig. 6.5: RCC stem wall construction – completion

Fig. 6.6: Foundation platform for construction of LGSF structure

Fig. 6.7: Installation of LGSF frames

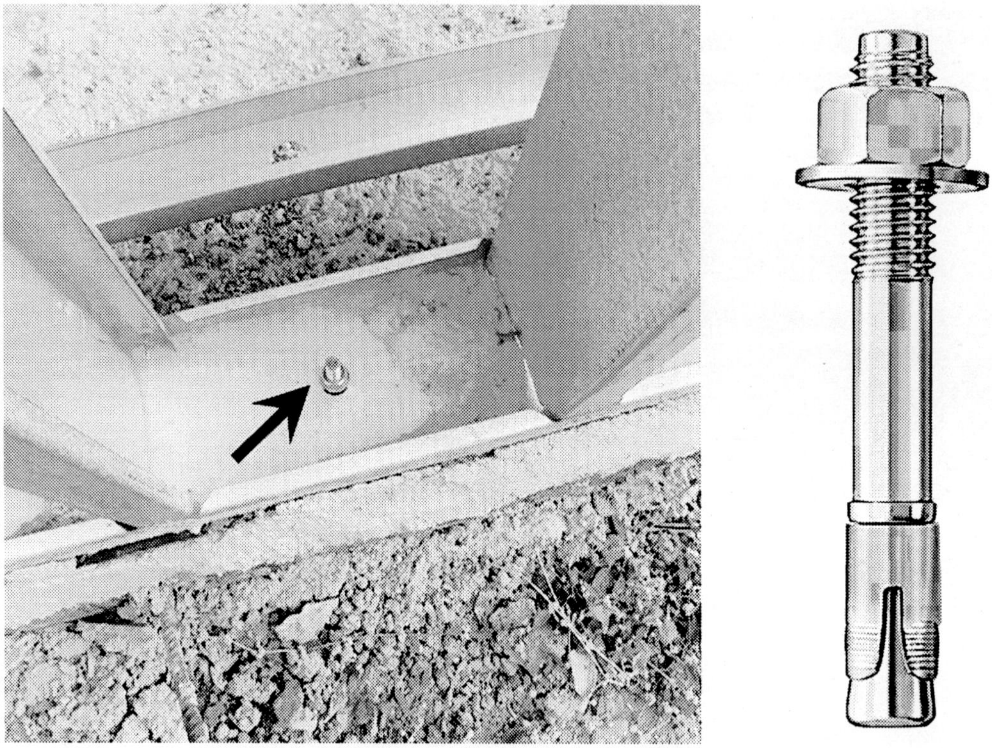

Fig. 6.8: Installation of LGSF frame can be done using mechanical anchor bolts (Courtesy: Hilti KB3 Expansion Anchor)

Fig. 6.9: Completion of LGSF frame for the ground floor

Fig. 6.10: Installation for floor deck panel for roof

Fig. 6.11: Installation for floor deck panel for roof

Fig. 6.12: Installation of LGSF frames for next floor

Fig. 6.13: Installation of sheathing boards (external cover) over LGSF frames

Fig. 6.14: Installation of sheathing boards (external cover) over LGSF frames

Fig. 6.15: View of the completed LGSF structure

6.3.4 Durability of Light Gauge Steel Framed Structures

The AISI (American Iron and Steel Institute) and (Cold-Formed Steel Engineers Institute) combindly carried a research to study the rate of corrosion of the Cold-formed Steel Structural member by realistic experiments. The testing procedure and the test results are as follows.

This summary result is a 7-year report from four test sites where the Cold-formed Steel Structure samples are kept in a severe exposure conditions. The NAHB Research Center commenced work on the project in February 1997 and established test sites in Miami, Florida; Leonardtown, Maryland; Hamilton, Ontario; and Long Beach Island, New Jersey. At each site numerous test samples were installed in building cavities where steel framing would typically be used (e.g., attics, floor systems, walls). The corrosion test samples consist of galvanized, galvalume, and galfan-coated flat plates and 1-inch (nominal) segments of C-section stud. Two sites were also equipped with electronic monitoring systems that measured and recorded surface temperatures, relative humidity, and time of wetness for a one-year period.

Test samples were scheduled to be retrieved from each test site at intervals of one, three, five, and seven years after installation. All batches of one, three, five, and seven-year exposure samples have been retrieved.

This data has been analyzed to determine if thermal and moisture conditions existed that would allow condensation to form on building components. The program was divided into two phases: Phase I of the program, included all sample and site preparation and installation. Phase II, involved processing the environmental data, retrieving and analyzing samples, and maintaining the sites. Phase I was completed in 1998. Phase II was initially completed in 2003 for a 5-year exposure (1-, 3-, and 5-year exposures) but was further extended to the end of 2005 to obtain data for 7-year exposure.

Coating loss measurements from the four sites have indicated minor mass loss rates for all sample types (e.g., studs, plates), all sample coatings (e.g., galvanized, galvalume, and galfan), and all sample colonies (e.g., crawlspaces, walls, attics, joists). All retrieved samples had a measured mass loss of 0.05 grams or less and an estimated average life expectancy of 574 years. The fastest coating corrosion rate observed for any of the four sites for any colony was 0.1306 microns/year for a galvalume plate installed in the crawl space of the Leonardtown, Maryland site after seven years of exposure.

The one-year environmental data from the Hamilton and New Jersey sites demonstrated that the surface temperatures of metal samples and actual building components remained above the local dew point with little exception. At one exterior wall location in Hamilton there were numerous instances of wall component surface temperatures falling below dew point. However, sample plates retrieved from this wall cavity after seven years of exposure showed an average mass loss of 0.02 grams. The executive summary of the results is shown as follows in Table X.

Finally, the conclusion of this study indicates that the cold-formed steel with an appropriate galvanized coat will lost for hundreds of years.

Table X Predicted average life span of cold-formed steel structures based on the performance of seven years severe exposure conditions

Coating	Coating specification	Average life span of cold-formed steel structures (in years)		
		Due to average mass loss (with actual coating thickness)	Due to maximum mass loss (with actual coating thickness)	Due to maximum single mass loss (with nominal coating thickness)
Galvanized 1	Z180 or G60 (38 microns thickness and 7.14 g/cm³)	788	815	404
Galvanized 1	Z180 or G60 (29 microns thickness and 7.14 g/cm³)	666	569	490
Galvalume	AZ180 or AZ60 (60 microns thickness and 3.75 g/cm³)	822	425	387
Galfan	AZ180 orAZ50 (45 microns thickness and 3 g/cm³)	886	697	608

6.3.5 Design Standards For Light Gauge Steel Framed Structure

Though we have discussed about the available design guidelines for the construction of LGSF Structures, it is necessary to know about the history of development of design specifications for LGSF structures. The first design code on cold-formed steel was developed in 1946 by American Iron and Steel Institute.

First design code: American Iron and Steel Institute: Specification for the Design of Light Gage Steel Structural Members, Washington, DC, Apr. 1946.

However in the recent times the American Iron and Steel Institute has developed a design standards for various structural components as follows:

- Cold-Formed Steel Wall Assemblies
- Screw and Bolted Connections
- Standing Seam Roof Systems
- Fastening of CFS Track to Concrete Base Materials
- Reinforcement Schemes for CFS Joists
- Connections for Cold-Formed Steel Framing to Insulating Concrete Form Walls
- Durability of Cold-Formed Steel Framing Members

- Welding Cold-Formed Steel
- Bracing of Cold-Formed Steel Trusses
- Fire Assemblies of Cold-Formed Steel Construction
- Code of Standard Practice for Cold-Formed Steel Structural Framing

The above publications are available at https://www.cfsei.org/publications and https://www.cfsei.org/free-publications-by-development

The following sections illustrate the design formulas for the design of cold-formed steel beam and column.

6.3.5.1 Design equations for Design of Cold-formed Steel Columns

The design rules and expressions of the direct strength method (DSM) of AISI (2016) for CFS axial compression member are summarized as follows. The AISI DSM design rules are also adopted in Australian/New Zealand standards AS/NZS (2005). The unfactored or nominal axial strength (Eq. 4) of the CFS column member (P_{DSM}) is the minimum of nominal axial strength for local buckling (P_{nl}), distortional buckling (P_{nd}) and flexural/flexural-torsional buckling (P_{ne}).

$$P_{DSM} = \min (P_{nl}, P_{ne}, P_{nd}) \tag{4}$$

The nominal axial strength of the CFS column for local buckling can be determined in two ways [Eqs. (5 and 6)], the first method is consideration of element local buckling alone (λ_1) [Eq. (5)] and the other method is considering the global-local interactive buckling (λ_{1-e}) [Eq. (6)].

$$P_{nl} = \begin{Bmatrix} P_y & \text{if } \lambda_1 \leq 0.776 \\ P_y \left(\dfrac{P_{crl}}{P_y}\right)^{0.4} \left[1 - 0.15\left(\dfrac{P_{crl}}{P_y}\right)^{0.4}\right] & \text{if } \lambda_1 > 0.776 \\ \lambda_1 = (P_y / P_{crl})^{0.5} \text{ [local buckling alone]} & \end{Bmatrix} \tag{5}$$

$$P_{nle} = \begin{Bmatrix} P_{ne} & \text{if } \lambda_{1-e} \leq 0.776 \\ P_{ne} \left(\dfrac{P_{crl}}{P_{ne}}\right)^{0.4} \left[1 - 0.15\left(\dfrac{P_{crl}}{P_{ne}}\right)^{0.4}\right] & \text{if } \lambda_{1-e} > 0.776 \\ \lambda_{1-e} = (P_{ne} / P_{crl})^{0.5} \text{ [global – local interactive bucking]} & \end{Bmatrix} \tag{6}$$

where, P_{nl} and P_{nle} are the nominal axial strength for local buckling and global-local interactive buckling, P_y is the axial strength for yield stress, P_{crl} is the elastic critical buckling stress for local buckling that can be determined from Thinwall software (Papangelis and Hancock 1995) and P_{ne} is from Eq. (7). It should be noted that the elastic critical local buckling stress for calculating of P_{crl} should be obtained for the individual cross section as per the suggestions of Young and Chen (2008) and Selvaraj and Madhavan (2019).

The nominal axial strength of the CFS column for flexural buckling/flexural buckling (P_{ne}) and distortional buckling can be determined in accordance with the Eq. (7 and 8).

$$P_{ne} = \begin{Bmatrix} P_y(0.658^{\lambda_c^2}) & \text{if } \lambda_c \le 1.5 \\ P_y\left(\dfrac{0.877}{\lambda_c^2}\right) & \text{if } \lambda_c > 1.5 \\ \lambda_c = (P_y/P_{cre})^{0.5} & \end{Bmatrix} \quad (7)$$

$$P_{nd} = \begin{Bmatrix} P_y & \text{if } \lambda_c \le 0.561 \\ P_y\left(\dfrac{P_{crd}}{P_y}\right)^{0.6}\left[1-0.25\left(\dfrac{P_{crd}}{P_y}\right)^{0.6}\right] & \text{if } \lambda_c > 0.561 \\ \lambda_d = (P_y/P_{crd})^{0.5} & \end{Bmatrix} \quad (8)$$

where, P_{cre} and P_{crd} are the elastic critical stresses for global and distortional buckling, respectively and can be obtained from the Thinwall software or section E2 of AISI 2016.

6.3.5.2 Design Equations for Design of Cold-formed Steel Beams

The nominal flexural moment or unfactored design moment (M_{DSM}) of the CFS structural member as per AISI (2016) is a minimum of LTB moment (M_{ne}), local buckling moment (M_{nl}), and distortional buckling moment (M_{nd}). The design expressions of DSM method as per AISI (2016) section F [15] are summarized as follows:

$$M_{DSM} = \min(M_{ne}, M_{nl} \text{ and } M_{nd}) \quad (1)$$

Lateral-torsional buckling moment *(M_{ne})*

$$M_{ne} = S_f F_n \le M_y \quad (2)$$

$$F_n = F_{cre} \text{ for } F_{cre} < 0.56 f_y \quad (3)$$

$$F_n = \frac{10}{9} f_y\left(1-\frac{10 f_y}{36 f_{cre}}\right) \text{ for } 2.78 f_y \ge f_{cre} \ge 0.56 f_y \quad (4)$$

$$F_n = f_y \qquad \text{for } f_{cre} > 2.78 f_y \quad (5)$$

Local buckling moment *(M_{nl})*

$$M_{nl} = M_{ne} \qquad \text{for } \lambda_l \le 0.776 \quad (6)$$

$$M_{nl} = M_y + \left(1-\frac{1}{c_{yl}^2}\right)(M_p - M_y) \qquad \text{for } \lambda_l \le 0.776 \text{ and } M_{ne} \ge M_y \quad (7)$$

$$M_{nl} = \left[1-0.15\left(\frac{M_{crl}}{M_{ne}}\right)^{0.4}\right]\left(\frac{M_{crl}}{M_{ne}}\right)^{0.4} M_{ne} \quad \text{for } \lambda_l > 0.776 \tag{8}$$

Distortional buckling moment (M_{nd})

$$M_{nd} = M_y + \left(1-\frac{1}{c_{yd}^2}\right)(M_p - M_y) \quad \text{for } \lambda_d \le 0.673 \tag{9}$$

$$M_{nd} = \left[1-0.22\left(\frac{M_{crd}}{M_y}\right)^{0.5}\right]\left(\frac{M_{crd}}{M_y}\right)^{0.5} M_y \quad \text{for } \lambda_d > 0.673 \tag{10}$$

where, M_{ne} = nominal lateral-torsional buckling moment; S_f = gross section modulus (first yield); F_n= elastic lateral-torsional buckling stress; M_y = member yield moment; $M_y = S_f\, f_y$; f_y = yield stress obtained from tensile coupon tests; f_{cre} = critical elastic lateral-torsional buckling stress; M_{nl} = nominal local buckling moment; $\lambda_l = \sqrt{(M_{ne}/M_{crl})}$; M_{crl} = critical elastic local buckling moment; $M_{crl} = S_f\, f_{crl}$; f_{crl} = critical elastic local buckling stress; $C_{yl} = \sqrt{(0.776/\lambda_l)} \le 3$; M_p = member plastic moment; $M_p = Z_f\, f_y$; Z_f= plastic section modulus.

It should be noted that the value of shape factor (η) for determining the plastic section modulus from the elastic section modulus is based on the cross section. The value of shape factor (Z_f/S_f) for the hollow cross section is 1.15 as obtained from MassPlus software. M_{nd} = nominal distortional buckling moment; $C_{yd} = \sqrt{(0.673/\lambda_d)} \le 3$; $\lambda_d = \sqrt{(M_y/M_{crd})}$; M_{crd} = critical elastic distortional buckling moment; $M_{crd} = S_f\, f_{crd}$; f_{crd} = the critical elastic distortional buckling stress. It should be noted that the critical elastic buckling stresses (f_{cre}, f_{crl} and f_{crd}) used in the DSM expressions are obtained from the elastic buckling analysis software Thinwall (Papangelis and Hancock 1995).

6.3.5.3 Cold-formed Steel Built-up Structural Members

Although the primary advantage of the cold-formed steel structural members is the strength-to-weight ratio, they are structurally weaker and / or ineffective when the slenderness is high, and the cross section is unsymmetrical about the loading axis. Most of the CFS structural member's geometry is open cross-sections such as C-shape (Fig. 2) (singly symmetric sections) and Z-shape (point symmetric sections), and are highly vulnerable to fail in torsional buckling due to the low torsional resistance. The vulnerability increases with the increase in slendernesses since the geometric imperfections are high in magnitudes for the slender members. The high slenderness and torsional resistance issues in the open cross-section CFS members can be avoided or significantly reduced when they are used in the wall panel with the bracing effect of the sheathing included. The application of CFS in industrial structural frame construction (long and tall) or in situations where high magnitude live loads are expected, the open cross-sections of the CFS structural members can be converted to closed or doubly symmetric cross sections (Fig. 16) to increase the structural resistance. This transformation of the open cross-section to a closed or symmetric cross section (about loading axis) will be highly effective in torsional resistance; the transformation effect will be significant for the slender (global) members compared to the shorter or stocky members. The possible types of CFS built-up structural members with different cross-sections can be chosen depending on the requirement as shown in Fig. 16. These built-up cross sections can be fabricated with minimal effort using self-drilling screws or interconnection spot welding (arc welding) with regular spacing (AISI 2016). Although the built-up members are widely used in the industry, the structural behavior of many built-up cross sections shown in Fig.16 under flexural loading is still unknown; the codification of design method for them is under investigation. However, we can adopt the following design recommendations for the design of CFS built-up members as they were published in the reputed journals and successfully used by the renowned industries.

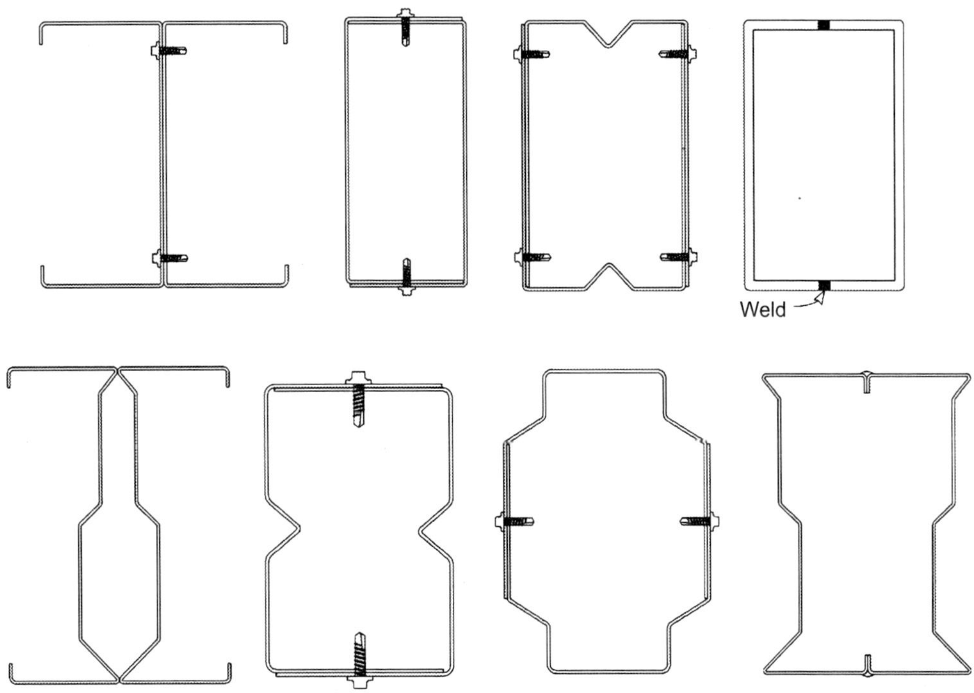

Fig. 6.16: Cold-formed steel structural members, built-up cross sections

6.3.5.4 Design Recommendations for Design of Cold-formed Steel Beams

In general, the DSM design method is based on the slenderness of the member irrespective of the shape and size. Therefore, whether it is an open cross-section or a built-up cross section it is about how to accurately determine the behaviour of the member is Finite Strip Analysis and incorporate the appropriate slenderness in the design expressions. The following are the recommendations on how to use the finite strip analysis for determining the critical elastic buckling stress of the CFS cross-sections.

1. The global buckling stress (P_{cre} and f_{cre}) can be determined by using the full built-up cross section (Figs. 17 (a) and (c)).
2. The local and distortional buckling stresses (P_{crd}, f_{crd}, P_{crl} and f_{crl}) shall be determined by using an individual/single cross section which was used to fabricate the built-up cross section (Figs. 17 (b) and (d)).

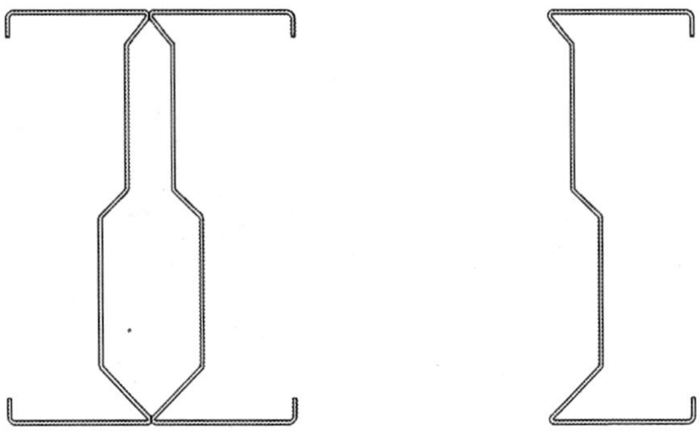

(a) Elastic buckling model for f_{cre} and P_{cre}

(b) Elastic buckling model for f_{crd}, f_{crl}, P_{crd} and P_{crl}

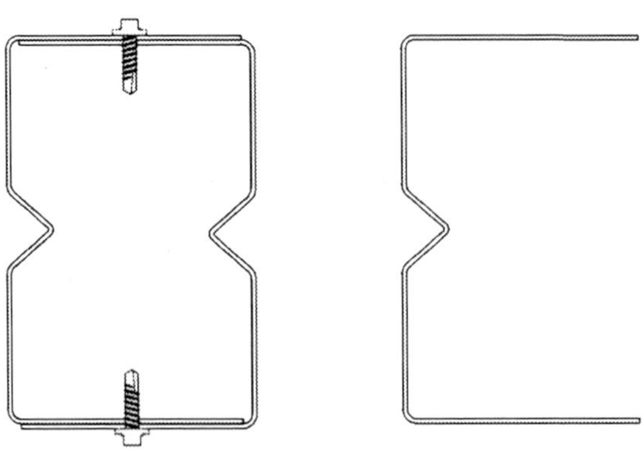

(c) Elastic buckling model for f_{cre} and P_{cre}

(d) Elastic buckling model for f_{crd}, f_{crl}, P_{crd} and P_{crl}

Fig. 6.17: Elastic buckling model and design procedure for CFS built-up sections

6.3.5.5 Cold-formed Steel Wall Panel Design

Sheathings and roof coverings are commonly employed in the cold-formed steel joists, wall studs and purlins as a protection from the external environment to the shelter. The most common sheathing types are oriented strand board (OSB), gypsum boards, fiberboard, pulp board, plywood and light gage steel sheets. The sheathings are attached by the self-tapping screws or fasteners at intermediate spacing. The CFS joists, studs and purlins are typically open sections such as C-sections and Z-sections. These CFS structural members have weak torsional rigidities and are prone to fail by torsional buckling. There are also many failure modes associated with these open section CFS members based on their local and global slenderness and loading conditions. The various failure modes of the unsheathed CFS structural members subjected to axial compression and bending (out-of-plane lateral loading) are shown in Figs.18a and 19 (a-f).

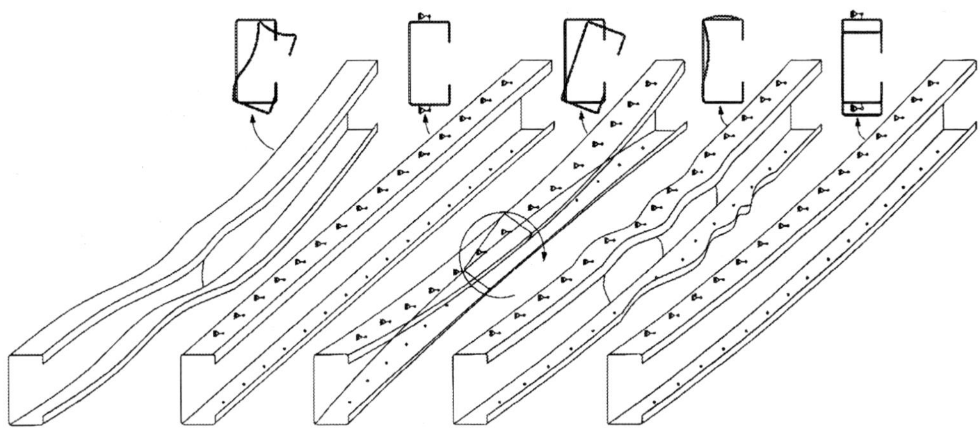

(a) GD interaction buckling (b) Beam with idealized sheathing restraint (c) Lateral torsional buckling (d) GL interaction buckling (e) Major axis buckling

Fig. 6.18: Cold-formed steel structural members subjected to out-of-plane bending - failure modes (GD - global and distortional; GL - global and local)

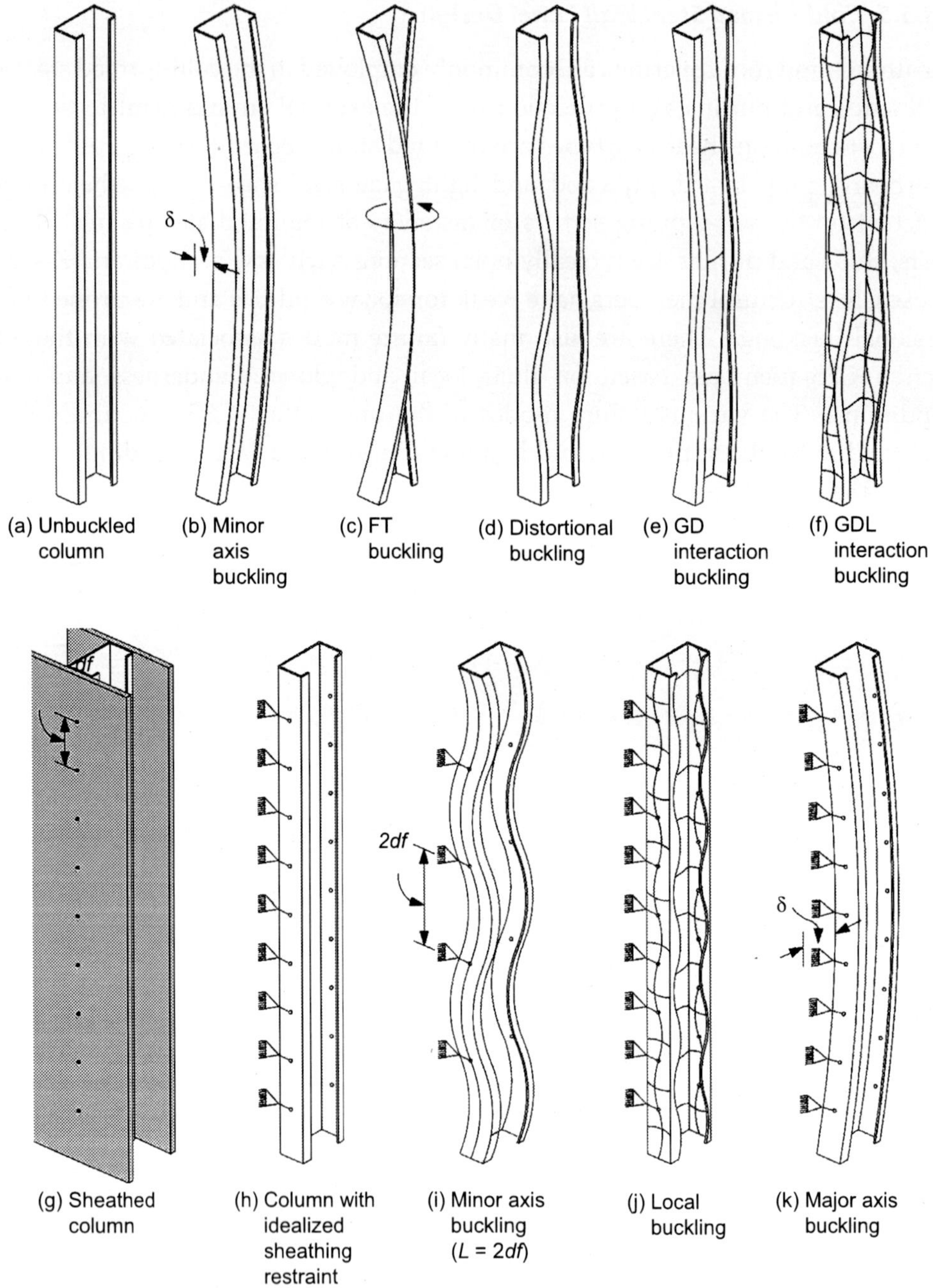

Fig. 6.19: Cold-formed steel structural members subjected to axial compression - failure modes (FT - Flexural torsional; GD - Global and distortional; GDL - Global, distortional and local)

The Direct Strength Method (DSM) from AISI S100 and AZ/NZS predicts the design strength of the open CFS unsheathed structural members conservatively and over conservatively respectively for highly slender members. The failure modes associated with the open CFS structural member changes significantly when they are attached to the sheathing thereby increasing the strength depending on the member slendernesses as shown in Figs. 19(g-k) and Figs. 18(b-e). In addition, the research results presented in Winter suggests that the sheathing configuration must satisfy the following requirements in order to consider the effect of sheathing in the design of CFS structural member. The requirements are (i) The fastener spacing (df) must be close enough to prevent the stud from buckling; (ii) The sheathing material must be rigid enough to minimize the deflection of the stud; (iii) The sheathing fastener connection should be capable of resisting the buckling load without any failure. The sheathing requirements suggested by Winter has been adopted in AISI specifications for the design of CFS structural members. The increase in strength due to the sheathing's bracing effect also depends on the slenderness of the CFS stud. Typically, C channels with high global slenderness fail due to flexural-torsional buckling or lateral-torsional buckling (LTB) in axial compression and flexural loading respectively. Such highly slender members (global) will have low resistance against any loading conditions. However, if such specimens are sheathed, especially on both the sides, the increased strength due to the bracing effect will be significant thereby the structural economy will improve substantially.

In wall panel construction, there is a need for using CFS members with high global slenderness due to the height and thickness limitations. The height and thickness of the wall panel range from 8-10 feet (2400 mm to 3000 mm) and 3-5inches (75 mm to 125 mm) [inclusive of two-sided total sheathing thickness of 1 to 1 $\frac{3}{16}$ inches (24 mm to 30 mm)] respectively. Therefore, the CFS members used in the wall panel becomes highly slender. It should be noted that the governing slenderness of the CFS members in the wall panel can also be reduced by providing bridging and blocking as shown in Fig. 20. At the same time, provision for bridging and blocking results in a perforation in the CFS structural member (inset view-I in Fig. 20) or sometimes the bridging and blocking themselves will have perforations as shown in inset view-II of Fig. 20 to allow the continuity of the CFS structural members. Such effects should be considered in the design in addition to the electricity service perforations. However, the need for bridging and blocking can be significantly reduced when the contribution of the attached sheathing is considered in the computation of design strength. This results in an added advantage in terms of reducing the cost of the structure and eliminating the necessity of providing larger perforation for bridging and blocking which eventually reduces the strength. In addition, the wall panel in the residential buildings should have resistance against both compression (live and dead loads from the roof) and flexure (out of plane lateral loadings due to wind). Hence, the increase in design strength due to the bracing effect of sheathing in the wall panel will be effective in terms of economical design.

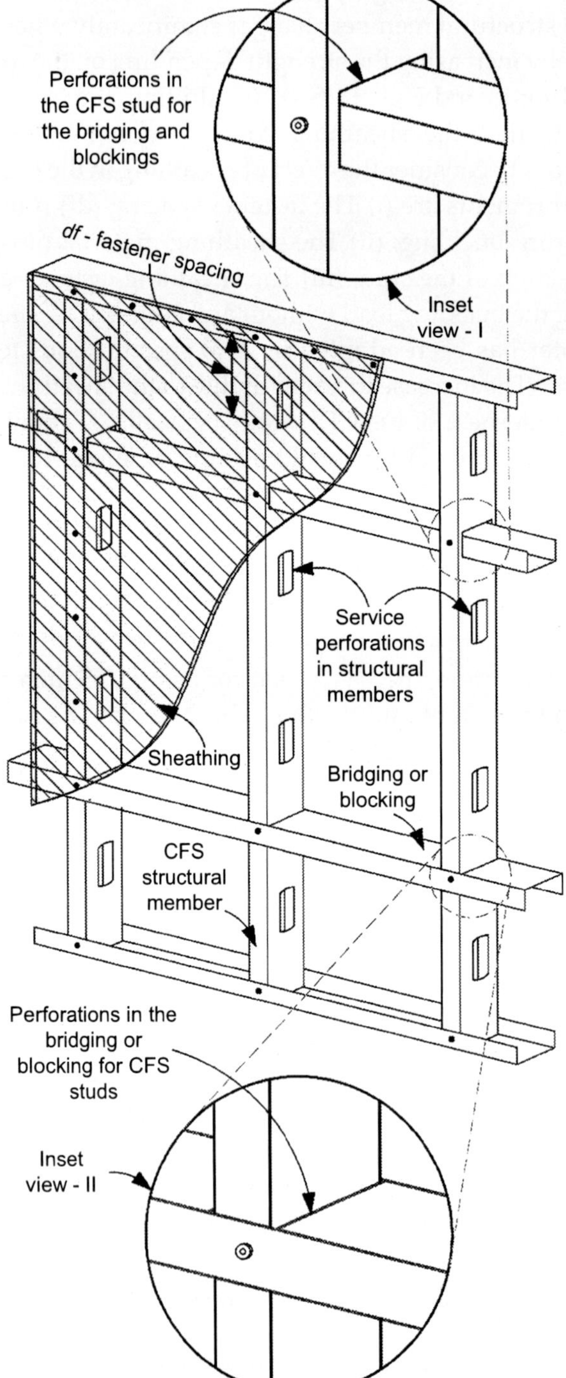

Fig. 6.20: Cold-formed steel structural members with perforations (service openings and openings for continuity members)

In the past, several researchers studied the design of sheathed CFS structural members that are subjected to axial load. Recently, a combination of both lateral and axial compression was considered for the experimental investigation by Peterman and Schafer. The research results indicate that the sheathing attached to the CFS studs resist the weak axis buckling and other buckling modes of the highly slender unsheathed CFS studs and enforces strong axis buckling thereby increasing the design strength. The proposed design method by AISI also suggests the same for the design of sheathed CFS panels subjected to axial loading by considering either the major axis buckling strength or the next governing mode's (local or distortional) buckling strength.

The following are the statements from the design specifications documents

AISI S100:

Wall stud assemblies using a sheathing braced design shall be designed assuming that identical sheathing is attached to both sides of the wall stud and connected to the bottom and top horizontal members of the wall to provide lateral and torsional support to the wall stud in the plane of the wall. Wall studs with sheathing attached to both sides that is not identical shall be designed based on the assumption that the weaker of the two sheathings is attached to both sides.

NAHB (1997)

Exterior load bearing walls with a minimum of 1/2 inch (13 mm) gypsum board on the inside and 7/16 inch (11 mm) OSB or plywood on the outside, and interior load bearing walls with a minimum of 1/2 inch (13 mm) gypsum board on both sides may use the next thinner stud but not less than 33 mils (0.84 mm).

Precisely as per Selvaraj and Madhavan 2018c

(i) If the CFS member is slender in both global and local buckling ($\lambda_e >> 1$ and $\lambda_l >> 1$) or slender only in global buckling ($\lambda_e >> 1$ and $\lambda_l << 1$), the provision of steel bracing will decrease the global unbraced length of the CFS stud in the minor axis from "*L*" to "a" (vertical spacing between the bracings) as shown in Fig. 19 (i), resulting in a significant increase in member strength. However, the increase in member strength should not be higher than the major axis buckling strength.

(ii) When the CFS stud is locally slender ($\lambda_l >> 1$) and has a strong resistance against the global buckling ($\lambda_e << 1$), the bracing effect will not improve strength to the CFS stud as shown in Fig. 19 (j).

6.3.5.6 Design Procedure for LGSF Wall Assembly or CFS Wall Stud

The LGSF Wall Assembly or CFS wall Stud can be designed as a common bracing system as the sheathing boards are behaving as an external bracing to the wall frames. The concept of beam bracing originated from the column bracing expressions developed by Winter (1960). In general, the concept of bracing design is simply to meet the stability requirement by the bracing member. The objective of installing a bracing system in beams is to achieve the full capacity of beams (yield moment capacity) (Selvaraj and Madhavan 2018a,2018b and 2018c). It was shown by Winter (1960) that both the stiffness and strength of the member is important. If the bracing design rules are based only on either strength or stiffness, the bracing system will be inadequate (Yura 2001). Therefore, it is necessary to check both the stiffness and strength requirements of the beam bracing systems (Wang and Nethercot 1990).

The beam bracing arrangements and design are complex and requires detailing when compared to the column bracings (Yura 2001; Selvaraj and Madhavan 2019a and 2019b). The design of beam bracing should be based on the failure mode of the beam; the failure of the beam combines both torsion (cross section twist) and flexure (vertical deflection) (Selvaraj and Madhavan 2019b). The bracing system of beams can be classified as lateral bracing and torsional bracing. An adequate lateral bracing inhibits the lateral deflection of the beam; however, the effectiveness of the lateral bracing depends on the location of center of twist of the beam and that of the lateral bracing. In addition, an effective beam bracing depends on the support condition of the beam as well. An additional advantage of the effective beam bracing is the elimination of the transverse stiffeners in the beam. The failure mode of the beams with different support conditions and effect of bracings are pictorially represented in Fig. 21. Torsional bracing, as the name implies provides restraint against cross-sectional twist of the beam about its longitudinal axis.

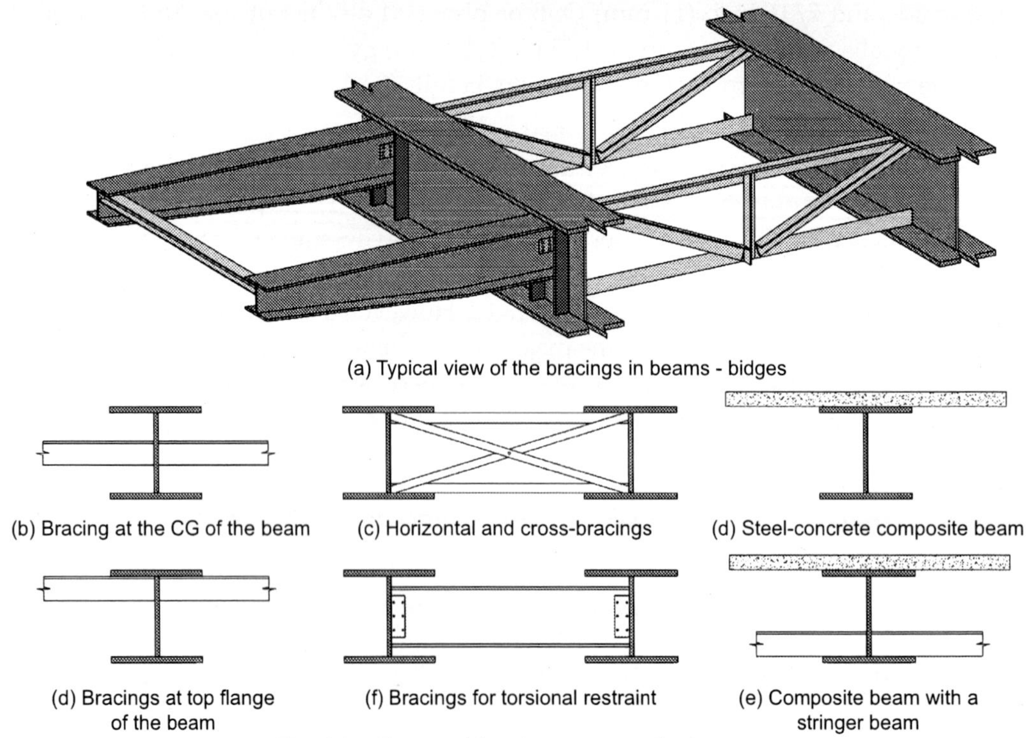

Fig. 6.21: Types of bracing systems for beams

An example of torsional bracing may be a concrete slab on the composite steel beam. However, the concrete beam arrests both the lateral displacement and cross-sectional twist of the beam. The bracing that inhibits both the displacements is much more effective and preferred in the design. Though the single bracing system can be sufficient for restraining the beam from lateral-torsional buckling, the bracing requirement for arresting lateral translation and twist shall be determined individually as it is more practical and conservative. Therefore, the bracing requirements are discussed separately as follows:

6.3.6 Lateral Bracing of Beams

6.3.6.1 *Effectiveness of the Lateral Bracing*

As mentioned previously, the effectiveness of beam bracing depends on the various factors such as location of the beam bracing, beam support conditions and loading pattern. The behaviour of the beam cum bracing with the above interdependent factors are described as follows. For a beam subjected to uniform moment, the lateral bracing at the top flange will be much more effective compared to the lateral bracing at the centroid of the beam. This is due to the fact that the center of twist of the simply supported beam lies well below the tension flange; therefore the bracing away from the center of the twist will experience a smaller force. Now consider the beam with a concentric load at the mid span of the beam. In this case, the beam will not have a uniform moment along the length of the beam, however, due to the load concentration, the ultimate moment at the mid span of the beam is significantly higher than the uniform moment case. As the moment increases the strength and stiffness of the bracing requirement increases significantly compared to the uniform moment condition. It should be noted that all the above cases are for the load applied through the center of gravity of the specimen.

The next interdependent factor is the load applied through the top flange of the beam. In this case, the ultimate capacity of the beam significantly decreases even with top flange bracing. The significant decrease in the effectiveness of the bracing is due to the change in the center of twist of the beam due to the top flange loading. The center of twist is close to the center of gravity of the beam. Therefore, the bracing at the centroid of the beam is ineffective. As described, the bracing requirement increases significantly with decrease in the distance between the center of twist to the location of the bracing. Therefore, it is clear that the application of load position must be considered in the design of beam bracing systems. In the design of the lateral beam bracing systems, the strength requirement as well as the stiffness requirement should be met as per the following section.

6.3.6.2 *Strength Criteria for Lateral Beam Bracings*

The required strength for each bracing is determined by the bracing design method developed by Yura. This bracing design concept was initially developed by Winter for sheathing braced design of CFS members subjected to axial compression. However, in 2001, Yurahad made modifications in the design approach of Winter to account for the following design parameters: (i) different loading cases; (ii) number of bracings; (iii) single and double curvature; and (iv) discrete and relative bracing. It should be noted that the current bracing is a discrete one. The modified formula by Yura for determining the bracing strength for the discretely braced structural member (F_{br}) is given in Eqs. (1) and (2) respectively.

$$F_{br} = 0.01\ C_L C_d M_f / h \tag{1}$$

$$F_{br} = 0.004\ C_L C_d M_f / h \tag{2}$$

where, C_L is the modification factor to account the top flange loading effect, equal to unity for normal loading and C_L is 1+(1.2/n) for top flange loading; n is the number of bracings; C_d is the additional modification factor to account the number of curvatures (single or double), equal to unity ($C_d = 1$) for single curvature and is equal to $1+(M_S/M_L)^2$ for double curvature; M_S and M_L are the moments causing compression in the top and bottom flanges respectively; M_f is the design moment capacity of the structural member; h is the depth (outtoout) of the member or distance between the centroid of the force to the location of the bracing, whichever is conservative. Since the objective of the work is to avoid the lateral torsional buckling of the steel girder, the design moment (M_f) has been taken as equal to yield moment capacity [M_y = section modulus (S_x or S_y) × yield stress (f_y)]. If the strength of the bracing is higher than the strength required (F_{br}) to achieve the design moment (M_f), then it can be assumed that the beam will attain the yield moment capacity.

6.3.6.3 Stiffness Criteria for Lateral Beam Bracings

The Yura's method of required bracing stiffness calculation is from Winter's ideal lateral brace stiffness method which was developed for sheathed CFS columns. The Winter's method of bracing stiffness calculation is based on the elastic buckling stiffness of the column, where an increase in buckling load results in a corresponding increase in the stiffness required to brace the column. The modified formula for required bracing stiffness (β_i^*) is given in Eq. 3.

$$\beta_i^* = 2\frac{N_i C_b P_f}{L_b} C_d C_L \tag{3}$$

where, numerical 2 is a factor of safety as suggested by Yura; N_i = coefficient depending on the number of braces (n), as recommended by Winter, for discrete bracing $N_i = 4 - (2/n)$ and for relative bracing $N_i = 1$; n = number of bracings; C_b = bending coefficient, for uniform loading $C_b = 1$ and for three-point loading $C_b = 1.75$; $P_f = (\pi^2 E\ I_{yc})/L^2$; E = Young's modulus of the steel beam; I_{yc} = moment of inertia of the compression flange; L = unbraced length of the structural member requires bracing; C_d = additional modification factor to account the number of inflection points (single or double curvature), equal to unity for single curvature and $C_d = 1+(M_S/M_L)^2$ for double curvature; M_S and M_L are the moments causing compression in the top and bottom flanges respectively; C_L = modification factor to account the top flange loading effect, equal to unity for normal loading and $C_L = 1 + (1.2/n)$ for top flange loading; L_b = is taken as the distance between the two bracing points. It should be noted that the stiffness required $\left(\beta_i^*\right)$ should be matched by the axial stiffness of the bracing in order to restrain the steel beam from failure due to LTB.

6.3.7 Torsional Bracing of Beams

6.3.7.1 Effectiveness of the Torsional Bracing

The twist of the beam can be restrained by one of three ways: (i) By providing beams with a similar cross section in the transverse direction (Fig. 21f) (ii) By providing cross frames that connects both top and bottom flange of the beam (Fig. 21c) or (iii) By a steel-concrete composite beam along with floor/stringer beams at the bottom flange (Valentino and Trahair 1998; Braford and Pi 2002; Mohebkhah and Showkati 2005 and Park and Stallings 2003). It should be noted that the provision of torsional buckling need not necessarily arrest the lateral movement of the beam. However, the beam will have a relative displacement or move as a whole as shown in Fig. 22.

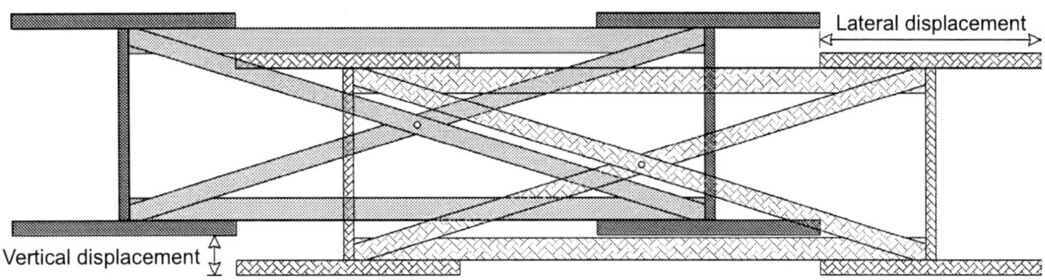

Fig. 6.22: Lateral movement of the beam with torsional bracing

It should be noted that for effective torsional restraint, it is essential for both the individual top flange and bottom flange to be braced. In addition for torsional bracing, the difference in the effectiveness of bracing under the top flange loading and centroid loading is insignificant (Yura 2001). Similar to lateral bracing design, the torsional bracing should also be designed for both strength and stiffness.

6.3.7.2 Strength and Stiffness Criteria for Torsional Beam Bracings

The force and stiffness requirement for the torsional beam bracing is shown in Eqs. (4) and (5), respectively as per Yura (2001).

$$F_{br} = \frac{0.005\, LL_b M_f^2}{(nhEI_{eff} C_{bb}^2)} \tag{4}$$

$$B_T^* = \frac{2.4LM_f^2}{(nhEI_{eff}C_{bb}^2)} \tag{5}$$

where, F_{br} and B_T^* is the force and stiffness required to brace the beam from torsional buckling; L is the beam span; L_b is the unbraced length (between the bracing points); M_f is the design moment of the beam; I_{eff} is the governing moment of inertia for bracing design; typically moment of inertia of the compression flange; C_{bb} is the bending coefficient (bending moment modification factor), n is the number of intermediate braces and h is the distance between the centroid of the two flanges.

6.3.7.3 Further Discussion on Bracings

Though the Yura work on bracing is significant and is currently being followed in the design of beam bracing systems, the recent work on sheathing bracing design for cold-formed steel beams by Selvaraj and Madhavan (2019d) validates the same by experimental results. In particular, the experimental results indicate that the effect of bracing varies significantly for members that fail in minor axis buckling and lateral torsional buckling. Therefore, a new design expression for predicting the sheathing stiffness against the pull through failure is proposed. The equation proposed by Selvaraj and Madhavan (2019d) may be used in the design of bracing for the floor joist where the wood or cement sheet is used as a deck (Fig. 23a). As the concept of bracing system design is simply a demand and supply approach, the bracing demand for the floor joist shall be obtained from Yura (2001) and the strength and stiffness of the wood or cement sheet may be obtained from Selvaraj and Madhavan (2019d).

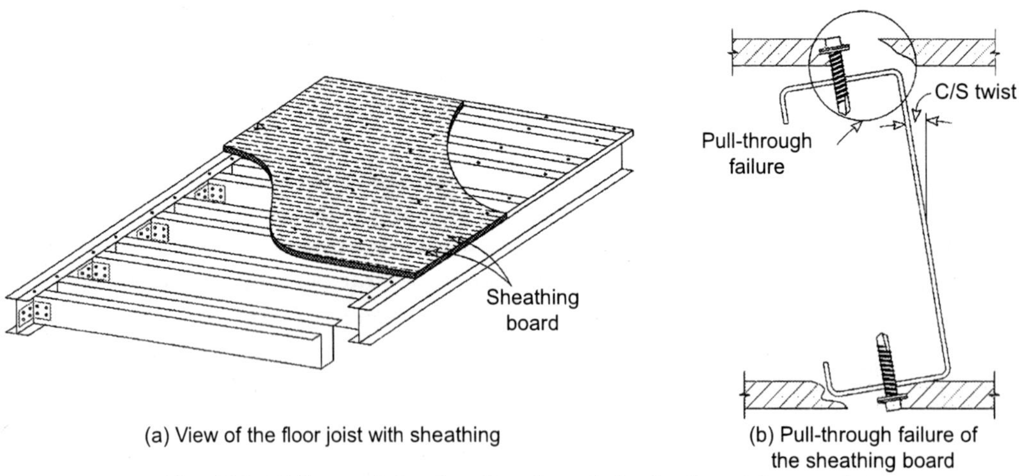

(a) View of the floor joist with sheathing

(b) Pull-through failure of the sheathing board

Fig. 6.23: Stiffness of the sheathing boards in the floor joist panels

The generalized expression for predicting the stiffness of the sheathing board against the pull-through failure (due to the lateral torsional buckling of the CFS stud - Fig. 23b) is shown below.

$$k_p = \frac{\left(\dfrac{E}{58.4}\right)e^{(-0.106(d/2))}}{A.\left(\dfrac{6274.40}{E_S}\right)e^{(Bd/2)}} \tag{6}$$

$$A = 3112.4\ E_s^{-0.909} \tag{7}$$

$$B = \frac{E_S}{142857.1} - 0.0437 \tag{8}$$

The proposed Eqs. (6-8) for predicting the magnitude sheathing stiffness is valid only in SI units, where E and E_s are Young's modulus of steel in N/mm^2 and tensile modulus of sheathing board in N/mm^2, respectively; d is the depth of the CFS stud in millimetres.

6.3.8 Construction Procedure For Residential Building Using Light Gauge Steel Structure

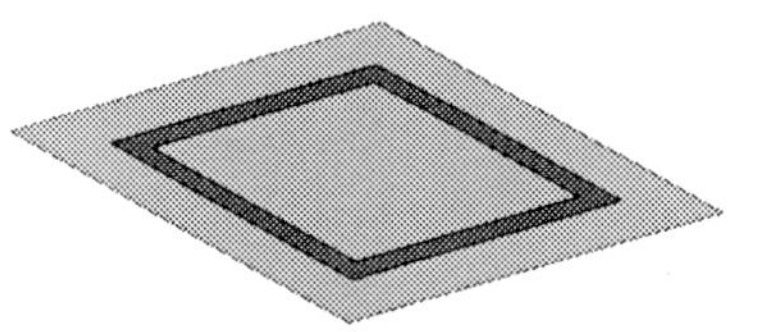

Foundation layout

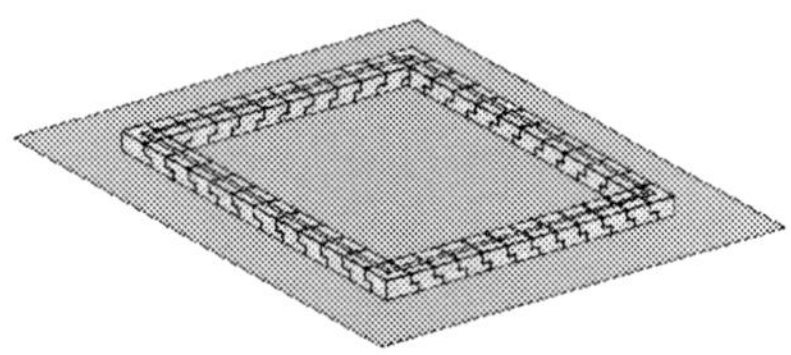

Construction of foundation concrete for LGSF structure

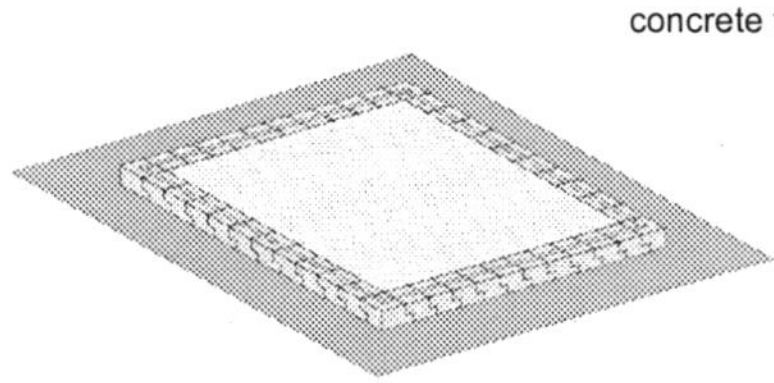

Typical earth filling and flooring inside the foundation panel

Fig. 6.24: Preparation on foundation for installation of LGSF frames

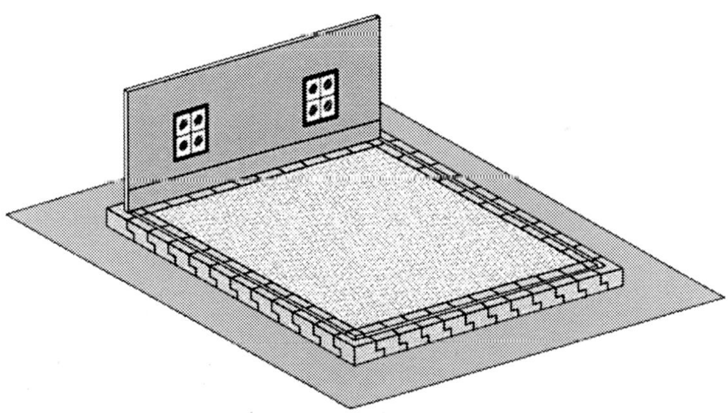

Fig. 6.25: Installation of wall panels and frames

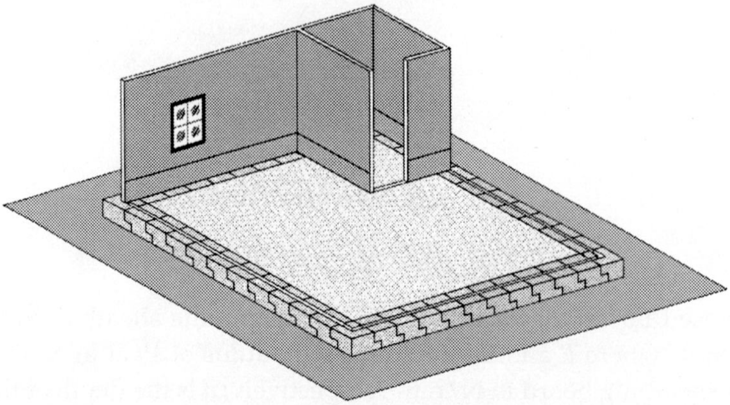

Fig. 6.26: Installation of corner wall panels and frames

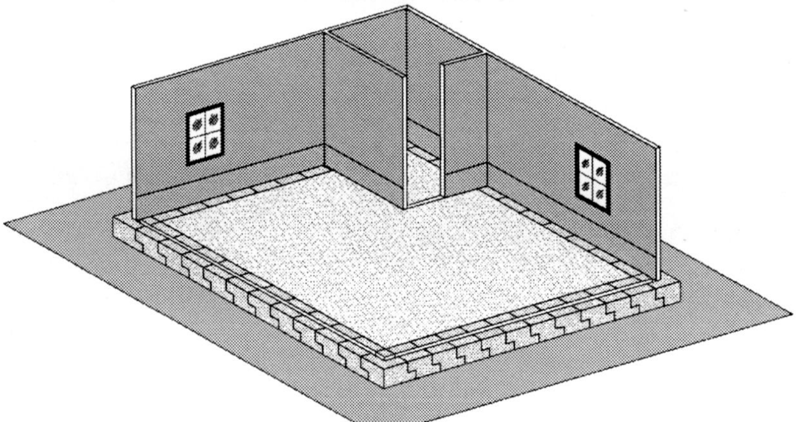

Fig. 6.27: Installation of continuous wall panels and frames

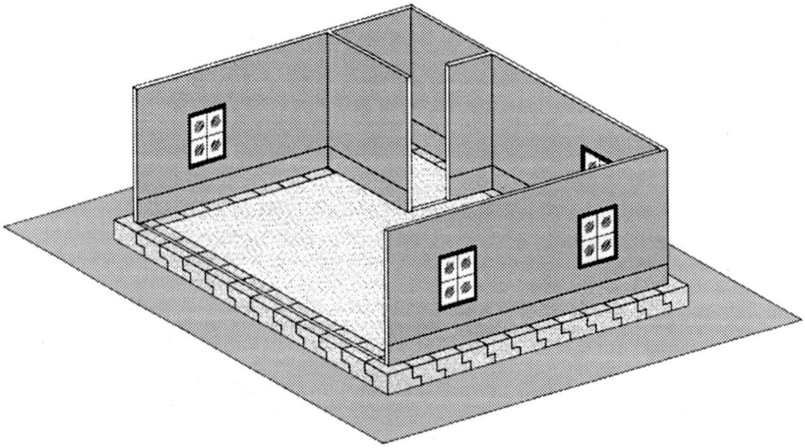

Fig. 6.28: Installation of continuous wall panels and frames

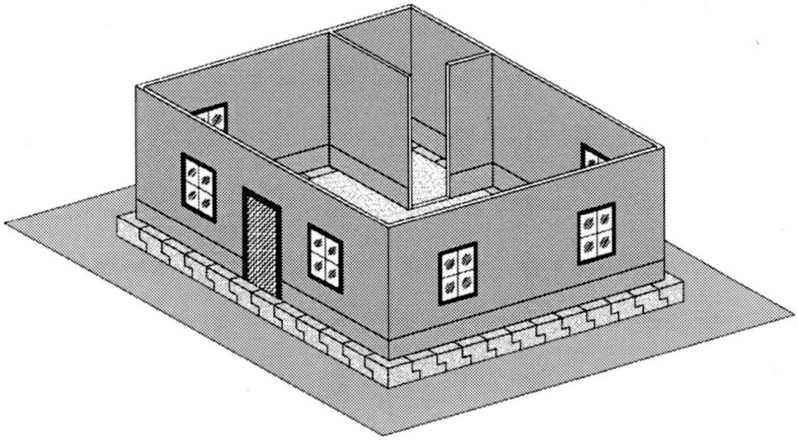

Fig. 6.29: Installation of continuous wall panels and frames

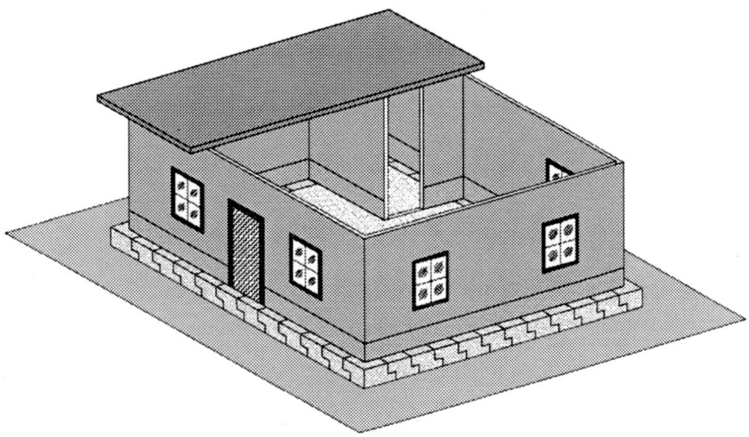

Fig. 6.30: Installation of roof panels

Fig. 6.31: Installation of roof panels

Fig. 6.32: View of the residential building constructed using LGSF structure

Fig. 6.33: View of the residential building with toilet constructed using LGSF structure

6.3.9 Construction Procedure for Residential Building using Hot-rolled Steel and Light Gauge Steel Structure

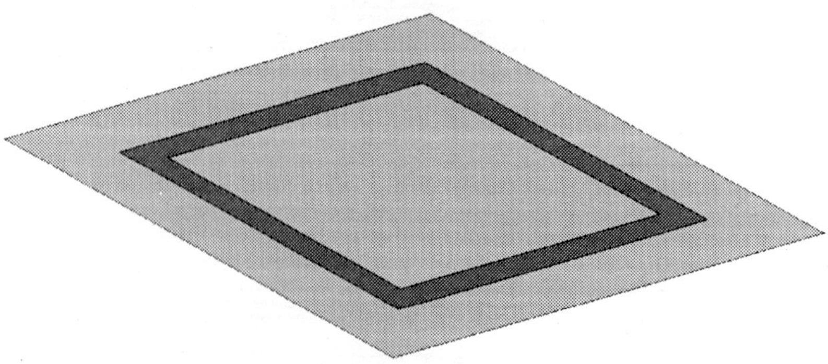

Building layout

Fig. 6.34: Preparation on foundation for installation of hot-rolled steel and light gauge steel structure

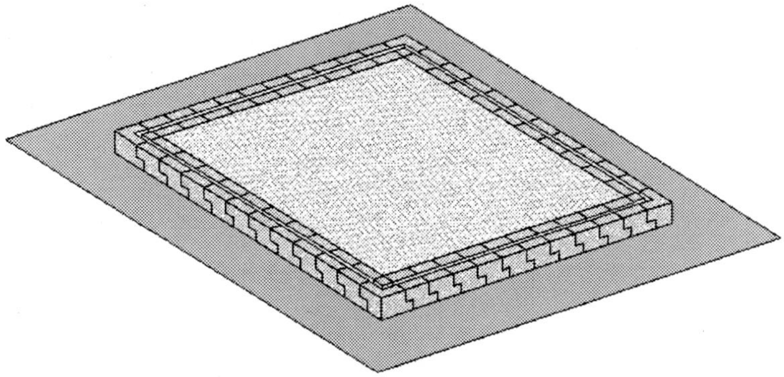

Building foundation layout

Fig. 6.35: Preparation on foundation for installation of hot-rolled steel and light gauge steel structure

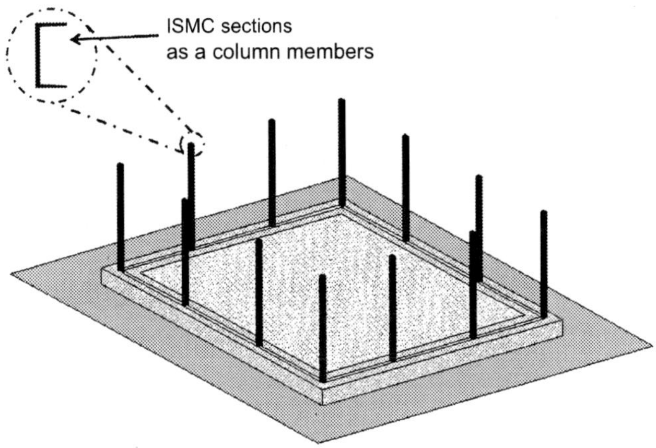

Rise of superstructure

Fig. 6.36: Erection of hot rolled steel structure (columns - loading member)

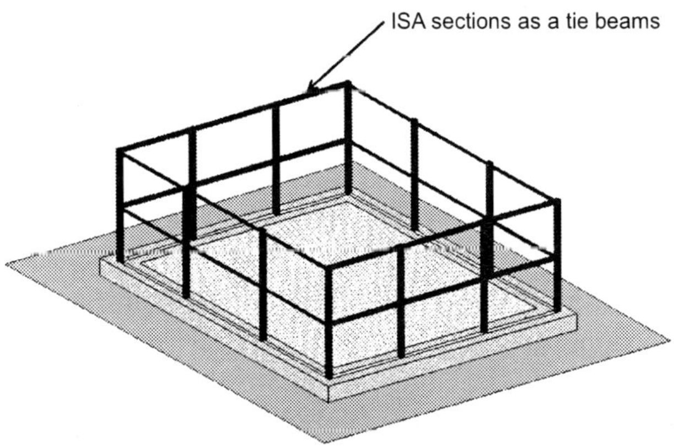

Rise of superstructure

Fig. 6.37: Erection of hot-rolled steel structure (beams - loading member)

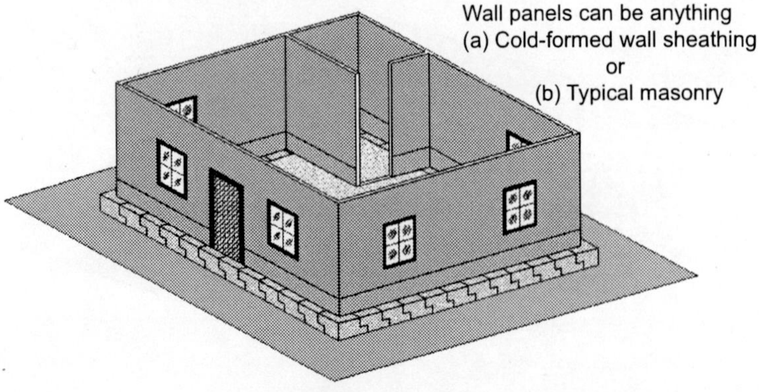

Fig. 6.38: Erection of wall panels fabricated using LGSF (non-loading member)

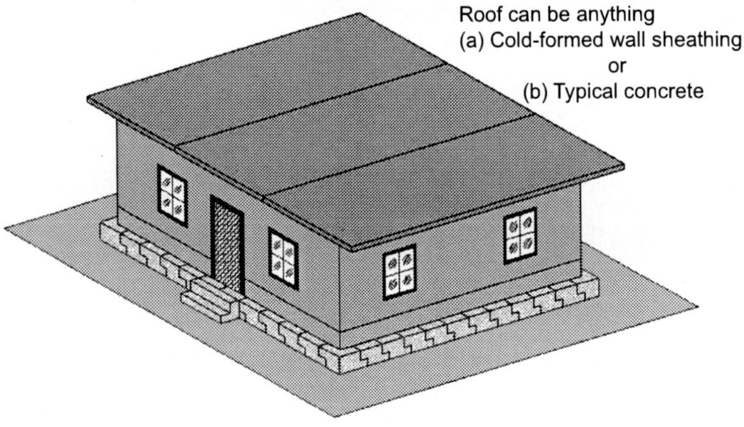

Fig. 6.39: Erection of roof panels fabricated using LGSF (loading member)

REFERENCES

1. Yu, W.W., (2000). "Cold-formed steel design". John Wiley & Sons.
2. Rasmussen, K. J. R., and G. J. Hancock: "Geometric Imperfections in Plated Structures Subject to Interaction between Buckling Modes," *Thin-Walled Struct.*, vol. 6, no. 6, 1988.
3. Selvaraj, S. and Madhavan, M., (2014). September. Study on partially closed built-up sections using cold formed steel with geometric imperfection combinations under axial compression. In 7th international conference on thin-walled structures, Busan, Korea (Vol. 28).

4. Selvaraj, S., and Madhavan, M. (2018a). "Geometric Imperfection Measurements and Validations on Cold-Formed Steel Channels using 3D Non-contact Laser Scanner." *J. Struct. Eng.* DOI: 10.1061/(ASCE)ST.1943-541X.0001993
5. Zhang W, Mahdavian M, and Li Y, Yu C. (2016). "Experiments and Simulations of Cold-Formed Steel Wall Assemblies Using Corrugated Steel Sheathing Subjected to Shear and Gravity Loads". *J. Struct. Eng.*,143(3):04016193.
6. Selvaraj, S. and Madhavan, M. (2018b)."Studies on Cold-formed steel stud panels with gypsum sheathing subjected to out-of-plane bending," *J. Struct. Eng.*, 144 (9). DOI : 10.1061/(ASCE)ST.1943-541X.0002069.
7. Selvaraj, S. and Madhavan, M., (2018c). "Improvements in AISI Design Methods for Gypsum Sheathed Cold-Formed Steel Wall Panels Subjected to Bending". *J. Struct. Eng*, 145(2), 04018243.
8. Selvaraj, S. and Madhavan, M., (2019a). "Sheathing Bracing Requirements for Cold-formed Steel Wall Panels: Experimental Investigation". Structures (Vol. 19, pp. 258-276). Elsevier.
9. Selvaraj, S and Madhavan, M (2019b). "Bracing Effect of Sheathing in Point symmetric Cold-formed Steel Flexural Members," Journal of Constructional Steel Research, Accepted for publication. Article no: JCSR_2018_1172.
10. Selvaraj, S. and Madhavan, M., (2019c). "Investigation on sheathing effect and failure modes of gypsum sheathed cold-formed steel wall panels subjected to bending". Structures. Elsevier. https://doi.org/10.1016/j.istruc.2018.09.013.
11. Selvaraj, S. and Madhavan, M., (2018d). Retrofitting of Structural Steel Channel Sections Using Cold-Formed Steel Encasing Channels. Journal of Performance of Constructed Facilities, 32(4), p.04018049.
12. AISI. (American Iron and Steel Institute) (2016). "North American Cold-Formed Steel Specification for the Design of Cold-Formed Steel Structural Members." AISI-S100-16, Washington, DC.
13. Niu, S., R. Rasmussen, K. J., and Fan, F. (2014a). "Local-global interaction buckling of stainless steel I-beams. I: Experimental investigation." *J. Struct. Eng.*, 141(8) 04014194.
14. Niu, S., R. Rasmussen, K. J., and Fan, F. (2014b). "Local-global interaction buckling of stainless steel I-beams. II: Numerical Study and Design." *J. Struct. Eng.*, 141(8) 04014195.
15. Su, M.N., Young, B. and Gardner, L. (2014). Deformation-based design of aluminium alloy beams. *Eng. Struct.*, 80, 339-349.
16. Wang, L. and Young, B., (2015a). "Behavior of Cold-Formed Steel Built-Up Sections with Intermediate Stiffeners under Bending. I: Tests and Numerical Validation." *J. Struct. Eng.*, 142(3), p.04015150.

17. Wang, L., and Young, B. (2015b). "Behavior of Cold-Formed Steel Built-Up Sections with Intermediate Stiffeners under Bending. II: Parametric Study and Design." *J. Struct. Eng.*, 142(3) 04015151.
18. AISI. (American Iron and Steel Institute) (2012a). "North American Cold-Formed Steel Specification for the Design of Cold-Formed Steel Structural Members." AISI-S100-12, Washington, DC.
19. Wang, L. and Young, B., (2018). "Behaviour and design of cold-formed steel built-up section beams with different screw arrangements". *Thin-Walled Struct.*, 131, 16-32.
20. Zhang, J. and Young, B., (2018). "Finite element analysis and design of cold-formed steel built-up closed section columns with web stiffeners". *Thin-Walled Struct.*, 131, 223-237.
21. Papangelis, J. P. and Hancock, G. J. (1995). "Computer analysis of thin-walled structural members." *Comp. & Struct.*, 56(1) 157-176.
22. AS (Standards Association of Australia). 1998. Steel structures. AS 4100. Homebush, NSW, Australia: AS.
23. AISI. (American Iron and Steel Institute) (2012b). "North American Standard for Cold-Formed Steel Framing - Wall Stud Design." AISI S211-07, 2007 Edition (reaffirmed 2012).
24. ASCE. (2010). "Minimum design loads for buildings and other structures." *ASCE/SEI 7-10*, ASCE, Reston, VA.
25. AS/NZS (Australian/New Zealand standard) (2002). "Structural design actions. Part 0: General principles. *AS/NZS 1170.0:2002*, Standards Association of Australia, Sydney, Australia.
26. Schafer, B.W. (2006). "Designing cold-formed steel using the Direct Strength Method." *Eighteenth Intl. Spec. Conf. on Cold-Formed Steel Struct.*, Orlando, FL.
27. Pham, C.H. and Hancock, G.J., 2013. Experimental investigation and direct strength design of high-strength, complex C-sections in pure bending. *J. Struct. Eng.*, 139(11), pp. 1842-1852.
28. Selvaraj, S. and Madhavan, M,. (2019)."Structural Design of Cold-formed Steel face-to-face Connected Built-up beams using Direct Strength Method," Journal of Constructional Steel Research, DOI: https://doi.org/10.1016/j.jcsr.2019.05.053.
29. Bradford, M.A. and Pi, Y.L., 2002. Elastic flexural-torsional buckling of discretely restrained arches. *Journal of Structural Engineering*, 128(6), pp. 719-727.
30. Mohebkhah, A. and Showkati, H., 2005. Bracing requirements for inelastic castellated beams. *Journal of Constructional Steel Research*, 61(10), pp. 1373-1386.
31. Park, J.S. and Stallings, J.M., 2003. Lateral-torsional buckling of stepped beams. *Journal of structural Engineering*, 129(11), pp. 1457-1465.

32. Valentino, J. and Trahair, N.S., 1998. Torsional restraint against elastic lateral buckling. *Journal of Structural Engineering*, 124(10), pp. 1217-1225.

33. Wang, Y.C. and Nethercot, D.A., 1990. Bracing requirements for laterally unrestrained beams. *Journal of Constructional Steel Research*, 17(4), pp. 305-315.

34. Winter, G. 1960. "Lateral bracing of beams and columns." *J. Struct. Div.*, 125 (1): 809-825.

35. Yura, J.A., 2001. Fundamentals of beam bracing. *Engineering Journal-American Institute of Steel Construction*, 38(1), pp. 11-26.

For more details about the cold-formed steel research activities the reader can contact Prof. Mahendrakumar Madhavan, IIT Hyderabad at the following address.

Division of Structural Engineering

Department of Civil Engineering, IIT Hyderabad

Kandi (V), Sangareddy (M), Medak Dist-502 285, Telangana, India

Phone: 9490782690

Personal Website: https://sites.google.com/view/iithmkmsteelsite

Recommended Books for Light Gauge Steel Frame Systems Design

- ***Cold-Formed Steel Design*** by Wei-Wen Yu, Roger A. LaBoube, Helen Chen
- ***Cold-Formed Steel Structures to the AISI Specification*** by Gregory J. Hancock, Thomas Murray and Duane S. Ellifrit.

Useful Websites for Light Gauge Steel Frame Systems

- https://www.cfsei.org/
- https://www.steel.org/
- https://www.asce.org/
- http://www.ssma.com/
- https://www.mbma.com/
- http://cssbi.ca/
- https://www.sdi.org/
- http://cfsrc.org/
- http://steeli.org/
- https://www.ce.jhu.edu/cfsnees/
- http://www.ssrcweb.org/

7
Precast Concrete Construction Systems

7.1 PRECAST CONCRETE CONSTRUCTION SYSTEMS

7.1.1 Introduction

There are different types of precast concrete buildings, which can be grouped as total precast, partial precast and mixed construction structures.It is necessary to study each system for better understanding, and to arrive at an appropriate application. Total precast building comprises various precast components such as footings, columns, beams, slabs, walls, façades etc. A partial precast building can be made of precast concrete components, and cast-in-place (CIP) (or, cast-in-situ) concrete members. This type of building is also referred to as hybrid construction. Mixed construction building comprises of precast components along with CIP concrete or steel or masonry or timber members. Here, description of the different types of precast building is followed by illustrations of the various types of precast components. An introduction to mixed construction is provided.

A system refers to a collection of components which interact together to perform a specific function. The different systems of precast concrete buildings can be grouped under the following headings.

- Overall structural systems
- Systems for lateral load resistance
- Roof and floor systems

7.1.2 Overall Structural Systems

The *structural system* of a building is that part of the building which resists the loads acting on the building. First, this system has to continuously resist the vertical loads due to gravity, such as the self-weight of the different components of the system (termed as the *dead load*), weight of the additional components outside the system but acting perpetually (termed as the *super-imposed dead load*), and the fluctuating weight of the occupants or contents of the building (termed as the *live load*). Second, the structural system has to resist the horizontal (lateral) loads due to several causes such as wind, earthquake, and soil pressure. Third, it is required to resist the loads generated due to the effects of other factors, such as creep and shrinkage of concrete, variation of ambient temperature, differential settlement of the foundations supporting the building, etc.

The overall structural systems of precast concrete buildings can be broadly classified into four groups, as shown in Figure 1. Typical examples of framed and large panel constructions are shown in Figures 2 and 3, respectively.

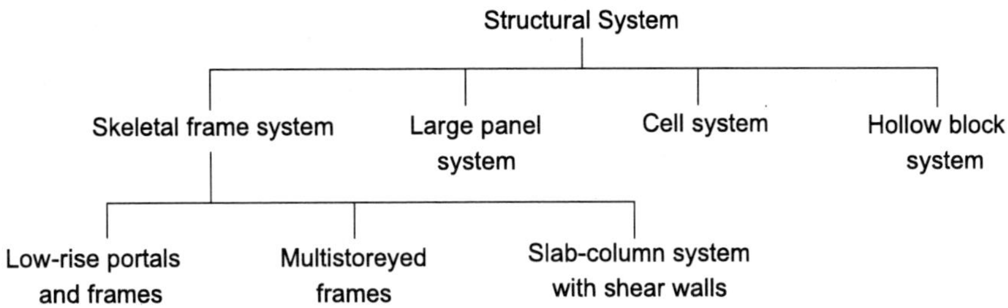

Fig. 7.1: Classification of structural systems for precast concrete buildings

Fig. 7.2: Framed system: Terminal building at Bangalore airport

7.1.3 Systems for Lateral Load Resistance

In this section, the system of components in a building that is designed to provide resistance to lateral loads is separately explained. This is termed as the *lateral load resisting system* (LLRS) for the convenience of conceptualisation, analysis and design. Each of the structural systems described in the previous section can have a single type of LLRS, or a hybrid of more than one type of LLRS. Here, the various types of LLRS are described with reference to the overall structural systems.

Fig. 7.3: Large panel system: High-rise apartment buildings at Mumbai

7.1.3.1 Low-rise Portals and Frames

The resistance to lateral loads can be provided by the following types of LLRS.

Cantilever columns fixed to the foundation: The system consists of columns acting like vertical cantilevers, which are connected at the top by the roof system. The roof acts as a diaphragm to mobilise the columns to act together and thereby to share the total lateral load acting on the roof. Depending upon the location, the system is suitable for up to 3 storeyed buildings.

Portal made of sub-assemblages: The system consists of sub-assemblages of portal frame members, where the connections of the members are rigid. The sub-assemblages are isolated near the locations of reduced bending moment (a point of inflection under a certain load case). The connection of the sub-assemblages can be pinned or moment resisting. The bases of the columns need not be fixed, and isolated pad footings can be adequate.

7.1.3.2 Multistoreyed Frames

The resistance to loads in a conventional CIP multi-storeyed multi-bay frame generates from the frame action of the beams and columns, and rigidity of the beam-to-column joints. For a frame made of precast members, the resistance to lateral loads depends on the nature of connection of the members. The following classification of the frames is based on the type of connections.

Frames with rigid beam-to-column connections: The individual precast members are provided with dowel bars at their ends. At the site, the bars of the beams and the columns at a joint are overlapped, and concrete is cast to emulate a rigid connection. The behaviour of an emulative frame is similar to a CIP frame. The adequacy of the lateral load resistance depends on the location and height of the building.

Frames with dry-jointed beam-to-column connections: To avoid on-site concreting, the precast members can be connected by steel inserts and elements. This type of connection is also referred to as a dry connection. The common option is to support the beams of the intermediate levels on corbels of the columns, with adequate restraint against unseating or toppling. Non-prestressed bars are used to introduce continuity at the top of each beam, thus generating resistance for partial moment transfer. In analysis, this type of beam-to-column connection is idealised as pinned or semi-rigid. In the absence of adequate moment transfer from the beams to the columns, additional lateral load resistance is provided by braces, shear walls or core walls.

Dual system: A *dual system* points to the sharing of lateral load between the frames and additional components, such as braces, shear walls and cores. The proportion of sharing of the lateral load depends on the relative lateral stiffness of the frames and these additional components. The sizes of the columns can be reduced in presence of these components.

7.1.3.3 Wall System

The resistance to lateral loads comes from the jointed panels that behave like shear walls. There can be two types of layout of the walls. In the first type, load-bearing or structural walls are provided in orthogonal directions. This generates adequate lateral load resistance in both the directions. In the second type, to retain flexibility in the usage of space, interior structural walls are provided in only one direction, which is referred to as the longitudinal direction. Non-structural cross walls are provided for partitioning of space. Since the lateral load resistance in the transverse direction is generated only by the exterior structural walls, cores are provided to supplement the resistance.

7.1.3.4 Roof and Floor Systems

The roof and floor systems are described separately to illustrate the transfer of loads between the several components.

Roof systems: A precast horizontal roof system can be similar to that of a floor system (described subsequently), with additional weather-proof course. A mild slope can be provided by using roof girders with camber, or with girders with varying depth (referred to as a saddle girder). In a sloping roof system, precast concrete units (subsequently referred to as roof units) or metal sheets can span longitudinally between the saddle members or the rafters of portal frames, or the top chord members of trusses.

Elegant precast roof system can be made of arches, shell units or folded plate units. Apart from providing large clear space, there can be provisions of sky light. Roofs made of trusses, arches, shells or folded plates are suitable for industrial and commercial buildings, convention centres, airport terminals and storage facilities. Figures 4 to 6 illustrate a few types of precast concrete roof systems.

Fig 7.4: Slab units on trussed purlins, supported on rafters of A-frames (Silo at Thoothukudi)

Fig. 7.5: Slab units on arches in a vaulted roof (Silo at Jagdishpur)

Fig. 7.6: Folded plate units on girders (Chemical plant at Ongole)

Floor systems: Concrete floors can be made of CIP concrete or precast concrete units. In a large panel system building, if the bay size is small, a two-way single precast concrete slab unit can span between the walls and have emulative connections with the walls. The slab acts similar to a CIP concrete floor. But in a skeletal frame system building, due to large bays, a floor is made of multiple one-way precast concrete units. In this situation, the floor is not inherently monolithic. Under gravity loads there may be uneven deflections of the units, which can affect the serviceability. Under lateral loads, a floor needs to act as a horizontal diaphragm to mobilise the vertical components of the LLRS, such as the frames, braces or walls.

The components of the floor system are:

- Floor units
- Spandrel units
- Interior beams

In addition to the flexural reinforcement in the floor units, reinforcements are provided for the diaphragm action. They are grouped under four categories.

- Stitch reinforcement
- Chord reinforcement
- Shear reinforcement
- Collector reinforcement

Figure 7.7 illustrates the use of precast hollow core units.

Fig. 7.7: Floors made of precast hollow core units (Canteen building, Pune)

7.1.4 Summary

The write-up presents the different systems adopted in precast concrete construction. First, the classification of the overall structural systems in to skeletal frame system, large panel system, cell system and hollow block system is presented. Each of these systems has benefits depending on the type of building. The frame system can be further sub-divided in to low-rise portals and frames, multi-storeyed frames and slab–column system. The layouts of these buildings provide large column free space. On the contrary, the large panel system is typically used in residential construction, where close partitioning of space is required. The hollow block system can be used in place of masonry construction, for low-rise buildings.

The second set of systems is related to resistance to lateral loads. A portal generates lateral load resistance either by cantilever columns, or frame action of the portal. In a multi-storeyed frame, the connections of the precast members can be emulative to that of cast-in-place construction, to generate lateral load resistance. Else, in case of dry-jointed connections, supplemental lateral load resistance may be provided by braces, shear walls or core walls. In a wall system, the structural walls provide adequate lateral load resistance.

The third group of systems describes the roof and floor systems. Each of these systems has several components, whose integral action provides the resistance to gravity and lateral loads.

REFERENCES

1. FIB Bulletin 19 (2002), *Precast Concrete in Mixed Construction*, International Federation for Structural Concrete (FIB), Switzerland.
2. FIB Bulletin 27 (2003), *Seismic Design of Precast Concrete Building Structures*, International Federation for Structural Concrete (FIB), Switzerland.
3. FIP *Planning and Design Handbook on Precast Building Structures* (1998), International Federation for Prestressing.
4. *Handbook on Precast Concrete for Buildings* (2018), ICI Bulletin 02, Indian Concrete Institute.
5. *PCI Design Handbook* (2010), Precast/Prestressed Concrete Institute, USA.
6. Proceedings of the *One Day National Workshop on Precast Concrete Buildings in India* (2011), Organised by Indian Concrete Institute and Indian Institute of Technology Madras, Chennai, 6th August.
7. Bachmann, H. And Steinle, A. (2011), *Precast Concrete Structures*, Ernst and Sohn.
8. Elliott, K. S. (2002), *Precast Concrete Structures*, Butterworth & Heinemann.
9. Elliott, K. S. and Tovey, A. K. (1992), *Precast Concrete Frame Buildings*, British Cement Association.
10. IS 15916:2010 Code of practice for building design and erection using prefabricated concrete.
11. NBC 2016 - Part 6, Section 7 Prefabrication, System, Building and mixed/ composite construction.

Acknowledgements

The author wishes to gratefully acknowledge the photographs and data received from M/s Larsen & Toubro Limited.

HANDBOOK ON PRECAST CONCRETE FOR BUILDINGS – AN INTRODUCTION

Introduction

The use of precast concrete is considered to be a solution for the construction of mass housing in India. Under this context, the Indian Concrete Institute published the *Handbook on Precast Concrete for Buildings* for the benefit of professionals involved in construction of buildings using precast concrete [1] (Fig. 1). The objective of the handbook was to cover wide ranging topics of precast concrete, with a simple to read and easy to comprehend approach. To maintain brevity, information that is commonly used in design and construction of reinforced concrete structures was not covered. There are references in the handbook which can be accessed for additional material. The different chapters of the handbook were authored by professionals from the construction industry, scientists from a research organisation, and academicians involved in education and research related to precast concrete. This paper briefly presents the content of the handbook chapter wise. Important statements are highlighted in boxes.

Fig. 1: Cover of the "Handbook on Precast Concrete for Buildings"

1. Precast Concrete in Buildings and Urban Infrastructure

> *"Though the Indian construction industry is sizeable and contributes significantly to the development of the country, it has many challenges to improve the productivity in the construction sector. Hence, mechanised construction, predominantly known as precast concrete construction, will facilitate buildings which are faster in delivery with the best quality. Economy is achieved by saving in the construction time predominantly and adoption of forms which are not possible in conventional design."*

The benefits of precast concrete can be summarised under the following categories.

Quality

- Better control in a factory environment
- Suitable during inclement weather
- Efficient quality management
- Accuracy in dimensions
- Possibility of textured finish

Time

- Rapid construction with robust planning
- Use of mechanised ways, such as extrusion, battery and tilting moulds, etc.
- Suitable for modular and repetitive construction

Cost

- Optimum use of materials
- Limited use of temporary supporting structures, such as scaffolding
- Multiple use of formwork
- Availability of standard shapes
- Reduced maintenance leads to reduced life cycle cost

However, there are challenges also in precast concrete technology. These are:

- High initial costs for setting up factories
- High transportation costs for delivery of precast components
- Erection of components
- Excise duty of precast products

The chapter provides the potential for use of precast concrete, with reference to the developments in the countries which are advanced in this technology. The special types of formwork that can be used are large area forms, wall forms, climbing forms, slip forms, automatic hydraulic forming systems, heated tunnel forms, etc. Large projects undertaken in the past are highlighted.

2. Precast Concrete Building Systems: An Overview

There are different types of precast concrete buildings and hence, it is necessary to classify them for better understanding. In this chapter, the different systems adopted in precast concrete buildings are elucidated, namely, overall structural systems, systems for lateral load resistance, roof and floor systems. The systems are illustrated using photos of constructed facilities.

The structural system refers to the combination of the primary components of a building that resist the loads acting on the building. First, the different types of systems to resist the gravity loads are presented under overall structural systems. The systems are classified as skeletal frame system, large panel system and cell system. Second, the systems to resist the lateral loads due to earthquake and wind, are grouped as low-rise portals and frames, multi-storeyed frames, and wall system. The roof and floor systems are presented separately to explain the transfer of loads among the several components.

Various types of individual precast components for buildings are also described briefly. These include beams, columns, and units for the roofs, floors, walls and foundations. Comparative statements relating to suitable spans and material consumption are tabulated for ready reference.

3. Foundation and Underground Structures

Precast concrete can be adopted both for shallow foundations such as individual pad footings, and deep foundations such as piles. Apart from the general advantages, the advantages of adopting precast concrete for the foundations are:

- The foundation stratum is exposed for a minimum period. The backfilling can be carried out immediately after placing the footing component.
- The excavation size can be reduced.

However, the connection of the superstructure with the foundation needs appropriate detailing. The chapter provides the design considerations for the pad footings and the piles. Apart from the building structures, precast concrete can be used for other underground structures such as pipes, drains, culverts, tunnels, in-take wells, etc. Precast concrete is extensively used in other geo-structures such as facial elements in reinforced earth walls, interlocking blocks in pavements, liner elements in canals and water reservoirs.

4. Structural Analysis and Design

The structural analysis and design of precast concrete buildings follow the same principles as used in conventional construction. However, attention is required to model the structure appropriately considering the behaviour of the joints of the members. The modelling of the joints should be based on the adopted type of design. First, the chapter provides an overview of the loads based on the provisions of the Indian codes IS 875 Parts 1 to 3, and IS 1893 Part 1. Next, the analyses of frames are presented for a few typical types of frames. The design and detailing for the tie reinforcement required to avoid progressive collapse, is highlighted.

> *"While in an in situ construction, isolated sections in a structural element showing inadequacy of strength or defective detailing cannot cause serious consequences on the structure as a whole, because of redistribution of forces made possible by the monolithicity of construction, this is not the case in precast construction. The individual precast components might have been designed properly and might possess the required strength, but in spite of this, if they are not properly assembled and connected together so as to satisfy the assumptions made in their analysis and design, the safety of the whole structure or a major part of it may be jeopardised, particularly in situations where lateral loads play a dominant role."*

5. Prestressed Precast Concrete

The major advantages of prestressing precast concrete members in buildings are:

- The span-to-depth ratio of a flexural member can be increased. With reduced depth, the amount of concrete and self-weight decrease. The section tends to be aesthetically appealing. There can be large column-free space.
- Under service conditions, the members may remain uncracked. This leads to increase in section stiffness and durability. The shear capacity near the supports also increases.

The common applications of prestressing are hollow core slabs, composite slabs, beams, double tee girders, folded plate and shell members, roof trusses, piles and miscellaneous components. However, the limitations for prestressing include the availability of prestressing bed or self-straining benches, auxiliary equipment, good quality material and skilled labour.

> *"Generally, for prestressing, construction follows design closely, in terms of detailing (local effects), sequence (order of stressing, etc.), time durations (for creep and shrinkage effects), etc., and close control is required."*

The chapter provides the essentials of the analysis, design and construction of prestressed members.

6. Seismic Design of Precast Structures

The failures of precast concrete structures in past earthquakes have raised the concern of the use of such structures in earthquake-prone areas. It has been observed that the failures are primarily triggered by those at the joints of the precast components. The seismic design of a precast structure covers the overall seismic analysis of the structure, the design of the components, detailing of joints and providing integrity reinforcement. The first two aspects are similar to those of conventional reinforced concrete structures. There are two basic approaches for the detailing of the joints.

(a) Emulative or wet joints

(b) Dry joints

In the wet joints, reinforcement protrudes from the adjacent components, and on site concrete or grout is used to connect the components. The design aims to emulate or mimic the behaviour of cast-in-place construction. On the contrary, dry joints consist of metallic connectors with adequate corrosion protection.

> *Regarding wet joints:*
> *"However, these systems do not have all of the economical advantages of precast concrete technology because of the use of in-situ concrete. Furthermore, precast concrete systems that emulate the cast-in-place concrete systems have joints that are typically proportioned with sufficient strength to avoid inelastic deformations within these joints. Plastic hinges in these systems are forced to develop in the precast members, which does not lead to an economical design."*

The chapter first covers the basics of seismic analysis and design of buildings. Next, the detailing of joints is covered based on the different types of components to be connected. The detailing for slabs as floor diaphragms is also provided.

7. Materials, Properties and Products

The common materials used in making concrete are aggregates, cement, supplementary cementitious materials, chemical and mineral admixtures, and water. Reinforcing bars, prestressing strands, welded wire mesh and splice sleeve couplers are used as reinforcement. Ducts, grouts, dry packs, looped wire ropes, metallic inserts and plates are used in the joints. The selection of materials with appropriate properties is necessary for the mechanised manufacturing of the precast components. A few important requirements of precast concrete are as follows.

- early high strength for release of the components from the moulds;
- high flow mix or even self-compacting concrete in case of components with dense reinforcement; and
- stiff mix to facilitate extrusion in hollow core slabs and finishing in flat works.

Special types of concrete are used based on the applications, such as coloured concrete, textured concrete, light-weight concrete, high performance concrete, aerated concrete, etc. Sandwich wall panels with expanded or extruded polystyrene are used for thermal insulation. Typically, the cast components are subjected to accelerated curing, such as steam curing, electrical resistance curing or hot air/water curing.

> *"Precast concrete properties are different from that of general in-situ concrete used. It is mostly because of controlled mechanisation operation and ease in higher productivity of elements in a highly mechanised environment."*

8. Joints and Connections in Precast Buildings

As mentioned under seismic design, that joints are the vulnerable parts of a precast concrete structure. A connection is defined as an assembly of joints between two precast components. The chapter describes the design of joints based on the flows of forces that arise in the different types of components to be connected.

- Column to foundation
- Column to column
- Beam to column
- Slab to beam
- Slab to slab
- Wall panel to wall panel

There is a section on components in joints such as couplers, dowels, headed studs, bolts, inserts and bearing pads.

9. Production, Handling and Erection of Precast Elements

The setting up of a factory for production of precast concrete components needs careful planning.

> *"For establishing a factory, a detailed project report explaining the details of business model, market analysis, company background, infrastructure, plant capacity, marketing and sales turnover with time periods, and types of products and their ranges is required."*

The common types of moulds that are used for precast concrete are:

- Column moulds: with or without corbels
- Beam moulds
- Wall moulds: flat/table moulds, vertical moulds, battery moulds, tilting moulds
- Slab moulds: hollow core slab bed moulds, plank moulds
- Staircase moulds
- Moulds for miscellaneous non-structural components

The chapter describes the moulds and their tolerances. The typical production process is explained using a flowchart. Equipment for curing, storage, transportation, handling and erection are briefly presented. The installations of various components are described.

10. Quality Control and Assurance in Precast Products

> *"Quality assurance system provides means and methods by which product fitness is guaranteed. In a precast factory the technical and engineering skills in planning, design of precast concrete elements, moulds for production and design of processes for fast production, delivery of the product and integration of elements at site are the major competencies, and the net result should culminate into product fitness or acceptance to the standards specified by the customer."*

The chapter provides the aspects of quality control of raw materials and their storage, production process, the finished products and the testing procedures.

11. Contracts and Taxation

First, the chapter briefly describes the general types of contracts.

- Item rate contract
- Lump sum or design-and-build contract
    - (a) Turnkey contract
    - (b) Engineering procurement and construction (EPC) contract
- Cost-plus contract

Considering lean construction concepts, the following variants are possible.

- Target value design
- Integrated project delivery
- Alliance contracting

Next, the chapter provides the aspects of contracts that are relevant to precast concrete construction. The taxation system for precast concrete construction in India is covered.

12. Information Technology in Precast Construction

The use of building information modelling (BIM) in precast concrete construction is described under the following sections.

- Creating a conceptual model and generation of tender quantities
- Integration with analysis and design applications
- Precast element connections and detailing
- Creating drawings, reports and bill of materials
- Change management
- Generating automated deliverables
- Automated detailed drawings
- Site and delivery scheduling
- Field erection

13. Case Studies

Two case studies are provided to elucidate the various aspects of the design of precast concrete structures.

- Canteen building constructed for an information technology hub
- Multi-level vehicular parking garage for an international airport

The architectural layout, structural systems, structural analysis models, adaptation of precast system, components used and the erection scheme for each of the above projects are explained.

Closure

The use of precast concrete leads to better quality, faster and economical construction of buildings. Further development of this industry will provide prefabricated prefinished volumetric construction, as is being adopted in certain countries.

The *Handbook on Precast Concrete for Buildings* is a source of compiled information. For better understanding, it provides several illustrations and sketches. The references in each chapter can be accessed for additional information.

REFERENCE

1. *Handbook on Precast Concrete for Buildings* (2018), ICI Bulletin 02, Indian Concrete Institute.

Acknowledgements

The contributions of the authors of the different chapters of the Handbook, and the support from the editorial members of *The Masterbuilder*, Chennai, are gratefully acknowledged.

Bibliography

1. **Agrawal, Shailesh Kr.**, S.K.Gupta, Dalip Kumar (2018), **Building Materials and Housing Technologies for Sustainable Development**, Proceedings of the National Seminar on Emerging Building Materials & Construction Technologies, February 22-23, 2018, New Delhi.
2. Murthy Ramachandra D.S & **Agrawal, Shailesh Kr.** (2017) **Alternate Technologies for Housing,** Dipti Press (OPC) Pvt, Ltd, Chennai.
3. **Agrawal, Shailesh Kr.,** J.K.Prasad, S.K.Gupta, Dalip Kumar (2016), **Emerging Building Materials and Construction Technologies,** Proceeding of the International Seminar on Emerging Building Materials & Construction Technologies, March 21-22, 2016, New Delhi.
4. **Agrawal, Shailesh Kr.,** Rai Amit (2009), **Waste to Wealth, Green Building Materials and Construction Technologies using Agricultural and Industrial Waste,** Proceeding of the International Seminar on Waste to Wealth, November 12-13, 2009, New Delhi.
5. **Agrawal, Shailesh Kr,** (2004), A Book on **Earthquake Designer Manual for Practicing Engineers,** CBRI, Roorkee, December, 2004.
6. **Agrawal, S.K.** Chourasia, Ajay, Agarwal, Pankaj (2004), A Book on **Earthquake Resistant Design & Construction,** CBRI, Roorkee, March 2004.
7. **Strengthening Technological Base of Building Materials Industry,** Building Materials & Technology Promotion Council, Ministry of Housing & Urban Poverty Alleviation, Government of India, 2008
8. **Earthquake Hazard Map of India -** Brought out the Andriod and iOS based Mobile App on Earthquake Hazard Map of India. The Mobile App has been developed by BMTPC jointly with NDMA. As a part of Digital India programme of Government of India, the Mobile App will be helpful in providing necessary information with regard to earthquake zonation of the country to the professional in particular and other users in general.

9. **BAMTECH -** BMTPC jointly with South Asia Bamboo Foundation, Guwahati has developed Mobile App on "Bamboo Housing & Construction" which provides information on technologies and process related to construction of bamboo housing besides other related information. This app will be useful particularly to the bamboo workers and other related professionals for construction houses using bamboo.
10. **Indian Concrete Institute,** Technical Committee (ICI-TC/02) **Precast Concrete for Building,** First edition, 2016
11. **Town and Country Planning Organization (TCPO) Ministry of Urban Development, Govt. of India** "Model Building Bye-Laws, 2016
12. **Central Public Works Department (CPWD)** 'Government of India **'Analysis of Rates for Delhi (Vol-1)/ Vol-2) 2019**.
13. **Central Public Works Department (CPWD), Government** of India ' **Delhi Schedule of Rates (Vol-4) & Vol-2) 2018.**
14. **Central Public Works Department (CPWD)** 'Government of India ' **Schedule of Rates 2018 - For New & Innovative Technologies , 2018.**
15. **Holman, J.P,** Gajda, W.J "**Experimental Methods for Engineers** (Fifth edition) McGRAW-HILL International Edition , 1989.
16. **Meghashyam, Er Kollegal K. ' Compilation of Analysis of Rates and Estimation Techniques for Civil Works 2019 (Vol-1)** May 2010.
17. **Jain, Nabhi Kumar, Commentary on CPWD Specifications Vol-1** Nabhi Publications, New Delhi September, 2002.
18. **Bureau of Indian Standard (BIS) 'National Building Code of India 2016** (Vol-1) 2016.
19. **Kong, F.K.,** Hvans, R.H **'Reinforced and Prestressed Concrete '** 2nd edition, 1980.
20. **Chopra, Anil Kumar, 'Dynamics of Structures Theory and Applications to Earthquake Engineering'** 2nd Edition, 2001.
21. **Pillai, S.Unnikrishna,** Menon, Devdas ' **Reinforced Concrete Design' 1998.**
22. **Prof. Singh, Yogendra 'Structural** Stability Assessment and Development of Design Guidelines for Expanded Polystyrene Core Panel System towards Safe and Affordable Housing' by Earthquake Department, IIT Roorkee .
23. **Sharma, Umesh Kumar.,** Chauhan, Aditi 'Durability and Serviceability Assessment of Concrete Sandwich Expanded Polystyrene Core Panels ' by Civil Engineering Deptt,. IIT Roorkee , March, 2017.
24. **Jagdish, K.S ' Sustainable Building Technologies -** A Joint Publication of BMTPC & I.K International Publishing House Pvt. Ltd 2019

25. **Agarwal, Pankaj** , Shrikhande Manish ' **Earthquake Resistant Design of Structures** ' by Deptt. of Earthquake Engg, IIT, Roorkee 2011 published PHI Learning Pvt. Ltd , August, 2011.
26. **Development of Draft Protocol for Testing of Structural Components and Systems** (*a joint initiative of MoHUPA under Technology Sub-Mission of Pradhan Mantri Awas Yojana & IIT Kanpur)* 'Workshop on Performance Evaluation of Housing Units, IIT Kanpur Extension Centre, Noida 21-22 July, 2017.
27. **PAC No. 1006-A/2011** Performance Appraisal Certificate issued by BMTPC on Formwork for Monolithic Construction
28. **PAC No. 1018-S/2015** Performance Appraisal Certificate issued by BMTPC on Modular Tunnelform System
29. **PAC Nos. 1029/S/2017 & 1036-S/2018** Performance Appraisal Certificate issued by BMTPC on Insulating Concrete Forms (ICF) / Monolithic Insulated Concrete Systems (MICS)
30. **PAC No. 1035-S/2018** Performance Appraisal Certificate issued by BMTPC on Structural Stay-in-Place Formwork System (Coffor Technology)
31. **PAC No. 1034-S/2018** Performance Appraisal Certificate issued by BMTPC on Lost-in-Place Formwork System – Plaswall Panel System
32. **PAC No. 1033-S/2018** Performance Appraisal Certificate issued by BMTPC on Lost-in-Place Formwork System – Plasmolite Wall Panel
33. **PAC No. 1025-S/2016** Performance Appraisal Certificate issued by BMTPC on Sismo Building Technology
34. **PAC Nos. 1008-S/2011 & 1009-S/2012** Performance Appraisal Certificate issued by BMTPC on Glass Fibre Reinforced Gypsum (GFRG) Panel Building System
35. **PAC No. 1044-S/2019** Performance Appraisal Certificate issued by BMTPC on Stay-in-Place PVC Wall Forms
36. **PAC No. 1010-S/2014** Performance Appraisal Certificate issued by BMTPC on Advanced Building System – EMMEDUE
37. **PAC No. 1026-S/2016** Performance Appraisal Certificate issued by BMTPC on Rapid Panels
38. **PAC No. 1020-S/2015** Performance Appraisal Certificate issued by BMTPC on Reinforced EPS Core Panel System
39. **PAC No. 1019-S/2015** Performance Appraisal Certificate issued by BMTPC on Quickbuild 3D Panels
40. **PAC No. 1031-S/2017** Performance Appraisal Certificate issued by BMTPC on Concrete Panel System

41. **PAC No. 1032-S/2017** Performance Appraisal Certificate issued by BMTPC on Rising EPS (Beads) Cement Panels
42. **PAC No. 1042-S/2018** Performance Appraisal Certificate issued by BMTPC on Flyash EPS (Beads) Cement Sandwich Panels
43. **PAC No. 1041-S/2018** Performance Appraisal Certificate issued by BMTPC on Baupanel System
44. **PAC No. 1045-S/2019** Performance Appraisal Certificate issued by BMTPC on V-Infill Wall (Light Weight EPS Wall)
45. **PAC No. 1030-S/2017** Performance Appraisal Certificate issued by BMTPC on Prefabricated Fibre Reinforced Sandwich Panels (AEROCON)
46. **PAC No. 1039-S/2018** Performance Appraisal Certificate issued by BMTPC on PIR Dry Wall Pre-fab Panel System
47. **PAC No. 1047-S/2019** Performance Appraisal Certificate issued by BMTPC on Nano Living System Technology
48. **PAC No. 1014-S/2014** Performance Appraisal Certificate issued by BMTPC on Light Gauge Steel Framed Structures (LGSF)
49. **PAC No. 1028-S/2016** Performance Appraisal Certificate issued by BMTPC on Light Gauge Steel Framed Structure with Infill Concrete Panel (LGSFS-ICP)
50. **PAC No. 1011-S/2013** Performance Appraisal Certificate issued by BMTPC on Factory Made Fast Track Modular Building System
51. **PAC No. 1013-S/2014** Performance Appraisal Certificate issued by BMTPC on Speed Floor System
52. **PAC No. 1038-S/2018** Performance Appraisal Certificate issued by BMTPC on Continuous Sandwich (PUF) Panels with Steel Structure
53. **PAC No. 1021-S/2015** Performance Appraisal Certificate issued by BMTPC on SRPL Building System (Waffle Crete)
54. **PAC No. 1027-S/2016** Performance Appraisal Certificate issued by BMTPC on Precast Large Concrete Panel System
55. **PAC No. 1022-P/2015** Performance Appraisal Certificate issued by BMTPC on Walltec Hollowcore Concrete Wall
56. **PAC No. 1043-P/2019** Performance Appraisal Certificate issued by BMTPC on K-Wall Panels
57. **PAC No. 1040-S/2018** Performance Appraisal Certificate issued by BMTPC on Robomatic Hollowcore Concrete Wall Panels
58. **PAC No. 1046-S/2019** Performance Appraisal Certificate issued by BMTPC on Precast Construction Technology
59. **Guidelines** on Monolithic Concrete Construction by BMTPC, 2011

60. **Agreement No. 2569** relating to New Materials and Non-traditional Construction Processes between Cashiers of the C.S.T.B, Paris, France and Outinord, Company, S.A.
61. Application of accelerated curing to Apartment Formwork System - **Advisory Note** from British Cement Corporation
62. **Technical Assessment No. 16/10-607** of Coffor Structural Formwork by CSTB, Paris, France
63. **Structural Evaluation** of Prefabricated Concrete Wall System made of Coffor Steel panels comprising tests of Lateral load, Flexural strength and Axial load of the Panels by IIT Bombay
64. **Project Report** of Flexural, Compression, Shear & Deflection tests by Geo Test House, Vadodra
65. **Sismo technology:** Plain concrete in high rise buildings by Sismo Engineering, Belgium
66. **Guideline for European Technical Approval** of 'Non-load bearing permanent shuttering systems based on hollow blocks or panels of insulating materials' by EOTA, Brussels, Belgium
67. **Experimental Research** in 92-93 & 93-94 by Sismo Engineering & CE Deptt., University of Leunen, Belgium
68. **GFRG / Rapidwall Building Structural Design Manual**, prepared by IIT Madras, published by BMTPC, New Delhi.
69. **Schedule of Item & Rate Analysis for GFRG** Construction, BMTPC, New Delhi.
70. **Manual on M2 System** by EMMEDUE, S.P.A. Italy.
71. **Manual on Schnell Home**, Schnell Wire, Italy.
72. **Certificate No. 06/0241,** Irish Agreement Board, Ireland.
73. **Technical Report** on Experimental Evaluation of Building System M2 by Structure Lab. Department of Engineering, Ponitificia Universidad Catolica Del, Peru.
74. **Review of EVG-3D Technology** for residential buildings in India, IIT Mumbai, India.
75. **Report on Performance Tests** conducted on EMMEDUE Panel System at Hesarghalta, Bangalore Civil Aid Techno Clinic Pvt. Ltd., Bangalore.
76. **Legacy Report** by ICC Evaluation Services Inc., USA
77. **Construction Manual** by WorldHaus Construction Ltd., USA
78. **Axial Compression Test and Static Flexural Test** on Panels as Wall elements and Roof or Slab elements respectively by IIT Madras
79. **Pull off test on plastered surface** of structural concrete insulated panels at Bangalore by Civil-Aid Technoclinic Pvt. Ltd. Bangalore

80. **Report on Shaking Table Test** of a 1:2.35 Scale 4-Story Building Constructed with 3D Panel System University of Technology, Iran.
81. **Design and Construction** of "2 Police Constables Quarters (G+1) building for Karnataka State Police Housing Corporation Ltd., Bangalore"
82. **Technical Report** on "Light Gauge Steel Frame Structure with Infill Concrete Panels for Fast Tack and Disaster proof Housing"
83. **Structural Analysis Report** for "G+2 storey building constructed using LGSFS-ICP Technology" by M/s Nagesh Consultants, Bangalore
84. **Report** of Seismic Evaluation of Model of G+7 CRC framed structure for a ground motion compatible to zone V spectrum by SERC, Chennai.
85. **Suitability of Precast Concrete Large Panel system** for Mass Housing Projects by IIT Madras
86. **Design & Construction Methodology Review** for Rehab Bhiwada Precast Project, Mumbai by IIT Madras
87. **Verification of Thermal Performance Reports** - Evaluating RCC Wall apartments in Ahmedabad & Chennai by Indian Institute of Science, Bangalore.
88. **ACI 318:2014** Building code requirements for structural concrete, structural design for flat wall ICF systems
89. **AS 2327(Part1) :1996** Design of simply supported Composite structures
90. **AS/NZS 1170-2 (Parts 0 & 2) : 2002** Structural Design Actions—General principles and Wind actions
91. **AS/NZS 4600:2005** Design of Cold Formed Steel Structures
92. **AS/NZS 4671: 2001** Specifications for Steel reinforcing materials\
93. **ASTM - A 792/792 M -13** Specification for steel sheet, 55% aluminium zinc alloy coated by hot dip process
94. **ASTM - A 875/875 M -13** Specification for steel sheet, zinc 5% aluminium alloy coated by hot dip process.
95. **ASTM - A653/ A 653 M -13** Specification for steel sheet, zinc coated (galvanized) on zinc - iron alloy coated by hot dip process. \
96. **ASTM 322:09** Standard test method for thermal conductivity
97. **ASTM A 568** Standard specifications for thickness tolerances of cold rolled steel sheets & coils
98. **ASTM A 653(9)** Standard specifications for steel sheet, zinc coated or zinc-iron-alloy coated
99. **ASTM C 1185(08):2016** Standard test methods for sampling and testing non-asbestos fibre cement flat sheets
100. **ASTM C 293** Standard test method for determination of flexural strength of concrete
101. **ASTM C 423** Standard test method for sound absorption by reverberation room method

102. **ASTM C 495** Standard test method for determination of compressive strength of concrete
103. **ASTM C 518** Standard test method for steady state thermal transmission properties by means of heat flow meter apparatus.
104. **ASTM C 518:2017** Standard test methods for steady state thermal transmission properties by means of heat flow meter apparatus
105. **ASTM C 518-02** Standard test method for steady state thermal transmission properties by means of heat flow meter apparatus
106. **ASTM C 578:2015** Standard specifications for rigid, cellular polystyrene thermal insulation
107. **ASTM C 955:2007** Standard specifications for load-bearing (transverse and axial) steel studs, runners (Tracks) and bracing or bridging for screw application of gypsum panel products and metal plaster bases
108. **ASTM C1513-10** Standard specification for steel taping screws - cold formed steel framing connections
109. **ASTM C518** Standard test method for steady state thermal transmission properties by means of heat flow meter apparatus.
110. **ASTM C779** Standard test method for abrasion resistance of horizontal concrete surfaces
111. **ASTM C873** Standard test method for compression strength of concrete cylinders
112. **ASTM C900** Standard test method for pullout strength of hardened concrete
113. **ASTM D 1621** Standard test methods for compressive properties of rigid cellular plastic
114. **ASTM D 1622:2008** Standard test methods for apparent density of rigid cellular plastic
115. **ASTM D 4226:2016** Standard test methods for impact resistance of rigid PVC building products
116. **ASTM D 570-08** Standard test method for determination of Water absorption
117. **ASTM D 638:2014** Standard test methods for tensile properties of plastic
118. **ASTM D 695-15** Standard test method for determination of Compressive strength
119. **ASTM D 790-17** Standard test method for determination of Flexural strength
120. **ASTM D1621** Standard test method for compressive properties of rigid cellular plastics
121. **ASTM D1622** Standard test method for apparent density of rigid cellular plastics
122. **ASTM D1623** Standard test method for adhesion properties of rigid cellular plastics

123. **ASTM E 119:2014** Standard test methods for fire tests of building construction and materials
124. **ASTM E 152-58** Non-combustibility test for materials and heat emissions from building materials
125. **ASTM E 2634:2011** Standard specifications for flat wall ICF systems
126. **ASTM E 72:2015** Standard test method for conducting strength test of panels for building construction
127. **ASTM E 84:2007** Standard test methods for surface burning characteristics of building materials
128. **ASTM E119-2019** Standard test methods of tests of building construction and materials
129. **ASTM E2179** Standard test method for lab measurement of effectiveness of floor coverings
130. **ASTM E413** Classification of rating of sound insulation and field transmission class
131. **ASTM F 1939:2015** Standard test method for radiant heat resistance of combination of materials
132. **BS 2750-3:1995** Measurement of sound insulation in buildings and of building elements — Laboratory measurements of airborne sound insulation of building elements
133. **BS 4370 (Part 2):1993** Method of tests for rigid cellular materials
134. **BS 476 (Part 20-22): 1987** Method of determination of fire resistance of elements of building materials and structures
135. **BS 476 (Part 21):1987** Fire tests on building materials and structures — Methods for determination of the fire resistance of loadbearing elements of construction
136. **BS 476 (Part 4):1970** Fire tests on building materials and structures — Method of test to determine classification of surface spread of flame
137. **BS 476 (Parts 5, 6, 7)** Fire Tests on Building Materials & Structures - Method of test of Fire Ignitability, Fire Propagation & Surface spread of flame of materials/ products
138. **BS 5234 (Part 2):1992** Specifications for performance requirements for strength and robustness of partitions including method of tests
139. **BS 5250:2002** Code of practice for control of condensation in buildings
140. **BS 5950 (Part 5):1998** Code of practice for design of cold formed thin gauge sections
141. **BS 6093:1993** Code of practice for design of joints and jointing in building construction

142. **BS EN 10326:2004** Code of practice for continuously hot dip coated steel strip and sheet
143. **BS EN 13163:2012** Thermal insulation properties of materials
144. **EN 14889-1&2-2006** Fibre for concrete, steel fibres - definitions, specifications and conformity
145. **EN 1609:2013** Specifications for thermal insulating products for buildings
146. **GB 8624:2012** Classification of burning behavior of building materials
147. **IS 158:1981** Ready mixed paint, brushing, bituminous, black, lead free, acid, alkali and heat resisting
148. **IS 277 : 2003** Specifications for plain and corrugated galvanized steel sheets (sixth revision)
149. **IS 383: 2016** Specifications for coarse and fine aggregates from natural resources
150. **IS 419:1967** (Reaffirmed 2009) Specifications for putty
151. **IS 456 : 2000** (Reaffirmed 2016) Code of practice for plain and reinforced cement concrete
152. **IS 516:1969** (Reaffirmed 2004) Standard test method for strength of concrete
153. **IS 712:1984** Specification for building limes (Reaffirmed 2014)
154. **IS 733 : 1983** Wrought Aluminium and Aluminium Alloy Bars, Rods and Sections (for General Engineering Purposes)
155. **IS 800:2007** (Reaffirmed 2013) Code of practice for general construction in steel
156. **IS 801:1975** (Reaffirmed 2010) Code of practice for use of cold formed light gauge steel structural members in general building construction
157. **IS 875 Part-1) -1987** (Reaffirmed 2008) Code of Practice for Design Loads (Other than Earthquake) for Buildings and Structures-Unit Weights of Building Materials and Stored Materials.
158. **IS 875 (Part 3):2015** Code of Practice for Design Loads (other than earthquake) for buildings & structures - Part 3 Wind Loads
159. **IS 875 (Part-2) -1987** (Reaffirmed 2008) Code of Practice for Design Loads (Other than Earthquake) for Buildings and Structures-Imposed loads
160. **IS 875 (Part-5) -1987** (Reaffirmed 2003) Code of Practice for Design Loads (Other than Earthquake) for Buildings and Structures - Special Loads and Load Combinations
161. **IS 1346:1991** Code of practice for waterproofing of roofs with bitumen felts (Reaffirmed 2016)
162. **IS 1363:2002** Hexagon Head Bolts, Nuts and Screws of Product
163. **IS 1367:2002** Technical Supply Conditions for Threaded Steel Fasteners
164. **IS 1542:1992** Specifications for sand for plaster (Reaffirmed 2014)

165. **IS 1642-1989** (Reaffirmed 2000) Code of practice for Fire Safety of Buildings (General): Details of Construction.

166. **IS 1786 : 2008** High strength deformed steel bars and wires for concrete reinforcement

167. **IS 1893 (Part 1) : 2016** 'Criteria for Earthquake Resistant Design of Structures (Sixth Revision), Part -1, General Provisions and Buildings.

168. **IS 1904:1986 (Reaffirmed 2015)** Code of practice for design and construction of foundations in soils: General requirements

169. **IS 1905:1987 (Reaffirmed 2007)** Code of practice for structural use of un-reinforced masonry

170. **IS 1950 : 1962** Code of practice for sound insulation of non-industrial buildings (Reaffirmed 2010)

171. **IS 2062:2011 (Reaffirmed 2016)** Specifications for hot rolled medium & high tensile structural steel

172. **IS 2095 (Part 1) : 2011** Specification for Gypsum Plaster Boards - Part 1 Plain Gypsum Plaster Boards (Reaffirmed 2016)

173. **IS 2185 (Part-1) 2005** Concrete Masonry Unit – Specification (Third Revision), Part 1 Hollow and Solid Concrete Blocks.

174. **IS 2185 (Part-II) : 1983** Specification For Concrete Masonry Units (First Revision), Part II Hollow and Solid Lightweight Concrete Blocks.

175. **IS 2185 (Part 3) : 1984** 'Specification For Concrete Masonry Units (First Revision), Part 3 Autoclaved cellular (Aerated) Concrete Blocks.

176. **IS 2185 (Part 4) : 2008** ' Concrete Masonry Units – Specification, Part 4 Preformed Foam Cellular Concrete Blocks.

177. **IS 2212: 1991** 'Brick Works – Code of Practice (First Revision)

178. **IS 2380 (Part 10):1977** (Reaffirmed 2013) Falling hammer impact test

179. **IS 2380 (Part 14):1977** Methods of test for wood particle board and other Ligno cellulosic materials – screw & nail withdrawal test (Reaffirmed 2013)

180. **IS 2380 (Part 2):1977** Methods of test for wood particle boards and boards from other lignocellulosic materials – Determination of dimensional stability (Reaffirmed 2013)

181. **IS 2380 (Part 4):1977** Methods of test for wood particle boards and boards from other lignocellulosic materials – Determination of flexural strength (Reaffirmed 2013)

182. **IS 2380 (Part 5):1977** (Reaffirmed 2013) Methods of test for wood particle board and other ligne cellulosic materials – tensile strength test.

183. **IS 2386 (Part 1 & 3):1963** (Reaffirmed 2016) Method of tests for aggregates for concrete

184. **IS 2386(Part 3):1963** Methods of test for aggregates for concrete - Part 3 specific gravity, density, voids, absorption and bulking (Reaffirmed 2016)
185. **IS 2547 (Part 1): 1976** Specification for gypsum building plaster: Part 1 excluding premixed lightweight plaster (Reaffirmed 2017)
186. **IS 2572 : 2005** Construction of Hollow and Solid Concrete Block Masonry – Code of Practice (First Revision)
187. **IS 2645:2003** Specifications for integral water proofing compounds for cement, mortar and concrete
188. **IS 2950 (Part 1):1981**(Reaffirmed 2008 Code of Practice for Design & Construction of raft foundation
189. **IS 2974: 1992 (Part 3)** (Reaffirmed 2006) Code of Practice for Design & Construction of machine foundations.
190. **IS 3346: 1980** (Reaffirmed 2017) Method of determination of thermal conductivity of thermal insulation materials
191. **IS 3792 : 1978** Guide for heat insulation of non-industrial buildings (Reaffirmed 2013)
192. **IS 3809: 1979** (Reaffirmed 2002) Fire resistance test for structures
193. **IS 3812 (Part 1):2013** Specifications for pulverized fuel ash - part 1 : for use as pozzolana in cement, cement mortar and concrete
194. **IS 3812 (Part 2):2003** Specifications for pulverized fuel ash - Part 2 : for use as admixture in cement mortar and concrete (Reaffirmed 2017)
195. **IS 3952 : 2013** Burnt Clay Hollow Bricks and Blocks for Walls and Partitions – Specification, (Third Revision).
196. **IS 4020(Part 1 to 16):1998** Door Shutters - Methods of Tests
197. **IS 4326 : 2013** Earthquake Resistant Design and Construction of Buildings – Code of Practice (Third Revision).
198. **IS 4671:1984** (Reaffirmed 2004) Specifications for expanded polystyrene for thermal Insulation purposes
199. **IS 4759:1996** (Reaffirmed 2016) Hot Dip Zinc Coating on Structural Steel Products
200. **IS 6041 : 1985** Code of Practice for Construction of Autoclaved Cellular Concrete Block Masonry (First Revision)
201. **IS 6042 : 1969** Code of Practice for Construction of Light-Weight Concrete Block Masonry
202. **IS 6072:1971** Specification for Autoclaved Reinforced Cellular Concrete Wall Slabs.
203. **IS 6073:2006** Autoclave Reinforced Cellular Concrete Floor and Roof Slabs - Specification (Reaffirmed 2017)

204. **IS 7215:1974** Tolerances for Fabrication of Steel Structures (Reaffirmed 2016)
205. **IS 7888:1976** (Reaffirmed 2008) Methods of test for Polyurethane Foam
206. **IS 8112:2013/12269:2013** Specifications for 43/53 grade ordinary Portland cement
207. **IS 9012:1978** Recommended practice for shotcreting (Reaffirmed 2016)
208. **IS 9103:1999** (Reaffirmed 2004) Specification for Concrete Admixtures
209. **IS 9142:1979** (Reaffirmed 2011) Specifications for light weight aggregate
210. **IS 9901(Part III):1981** Measurement of sound insulation in buildings and of building elements
211. **IS 9901:1981** (Reaffirmed 2007) Measurement of sound insulation in buildings and building elements
212. **IS 10151 : 1982** Polyvinyl Chloride (PVC) and its Copolymers for its Safe Use in Contact with Foodstuffs, Pharmaceuticals and Drinking Water
213. **IS 10262 : 2009** Concrete Mix Proportioning - Guidelines (First Revision) (Reaffirmed 2014)
214. **IS 10505:1983** Code of practice for construction of floors and roofs using precast concrete waffle units (Reaffirmed 2013)
215. **IS 11050 (Part 1):1984** Rating of sound insulation in buildings and of building elements - Part 1 : airborne sound insulation in buildings and of interior building elements (Reaffirmed 2017)
216. **IS 11239 (Part 1, 3, 4, 11 & 12):2009**/1985/1988/2014 Method of tests for rigid cellular thermal insulations
217. **IS 11239 (Part 1, 3, 4, 11 & 12):2009**/1985/1988/2014 Method of tests for rigid cellular thermal insulations
218. **IS 11384:1985** Code of Practice for Composite Construction in Steel and Concrete
219. **IS 11447:1985** Code of practice for construction of large panel prefabricates (Reaffirmed 2013)
220. **IS 12089:1987** Specifications for granulated slag for manufacture of portland slag cement (Reaffirmed 2013)
221. **IS 12269:2013** Specifications for 53 grade ordinary Portland cement
222. **IS 12436:1988** (Reaffirmed 2017) Specifications for performed rigid polyurethane foam for thermal insulation.
223. **IS 12440 : 1988** Specification for Precast Concrete Stone Masonry Blocks.
224. **IS 13000:1990** Specifications for Silica-Asbestos-Cement Flat Sheets (Reaffirmed 2015)
225. **IS 13920 : 2016** Ductile detailing of reinforced concrete structures subjected to seismic forces - Code of practice (First Revision)

226. **IS 13920-1993** (Reaffirmed 2008) Ductile Detailing of reinforced concrete structures subjected to seismic forces –code of practice.
227. **IS 14213 : 1994** Construction of walls Using Precast Concrete Stone Masonry Blocks Code of Practice.
228. **IS 14246:2013** Specifications for continuously pre-painted galvanized steel sheets and coils
229. **IS 14687 : 1999** Falsework for Concrete Structures - Guidelines (Reaffirmed 2014)
230. **IS 14862:2000** Specifications for Fibre Cement Flat Sheets (Reaffirmed 2015)
231. **IS 15916:2010** Code of practice for building design and erection using prefabricated concrete (Reaffirmed 2013)
232. **IS 15917:2010** Code of practice for Building design and erection using mixed/ composite construction (Reaffirmed 2014)
233. **IS 16700:2017** Criteria for structural safety of tall concrete buildings
234. **ISO 179 (Part 2):1999** Determination of properties of charpy impact strength
235. **ISO 2796:1986** Cellular plastics -- Test method for dimensional stability of rigid materials
236. **ISO 2896:2001** Cellular plastics --Test method for water absorption of rigid materials
237. **ISO 9705:1983** Fire tests for evaluating contribution of wall & ceiling interior finish to room fire growth
238. **NZS 3101(Part1): 2006** Design of Concrete Structures
239. **NZS 3404 (Part1):1997** Design of Steel Structure

Index